Life Cycles

LIFE CYCLES
your emotional journey to freedom and happiness
By Christine DeLorey

Published By Osmos Books
P.O. Box 1916
Hallandale Beach, FL 33009

E-mail: numerology@freesoul.com
Web Site: http://www.numerology.freesoul.com

ISBN: 0-9673130-9-0
Library of Congress Catalog Card Number: 99-90582

Cover design by Fisher Graphics, Inc.
West Palm Beach, FL

Special thanks and appreciation to Jack Tempchin
for permission to reprint lyrics from "Already Gone."
Copyright Jack Tempchin. All rights reserved

"Beautiful Boy (Darling Boy)"
Words and music by John Lennon
(c) 1980 LENONO MUSIC
All rights controlled and administered by EMI BLACKWOOD MUSIC
All Rights Reserved. International Copyright secured. Used by permission

First Edition

Life Cycles

your emotional journey
to freedom and happiness

CHRISTINE DELOREY

OSMOS BOOKS

Table of Contents

... PART TWO ...

... PART THREE ...

with love and thanks

To my partner, husband, lover, and best friend, MIKE DELOREY, without whose love, patience, generosity, and belief in me, this book, quite simply, could not have been written.

let there be peace

let there be peace
let there be trust
let there be compromise
we know we must
and if we don't
answer this call
there will be nothing left
at all
let there be peace, love, understanding

let there be peace
let there be calm
let there be tolerance
no more alarm
free the hate
you hold within
learn to forgive
and let love in
let there be peace, love, understanding

let there be peace
in every place
and so evolves
the human 'race'
free the fear
free the pain
nothing to lose
the WORLD to gain
let there be peace, love, understanding

let there be peace
let there be truth
let us be free
to live as we choose
with borders and warriors
a thing of the past
and love for each other
the fuel of our hearts
let there be peace, love, understanding

there is no prize
no first place
here at the finish line
of the 'race'
and when we see
that no one can win
that's when HUMANITY
begins
let there be peace, love, understanding

CHRISTINE DeLOREY

iNTroduCTion

what are
life cycles?

*Life is like a game of cards.
The hand that is dealt you
represents determinism;
the way you play it
is Free Will.*

JAWAHARIAL NEHRU

...wElcomE To Your world oF NUMbErS...

what are
life cycles?

One cannot discover new oceans
until one has the courage
to lose sight of the shore.
PATRICK WALKER

Human beings have always had difficulty embracing anything that is invisible to the eye. Yet, we know that our ability to see and understand extends far beyond the physical eyes alone. Vision is also possible through the eyes of one's mind; that marvelous ability we have to imagine - to *"image-in"* - the possibilities. But what is it that impels us to create what we have imagined?

Our natural creative drive is a form of sight which can only be described as our sixth sense. It is a powerful dimension which has the potential to enhance and, therefore, improve our entire experience of life. The new millennium brings us into the age of intuition: a new cycle of time and space in which we are learning to function, create, and excel, through the free expression of our *emotions.*

We are all living deeply emotional lives these days. We have entered a long cycle of the evolutionary journey in which we must face the stark realities of ourselves and this world. We are learning *how* to feel and, in the process, we are realizing the extent of our unused potential to create the lives we want to live. Our sixth sense - emotion - is the human *will* which, by its very nature, must be free.

We have also become aware that all life operates in clearly defined cycles of time and space which can be calculated and measured by numbers. Far from being predestined, our cyclical nature represents a road-map out of the present "system" to which we are all enslaved; out of those circumstances we thought were unchangeable, and in to the openness of Free Will. The quality of our lives, therefore, is determined by the quality and strength of our desires - our feelings.

> *The most beautiful thing we can experience is the mysterious.*
> *It is the source of all true art and science.*

ALBERT EINSTEIN

There is nothing supernatural about the science of numerology. Numbers are *natural* elements; major effects of space and time that enable us to measure and understand our world, and beyond it. Numbers are the pulse of nature and her endless cycles.

The numbers used in mathematics can be extremely complex and are used to measure and explain the physical realities of life. The numbers used in numerology are remarkably simple and are used to measure and explain the invisible tides and forces that lay beneath the physical. We are living at a time when vast quantities of new information are opening up to us at all levels. Every field of knowledge is expanding into higher levels of understanding. The numbers with which we measure *everything* in this world are no exception.

Today, we are using numerology as a concise and accurate way of understanding and improving our lives, minds, feelings, bodies, relationships, and circumstances. We travel through life on a sea of numbers. Understanding their deeper meanings can bring order and perspective to what we often believe is our chaos.

Ultimately, a deeper understanding of the cycles through which all human beings travel, cannot help but bring lasting and meaningful change to the world itself. We are learning to be the masters of our complexity instead of its victims.

> *All men will benefit if we can invoke*
> *the wonders of science instead of its terrors.*
> JOHN F. KENNEDY

Most importantly, we are learning that we still have so much more to learn. We are finding it easier to say "I don't know" instead of believing that we must always have an answer. We are realizing that many of our so-called leaders and experts have, for decades, been leading us in the wrong direction with their extremism, manipulation, disinformation, and hunger for the control of this Earth. We are realizing that this purely economically based existence is shallow, hollow, and unacceptable as the foundation of human life.

People, everywhere, are seeking an alternative way to live. They are independently seeking the truth, sometimes in areas that were once considered the realms of crackpots, eccentrics, and idealists. But it wasn't so long ago that the fields of psychology, physical fitness, and holistic medicine were thought of in this way. In fact, it wasn't so long ago that we thought the world was flat.

Perhaps the use of numbers to better understand ourselves is not such a far fetched idea after all. After twenty years of deep research, I believe that numbers represent the framework of humanity's glorious creative potential.

> *God hath numbered thy kingdom, and finished it.*
> THE BOOK OF EZEKIEL

The roots of numerology can be found in the ancient civilizations of China, Egypt, Greece, Babylonia, Britain, Tibet, and others. Its principles have been embraced by scientists, philosophers, theologians, and mathematicians through the ages. The theories of Pythagoras, Plato, and even Einstein and Planke are numerologically based. They believed that *all is arranged according to number.*

If God created all, then numbers are a vital element of God's creation. If we are 'created in his image', then our purpose as human beings must also be a creative one.

> *To every thing there is a season,*
> *and a time to every purpose under the heaven.*
> ECCLESIASTES

Today's numerology has broken through its traditional boundaries to a level of knowledge that is quite astonishing. We are now able to define the higher purpose of numbers way beyond anything the 'ancients' could possibly have perceived. This is because only now, as we embrace a new cycle of time, can the average human mind comprehend metaphysical realities in practical terms. We are breaking through our self-imposed boundaries which have retarded the human learning process for so long.

Numerology is no longer part of the unknown. What we know about this science today has uncovered a vital link between the cycles of time and the emerging power of our feelings. It is important to understand, from the very beginning, that this is not a book about psychic prediction or fortune telling. It is not even *about* numerology. This book is about YOU, and this ever changing world in which you are making your own unique voyage of discovery.

Nor is this a technical book. It was written for those who do not necessarily want to learn a new science but simply wish to benefit from what it can do for them. Similarly, when they switch on a light, they may not wish to learn about the intricacies of electricity but simply want the advantage of the light it produces. We all need to shed light on our paths, and *Life Cycles: your emotional journey to freedom and happiness* will help you do just that.

> *So often times it happens that we live our lives in chains*
> *And we never even know we have the key.*
> JACK TEMPCHIN/THE EAGLES - "ALREADY GONE"

By knowing the nature of the cycle you are in, at any given time, you will understand what is really happening in your life and how to deal with it effectively. Of course, the key is to look at your life more honestly; to think and feel more deeply so that you can see the whole picture and not just the issues you automatically perceive as problems.

You need to look at your entire reality: how your past led you to your present circumstances, and how the decisions you make now, in the present, will determine the quality of your future. Only when you recognize what you are doing wrong can you put things right. And when things are going well, you will not want to sabotage your situation by repeating the same old mistakes you have always made.

The road to Free Will can seem dark and confusing at times because every decision you make must be your own. Allow this book to illuminate your unique and special path so that you can understand what your reality and your potential actually are.

Life Cycles is designed to bring your life to its own natural pace. Sometimes, it will ask you to slow down, stop, or go back into your past. Sometimes you will be urged to speed up, move forward, assert yourself, and get things done. Living your life at the same speed as the cycle you are in brings you to that ideal pace and measure of awareness that enables you to sense your way through life, instead of relying on others to tell you how to live. Listen to and *feel* what each cycle has to say. Then, consciously apply this information to your circumstances in a way that feels right for you.

There are 9 yearly cycles, and 108 monthly cycles which run concurrently. Yes, it will take nine years to experience all of them. But, in the awesome process of creating your own destiny, 9 years is a small drop in the great ocean of time. As you build the confidence that comes with sensing your way through life, and as your goals materialize into reality, you will know that each goal is just a stepping stone to much greater goals such as freedom, creativity, longevity, peace, love, and understanding. The numbers are not our masters unless we allow them to be. We must master the numbers by constructively using the powers they offer.

We have cycles like the planets.
We come from these waves and cycles.. Why wouldn't we?
DAVID DUCHOVNY

Each month brings a new energy, a new situation, a new point of view, and a new wave of understanding to gain. You may not always be able to relate to a particular cycle. At these times, you must assess your reality more objectively so that you can see what you are refusing to see, think what you are refusing to think, and feel what you are refusing to feel. This book will help you to do this. It will also help you to manage the fear that facing one's reality often produces. Why, you may ask, would you choose to face reality when reality is so hard to look at? Because, if you do not know what your reality is, you will never be able to change those parts of it that you do not like.

Life is NOT an illusion. But the slave-like way in which we live our lives, where only the material is accepted as real, is certainly an illusion - a horrible nightmare - from which we are now waking up! As we awaken, one by one, we realize not only how loathsome we have allowed our world to become, but also how wonderful it could become if we were courageous enough to end our denial of reality and see life as the multi-dimensional miracle that it is.

As you start to recognize the various cycles of your life, there may be aspects you want to ignore because you think they do not apply to you. These are probably the very same aspects you are ignoring and denying in your everyday life, the very issues and emotions which are causing, and have always caused, your biggest and most consistent problems. These are the challenges that are standing between you and the fulfillment of your dreams. These are the cause of your personal nightmare, whatever that may be. First you must admit that these aspects of yourself do indeed exist. *Life Cycles* will help you to face them, accept them, and heal them.

Most of the harm that occurs in this world comes from our fear of being powerful individuals. Others use this fear to exert their power over us. This is the barrier we put up against our own Free Will. Each month, you will have an opportunity to strengthen your natural powers by releasing yourself from a specific emotional or mental shackle.

Reading ahead of the cycle you are in can be helpful for visualizing, planning, and sensing the course of your journey. However, you cannot judge a particular cycle until you are in it. In fact, looking too far ahead can distract you from what needs to be seen immediately in the here and now. As you travel the monthly segments of your journey, return regularly to the initial description of the current year, as a reminder of its basic principles. If you are starting this book at any time other than the beginning of the year, do not discount the months that have passed. Each month contains a set of valuable insights which may still need to be felt.

*Believe in yourself and your heart and find out
what makes you empowered. You have to create your own destiny
and not just sit back and watch life pass you by.*
DREW BARRYMORE

You cannot hope for a smooth ride through life when you are struggling *against* your cyclical tides. Going with the flow means flowing freely with your own individual energies, desires, and feelings. This can only be achieved by feeling and expressing every single feeling you have, fully and completely. Only then can you know what your deepest desires actually are.

This book is a personal blueprint, a road map of your natural energy cycles. It contains constructive guidance to whatever happens to you at any time in your life. It enables you to know what your own energy, your own magnetism, *feels* like. It holds the same importance as knowing where you are in any journey into unknown territory. And by reading about the cycles of the other people in your life, you can gain a much deeper understanding of your various relationships.

This voyage into your own reality will have some exhilarating moments. Not only will love be felt deeply, but different *forms* of love will make themselves known to you. You will also become astutely aware of those aspects which are preventing love, peace, happiness, and prosperity from entering your life.

*When an inner situation is not made conscious
it appears outside as fate.*
CARL G. JUNG

Of course, there is no book in the world that can improve your life if you ignore the information given. The accuracy of this work cannot be judged by merely reading it. Its content cannot be assessed as accurate or inaccurate until it has been consciously applied to your circumstances. Problems begin, continue, or multiply when these insights are ignored. When we deny the existence of a problem, there can never be a solution.

If at first you cannot associate a particular cycle with your own circumstances or feelings, don't give up. It is a matter of recognizing what your circumstances and feelings actually are. All you need is the firm intent - *the feeling of desire* - to do so.

Life Cycles does not create the experience for you. It does open you up to experiences you are already having, but may be unable to understand or even acknowledge. And, as you feel and express the emotions that arise in each cycle, you will experience the physical, intellectual, and emotional sensations of human growth. You will experience your own magnificent evolution.

Life Cycles **is divided into three parts:**

WHO YOU ARE:

PART 1 - DESTINY NUMBERS. This explains the energy you were born with; the natural power that you take with you at all times, no matter where you happen to be in the cyclical journey. It does not represent your destiny itself, but the path on which you emerged at birth; the path which provides the experiences you need so that you *can* create the destiny of your choice. Your destiny number is the fundamental and guiding energy of your unique passage through life.

WHERE YOU ARE:

PART 2 - THE JOURNEY takes you year by year, month by month through 108 cycles of your life. It explains the hidden forces behind your various circumstances and how to change or maintain course according to your personal needs and desires. When you have completed the nine yearly cycles, the journey does not end there. At that point, you start again from the beginning. But, instead of merely going around in circles and repeating the same old cycles of the past, you will be embarking on a new, evolved, and *spiraling* journey toward expanded freedom and happiness. You will find that *Life Cycles* is a book which has no end, and that your potential is as rich and limitless as you choose to make it.

HOW YOU ARE:

PART 3 - LIFE, LOVE, AND LIBERTY IN THE NEW MILLENNIUM: The Healing Power of Emotion. This section explains why your emotions are the driving force behind everything that happens to you. How you *feel* dictates all that you create and all that you destroy. Your ability to balance the expanding power of your emotions, in harmony with the expanding power of your mind, sets you free to create the life you want for yourself. This section also explains why *peace on earth* must be humanity's primary focus in the new millennium, and why true peace *begins* within each individual. This information is not always understood immediately. Please read it gradually, slowly, and only when you feel drawn to it. Each time you read it, however, you will learn something new and your life will change - for ever.

Have a wonderful journey, my fellow traveler.

PART 1

destiny numbers

Destiny is not a matter of chance,
it is a matter of choice;
it is not a thing to be waited for,
it is a thing to be achieved.
WILLIAM JENNINGS BRYAN

Your Destiny Number

a simple calculation

The DESTINY NUMBER, despite its name, does not tell you what your destiny will be. You yourself must decide what you want to do with your life. The options are infinite. The destiny number is, however, the path which will lead you to the destiny or destination of your choice. It represents the cyclical energy into which you emerged on the day you were born.

This number cannot be changed, even if at first you may wish you had a different or easier path to follow. This is the number - the energy - which stays with you for your entire life, no matter what other cycles you find yourself traveling. When your destiny number is accepted and properly understood, and when its challenges have been faced and overcome, its energy becomes your greatest strength.

Your destiny number is comprised of all the numbers contained in your date of birth. Calculating your destiny number is a matter of simple addition. For example, if you were born on November 27 1951, you would add together all of those numbers, like so:

Month   11
Day   27
Year   <u>1951</u> (the year must always consist of four digits)
Subtotal   1989
(now add these together)
1 + 9 + 8 + 9 = 27.
Keep adding until a single digit is obtained:
2 + 7 = 9.
In this case, the destiny number is 9.

Now calculate your own destiny number and be sure to double check your results. After all, this is your journey - your life - we are talking about, and you need to set off in the right direction.

It is also a good idea to familiarize yourself with the destiny numbers of other people in your life. Relationships of every kind can benefit by the acceptance of each other's individuality.

The 1 Destiny
the life-long path of the pioneer

No bird soars too high if it soars with its own wings.
WILLIAM BLAKE

The 1 path will teach you the importance of believing in yourself and of satisfying your need for independence. You want to lead your own life and you tend to do this by using your individuality and originality to draw success to you. You are able to take care of yourself, stand on your own two feet, and get what you want out of life. And what you want can be most unusual.

1 is the number of progress. This implies that steps must be taken, one at a time, which lead to higher goals. You know that each step is a goal in itself, and your foresight here, your knowing what you want and how to get it, can result in the achievement of large-scale ambitions.

Others may see you as self-centered, inconsiderate, or even greedy. They may resent your positive forward-drive, all the time wishing they possessed some of this energy themselves. Your self-centeredness is inevitable because the *self* is precisely what you came into this lifetime to learn about. Those who do not understand this will often be jealous of or angry with you. You must learn to appreciate who you are and accept that some negativity from others is inevitable on this path. But it is also avoidable once you are more comfortable in your role of leader and pioneer.

The 1 destiny provides the physical and mental energy which keeps you so busy and urges you to be wherever the action is. You must lead your own life without the constant influence of others. You can never be happy while you need their approval. But you will gain their admiration when they realize that their approval is not what you are seeking.

The feeling of having to go it alone is common because others can be so resistant to the new, the progressive, and the different. Sometimes, the only person you *can* lead is yourself. However, your tendency toward impatience must be recognized and toned down. The 1 pace is sometimes so fast that others find it difficult to keep up with you. But you do need an appreciative audience. How can you be a leader if no one is following? However, when your following starts to slow you down or distract you from what you really want to do, you are likely to break free abruptly, leaving others feeling hurt, abandoned, and confused. It may seem as if you are retreating or running away from everything. Usually, though, it is a matter of you pushing others back so that you can reclaim the space you believe is yours. Yes, patience is something you really do need to develop on the 1 path.

It can be lonely at the top. But do be honest with yourself here. The top is exactly where you want to be. It is where you are meant to be. You also need frequent periods of isolation so that you can focus on what is important to you. To meditate is to focus, which means that you are often meditating without consciously trying to. Concentration is one of the splendid gifts of the 1 destiny and is the key to achieving your desires, particularly once you learn to focus on the big picture instead of only small segments of the whole.

When you do find the courage to go your own way and do what you instinctively *feel* is right for you, those who were once unable to appreciate your unusual vision will suddenly be only too willing to jump on your bandwagon and applaud your independent manner. Do not deter these people with an attitude of superiority, intolerance, or resentment. Learn the art of leadership by welcoming and encouraging your self-made following, while confidently and patiently maintaining your position as originator and leader. Others will soon realize that you will not be forced or tricked into anything that goes against your grain.

The very thought of having to depend on someone else for your happiness, security, or success, is probably repugnant to you. You do not take kindly to others who depend on you to the extent that they distract you from what *matters* to you. Other people do play a very important role in your life, but dependence, in any form, is unnatural for you. This does not mean that you cannot be an excellent partner, spouse, parent or team mate. Roles, schedules, and purposes do need to be defined, and parameters may need to be set as to how much of yourself you are comfortably able to give. Others need to know that while you will make sacrifices that are necessary, you will never sacrifice yourself, your time, or your money for those who refuse to help themselves. You thrive around those who also possess an independent and creative nature.

The 1 destiny makes you a dynamo of energy which is usually positive. But you must be careful not to deny life's negative aspects because they do, indeed, exist. Unless a problem is accepted as a problem, a solution may never be found. One of the most often denied negatives on the 1 path is that of becoming addicted and attached to things, situations, and people that enter the life alluringly, only to become major challenges to your independence.

Always remain aware of your own addictions. Some will be obvious, while others will control you more subtly. It is necessary to recognize, admit to, and overcome these challenges. Your dependencies are what stand between you and the creation of a fulfilling destiny. These are traps that you, yourself, have set in place because you are afraid of your own potential for *greatness*.

It may be difficult to accept that this fear exists. To you, fear denotes weakness. Try not to deny your fear of being special. It is only by accepting and loving your uniqueness that you will be able to sense and avoid unwanted situations. Your denial of fear will slow down your progress to the extent that you will be unable to take important steps unless you have the approval of others.

Your very nature is to move progressively, step by step, with each step falling into place; creating yet another new foothold, and then another, which will lead to something greater. Yours is the nature of constant forward movement, and you cannot allow your denial of fear, or your denial of guilt, to stop your natural progression from taking place.

When you are unsure of yourself, you may still want to lead, but you will have no idea of where you are headed. In this case, others may reject you, your ideas, your beliefs, your methods, or your lifestyle. Once you stop depending on the approval of others for the results you want, you will gain an acute sense of direction, and you will be able to accept meaningful leadership roles when life offers them to you.

Other people are already aware of your independent essence as well as your many impressive abilities. But what others see in you is not the point. You yourself must recognize your talents and use them whenever you can, without compromising your individuality.

Learn to follow your driving force - your WILL - your feelings. When you reach this level of confidence, substantial opportunities present themselves which will lead to the recognition and all the material and financial rewards you desire.

Natural gifts of the 1 destiny are those of courage and assertiveness. You have strong personal needs which you see as goals and ambitions. Often, your goals can seem impractical, trivial, or grandiose to others. And, because they may sometimes consider your ideas to be too egotistically, financially, or whimsically based, it is often necessary for you to ignore their criticism and follow your own convictions. How else can a pioneer operate?

The other people in your life can disappoint you because they do not seem to share your passion for some of the things you hold dear. You may sense a lot of resistance from them. There seems to be no apparent reason why others disapprove of you so often. You dare to be yourself. Your Will is strong and active. You get things done. So why don't they accept you as you are? Perhaps you must learn that everyone's needs, desires, and levels of consciousness are different. What interests you does not automatically interest them.

Everyone is evolving at varying speeds and under different circumstances. Everyone's personal nature is different. Although you are a wonderful representative for Free Will most of the time, you must learn to allow others to be who *they* are and realize that there are no set ways for individuals to live and evolve. Once you have accepted yourself for who and what you are, you will be able to teach and inspire others about the importance of *their* individuality and *their* need to be original and independent.

The world has outgrown its need for idols and heroes. Humanity requires truthful information instead that encourages people to live their own lives. You have so much to teach about self-acceptance, determination, Free Will, creativity, and personal satisfaction. But you can only fulfill this potential by *being* self-accepting, independent, creative, satisfied with your own progress, and eager to forge the way for others.

You may hide your self-centeredness very well, but it is there anyway. In some people, this could be viewed as a negative trait. In you, however, self-centeredness is totally natural and beautiful when it is balanced with genuine consideration for others.

Learn the difference between self-centeredness and selfishness; egotism and self-deflation; impatience and indifference; being too trendy and too old fashioned; being too rigid and too easygoing.

One of the most difficult lessons you may have to learn on this path is that of EGO. Without an ego, it is impossible to know who you are or what you are capable of doing. People who say we must bury our egos in order to be spiritually 'whole', forget that in order to be whole, the ego must be allowed its right place. The ego is *part* of the whole. We cannot exist without our egos, without denying a part of who we are. The lesson you must learn about your ego is that of *balance*. This means balancing your personality between having too much and too little ego and regularly allowing your ego to rest so that meaningful relationships and free creative expression can be experienced.

You need to develop a realistic sense of your own importance. You are here to learn about yourself. Therefore, it is natural for your ego to fluctuate wildly at times so that you can learn how to balance it. You need to be honest as to how you really feel about yourself. There is a lot to think about here.

The 1 energy allows for a much easier trip through life than the other destiny numbers, but only if you allow this 'ease' into your life. If you think that life is a struggle, you are probably struggling with a dependency of some kind. And you do tend to deny your addictions even when they are obvious.

When you are truly being yourself and following your heart, life and love will flow very easily for you. Problems will always arise when you are dependent on someone or something, or when you deny or exaggerate your feelings. Being yourself means being *comfortable* with yourself, exactly as you are.

One of the principle gifts of the 1 destiny is your ability to influence others without actually trying to. At the same time, other people often view you as someone who could do a lot better if you would only push yourself a little harder. They are more aware of your rich potential than you are. They sense what you are truly capable of. But you prefer to live your life on your own terms. You do not want others setting your goals or agendas for you. You have your own ideas of where you want to go and how to get there. You can be stubborn. Yet, in a crisis, you can amaze everyone, including yourself, as you step in and efficiently save the day.

Recognize just how special, different, and powerful you are. This may sometimes leave you feeling that you are the only one who is putting any effort into a situation. This can make you feel as if you are very much alone in the world. But, only by knowing yourself can you truly know another. We are only just learning, as a species, that we are all connected and related. Until this is learned on a global level, until more individuals understand the new information that is making its way into the world, we *are* alone, and there are no guarantees for anything.

Your awareness of this reality gives you a distinct edge over those who seem forever dependent on outside factors for their information and their security. Your sense of aloneness can be used to your advantage by realizing that you were never meant to follow the crowd. Instead, you must find your own truths and understand that it is your role in life to be original, creative, innovative, influential, and self-satisfied. It is your place in life to stand alone - *ahead* of the crowd - and to create your own satisfying reality as you go.

Be yourself, be original, take the initiative in all your life's affairs. Liberate and strengthen your Will by denying nothing about yourself and others. Express your feelings spontaneously. Accept your freedom, your independence, your individuality, your uniqueness. Take care of your own needs first and, when necessary, you will be able to take care of others with an uncommon degree of compassion, humility, and understanding.

Intent is such a powerful energy. If your intent is loving, love will materialize in your life. Your personal relationships need to be looked at realistically because they will only flourish with those whose egos are already balanced; or with those who are actively working on balancing their egos; those who appreciate and encourage your creative and pioneering spirit; and those whose own sense of purpose is as intense as yours. You are a strong and ambitious person who is attracted to the strength and ambition of others. These are the people you love. By loving them as you would like them to love you, love itself will flow in great abundance.

The 2 Destiny
the life-long path of the sensitive

Every civilizing step in history has been ridiculed as sentimental,
impractical, or womanish, by those whose fun, profit,
or convenience was at stake.
JOAN GILBERT

The 2 destiny means that you will spend this lifetime learning about the feminine aspects of life, sexual equality, relationships, deep emotional awareness, intuition, healing, cooperation, patience, diplomacy, and meticulous attention to detail.

In the new millennium, the 2s of this world are beginning to lead the way through their refined powers of persuasion, their ability to inspire on an emotional level and, most importantly, their desire to bring PEACE to this planet.

In order to lead successfully, you must develop a calm and gracious approach that takes into account the needs and feelings of all concerned. Yours is the all-important task of *connection*. Therefore, you must be able to see, very clearly, how the big picture is influenced by seemingly minor details.

You are the one who encourages and promotes those who have something valuable to offer. You are the one who takes care of details that others are unable or unwilling to handle. This makes you the ultimate networker and agent, providing a service which enables others to move forward. You are the indispensable behind-the-scenes powerhouse on whom others rely, and you will be given much opportunity to fulfill your own ambitions and dreams along the way.

2 provides you with the power of *illumination*. When you focus that special light of yours on others, it enlivens and inspires. You, in turn, become inspired by your many relationships and experiences.

No matter how you think you fared in the 1000s, it is now in the 2000s that life becomes your oyster and the world becomes your stage. However, the way you live your life, feel your feelings, think your thoughts, make decisions, and reach for your dreams, may be quite unusual. It is from your example that others can learn, emulate, and embrace a brand new way of living which makes peace, love, and understanding their top priorities.

It is now time to bring forward those ideas of yours which were once considered idealistic but are, in fact, major evolutionary elements of life.

Remain true to your feelings and have the courage to question so-called authority and tradition. You must learn to do this without force. Use your natural ability to *persuade* instead.

PEACE is the objective of the 2 energy, which is why the 2000s is *your* time to excel. It is necessary to situate yourself close to those in positions of power so that you can gain their attention and trust. You have little inclination toward control, aggression, competition, or selfishness but, without peace as your motivation, there may be some confusion as to where you actually stand in this competitive and aggressive world.

Whatever your talents may be, they are the stepping stones to accomplishing your vital mission. Your emotional nature provides you with a vital intelligence, and lets you know how peace can be created out of chaos. You have the ability to feel, intuit, and sense your way through life. You must become comfortable with this gift, or you may become overwhelmed by your own feelings.

Your recognition of reality is what makes you so sensitive in the first place. But it is your acceptance of reality and your burning desire to *change*, rather than camouflage, realities that are painful, which can place you in a position of power.

Our misunderstanding of emotion has led us to deny our true feelings to an alarming degree. Most people have forgotten *how* to feel. They do whatever they can to suppress any feelings that may arise. The drug industry, for one, is tapping in to humanity's fear of feeling, and its fear of facing reality. There are now all kinds of "happy pills" which have no other purpose than to cut us off from reality, our emotions and, therefore, from FREE WILL. Acceptance of reality is intelligence and is the key to success and happiness.

2s tend to gravitate toward one extreme or another. Some are oversensitive, humble, passive, and self-depreciating, while others are overly aggressive, angry, controlling, judgmental, and even cruel. 2s often pendulate back and forth between the two extremes before a balance is achieved. Both extremes are created by your various fears, which must be faced head-on. Only then will you know what needs to be feared, and what does not. There is an inherent shyness in most 2s. But when you remain true to yourself and follow your deepest feelings, your humility turns to radiance and dignity.

2 is the number of *relation*. Your sense of self is often overshadowed by your need to interact with and understand other people and their situations. Your various circumstances will teach you to *relate* one thing to another so that a meaningful connection can be made. You will need to understand your position within all of your relationships. It is from these connections that you will both give and receive unprecedented love.

Relatives are likely to play an important role in your life, even though you do not believe you owe allegiance to certain people just because you are related by blood or law. You are able to *relate* to others by sensing their needs, their motivations, and the causes of their problems. You realize that, in some way, you are related and connected to all human beings. You are able to clarify and relate your feelings about other people, verbally and/or artistically.

2 is also the number of COOPERATION. The 2 destiny provides opportunities for you to become an organizer, facilitator, and peacemaker. You may often find yourself in situations where all-round cooperation is required. This does not mean submitting yourself to the demands or negativity of others. It means operating in your own right, usually within a team or group in which everyone involved has a particular talent to contribute or role to play. CO-operation means operating *together*.

You are here to connect other people to each other. Your friends and family are such a diverse collection of characters who have little in common except for the bond they share with you. You *are* what they have in common. You may not be the leader of this pack, but without you there to keep making the connections, the pack may not have existed in the first place.

It may be difficult to fathom, since you were born on the 2 path of peace and understanding, why you were thrown into such a harsh, chaotic, or insensitive childhood. Although your efforts were visible, you may not have received full recognition for your intelligence, contribution, or talent. You probably came up with some great ideas which were discounted or put into action by someone else. You may have found yourself seeking a position of leadership, only to realize that your ideas were too idealistic for this aggressive, judgmental world.

Try to understand and accept your past. This will release you from the pain, grief, anger, fear, guilt, and blame you have dragged with you into adulthood. Your early experiences were necessary to instill in you a burning *desire* for peace. This desire is the driving force for all that you aspire to in life today.

Understand that that was then. Now is quite a different story. In the 2000s, we are living in a new cycle of time in which the 2 energy takes center stage. It is your diplomatic brand of leadership which will attract the largest following. Your innate knowledge of human behavior will help you to become comfortable with your important role in bringing people and ideas together and making things work harmoniously.

The 2 energy requires *patience*, and this is something you possess in abundance. You must be patient and observant as you watch others achieve their results with a force that you simply do not possess. Whenever you try to imitate the aggressive tactics of others, you will end up with many unnecessary problems.

Others are sometimes tempted to take the credit for *your* ideas and efforts, or to use you and your talents without giving due compensation. You may believe that you just don't have what it takes to enjoy the kind of success others seemed to acquire with ease. But this is a temporary situation in which you will learn what needs to be learned. Eventually, you will emerge in your own right, with the added satisfaction of knowing that your success has enabled others to succeed too.

You are a natural diplomat, with a deep consideration for others. However, when 2s become frustrated with their slower path, they are also capable of turning diplomacy into guile and deceit. If you are ever caught in this maneuver, you could well find yourself with the reputation of being sly, slick, or two-faced. You can be extremely clever at hiding the fact that your gift of persuasion has become the knack of manipulation. And rather than apologize, you can twist a situation around and make the person you have offended feel guilty instead. This is your own guilt in reverse. It is called blame. Yes, 2s can send the rest of us on some confusing guilt trips which, frankly, dear 2, we could do without.

While you are very sensitive to the feelings and needs of others, your own feelings can be all too easily hurt. This need not be the case once you have learned to relax with yourself and with the realities that surround you. Most 2s want to retreat from situations where others are insensitive, indifferent, or unkind. But in doing so, they may deprive themselves of many beneficial experiences.

You must learn to deal courageously with the insensitivity of other people. You belong out there in the big and bustling world making things happen for others and, of course, for yourself. But do remember that tireless, patient, and meticulous attention to detail is essential on the 2 path.

You like to think of yourself as a good friend, and you usually are. You also need to know that you are loved by others. You may give the appearance of self-confidence but, inwardly, you may be intimidated by those who somehow seem more capable than you.

There may also be times when you question your own desirability or talent. These are the times when your powers of persuasion become reversed, enabling others to talk you into things that go against your grain. Here, life is trying to teach you to respect your Free Will and say 'no' when 'no' is what you really want to say. Be careful not to give in to the pressures of others simply to avoid confrontation. Your sense of self-worth must be developed so you can face people and issues with confidence and authority instead of aggression, blame, or fear.

Your strengths can be found where other people's are lacking. By doing for them what they cannot or will not do for themselves, in some kind of service, you will create a powerful position for yourself in which you will be considered *indispensable*.

Not only is the 2 energy extremely powerful in its own unique way, but it is becoming even stronger in the 2000s - and so are you. It is providing you with what you need, not only to survive the drastic changes that are occurring, but also to understand and be constructively involved in them.

Nervous tension is inevitable because you may not be able to understand where this power is coming from or what you are supposed to do with it. You may question whether it is real or not, or whether you are somehow deceiving your admirers and followers. If you back away from this exciting but demanding role, you will be dissatisfied because you will know that you are capable of so much more; frustrated with yourself for dreaming about what could be, instead of just creating it.

A strong intuition is one of 2s principal gifts. In order to hear your intuitive voice, it is necessary for you to relax with *everything* that is going on inside you and around you. Do what you want to do in life without dominating a situation or hiding your light under a bushel.

You have probably always been aware of your special qualities but were unable to define them or put them to constructive use in your younger years. This is because you could not bring yourself to believe in your potential for acclaim and personal power.

As time passes and your emotional nature becomes more accepted by your spiritual mind, you will feel the power, and the peace, that comes with this balancing of your mental and emotional energies.

Reduce the stress in your life. 2 is a slow-moving and gentle energy. The pressure that comes from trying to speed things up against its deliberately slow current can make you physically, emotionally, or mentally ill. Whenever you feel intolerable pressure, you can be sure that you are pushing too hard. You may have a lot to do in life, but you will probably do it more efficiently if you do it at a slower pace and observe the *details* involved.

2s instinctively know that spirituality has nothing to do with religion or philosophy. There can be no monopoly on something as personal as the evolution of your own consciousness and your own Will. Although the spiritual journey is a vital and life-giving one for us all, for you it is a unique experience which can be taken as far as you want to take it - or completely ignored. For some, life is a spiritual journey which eventually leads to the understanding of emotion. Yours, however, is a deeply emotional journey which will bring you deep into the spiritual realities of life.

Never deny what you are feeling. It is not the feelings you hide from others that are important here but, rather, those feelings you hide from yourself. *Feel* your feelings so that you can understand what has caused them, and how they need to be expressed. So much new intelligence can be gained from this ongoing experience. It is not enough to simply acknowledge your emotions on an intellectual basis. You must *experience* them. Let them pass through you and out of you. Only by truly feeling your feelings will you be able to navigate the 2 path successfully.

You *are* special! You are capable of great accomplishment which, for some, is to find fame and fortune. For others, it may be to live comfortably and quietly in an atmosphere of love and creativity. Some 2s want to do something specific to change the world. Whatever your aspirations, they can only be achieved through Free Will. Without the freedom to create our own realities, neither love nor peace can prevail. You are able to inspire others by your example, simply by being yourself and doing what you want to do. You have more potential than most to learn from the drastic changes that are now taking place on earth, and to show others the way to peace.

The 3 Destiny
the life-long path of communication

*Like smudges on a pair of spectacles, (words) have the
ability to blur everything you do not make crystal clear.
Listen with great care to what is being said and choose
your own words as if they were diamonds.*
SALLY BROMPTON

COMMUNICATION is your purpose in this lifetime, and you are learning how to communicate *effectively*. You will find that problems arise from lack of communication or when you express yourself inappropriately. Words are the key to your success and happiness. But until you learn what must be learned on this path, words can also be your downfall.

You entered this lifetime for the purpose of communicating something specific and important. However, it may take you a long time to *remember* what it was you came here to express. It may take you even longer to find the most convincing way to express it. Until you take this vital mission seriously, you may talk incessantly while giving no one else a chance to speak. Or, you may be too afraid to express yourself at all. Whichever extreme you fall into, it is because (1) you are overly concerned about how others perceive you, and/or (2) you do not know how to *listen*.

Communication is an ongoing exercise in output and feedback; receiving and delivering valid information. If you do not understand this, you may easily gain the reputation of being 'shallow'.

Whatever your most constant problems are, they are clues to the direction your communications should take. You have used words to talk your way out of many a sticky situation, haven't you? What you may not realize is that it was your own words that caused many of your sticky situations in the first place. The point is, 3, you must find a purposeful outlet for this wonderful ability.

The following 3 destiny people have unusual and memorable voices, and they have the ability to use their voices in unusual and creative ways: *Bill Cosby, Melanie Griffith, Barbara Walters, Alan Alda, Dionne Warwick, Rod Stewart, Joan Rivers, Kevin Spacey, Tracy Ullman, Katie Couric, Pierce Brosnan, Jerry Hall, Connie Chung, Billy Dee Williams, John Travolta, David Bowie, Robert Townsend, Johnny Mathis, Harry Belafonte, Celine Dion, Jodie Foster, Gloria Gaynor, Peter*

Graves, Herbie Hancock, Hillary Rodham Clinton, Phil Collins, and *Dr. Ruth Westheimer,* to name just a few.

Similarly, people remember your voice because there is something unusual about it. When you do recall what you are supposed to be communicating, and when you do find the appropriate words, you will be listened to and *remembered.*

3s have a tendency to play down how they really feel. They are more concerned with giving the *appearance* that everything is okay, even when their problems are obvious. Others can be impressed with the way you seem to bounce back from adversity as if nothing ever happened. Until they get to know you....

Eventually they realize that you have been holding all that emotion *in,* instead of expressing it out. Friendships are often lost because others feel you do not want to help yourself. Of course, they do not understand your complex nature. They do not understand your horrible fear that friends will be lost if you burden them with your problems. 3s are notorious for keeping up appearances. They desire popularity and social acceptance. They have a tendency to turn their problems into jokes. Why? Because they are desperately afraid of what other people think of them.

This guilt exists because 3 is the energy of joy. Many 3s mistakenly believe that they are not allowed to show any emotion other than happy exuberance. But when 3s dare to go beneath their own surface and accept that their emotions are as real as anyone else's, their lives become deep, indescribably beautiful, and richly creative. You are attracted to creative people because you secretly admire their ability to *feel.*

The trick is to take yourself seriously without becoming too serious. Humor, lightheartedness, and laughter are vital ingredients of your personality and of what you are meant to communicate. But you will be unable to use these talents until you are able to feel happiness yourself. And that's the problem. There is a huge difference between humor and happiness. Ask any professional comedian about that. Ask yourself why the clown is so often portrayed with an exaggerated painted smile which is nothing more than camouflage for his tears.

You will never be able to feel and experience genuine happiness until you let go of all that *sadness* that is buried deep inside; the grief you are refusing to express, and all that anger and fear you are burying under what you call your sense of humor.

3s need to be popular, and there is no more popular position on Earth than that of making others feel good about themselves. This is the position you came here to fill. However, it is your experience in the field that will decide whether or not you get the job. How much experience with genuine *happiness* have you actually had?

3's gain this experience by having the courage to do what they want to do; not what they hope will please or impress others; not what they believe they are limited to because of lack of opportunity, funds, or education.

Self-approval, and not just its *appearance*, is what you must strive for. Then you can live free from the worry of who you should be trying to impress. Learn to impress, please and *be* yourself. Worrying about what others think of you has always been a source of great unhappiness in your life. You are afraid of your emotions because they are so intense. But your feelings are nothing to be afraid of. The most emotional people in the world are also the most creative and successful. Why? Because they are driven by what they *feel*. And you are so attracted to these people.

Physical appearance plays a large role in your life. You *need* to feel attractive, popular, and appreciated. But you tend to cling to the trivial and mundane because you are afraid of taking anything too seriously. Rather than risk the pain being *wrong*, you often view opportunity as potential trouble rather than potential joy. Remember all the serious opportunities that have slipped through your fingers over the years and, all too often, into the hands of someone you thought was a friend.

And that brings us to the next aspect of the 3 destiny. *Friends.* People change along with their priorities. So do the feelings people have for one another. It can be painful when 3s realize they no longer have anything in common with someone they believed was a friend. Or frightening when they suddenly realize that they actually like someone they thought they hated. 3s are highly influenced by the opinions and lifestyles of other people. So much so that, sometimes, they do not bother to use their creative powers to be original. This is when friendship can turn to resentment.

These are not easy aspects for you to accept, let alone admit, but only by facing these issues will you be able to see the enormity and sheer beauty of your higher self. And isn't the quest for your higher potential the reason you're reading this book in the first place?

Remember that it is not your role to keep everyone happy, or to sacrifice your freedom in the name of friendship or social acceptance. This is the negative side of the 3 destiny in which the joy you need to experience will forever elude you. Yes, you are a natural performer, but there is no need for you to be *on-stage* all the time. You thrive best in natural surroundings. When you are calm and centered, your greatest inspiration comes from nature itself.

Part of learning how to communicate is to listen, to accept feedback, and to change your 'act' when the feedback is less than enthusiastic. Deep down, 3s know they are meant to communicate. Some assume that they must, therefore, always be right. If you do not hear what others have to say, you will miss the other side of the story. Without the input of others, you cannot learn anything new. This is a difficult lesson for a 3, especially when you realize that your need to be always right actually stops communication in its tracks.

Do not be swayed by popular opinion. We are living in times of monumental change. What may have been true yesterday may not be true today. Be willing to learn new things and your communications will always be fresh, entertaining, and inspiring. There is no need to be constantly talking, gesturing, making people laugh, gossiping, or repeating what you have heard about people and popular trends. Form your *own* opinions instead of merely being opinionated.

3s are naturally brilliant designers, which is why they are so often found in the beauty business or other creative fields. This is a good start. But, surface beauty is an illusion. Your true talents will emerge when you look *beneath* the surface of things and people. Only when you see and accept the reality of what you are dealing with will you be able to express your spectacular originality. Never judge a book by its cover, or a person by their "look". It is all veneer. Beauty is a matter of what is going on *inside*.

Creativity is one of the most precious gifts the 3 energy offers. When your imagination is free from the masochistic bonds of peer pressure, your creative abilities will astonish you and everyone around you. Your approval is the only approval you need. It will come when you realize just how much positive and creative energy exists inside you - *under the surface*. It will come when you allow this energy to express itself freely. Then, there will be no question as to whether you take yourself seriously or not. No one has more potential for creative genius than a 3. Unfortunately, no one is more prone to wasting this potential than a 3. This does not have to be the case once you start taking yourself more seriously.

Your urge to follow popular things and people and to establish a position for yourself in society is not without significant reason. Your desire to be popular is part of the 3 experience. You need to be liked. But you spend so much time trying to please everyone else that you have no time to figure out what you would like to do for *yourself*. Many 3s give the appearance of being superficial when, in fact, their feelings - and talents - run very deep indeed.

It can be difficult for you to focus on one thing at a time. Your well disguised self-consciousness often outweighs your ability to concentrate. You tend to spread your energies in too many directions. Your ability to start things is impressive. Finishing things is another matter. Ironically, one of the reasons you cannot focus on one thing long enough to complete it is that you are seeking the approval of others in the first place. This can be a vicious circle until you learn to take full responsibility for your own mistakes, your own happiness, your own success, and your own life.

When you worry about what others think of you, your imagination becomes stifled. It cannot produce the creative wonders that it is capable of producing. A free imagination is limitless. You may believe that you are already creative. Others may see your talent too. But it is probably only a pale reflection of your true potential. If your ideas are not *original* then your imagination is not free. Your ideas cannot be original if they are based on pleasing others.

Many 3s are unable to tolerate silence. They are so self-conscious in quiet atmospheres that they will talk about *anything* in order to fill the silent void. Then they find themselves on one giant verbal roll and have difficulty ending the conversation. They feel that they *must* communicate, even when they have nothing to say.

Watching and listening to 3s telling a story is quite an experience in itself. The pitch of the voice changes according to the attention being received. Watch how the 3 reacts to and interacts with an audience, how he physically moves into the audience to maintain its attention. He can repeat the same story over and over, along with the same mannerisms, the same sound-bites, and the same enthusiasm as when the story was first told. If the listeners tire of the story, embellishments are added to keep it exciting.

When a 3s communication skills are not developed, we see and hear a person who constantly repeats the same old stories as if they are stuck in the past and unable to move on. Some 3s, when they feel out of their depth, feign interest in what is being said. They are not *listening*. They are waiting for the first opportunity to change the subject to one they feel more comfortable with. And, there you have it! Communication is destroyed.

However, when 3s realize that intelligent, timely, and purposeful communication is their function in life, we see and hear a person who has the power to learn new things and to influence and inspire the entire world. Oh, yes, 3, that is precisely why you are here, and it is a serious mission indeed.

When you do focus for a prolonged period on something you feel passionate about, you are truly a beauty to behold. Your opinion remains fresh and alive.

You need to establish what you want from life and to surround yourself with others who are pursuing similar goals. Finding what you want to do; that thing that makes your heart beat faster and makes time stand still, signifies a vital turning point in the 3 destiny which leads to pure joy.

You belong in a lifestyle that appreciates and contributes to creativity and offers an abundance of social contact. If you are not involved in creative pursuits, then you need to be around those who are. You are meant to be with creative, passionate, emotional people so that you can understand the creative process, learn to take your emotions seriously through *their* example, and find your own passion, your own creative dream, along the way.

Recognize your tendency to criticize, especially in your younger years, and especially in reference to other people's *appearances*. These antisocial traits need to be turned around into genuine friendliness. You can hurt others with your careless use of words, but if others criticize you, you can be cut to the quick. Never dish out what you cannot take.

3 is the energy of appearances. Your own appearance has manifested to make you *memorable*. The way you look is important to you, but there is likely to be at least one aspect that causes you concern. 3 is the number of *attraction*. You are at your most attractive when you are being yourself. When your emotions are free, your physical appearance changes to meet your own approval. In other words, if you believe you are beautiful, so will everyone else. But remember we are talking about belief: not pretense, not the *appearance* of belief.

Remember that as life proceeds, appearances change. 3s often get stuck in time-warps, causing them to cling to people and styles that are now out of place. Popularity is important to you, but it can only be maintained in the *present*, otherwise the only people you will attract are those who are also stuck in some long-gone era.

The only way to release yourself from the anchors of the past is to release those old unexpressed emotions that are holding you there. Eventually you will learn that your appearance - your physical presence - is a matter of what you are feeling on the inside. Once you recognize your self-consciousness and learn to relax with yourself, *inside and out*, you will start to attract the very people you need and desire, instead of a string of superficial acquaintances who are going nowhere and have nothing to offer.

You have the gifts of words, attraction, sociability, creativity, optimism, memory, friendship, and humor. Use these precious talents to see beyond what others see. Break through the chains of popular opinion and dare to follow your own heart.

Seek the JOYS of life, and not just the *appearance* of joy that many 3s seem content with. Discover internal happiness through your own experience and communicate it externally to others. You have the power to lift others out of that negative downward spiral of gloom and doom in which so many are trapped.

Find your own happiness and others will realize that they can find theirs, too. Take yourself and your 3 destiny seriously, because what the world needs more than anything right now is a serious dose of 3's optimism, beauty, creativity, and laughter.

The 4 Destiny
the life-long path of breakthrough

If you run into a wall,
don't turn around and give up.
Figure out how to climb it,
go through it, or work around it.
MICHAEL JORDAN

The 4 destiny means that you will spend this lifetime learning about your identity or purpose in this world. The work you do is likely to play a major role. 4 is the destiny of great accomplishment through hard work, attention to detail, and belief in yourself.

Your 4 personality cannot stand doubt or disorder, even though you are well aware that nothing in life is certain. 4s often become frustrated by issues that others find trivial. But, until you learn to accept life's harsher realities, both mentally and emotionally, feelings of restriction or loneliness are bound to arise.

The 4 destiny creates events and circumstances which enable you to learn self-discipline, craftsmanship, industriousness, practicality, and leadership. Throughout your life, you will experience people and situations that will teach you the value of determination, effort, simplicity, and dependability.

This can be a path of great reward and inspiration - *or* - it can be one of limitation and narrow-mindedness. It all depends on what you believe is available to you. So, let me tell you what really is available to you on the 4 destiny path:

When you accept the gifts that 4 offers, you will experience a wonderful feeling that everything is "clicking" and coming together exactly as it should be; a feeling that everything is in the right place, and that your timing is right on target. It is a feeling that although obstacles are bound to occur, you will be able to deal with them effectively and, often, turn them to your advantage. It is a feeling that there is no challenge you cannot handle, even though you do not seek out these challenges.

4 produces a certain *knowing* that you are on the right road and are headed in the right direction. It is the feeling of succeeding in the materi-

al world while, simultaneously, achieving great inner satisfaction from what you are doing. In short, the 4 Destiny offers a feeling of self-confidence that few others are able to achieve.

When you learn to dispense with the limitations of guilt and blame that so many others place upon their relationships, love is inevitable on the 4 path. When you are confident about your ability to love, you need not worry about hurting others. Neither will you set yourself up for others to hurt you.

Unfortunately, very few 4s ever reach their extraordinary potential because they are just so cynical about it. Either they do not believe that such a condition is possible, or they do not believe it can be maintained. Well, it can be achieved, maintained, and even enhanced to higher levels, once you understand your own nature and recognize the choices available to you. It is never too late or too early to reach this understanding.

Some 4s use age - too old, too young - as an excuse for not doing what they want to do. In reality, 4 offers the opportunity for *agelessness*, if only you would allow yourself the experience of time standing still; the way it does when you're doing something you truly *love*.

Work is a major aspect of the 4 destiny, but if you do not love your work, then a huge chunk of love will be missing from your life. This doesn't mean that love cannot also come from intimate relationships. But you will find that when personal relationships inhibit your ambitions, happiness will be difficult to achieve in either area.

The problem is that 4 is the number of logic and intellectual reasoning. Deep feelings are often avoided, and relationships are then sought purely for social and emotional security. In fact, anything which does not appear to have a practical purpose can be rejected by a typical 4. With so much emphasis on work and effort, you may think that yours is a difficult path indeed. But it is you yourself who tends to make things difficult by wanting to do things in what you believe is the "proper" way.

You have a tendency to make the work much harder by obsessing over details. You may have to learn that most problems can be solved easily and that, in many cases, every tiny detail does not have to be scrutinized and analyzed. You must learn to simplify - not magnify. Finding a balance here may be difficult for you because of your natural tendency for detail, system, and orderliness. But a balance must be reached nonetheless.

Dealing with limitation is one of your most important lessons. Limitation is, in fact, what you are here to learn about and overcome. How are you limited by your own physical body? Your geographical location? Your general environment? Background? Responsibilities? Funds? Gender? Age? Qualifications? Beliefs? Personal history? Guilt? Fear?

Many restrictions can be eliminated or avoided by analyzing a problem and changing your *reaction* to it. To change one's point of view can seem like hard work, but this simply means recognizing your stubbornness, opening your mind, and accepting that alternatives *do* exist. You will find that many of your limitations are the result of your own inflexible beliefs and attitudes.

However, there will be some limitations in your life which appear to be immovable and unsolvable. These are the events and circumstances that life has placed on your path so that you can reach your so-called limits and then use your strong WILL to expand into broader horizons.

We all have limits which make us feel stopped in our tracks, boxed in, or even crushed under their pressure. But, by expanding your belief in yourself, you will produce an energy which creates more *space* around you. This pushes those limits up and out and away from you so that they no longer pressure you. And, if you encounter the same situation at a later time, it will no longer be a limitation but an area in which you have already gained *expertise*.

It is impossible to reach your limits and just crash through them. This would be like banging your head against a wall. You would be injured, killed or, at least, embarrassed. Accepting your tremendous capabilities and *using* them is the key here. Then, your capabilities cannot help but expand too.

Analyze your limitations so that options become apparent to you. Visualize the result you want, and take the actions that will draw it to you. With effort, not struggle, you will experience the elation of *breakthrough*. This will help to make your life happier, lighter, easier, healthier, more loving, and more successful.

One of your natural talents is that you are very practical, even though the word practical means different things to different people. You are very capable of managing and organizing. You can amaze people by taking what they see as chaos and turning it into order, priority, and logic. You are a born supervisor. You are able and usually willing to work long and hard. You have a great deal of patience with detail. You seem to prefer working with difficult problems rather than simpler ones. You are a dependable and conscientious worker whose efforts ensure that the work-at-hand is finished perfectly.

But do try to keep an open mind. Your way of doing things is not always the *only* way. Doing things the "proper" way has a definite place in your life, particularly where craftsmanship is involved, but unless this attitude is kept in perspective, it can also produce emotional, physical, and social problems.

Your frustration with others can sometimes turn into dominance or bossiness. You may focus your disapproving eye on one petty detail of someone else and fail to see the true value of the individual. You often criticize those whose lifestyles are different to your own. This can alienate you from those who have something valuable to offer. It may be difficult to tolerate certain people and, yet, if you look closely at other aspects of their lives, their sense of priority may just turn out to be more realistic than your own.

You must learn to accept others as they are and know that you are free to stay or walk away. Open your mind to life's natural diversity. Resist the urge to tidy everything up. The fact that you are a natural problem-solver can cause you to look for problems which, to others, are no problem at all.

You have a serious approach to most things, even though the other energies in your life may soften this tendency to some extent. You can have a fixed or dogmatic approach which can range from great courage and fortitude, to extreme pettiness and obstinacy. Even if you believe that you are footloose and fancy-free, even if you think you have a wonderful sense of humor, or that you exude creativity, there is a certain rigidity in your beliefs which is caused by your deep desire for a specific *identity*.

You may need to develop a lighter approach to who and what you are and a less rigid image of how you would like to appear to others. Your identity is not measured by the work you do. This may be difficult to fathom, since work is such a major aspect of your life. You must learn that work does not only pertain to what you do for a living. Your life's work - your destiny - is a matter of living in a state of freedom so that you can work at something for which you feel *passion*; something you truly love. Your identity, therefore, is not a matter of what you do for a living, but of living the life you want to live.

At times, you may find yourself going in the opposite direction of your desires by becoming disorganized, lazy, irresponsible, resentful, and with no sense of accountability or compassion. Of course, this is guilt disguising itself as blame. When these negatives arise, it is difficult to see that it is you, yourself, who is causing the problems. Remember that living an organized life includes making time for love, tenderness, enjoyment, creativity, social interaction, relaxation, and plain old fun. You must create a balance between work and play, seriousness and lightness, etc.

Not only does your life emphasize work, but you also possess a deep curiosity for *how* things work. 4s are often known for their love of gadgets, mechanical devices, psychology, sociology, religion, medicine, science, or metaphysics. Do not allow your tendency to do things the 'proper' way to confine you to old understandings which have since expanded. You admire and respect experts but you must realize that experts can only remain experts by keeping up with the times and increasing their knowledge.

So what is the purpose of a destiny that is so filled with limitations? By treating your limitations as accomplishable challenges and not unmovable barriers; by finding the opportunities that are always hidden within those limitations; its purpose - your purpose - is to learn how to live in a state of freedom *from* limitations.

Freedom from limitation means having the intelligence and the courage to realize that life is full of limitations, and that by *doing* whatever has to be done to deal with them, many can be eliminated. This requires effort and determination.

It also requires balance. Know when to take a break so that your energies can be replenished and your life can be *enjoyed*. 4s can be relentless workaholics who do not understand that, once in a while, they are supposed to stop, relax, luxuriate, and actually savor the fruits of their work.

Accept that you have limitless potential, and you will achieve the most significant material and spiritual goals. Become a *master* of the 4 path by combining your highest ideals with the enormous power that 4 gives you. 4 is the number of the architect and builder. Your dreams will be constructed, one piece at a time, through uncommon vision, well laid plans, and the passion to see those plans through to a satisfying conclusion. You have the potential to inspire and change the world with your constructiveness - or - create havoc with the abuse of this power.

Your destiny is one of *greatness*, and you will have to find a way to overcome a massive obstacle that stands in your way. This obstacle is easily definable. It is the inferiority complex that tells you that the desire for greatness is somehow "wrong" or that your large-scale ideas are nothing more than delusions of grandeur. No, my dear 4, it is your judgment against yourself that is wrong.

Let go of your cynicism. Believe in your vast capabilities. Believe in the miracle of life. There is nothing you cannot achieve if you give yourself the freedom to put your heart into it.

The 5 Destiny
the life-long path of experience

Our deepest fear is not that we are inadequate.
Our deepest fear is that we are powerful beyond measure.
It is our LIGHT, not our darkness that most frightens us.
We ask ourselves, "Who am I to be brilliant, gorgeous,
talented and fabulous?" Actually, who are you not to be?
You are a child of God. Your playing small does not serve
the world at all. There is nothing enlightened about shrinking
so that other people won't feel insecure around you.
We were born to make manifest the glory of God within us.
And, as we let our own light shine, we unconsciously
give others permission to do the same .....

NELSON MANDELA
FROM HIS **1994** INAUGURAL SPEECH

5 is the exhilarating path of RESOURCEFULNESS, CHOICE, CHANGE, FREEDOM, and the PHYSICAL realities of life. Being born with the 5 destiny means that you will learn, by trial and error, about your own physical presence on this Earth and the effect your presence has on others. The 5 energy emphasizes your physical body, your sexual intensity, and the impressive way in which your body, mind, and emotions are able to adapt to changing environments.

You will learn, in various and unusual ways, that physical matter changes constantly and that you can either prosper from these changes or be overwhelmed by them. Learning about the physical aspects of you and of life in general, is one of your main purposes for being here.

Eventually, you will experience the freedom and relaxation that comes when your body, mind, and emotions have equal acceptance for each other. You see, this balance *is* freedom. Do not be afraid to admit that you really do need more freedom to think, move, and feel in a way you know is right for you.

The 5 energy enables you to change your outward appearance and your inner attitudes to suit a great variety of environments, contacts, and encounters. This gives you the ability to be all things to all people and to fit in, very naturally, to any situation.

It is true that your personality is not consistent. All this means is that you are brilliantly *adaptable*. Your ever changing personality *is* who you are. It is the result of being yourself, being honest with your feelings, and encouraging the same spontaneity in others. This quality is what makes others feel so relaxed around you and it should never be curbed by your own or society's misconceptions about free expression. Your adaptability is one of the principal talents that life has given you so that you can experience more variety than most others. It has been said that *variety is the spice of life*. It is certainly what will keep your life fresh and exciting.

5 is a very active and unpredictable path. It is so filled with sudden and unusual events and opportunities that you sometimes become confused by it or afraid of it. Consequently, you often miss out on the abundance of experience that the 5 path offers. In order to utilize this energy, you may have to reach a deeper understanding of the word *experience*.

Some 5s are so afraid of accidents and mistakes that, instead of flowing confidently with this exciting energy, they cling to the safe and familiar with all their might. Although they can see and feel the excitement that is passing them by at every moment, they are too afraid to let go, take the plunge, and see where life takes them.

Once in a while these 5s do let go, or the 5 current becomes so strong that they are swept away into some kind of drama, only to miss the excitement of it all because they believe they are simply out of control. They grab on to the first semblance of stability and settle there unfulfilled yet again. The freedom of 5 starts with a desire - *a need* - for adventure, which can only come from inside.

Yes, the pace of the 5 path can be unpredictable and wild at times but, like it or not, you are here to gain experience of it. You must allow dealing with unpredictability to become your second nature, your *expertise*. You can amaze others with your resourcefulness in a crisis, but you may also need to use this talent to take care of some basic needs of your own. There are times in the life of a 5 when the real crisis is nothing more than self-neglect.

Throughout your life, you will find that you constantly repeat the same old mistake over and over, even though it appears to be in a different form each time. Refusing to let go of what is safe and familiar so that you can discover *alternatives* is a large part of what causes a mistake to be repeated. Admitting to your mistakes can be a battle in itself. Accept that mistakes are inevitable in your life because that is how 5s learn and prosper.

Your stubbornness to admit your mistakes is actually the emotion of fear being denied. It is natural for you to be afraid when you don't know what you're dealing with. But you must learn to accept fear as a natural and often life-saving emotion. Until you learn to face your fears head-on, your denial of them will keep you from expanding and enjoying your life. Fear arises when you are not focused on the reality that surrounds you. Therefore, the ability to concentrate is one of the principal lessons to be learned on this path. Otherwise your attention will be scattered in too many directions, mistakes will be made but not acknowledged, your fear of the unknown will become your excuse, and nothing substantial will be achieved.

The only way you can progress, discover new realities, and broaden your horizons, is to allow yourself to learn what needs to be learned when a mistake is made. Some 5s do recognize their mistakes and promise that they'll never make this mistake again, but are afraid to make the *changes* that not repeating it requires. Consequently, they change one approach with another, which is usually just a different form of the same mistake.

Sometimes, a totally new direction must be taken, which means having the courage to let go. There will be a time in your life, or many of them, when you must make a giant leap of faith for which you have had no previous experience. By understanding that this is the way you are meant to proceed, you will find that both your focus and your confidence expand. Your fear of the unknown is then replaced with a sense of adventure and a brilliant insight into what really should be feared, and what need not be feared at all.

5s love the concept of adventure but, instead of enjoying their own fast-paced and unusual episodes, there is often a tendency to live vicariously through the exciting lives of other people. Again, it is unaddressed fear which is making them avoid their responsibility to live their *own* lives. This approach can never bring lasting happiness. 5 is the path of freedom and adventure. Yet, so many 5s tie themselves down to mundane routines and situations in which freedom cannot exist. In order to be happy, 5s need plenty of time and space which they can truly call their own.

Most 5s love to travel. If they do not actually get to travel the world, they usually satisfy this need by fantasizing about far off exotic places, or by allowing their minds to wander into some very unusual places - places that the rest of us could not even imagine. When the free and adventurous 5 imagination is put to practical use, however, great accomplishments follow.

In order to gain the experience of life you need, you must be totally honest about the mistakes you always make - those things you do which never work for you and *always* result in unhappiness, aloneness, and disappointment.

First you must stop repeating this mistake. Catch yourself in the act. Take a very different approach, the approach you should have taken all along but were afraid to. This is how you not only learn from a mistake, but also prosper from it. This is when a mistake is no longer a mistake, but *experience*.

This is the way in which your life must proceed - if it doesn't work this way, then try it another way - until you become experienced enough to travel the 5 energy with a greater degree of self-confidence. At this point, your life reaches calmer waters because you are no longer struggling *against* the tide and are able to see the broader picture and the abundance of unusual opportunity that is yours for the taking.

Many 5s never realize that life has given them the precious gift of freedom. They feel alone in this world. Or, they struggle with unsatisfying relationships or situations and wonder why this is their lot in life. It is important that you realize that you are not alone, and you are not tied down. The truth is that you are free to take care of your responsibilities in a way that will also accommodate your own needs.

The 5 path is an unconventional one which is meant to take you far from your birth place. So, if you feel out of place, know that your right place is out there in the big world, dreaming big dreams, achieving big goals, and embracing all that is different, unusual, exotic, and exciting. You are a citizen of the world. As such, you must learn to let go of prejudices and judgments, and embrace different cultures and realities without losing your unique identity.

There is a tendency on the 5 path to abuse one's physical or material freedom. This often includes overindulgence in food, alcohol, drugs, sex, spending, gambling, and other areas where a balance needs to be maintained.

Babies are often conceived at too young an age, and marriage is rushed into as a means of stability. It is not unusual for 5s to marry several times or make commitments that, eventually, cannot be upheld. Changes of heart and mind are frequent in the life of a 5. That is not to say that you cannot love or be loved on a very profound level. But it is likely that true and lasting love will be found along with maturity. But do remember that maturity has nothing to do with age but, rather, *experience*.

Remember that your physical body is an integral part of you - the vehicle that will transport you through this exciting journey of yours. Your body needs to be well maintained and lovingly cared for. Often it is fear of freedom that causes your overindulgences in the first place, a subconscious rejection of freedom that creates a need to become dependent instead. Too much focus on the needs of others, and a lack of focus on what *you* desire, causes you to deny your fear of freedom even further.

The trick here is knowing what you want, *focusing* on it, and refusing to become entangled in superficial matters that are not part of your desired course. It is important to have a goal and to realize that each step you take toward it is a goal in itself. Seek only those activities and people that will be of benefit to you. Learn not to waste your precious time and resources. Learn the difference between genuine excitement and recklessness because there are no punishments in the land of chance-taking, only consequences.

You will have many episodes where you are footloose, fancy-free, and without a specific goal, but the frustration of moving from place to place, from person to person, from mediocre opportunity to mediocre opportunity, will eventually outweigh the delight.

You are probably known for your resourcefulness and versatility, but in order to feel the great satisfaction that 5 offers, you will need to specialize and become an expert at something you *love* doing. Look to the new and progressive rather than the outdated and conventional. You are a quick thinker, with a real talent for analyzing and investigating, although you do not always use this talent to further your best interests.

Your curiosity, restlessness, and impatience can cause difficulties in staying focused. One of the biggest mistakes 5s make is to give up on an experience before enough time has passed to gain the expertise needed and then rush on to something new that will probably be dropped in the same way. It is impossible to truly know something if you have not experienced it.

And what about love? Romance? Marriage? Responsibility? Parenting? Stability? Success? Prosperity? Are these things even possible on such a self-motivated, fast-moving, and diverse path? Most definitely, yes!

Freedom is the ability to do whatever you desire. Therefore, all of these things, and anything else you truly desire, can be yours. Desire *is* Love. On the 5 path, you have more chance of finding love that is real because real love thrives in freedom. Freedom does not mean carelessly severing existing ties or rushing headlong into the unknown. It means freeing yourself from misconceptions and mistakes so that you can fulfill a dream that is *yours*. And there is no reason why your particular dream should not include deep and fulfilling relationships.

However, if your freedom starts to take away from someone else's, neither person can be free. You must consider your relationships carefully to allow for your free and open 5 personality. You cannot survive in a relationship of rules, insecurity, dominance, or mistrust.

You may have a difficult time in understanding your role in a relationship, and this creates a problem in itself. You see, your role is simply to be who you are. On the 5 destiny path, you will meet others who will love you simply for who you *are* and not for what you can do for them. Your free lifestyle will be part of what they love about you, instead of an intimidating factor. These people are not something you go out and look for. They appear, as if by magic, when you admit to yourself that freedom and adventure are what you *must* have in this lifetime.

Your desire for freedom makes you an attractive and broad-minded individual who is able to relate to people from all walks of life. Your collection of friends and acquaintances are probably a diverse bunch of individuals who are scattered all over the world.

Friendship is very important to you. There are certain people in your life who you may rarely see on a physical level, but your bond with them is unbreakable because of a mutual love of freedom, and of each other.

When you are a friend, you are a friend for life. You possess a very special knack for saying or doing something that comes from your big heart, which can profoundly change another's life. While it is true that nobody can own you, those you have touched with your special open expression will never want to lose you or be able to forget you because you exemplify what everybody wants - freedom, sweet freedom.

The 6 Destiny
the life-long path of balance

I love people. I love my family, my children
..... but inside myself is a place where I live all alone,
where I renew my springs that never dry up.......
PEARL S. BUCK

As a child and young adult, responsibility was always there, but you probably rebelled against it in some way. You may have felt overwhelmed by family or domestic responsibilities that you were too young to handle or take seriously. This changed as you got older, and those who knew you in your youth may now be amazed at your transformation into such a stable and responsible adult. Remembering your childhood circumstances will help you to understand today's young people, which is especially important if you have children of your own. If you do not, you will find that many of the adults in your life are, in some way, your children.

Parenting is a large part of what you will learn about in this life time. You are here to create and to learn that creativity has many forms. It is not confined only to the creating of a biological family. Creativity comes from the outward expression of what you are feeling inside. In your case, it is through your connection to your family that many of your creative lessons will be learned.

Your parents, and the conditions in which you were raised, are likely to have a major effect on you. There may be hard lessons to learn here. Perhaps you blame a parent or sibling disproportionately or feel accountable to them well into your adulthood and even after they have passed away.

You cannot stand to have your loyalty questioned, and it can be difficult to distinguish love from guilt and blame. You must learn that you are primarily accountable to yourself, that family members do not *own* each other, and that love thrives when it is able to flow freely in all directions. You will learn a great deal in this regard through your association with *relatives*. Family *relations* are very important to you.

Each step you take is directly *related* to the last one you took and to the next one you will take. As your life proceeds in this step-by-step fashion, you will realize that although you are walking a path of responsibility, you are not responsible for everyone and everything you encounter, including family members.

One of the principal lessons of the 6 destiny is that of *balance*. Imagine yourself walking a path which is divided into three lanes. The middle lane contains the energies of love, peace, belonging, and understanding. It provides you with impressive abilities to teach, heal, create, nurture, entertain, and solve problems. On either side are the *extremes* of life. These are made up of unresolved hatred, misunderstanding, control, conflict, cruelty, and dependency.

Although you will venture into the extremes from time to time, you will not be happy there and will yearn to get back to the stability and peace of the center path. You must seek and focus on love, peace, healing, and understanding. These are the elements that will make your journey outwardly and inwardly successful.

Of course, anyone can walk a three-lane path and stay centered if that is all they have to think about. But yours is a more arduous test. As your life proceeds, you will amass responsibilities and circumstances which have to be identified, sorted, distributed, and juggled, so that you can maintain your balance.

Many of your duties will be pleasant, and some will not. Much of the weight you find yourself carrying will turn out to be the responsibilities of others which have somehow landed in your lap. You are responsible for your own life and for those things, situations, and people you have created. When you are free of responsibilities that are not yours, your capacity to give and receive love expands to the most satisfying levels.

6 gives you the power of magnetism. You will attract whatever you focus on far more easily than most others. Of course, this can have its drawbacks. Focus on danger, and you'll end up in dangerous situations. Focus on nickels and dimes, and that's all you'll have. Focus on other's shortcomings and you'll be surrounded by negative behavior. Look for problems and, believe me, you will find them. Try to focus on the good in other people by replacing old judgments and outdated beliefs with new and more realistic understandings. Seek peaceful solutions to all problems, and allow others to live their lives without your constant input and criticism.

You are one of life's natural entertainers. People are attracted to your exciting aura. There you are, walking through life on a high-wire, perfectly balanced and at ease. Of course you have a variety of safety nets securely in place beneath you. After all, you are *responsible* for yourself. This is why you are usually able to bounce right back any time you fall.

Others will always help you regain your footing in life because they love to watch your clever juggling act. What a show you can put on when you are balanced. What a brilliant display of inner beauty you exude when you are judging your own steps instead of someone else's. What a positive example you set when you are doing what you love, in a state of balance. You are a superstar. Your personal world, perhaps the whole world, is your stage.

You must develop a clear idea of what you desire from life, otherwise you will find yourself accumulating unwanted responsibilities just because you were standing there with nothing else to do. While you have unfulfilled dreams of your own, your need to volunteer must be curbed unless, of course, it is your dream to volunteer.

You are a very capable *teacher*. You have a natural ability to teach others how to take care of their own needs, to be responsible for themselves, and that life does not punish but, rather, produces *consequences* for judgments and actions taken.

Just as you cannot remain balanced on this path while you are struggling with other people's burdens, you can also lose your footing if you become too judgmental, arrogant, or greedy. A tendency to *look* for problems can cause you to neglect your own basic needs or to interfere in other people's lives in the mistaken belief that you can, somehow, save them from themselves.

It is a humbling experience when a 6 is told to butt out of someone else's business. This will happen at least once in your lifetime. Others resent a know-it-all and judgmental attitude. But you will not get lost in this extreme for long. You need the stability of loving relationships. You pride yourself on giving sound advice, and you can be hurt when your input is ignored or belittled. You quickly learn the arts of listening, diplomacy, and right timing.

You really do want to *understand* things. You know that it is impossible to understand something that you have not experienced. This applies to your relationships too. You can live a lifetime with someone and not *know* them because a barrier exists that prevents you from *feeling* who they really are. Or, you can meet a stranger and *know* this person immediately. The quality of your relationships is determined by the extent to which you let go of judgment and open yourself to the one-on-one experience of the individual involved.

Which brings us back to family. To understand is to *familiarize*. Familiarization within your own family is where this lesson begins. Life will teach you that rules, staunchly upheld traditions, and the inability to accept that everyone *changes* as their lives unfold, retards the process of familiarization. And, as you now familiarize yourself with your 6 destiny, you will start to realize just how much you desire to be familiar with so many different aspects of life. You came into this life to understand and teach, and you would dearly love to understand and teach it *all*.

You are known for your responsible approach and impressive problem-solving skills. You may not always welcome those who look to you for solutions but, because your nature is parental, you usually oblige them graciously as part of the flock that you must guide. However, when you treat them not as the children they appear to be, but as respected equals with whom love and pleasure is shared, or from whom *you* may have something to learn, deep relationships are formed. Equality is just another form of balance.

These intimate experiences provide you with realistic understandings of emotion and judgment, and how individuals influence each other. You will form many relationships. Each will affect the other, and this is where your balancing skills are tested. Loyalty is one of your great attributes, until you must choose between two precious alliances. You will learn that your relationships are *yours* and that not everyone in your circle is going to get along.

Your magnetism, or charisma, is what draws people to you in the first place. This gift is developed by exuding outwardly the desire for peace you feel inwardly. This desire creates an aura around you that tells others that peace is your objective, and they cannot help but respect you for this.

When your power of magnetism is used correctly, it has a calming effect which creates the desire for peace in others too. You have the ability to calm even the most aggressive individual. When you are genuinely in this balanced, peaceful, and nonjudgmental place, you are able to *spread* peace to others and create an atmosphere of purpose, belonging, and mutual respect. This is why you are thought of as the stable one, the adviser, the problem-solver, and the peacemaker. It is why you are able to command the respect of others even though they may not be able to pinpoint why they respect you so much. When your friends become your 'family', they will want to help and protect you at all times.

There will, of course, be those times when others turn against you, or even hate you. These will be the times when you have strayed off the path of balance. Perhaps your ego has become inflated and you are trying to control or manipulate things. In fact, it is not uncommon for 6s to be regarded as 'control-freaks'. Maybe you are being too opinionated, aggressive, irresponsible, interfering, bossy, or can see only your side of the story. Maybe you are being judgmental instead of using your good judgment.

Others become disappointed or even afraid of you when you lose sight of your own loving nature. You will also encounter difficulties in relationships when your life becomes an act in which you preach peace and love while holding in - denying - your true feelings.

You must be totally honest with yourself as to what you are *feeling*. You may believe that it is impossible to love if you are feeling hate. But the truth is that you cannot love genuinely if you do not express outwardly any hatred you may be holding inside. Remember that BALANCE is the secret ingredient of a very happy and successful life for you. It is impossible to remain balanced while carrying the weight of your unexpressed feelings.

6 is a complex destiny in which stability and approval are desired. You need to feel an intimate sense of belonging within your home, family, and

community. You are more at ease when there are clearly defined rules and traditions which embrace security and enable you to play a parental role. But do not expect others to play by your rules. These are *your* safety nets.

You want to be seen as a stable, responsible, and caring pillar of the community who will volunteer to help if necessary. Many 6s do not believe they are governed by tradition, conservatism, or rules until they realize just how much they are motivated by a sense of duty and a need to do the right thing. You may not be traditional in the broad sense of the word but within your family and circle of friends, there are many traditions you do not wish to modify or change.

Your home is your castle. You are responsible for it and for those who live in it. You are the ruling monarch, chief caregiver, problem-solver, healer, educator, and provider. You expect total cooperation and cannot understand why others don't appreciate that everything you do is for *them*. But this causes guilt and resentment for all concerned because you are not doing what you need to do for *yourself*.

6s are often involved in situations where justice is questioned and analyzed, or where laws are staunchly upheld or defiantly broken. Be careful not to develop extreme approaches when it comes to justice and judgment, rules and regulations, right and wrong. It is here that many 6s meet their downfall. In order to remain balanced, you will have to take a center position and assess the relativity of all factors. You know only too well that no law can be absolute and that real justice takes place on a much higher plane.

When you enforce your rules on others, you lose your balance because you become dependent upon their cooperation. And then, when you realize just how unstable you have become, the fear of losing your authority can produce controlling and dictatorial behavior. Or, you can become pessimistic and timid. This approach creates an emotional paralysis which prevents you from moving forward. It causes you to seek the advice of so called experts, who may be even less informed than you, to tell you how to live.

You are here to learn about and exemplify balance. It is from this standpoint that your true purpose can be fulfilled. Yes, home, family, and community have much to do with your aspirations. It is from these experiences that you will recognize that the world is also your home and that everyone on Earth is your family. It is only in balance that humanity's love can flow freely.

You were born with judgmental tendencies to learn how inaccurate judgment can be. You were born to experience control over others to learn of its futility. You were born to take on responsibility to learn about freedom and that it is not freedom *from* responsibility that you desire, but the freedom to take care of your responsibilities with ease. You were born with the gift of magnetism to attract others to your entertaining example. You were born to understand the creative process and teach those understandings to others. You were born to make peace so that life can continue. Oh, what a spectacular mission yours is!

Yes, 6 can be a confusing path to walk at times: a path of changing realities, duties, and loyalties. But it can also be a journey of beauty and love if your intent is to protect and beautify life.

Remember that intent is such an awesome power. It is the fuel that drives you through life, and the gauge that sets your direction. No matter how many wars or misunderstandings you encounter, or even partake in, if your firm intent is for peace and understanding, the necessary lessons will be learned and the 6 destiny will take you wherever you want to go. 6 is the path of LOVE. It contains far more reward than you may have *judged* it to have.

The 7 Destiny
the life-long path of intellect

Simplicity is the most difficult
thing to achieve in this world:
it is the last limit of experience
and the last effort of genius.
GEORGE SAND

7 is the path of WISDOM, TRUTH, PERFECTION, and FAITH. It is taking you on an extraordinary journey in which your quest for understanding is the main factor behind everything you do and everything that happens to you. You are the reality-seeker who will accept nothing but the truth. But until you recognize and accept that the attainment of wisdom is your very purpose in life, you may be left confused and frustrated by the actions and attitudes of other people.

7s are seeking perfection. But, in this imperfect world, you can only aspire to what is perfect for *you* and, even when you have found what you believe is perfection, you will soon discover its flaws and become dissatisfied again. If you cannot, at first, recognize this trait in yourself, just study your own actions and needs for a while, or ask someone who knows you well. You will soon realize that you are, indeed, an exacting soul whose standards are often too high for others, and even you, to keep up with.

You may want to remove yourself from the frays of the common man so that you can maintain your dignity and privacy. To others, your need to be alone can appear to be secrecy or aloofness, and this can make you difficult to get to know or even approach. There is often a strangeness about you which others can find unnerving and intimidating.

Once you become comfortable with your differentness, others will realize that this is actually your uniqueness - your inner beauty - the very thing that enables you to stand out from the crowd and be remembered. This precious gift of the 7 destiny brings mystique to your personality. You are intriguing to a lot of people. Puzzles excite you, mainly because you, yourself, are a puzzle; a fascinating and sometimes confusing enigma. And unraveling the puzzle of *you* is an important part of what your journey is all about.

7s live in their minds, constantly going within to find answers to their constant and diverse questions, always looking for the truth which could bring about the changes they visualize. As a 7, you probably have profound beliefs and strong feelings about many aspects of life. 7s question authority and make impressive and moving arguments for change. Your active intellect often astounds others with its unusual perspectives and insights.

However, you are also prone to great stress and worry when matters go beyond your comprehension. It is not unusual for 7s to suffer from excruciating headaches, which are the result of the sheer pressure that comes from thinking so hard about matters for which there seem to be no acceptable answers, or from having to endure environments, people, or situations which go against their dignified grain.

Very often, your quest for answers simply produces more questions. But isn't that the basis of higher intelligence, answering questions with questions until the truth is uncovered? Just as the physical 5 destiny often places great stress on the body, the intellectual 7 destiny stresses the mind beyond what it believes is its capacity. Your headaches will continue until you learn what needs to be learned about *your* particular mind.

Your 7 mind must allow itself to expand and become so capacious - so open - that its boundaries do not press down on you and create physical pain. Developing an open mind is essential to your wellbeing and is a large part of your life's purpose. Alas, developing a truly open mind is not as easy as it sounds for a 7.

This level of intellectual openness can only be achieved when you learn to accept the *emotional* reality of every experience you have. It comes when you accept the imperfections that are in you as well as in other people. It comes when you do your learning *in private*, when you release your emotions *in private*, and when you accept the fact that you are actually a very sensitive and emotional person.

You, of all people, experience great pain and embarrassment if you think you are being scrutinized or criticized publicly. There is so much that others do, quite openly, that you must do behind closed doors. While 7s are not generally known for being open-minded, it must be repeated that open-mindedness is what you have come into this life to achieve.

Others may see you as a serious individual. But the only serious thing about you is your desire for respect, dignity, and truth. You prefer the company of those who are educated, refined, and tasteful. Your love of high quality is probably one of your better known characteristics. 7s possess a certain flashiness and panache which could never be mistaken for gaudiness.

Although you tend to place yourself in conservative environments, you answer to no clique, philosophy, or law, unless it is your own. With even the most foolish or undignified behavior to your discredit - yes, you too are prone to some negative behavior at times - you instinctively know that you are a wise soul who must dance to the beat of your own drummer.

You are a deep thinker, a clever planner and orchestrator, a keen investigator, a creative analyst, an accurate intuitive, and an impressive problem solver. In order to expand these gifts to their full potential, you must learn to be at peace with your thoughts and feelings. Indeed, you must learn to tell the *difference* between your thoughts and your feelings.

Much of your excessive worrying is caused by listening only to your mind and ignoring your feelings. Balance is achieved when your thoughts and feelings align and agree with each other. At this point, inner harmony is reached, solutions are found, and headaches disappear.

Paranoia is not an uncommon condition for a 7. Usually, however, the 'big brother' you think is always watching you is nothing more than your own feelings of fear which you have been too afraid to acknowledge. And what are you afraid of? Poverty is one of the monsters under your bed, and the very thought of having to endure scandal and indignity is another. But your ability to forge master plans, with no detail left to chance, can provide the inner security you need.

However, if your plans become plots and schemes, you place yourself in the vulnerable position of being caught. Then the paranoia starts all over again. There is always some form of intrigue in the life of a 7 because 7 is the number of secrets, conspiracies, and behind-the-scenes activities.

But you were never meant to live on the edge, 7. You were never meant to become involved in fast, loud, or chaotic activities or underhanded complicity. Your true potential cannot be realized in cold environments in which others are consumed by envy, aggression, or self-sabotage. You need quiet and elegant surroundings in which to think without interruption, to admire quality and artistry, and to soak up beauty and tranquility. You need calm and quiet, and you need *inner* peace, so that your remarkable power of intuition can be developed and strengthened.

Your intuitive skills give you the ability to sense or "feel" your way through any situation, with unexpectedly positive results. Unexpectedly for others, that is. When you listen to your inner voice - the voice of your *feelings* - positive results will come as no surprise to *you*.

While others sit perplexed and confused by a problem, you can produce the right answer, as if by magic, in one intuitive flash. And once you have the solution, your intuition will take you inward and backward to show you *how* you arrived at it.

Yours is the probing mind of the analyst and scientist who will not rest until a question is answered in full. And if someone tells you to do something without explaining why, there is a good chance that you will rebel in your own unique way. You simply must know WHY.

You are often afraid of your own thought process and of the depths to which you know your mind is capable of going. This means that you are afraid of your spirituality. And what exactly is your spirit? Spirit is your mind. It is your consciousness. It is your masculine energy. You can, however, become a master of spirituality, if you strive to expand upon this potential and incorporate your feminine energy, otherwise known as your Will, or the power of your emotions, into your personal equation.

7 is the number of science. It is the number of knowledge and intelligence. Those on its path must learn to accept their emotions as natural elements of life. They must address their unaddressed fear. It has been the denial of emotion which has always kept spiritual reality out of the realms of scientific explanation. True scientists are secretly trying to find God, the originator of life. But fear of what they may find has deterred the most brilliant minds from uncovering the truth. This makes the emotion of fear a challenge that neither they, or *you*, can afford to discount any longer.

Do not be afraid to be afraid. Feel your fears. Then you will be able to separate those things which really do need to be feared from those which do not. Without this understanding, a 7 can live an entire lifetime in a state of worry, concern, guilt, or paranoia. You may think you are not a scientist or you may think you are not a spiritual individual, but you cannot deny that you *love* to delve into that mind of yours to see what it is trying to show you.

But, oh, how you hate and fear the ordinary and the mundane. You can be a cruel critic at times. You can hurt other people's feelings or even lose love and friendship with that scathing tongue of yours. Or, perhaps, you are one of those 7s who does not confront others directly but waits until they are out of earshot before you tear them to shreds. Sorry, 7, but your tendency to criticize is one of your great imperfections.

Of course, this can be rectified. First, you must acknowledge that you are, indeed, extremely critical of those you feel do not meet your high standards and tastes. Then you must realize that your standards and tastes, although perfectly natural for you, are not just higher than average; they are extraordinarily lavish and uncompromising.

Do not lower your standards because it is your nature to seek perfection in all areas of your life. Realize, however, that very few others will ever meet your high expectations, even if they desire to. An understanding of your differentness here will help to curb that critical tongue of yours. It will enable you to replace your inadvertent snobbery with a remarkable dignity and presence which exudes warmth, friendliness, serenity, confidence, intelligence, and compassion. You are at your most beautiful and your most impressive when you express yourself with a little humility.

You may never truly understand how other people can accept less than the best, or how they can put up with situations which, for you, would be intolerable. Your criticism will not help others, but your genuine desire to understand them will earn you their respect. This, in turn, may trigger a desire in them to better understand themselves. Do not be surprised if some individuals try to follow your example and seek to become more like you. It may amuse or annoy you to see others copying your lifestyle, your look, your expression, or anything else of yours they admire.

Never forget that imitation is the highest form of flattery. And you can be sure that they will never pull it off with the same measure of perfection as you. When they can no longer keep up the pretense, they will probably turn the tables and criticize *you* for being so pretentious. But, of course, it is not you who is trying to keep up with the Jones'. You *are* Jones!

You are seeking wisdom on this 7 path of yours and one of the first great wisdoms that 7 has to offer is this: Do not shoot your mouth off if you are not sure of what you are about to say. Careless use of words can create havoc in your life. You are extremely intelligent and to be labeled a know-it-all or an ignoramus would be a devastating affront to your dignity.

Most 7s enjoy intelligent discussion and cannot bring themselves to partake of unsophisticated exchanges. Of course, this can leave you conspicuously silent at times, especially in debate or other forms of argument. 7s become introverted, shy, insecure, or boorishly loud and aggressive when they are unsure of themselves.

Whenever there is heavy or unproductive argument, the most intelligent 7s leave it to others to do the shouting and convincing. They sit quietly, look dignified, and appear to be listening. But what they are really doing is escaping from it all and venturing inward to the tranquility of their own mind. Or, they will get up and leave the scene entirely. There is always the element of the loner in a 7.

But when 7s really do know their stuff, not only are debates won, but also the respect of those with whom they are debating. This is because they have shared their wisdom instead of arguing their point.

Yes, you are seeking wisdom on this elegant and slightly eccentric 7 path of yours, but what is the point of amassing so much knowledge if it is not shared with those who need and want it?

When you realize how blessed you are within the 7 energy, when you learn something profound from each of your experiences, when you find the courage to share your knowledge and dreams with others, and when you realize that it's okay to want to be alone and that aloneness does not require you to be *lonely*, your impressive contribution to life will be recognized by others. You will be sought out for your special knowledge and compensated accordingly.

There will always be the mundane and the mediocre; the crude and the rough; the ignorant and the evil, but as long as you accept these aspects as part of life's reality, without ever compromising your own position, the 7 path can take you wherever you want to go.

The 8 Destiny
the life-long path of empowerment

*What this power is, I cannot say. All I know is that it exists
and it becomes available only when you are in that state
of mind in which you know EXACTLY what you want
and are fully determined not to quit until you get it.*
ALEXANDER GRAHAM BELL

The 8 destiny signifies a lifetime of investing in yourself and overcoming the judgments that stand between you and your very strong ambitions. You will learn that others can only dominate you if you allow them to, and that all circumstances can be changed by taking determined action. You are here to learn about and master life's material and financial aspects from a spiritual perspective.

You want to appear fearless. You may deny that your fear exists, even when it is obvious. As experience is gained, a certain fearlessness does develop but, first, you must learn to be *authoritative* instead of domineering. The only things you are meant to dominate are your own time and space. However, there will be times when you feel that the whole world is, or could be, your dominion.

Eventually you realize that fear is a natural emotion; the effect of something that requires *caution* on your part. It is impossible to exclude fear completely. This would deprive you of the information you need to keep yourself safe. Instead of denying fear, or dwelling in it, you will learn to welcome fear as the radar device it is supposed to be. You will learn not to be afraid to be afraid.

But matters of the heart can take fear, or denial of fear, to more difficult levels. Your fear of emotional pain makes you vulnerable inwardly, no matter how much confidence you exude outwardly, until you realize that love does not hurt. It is *loss* of love that causes pain.

Your childhood may have had some oppressive elements such as financial, intellectual, or emotional poverty. Your parents or other adults may not have appreciated your enormous potential for success. Perhaps your interests did not fit in with their expectations for you or with the reality of the world as it was then. There was either a strong emphasis on making something of yourself, or it was assumed that you would amount to nothing. Your determination to be 'somebody' and your dread of being 'nobody' is an 8 gift which now propels you to seek your own route to success.

8 children often experience problems with matters of entitlement. You're entitled to this; you're not entitled to that. In some cases, your very *title*, your name, is a problem. Childhood memories are vivid to an 8. They motivate all your goals of today. At some point, you will decide that your background can no longer stand in your way. And because you want to succeed, you probably lean toward ideals that exemplify dignity, economy, grace, and efficiency. You know that your behavior has a direct bearing on whether or not you will get what you want. You know how to behave. You know where your loyalties lie. And you know how to be discreet.

What a diverse collection of friends and acquaintances you have amassed. You cannot adapt to all of them. Therefore, you must present yourself in a way that does not offend anyone and allows you to be seen as steady and reliable. People enjoy your presence. And you *do* have a strong and seductive presence. Your charm and charisma represent more of 8s special gifts to you.

You came into this life to experience personal satisfaction. It is a feeling so wonderful and impelling that it's a pity many 8s never look beyond purely material and financial satisfaction and reach for the true power that inner gratification brings. It is not a matter of forcing yourself to be content with mediocrity or pretending that you're satisfied. It is a matter of going out into the world and manifesting what you desire on a material level. Desire is a form of *love*.

You do desire abundance. You want to make a *lot* of money. You are ambitious and energetic. You are also an excellent organizer, administrator and persuader, provided it is you who gets to call the shots. You are acutely aware of how others fit in with your own plans and ambitions. You have an impressive ability to take control and direct. You want the freedom and the status that comes with money, and it is unfair to deny yourself these natural 8 desires. It is also unfair to deny yourself the education, the learning process, which enables you to fulfill these needs and helps release you from the guilt and anger that has followed you through from childhood.

You will learn that it's NOT just about the money. It is your ability to manifest what you desire, with or without money, that is the true measure of your personal power. Sometimes there is no amount of money in the world that can give you what you want, since love and acceptance are your greatest desires. But money is a tool, and it is important that you learn how it works: accumulate it; "play" with it; and use it to get what you want, without allowing guilt to tell you that your focus on money and power is wrong.

Take only what you desire from life. 8s who hoard and take everything they can get their hands on are operating through greed. This brings no satisfaction whatsoever, even though they will deny their discontent. They will also deny that they feel guilt about their obsession with materiality. When guilt is denied, 8s natural *love of life* is replaced by manipulation and/or bullying.

During the 1980s, the entire world was under the influence of the 8 energy. The misuse of money and power *and* the hatred of money and power during that decade, created a heartless era of haves and have-nots which is still with us to this day. Negative 8s develop a dangerous obsession with power. They reach their goals, but exclude love from their accomplishments. The fact that they are despised simply adds fuel to their belief that ruthlessness is what it takes to be successful.

Then, there are those 8s who desire achievement and money but are too afraid to take the risks they believe asserting themselves would require. They feel dissatisfied, resentful, and limited but may deny these feelings completely, while the echoes of childhood tell them they do not have what it takes to succeed.

The negative elements of 8 can be avoided when you accept that there is nothing wrong with wanting something better from life. Just remember that too much emphasis on money can lead to limited thinking, stifled creativity, and missed opportunities. Driving yourself and others too hard, or trying to go it alone so you do not have to share, are destructive elements of the 8 energy.

You, dear 8, are one of the magicians of the material world. You can make things happen just by focusing on the desired result and taking action to attain it. Your power to manifest is an instinctive talent, the Midas touch, a strong magnetism that attracts material reward.

Although 8 is the most materially-driven energy, it reaches its true potential when its spiritual and emotional aspects are understood. You are here to discover personal satisfaction which can never be attained without *loving* intent. It is through the power of intent that you are able to manifest anything at all. Intent is desire, desire is love. So, what is it that you desire? What is it that you love? What brings a smile to your lips and a glow to your face? Always be aware of what you are trying to manifest and of how you are weaving your magic. You *will* get what you wish for.

You may think it is you who networks, organizes, convinces, connects, and ideates, but it is the 8 energy within you that brings you to the right place at the right time, introduces you to the right people, and sets you up in the right circumstances.

Once you realize this, you will be able to live and succeed by intuition - *emotional awareness* - the way you *feel* about things. Remember that balance is one of the key ingredients of all magic. The other is presence. This means *being* there; being focused.

You must learn that you *are* allowed to make mistakes. And you do learn quickly from those mistakes that you actually admit to. You are instinctively aware of the laws of cause and effect. You learn that if you do something this way, this is the result. If you do something that way, that will result. And results are what you constantly seek along the 8 destiny path.

Playing it safe is the logical step to take in most circumstances, but issues will also arise which require leaps of faith into the darkness of uncertainty. Learn to visualize the end result first. Then plan the steps you will need to take to reach your goal. Treat each step as a goal in itself. Graciously request the cooperation of others to take care of the smaller details while you focus on the larger ones. The resentment of others may be felt, but this can also be avoided. Delegate with fairness. Treat others with compassion and respect. Their input and their feelings *are* important.

You have an extraordinary ability to utilize the talents of others and manifest something much greater than you or they could ever achieve alone. The end result is something which bears the trade mark of *your* creative genius even though others did contribute to it. And so, you must learn to give credit where it is due.

You want the best of everything. When it comes to displaying your talent, you know that you must give only the very best. Your deep pride can be a positive force which prevents you from rushing into situations you are not ready for, or from assuming that you are more talented than you are. Your strong desire for status provides dignity which, in turn, becomes part of the magnetism that makes you so attractive. There may be aspects of you that are wild, but your sense of propriety will always bring you back to a more conservative and down-to-earth approach.

You need to be in an environment in which contact with powerful and wealthy people is possible. They can open doors for you. Life will provide opportunities for you to interact with such people. You have much to learn from them, and they from you.

You may also have friends who focus purely on humanitarian or artistic pursuits. It is you who can open doors for them. Many 8s travel this path taking only its rewards. Others *master* this path by taking its rewards and sharing them with others. You love success, and you can be as excited about someone else's success as you are about your own. Well, almost.

Did you know that you often talk in tangents? Once you get going verbally, there is little that can stop you expressing *everything* in that dynamic mind of yours. One sentence is often interrupted by a completely unrelated thought, shifting your conversation from one topic to another without even a pause to catch your breath. Then, you will ask yourself, *"What was I talking about?"* and, with a certain grace, you'll find a common link which will bring the topic back to its original focus.

You always want more; you always want to do better; and you always want a return on your time and investment. Or, you may deny that you are dissatisfied with your life because you are afraid to feel the guilt that wanting more invokes. Or, you may be too proud to admit your discontent, even to yourself. Eventually, your need to propel yourself forward and upward will force you to face reality and realize that self-denial is no longer an option.

Of course, satisfaction is never a permanent state of being. It is an ongoing series of stops in your journey in which to experience the sensation of happiness. It is a feeling of thankfulness for who you are, the way your life is proceeding, and for everyone who has contributed to it. These are the times when you feel compelled to stop what you are doing, realize how far you have traveled, how much love you give *and* receive, and feel the joy of genuine satisfaction. It is an exciting rush of warm emotion which saturates the mind and body. This is *love of life*, dear 8, and you will not want these intensely personal episodes to be interrupted by minor details such as your business agenda. This feeling is the reason - the main reward - for everything else you do.

You can make an excellent entrepreneur, but you prefer a more stable environment. Once a base is established, you do not want to take chances or make too many changes. You like to stick to what you know. You cleverly disguise your traditional approach by adding just enough pizzazz to keep things looking fresh and original. This is the part of your magic that keeps others enthusiastically coming back to something which is actually routine. You take the ordinary and make it extraordinary; you take what you *already* have and build upon it.

There is nothing ordinary about the 8 ego, however. It pendulates from massive over inflation to the depths of self-sabotage. These extremes occur when you forget that you are walking a path on which that thing called guilt often jumps out and attacks you.

Because guilt disguises itself in so many different forms, it can catch you off guard and leave you either insecure and overly humble, or insecure and overly arrogant. However, these feelings pass quickly because your sense of dignity eventually provides the balance your ego needs.

Of course, your need for dignity also has its negative side which produces feelings of superiority, a loathing for the mundane, a disgust for what you consider bad taste, a fear of scandal, and a terror of displaying emotional weakness.

When 8s admit to these fears, a certain calmness takes over as they discover their true strength; the power to *feel*. When fear is accepted as "normal", deep feelings of satisfaction are experienced, followed by new and higher goals.

You do not want to be told what to do, but others do become irritated when you ignore their well-intended advice only to, somehow, figure it out by yourself. You can ignore other people's ideas, only to incorporate them into something for which you are given credit. You do not deliberately steal other people's ideas, but you do hate to see a good idea go to waste. You simply do what 8s do. You *incorporate*. But it is when you incorporate *love* into your magic melting pot that you are able to manifest something which is loved by others. This is your key to success. Give people what they *love*.

Yes 8, love is a difficult issue for you to deal with. You may believe you are the most loving person in the world, but not everyone can relate to your businesslike manner. You want the best of everything, including intimate relationships, but your actions can prove painful for others when business, reputation, or money come between you.

Your own feelings can be hurt if a friend or family member oversteps your clearly defined social mark and does something to embarrass you. You may have already distanced yourself from those family and friends who don't fit in with your image. This is normal behavior for an 8, until a level of confidence is reached where you can accept the reality of your background without fear of being judged for it.

Your reputation is so important to you. Any form of rejection can leave you unable to function. If you feel slighted or shunned, you can go to extraordinary lengths to prove just how likable you are. This, too, is normal for 8s who are uncertain of their higher purpose.

Only you can determine your higher purpose through the way you *feel*. And it is only on the 8 path of manifestation, money, power, status, and satisfaction that you will ever discover what it is. You will know what it is when your activities create passion, love, and enthusiasm in you. And, still, the only way you will be able to fulfill your higher purpose is from a position of personal strength.

Elizabeth Taylor's destiny number is 8. In a 1996 interview with CNN's Larry King, she talked about her passionate efforts for AIDS research, and said: *"What good is all this fame and power if I cannot use it to help others?"* Perhaps she found her higher purpose in her powerful lifetime. Yours is entirely your own business - your own passion - your own calling. One thing is certain though: You *have* the power.

The 9 Destiny
the life-long path of letting go

The best and most beautiful things
in the world cannot be seen or even touched.
They must be felt with the heart.

HELEN KELLER

9 is a path of insight, generosity, emotion, compassion, global awareness, interpretation, diversity, and strength. 9 contains a little bit of all the
other numbers, as well as some unique characteristics of its own. Its influence makes you versatile and unusual.

To better understand 9s universal effect, add together the numbers
from 1 to 8. (1+2+3+4+5+6+7+8). The answer is 36. Add the 3 and 6 together, and you have 9. Add 9 to 9 and you have 18. Add the 1 and 8 together,
and you're back to 9. This is the only number that works in such a mysterious way. Just as 9 contains all the other numbers, you, yourself, are all
things to all people.

The 9 destiny enables you to live a life full of love, accomplishment, and
personal satisfaction. But you must accept that *feelings* are what you came
into this life to express and understand. The 9 destiny is, indeed, an emotional one.

9 is the most complicated of all the energies. It is the most difficult to
live with or make sense of. And, until you understand its emotional purpose, life can seem like an eternal roller coaster ride. Trauma after trauma
may have to be experienced until you finally *accept* that emotion is what
you are here to learn about.

The 9 mind expands and evolves in ways that most others will not experience. This enables you to feel love in its most profound and diverse forms.

You often have to travel in what seems like the wrong direction - backwards - in order to go forward. The 9 path is so complex that you cannot
help but become involved in the metaphysics of life. You have an insatiable
appetite for the spiritual and psychological.

A basic understanding of reincarnation is desirable because this lifetime
is likely to be your last. If that sounds a little ominous, you should know
that all 9s are very old souls who have lived many lifetimes. Haven't you
ever wondered why nothing really shocks you? It is because you have seen

it all before and done it all before. You have been every form, color, race, creed, and gender, and you have traveled every walk of life.

Deep down, you know you are here to conclude unresolved issues of the past so that you can move on to a higher existence. Yet you must live this life fully. You must finish everything you start, tie up all the loose ends, gain experience from your past and present mistakes, and leave nothing unfinished. All of this can seem like a daunting task. Or, in a different light, it can be an exciting and fulfilling adventure in which to experience love on a very profound level.

You can become frustrated and angry at the demands of others. Usually, you are the one who allows this to happen. You may not assert yourself as fully as you could. Your live-and-let-live attitude is a beautiful part of who you are, but it can also backfire on you. To counteract this, you must develop self-respect and, at the same time, be comfortable in your role of *giver*. When this is achieved, you will have no problem saying "no" when it is necessary, and you will be able to move away from the guilt that often plagues the 9 who does not know what it means to be a 9.

You can achieve anything for which you feel *passion*. You are probably aware of just how versatile you are. There is very little to which you cannot relate and you probably know a little bit about everything. However, while your versatility is a great asset, it can also create problems with regard to your sense of identity, making a living, and establishing a secure base for yourself. Therefore, it is necessary for you to specialize in something in which you are passionately interested. Otherwise, you cannot help but suffer the pains of feeling unfulfilled. Self-fulfillment, usually through creativity and/or helping others, is one of the beautiful gifts that 9 offers.

Your life tends to create circumstances to which you must constantly adapt. This makes it difficult for you to focus on one thing at a time. You may spread yourself too thin, unable to concentrate long enough to gain the necessary experience or expertise. You may find yourself bouncing from one thing to another without actually completing anything, unaware that completion is the very thing you came into this life to achieve.

You may already be doing pretty well in life, but there is no telling just how much you can accomplish with *focus*. It is always lack of concentration which prevents 9s from seeing their higher potential. It is up to you to recognize your specialty, that thing you feel impassioned about, and give it the focus it deserves.

Your life is often cluttered with useless projects, people, possessions, and memories. Stand back, occasionally, from the ongoing dramas of your life and assess any situations or relationships that need to be weeded out and ended. Go back to the past and release yourself from an unexpressed emotion which is holding you there.

It is no wonder that during the 1990s, when 9 was the dominant energy in the world, that humanity experienced the "retro" trend. That was a decade in which we realized that nobody knew what the future held and that the visions expressed by industry, politics, science, and religion were greatly lacking in compassion and imagination. With the future seeming so unacceptable, people turned and faced the past instead. They saw that the past had become the present and that what we choose to do now, in the present, creates the future. Even though the future never comes, both the past and the future are always NOW. By using nostalgia to go back into the past, you will be able to create a future of your own design.

Ultimately, you are learning how to *let go*. This can be a painful process until you understand its necessity. You may question how it is possible to be the loving and generous person you know you are when you may have to hurt people in the process of letting go.

The life of a 9 is never simple. 9 works in the most mysterious ways. Very often, the people you think you may hurt, actually need to be released so that their lives can unfold naturally. For you, partings are such sorrowful and frightening occasions, only to find, in retrospect, that it was the best thing for all concerned. On the other hand, by developing a greater tolerance for the individuality of others, the need to end certain relationships need never arise.

Accept the diversity of humanity and enjoy the richness of loving relationships in which a common goal takes the place of ego. It is hard for those who love you to share you with the world as they often have to do. The least you can do is to allow them to be who they are rather than who you want them to be. You can be frustrated with those who do not live up to your high ideals, but your disappointment is actually with your own intolerance.

9 is the number of giving, and the most precious gift you can bestow on anyone is your acceptance of them just as they are. This in no way implies lowering your standards or putting up with ongoing negative behavior. You must stay true to yourself and your principles. But your vision is a unique one, and you cannot expect others to see life as you see it. If you try to control other people, or if you are overly possessive, irresponsible, unemotional, or destructive, the 9 energy will work against you dramatically.

You will experience at least one major trauma, illness, loss, accident, scandal, or some other dramatic event which changes the course of your entire life. In retrospect, such painful events often turn out to be positive and significant turning points. They open you up to your emotional powers which, in turn, set you on a more meaningful path. When you express your emotions, life will provide you with many unusual and profound understandings and experiences. As your experience grows, you will become a philosopher of sorts, and you will want to share your insight with others.

There is nothing you cannot handle. You have had to face fear so often that you instinctively understand its purpose. The more you face your fears head-on, the more you will know what really does need to be feared and what does not. This makes you courageous, intelligent, and compassionate.

You may have to work hard at building this level of confidence. When you do, you will experience a massive shift of consciousness. Your emotions will become your power instead of your weakness, and you will develop a much deeper appreciation of your purpose as a human being.

With 9's emphasis on humanitarianism, some of your most natural characteristics are those of generosity and compassion. You may sometimes be taken advantage of by others who can sense your need to give, and must learn to give only because you want to and not because you feel you *should*. You cannot battle with guilt. You can only recognize it and move away from it. Remember that guilt is not an emotion. It is a wall of judgment which prevents you from feeling anything at all.

Take a good look at the way you have led your life and you will realize that you have been giving your whole life through, perhaps without even knowing it. There are so many ways in which to give. Few of them require sacrifice. You can give as a loving spouse or parent, you can give kindness and comfort to others, or money and material assistance to those in need, you can give friendliness, encouragement, opportunity, emotional support, guidance, and counsel; you can give of yourself through your particular field of work or service, or through your abundance of creative talent. Yes, you have been giving to this world all your life.

When you are not focused, you can be *all talk and no action*. Who can blame others for ignoring or even stealing your ideas when it is plain that you have no intention of putting them to use. You are a natural planner and dreamer, but you must also take the action which will actualize your goals. Only through an undaunted belief in yourself will you be able to do this.

Because 9 is made up of all the other energies, you must know what the other energies consist of so that you can incorporate their qualities into your everyday life:

1. INDEPENDENCE: knowing who you are, adapting to change, and leading your *own* life.
2. RELATION: cooperating with others, patience, tact, careful attention to detail, and developing intuition.
3. CREATIVITY: communication, friendship, beauty, and happiness.
4. BREAKTHROUGH: knowing that one's work must be what one *loves*.

5. FREEDOM: expanding your experience by learning from your mistakes.
6. RESPONSIBILITY: love; the ultimate balancing act.
7. WISDOM: inner development, spirituality, knowledge.
8. SATISFACTION: using your powers of manifestation.
9. COMPLETION: following your feelings to Free Will.

You can be perceived as many things, ranging from the nicest person in the world to an angry, self-centered alarmist. What seems to others as negative behavior is actually quite natural for one who is experiencing so many different aspects of life as intensely as you are. Be yourself. Let your feelings take their spontaneous course, through you and out of you.

You are able to see all sides of a situation and you realize just how nearsighted others can be. Even though you become frustrated by a world that is so gullible, your caring nature wants to open people's eyes to reality. Yes, you are a very intense person. You are here to learn about life from a broader perspective and then *interpret* your findings to others. You must find a way to communicate complex ideas in simple forms, otherwise your life will feel like one big ongoing struggle to explain yourself.

You can impress people with your versatility and broad knowledge. But, in the end, it is *you* who must be satisfied. Success is the result of many different factors being brought together at the right time, in the right place, and by the right people. First and foremost, you must have a clearly defined vision of what you want to achieve. You probably feel deeply about a lot of things which, somehow, are connected by a common thread. What you want can only be determined from what you feel, and how deeply you let yourself feel it.

Without a specific goal, you will be unable to change a thing. Once you develop the firm *intent* to fulfill a goal, you will notice opportunities you could not see before. Then you learn the progressive nature of reaching a goal, and resolve to take the steps which will lead you to it. It is not enough to merely wish for something. It is a matter of setting your sights on what you passionately desire and then drawing yourself closer to it, step by step, with patience and determination. As more steps are taken, new insight accelerates the process. Soon, you become so close to your goal that you can touch it, feel it. You *know* it is happening.

At this stage, you realize that this particular goal is only one step in a far greater process and that even higher goals are attainable. Be sure not to rush toward those higher aspirations without taking those last few steps which will ensure that the previous goal is realized. Otherwise you will fall back, hurt, disappointed, and disillusioned.

9's emphasis on endings means that you cannot progress until each step is concluded. You may often find yourself having to go back over ground you thought you had already covered. But once this lesson is learned, there is no telling what you can achieve, especially if your goals involve creativity or humanitarian issues.

You hate to be distracted when your heart is set on something. However, as you take one step and strive to complete it, other aspects of your diverse life will pull you in a multitude of directions. As you take your time to figure out which way to go, others may see you as lazy or scattered. But, if you truly believe in what you are doing, the criticisms of others will have little effect on you.

Eventually, both you and those around you will see that all those seemingly unrelated events in your life are actually connected in a vital way. They represent the link between the unknown and your very purpose in this lifetime. Leave nothing unfinished. Tie up all the loose ends. Know when you are finished and LET GO. Then move on. What a perfect journey yours can be when you know how to travel its powerful, unpredictable, and loving energy.

PART 2

the
journey

The winds, waves, and tides,
are the tools of the ablest navigator
EDWARD GIBBON

WHERE ARE YOU NOW?

Your life cycles began on the day you were born. To determine your present cycle, you must combine your day and month of birth with the year in which you are currently living, NOT the year in which you were born.

As an example, we can use November 28 as the day and month of birth and 2006 as the present year.

Add all these numbers together like so:

Month	11
Day	28
Year	<u>2006</u>
Subtotal	2045

Now keep adding until a single digit is obtained:

$2 + 0 + 4 + 5 = 11.$
$1 + 1 = 2.$

A person born on November 28 will be in the 2 year cycle throughout 2006. Please double-check your calculations.

The 1 Year Cycle

a journey of change, new beginnings, and independence.

Not everything that is faced can be changed,
but nothing can be changed until it is faced.
JAMES BALDWIN

The 1 year cycle is the first year of a brand new nine-year cycle of your life. It urges you to create the existence you want for yourself by recognizing the *new* potential that now exists for you. This is a time of great change and positive new beginnings.

Last year brought an entire nine-year cycle of your life to an end. It was a year of deep emotion and confusion. Those experiences were necessary, however, so that this year's new beginnings can take place. The past is certainly over, but you will need to release the feelings, attitudes, and beliefs that are still anchoring you to it. Then, instead of being shocked or confused by the changes that occur this year, you will instinctively understand their purpose in the grand scheme of your unfolding journey.

The 1 year cycle is a twelve month journey of new interests, experiences, goals, and understandings: about life, about you, where you have been, where you are now, and where you would like to be. And, because so much drastic change is required, you will also be learning the meaning of *courage*.

This year's events and circumstances will teach you about self-awareness, individuality, and the vital changes that must take place *within* you if you are to attain what you want out of life. You are learning about independence, leadership, and originality, and you will need great faith in yourself in order to take the appropriate action. You will encounter situations involving your deepest feelings, your unique mind and talent, and your need for more freedom.

You must learn to adapt to the changes taking place inside you and around you, while new circumstances test your ability to lead yourself and, possibly, others. Your desire for material and financial attainment will be helped along by unexpected opportunities and new understandings.

Start out by accepting the need for real and complete *change*. Develop a realistic sense of your own self-worth. Listen to and follow your feelings.

What you do this year will set the course for the next nine years. This should provide all the incentive you need.

By accepting the reality of your past, you become more aware of who you really are. In turn, this allows you to *be* who you really are. If you think you already know your true identity, be prepared for some astonishing new truths to emerge. You may start to doubt beliefs and attitudes you have always held as you realize they are no longer appropriate to your current circumstances.

You may start to feel out of place around people with whom you have always felt comfortable. You may question their continuing role in your life. Doubts may arise as to how you can be free when responsibilities or circumstances seem to stand in your way. Feel every feeling that arises around such issues so that new options can materialize. At some point, you will instinctively know that it's time to move in a completely *different* direction, even if it means doing it alone. Don't forget that this year you are learning to be independent. This is what the 1 energy is all about.

Attaining independence often brings feelings of isolation and loneliness. Those you thought you could count on may become unavailable to you. Attaining independence *always* produces guilt. This must be seen for the destructive force it is, otherwise you will become stuck in a painful rut of resentment, confusion, and blame.

Welcome new activities. Change those boring routines. Without change - *drastic change* - you may find yourself being buffeted around with no Will of your own for a long time to come.

The 1 year cycle gives you the opportunity to fix your bearings and choose the direction *you* want to take. It enables your Will to emerge as the only alternative to guilt and fear. Problems will arise for as long as you *resist* change. Stay flexible. Your firmest goals may be diverted into unexpected new directions. The only thing you can reliably expect this year *is* change. One change leads to another, and then another, transporting you physically, emotionally, and spiritually far from where you thought you would be. Do not allow others - or your own doubts - to deter you.

Consider what is best for *you*, what will make *you* happy, and then go ahead in that direction. Start afresh. Decide which direction you want your *long term* future to take and, even if it means starting small, take the necessary first steps toward these goals.

This year, the emphasis is on *you*. Therefore, you may feel self-centered at times. This is not a negative characteristic but a life-giving one during this 12-month cycle of self-awareness. Guilt will tell you that you are wrong to focus so keenly on yourself and will try to prevent the expression of your emotions which will lead to freedom. Guilt will tell you that ego is the problem. The solution is to *stop judging yourself.* This will enable you to balance your ego between over or under development.

Freedom for one cannot be achieved if it takes away the freedom of another. Similarly, if you are around people who disapprove of you or your plans, or those who are determined to exert control over you, you will need to break free from those chains. Know what you want, believe in yourself, and trust in your capabilities. If your capabilities are lacking in some way, then take the time to *learn* what is necessary to fulfill your intentions. As you strive toward freedom, you will notice that others become less dependent on you and less critical of you.

The more self-accepting you are, the happier everyone will be. Confidence is not an air or attitude you convey in order to hide or deny your fear or ignorance. Confidence is not an act. It is a natural feeling that comes from your acceptance of reality. Once you have accepted the reality of your desires and potentials, and what you have to do to fulfill them, you will find yourself on a course where everything falls into place, no matter what opposition arises.

Confidence is a feeling that even though you don't know all the answers yet, they will come to you because you have a genuine intent to learn and an openness which can utilize new information. Confidence is the ability to accept changes as they occur, and they *will* occur this year.

Imagine your endeavors to be the planting of seeds for your future happiness. Plant them where you want them to take root and grow. Keep the nature of a goal always in mind because now, in the millennium of the 2000s, nature itself is changing drastically.

Beware of laziness and procrastination. These habits not only retard forward movement but also effect your ability to think and express yourself. It is time to leave the past in its proper place - behind you. Focus on happiness and creativity. Always stay aware of what is going on locally and globally. Plan accordingly.

Begin something substantial this year. Failure to start a new project, activity, job, hobby, or even a new attitude, will result in a directionless frame of mind which will keep you tied to people, places, and circumstances that you just can't stand any more. At the very least, start a new phase of something already active in your life.

If you do not make changes where they are needed, they will be made for you, whether you want them or not. Without change, we struggle to hold on to situations and things that no longer serve a purpose. We then believe that life is a struggle. This year, you will learn that life is not a struggle but a continuous free-flowing journey of energy that moves, shifts, vibrates, spirals, and evolves through cycles of learning.

Focus on independence by considering any dependencies you may be holding on to. Imagine the freedom you would enjoy without them. These may include a dependence on others, a need to keep others dependent on you; a need for approval; on substances such as food, tobacco, alcohol, drugs; or distractions such as TV, computers, gambling, and extravagance. We are all experts at disguising our addictions so that they are quite unrecognizable, even to ourselves.

It is not easy to eliminate a dependency if you don't know its emotional *cause*. You may have to search your feelings very deeply, all the way back to your childhood, which is where most of your erroneous beliefs were ingrained, to find out *why* you need these things so badly. Knowing the emotional reason for a dependency makes it much easier to understand and leave behind. This will enable you to think and act for yourself once again, which is where independence begins.

Even though this year's emphasis is on you, your various relationships are vitally important. So much love and happiness can be experienced there. The 1 Year Cycle will teach you that all is attainable if you do not *depend* on anyone else for your happiness or success. Rely only on *you*. While you are surging ahead, understand that others may be trying to do the same. Try to surround yourself with realistic, freethinking people who do not judge and criticize your every move. Have the same consideration for them.

This is a year of action and forward movement in which patience is often required. Some results may not be realized until later in this nine-year cycle, but projects or ideas started three years ago can materialize as accomplishments *this year*, leaving you, and others, pleasantly astonished as loose ends from the previous nine year cycle are finally tied up.

Understand the need for time to pass between one experience and the next, and you will enjoy many pleasant surprises this year. Aim high, believe in your goals, and never give up the pioneering spirit that is so essential during the 1 Year Cycle. The massive changes taking place in the world will certainly have an impact on you. You may have to take action which, at first, seems difficult or even impossible to accomplish. Your fears will have to be faced head-on.

Do not be deterred by your inevitable mistakes. They may not be mistakes at all, but a means of gaining knowledge. We are all in unfamiliar territory right now. Mistakes are not mistakes if you learn from them and don't repeat them. Learning from mistakes is how *experience* is gained. Allowing guilt or blame to rule your life is, indeed, a mistake.

Work through your fears instead of denying them and you will be able to explore humanity with an open mind and promote your own desires and interests along the way. Much of what occurs in your life this year will be reflected back to you through events that are taking place elsewhere. Once you make that connection, you will be able to see exactly where you and your talents fit in and confidently claim the position you know you deserve.

~ January ~
1 Year - 2 Month

> *The great thing in this world is*
> *not so much where we stand,*
> *as in which direction we are moving.*
> OLIVER WENDELL HOLMES

Before you can know where you're going you must know where you are. So much occurred in your emotional life *last year* that you now need an interim period in which to let the dust settle and find your bearings. Reality must be faced and feelings must be deeply experienced. The past must be accepted as part of the continuing journey of your life, instead of a guilty barrier which will prevent you from moving forward.

Instead of forging ahead into the unknown, wait for developments to occur of their own accord. This will enable you to determine where you actually stand. This is a time to be patient and observant. It is a time to relax. Consider the other people in your life, see what they need and try to provide it.

Explain to those close to you that you are making a fresh start this year, and that something, or everything, must change. Clearly communicate your intentions. Most importantly, allow others to express their feelings too. You may need each other's support throughout the year.

2 is the energy of cooperation. This month, you must both request it *and* provide it. Try to find some common ground which creates a spirit of teamwork. Make an effort to get the support of others. No matter what their reaction, do not be deterred from your desire to change the direction and the quality of *your* life.

2 is the vibration to which all of life is evolving. It is the key to understanding what will work in the future and what will not. In the years to come, we will all be made aware of the absolute *connectedness* of life. We will know that when an action is taken in one area, it creates ripples of energy which effect all areas.

It is not enough to look at your life's complexities and say, *"There's a reason for everything so if I just leave it alone it will work itself out"*. Yes, there is a reason for everything, but this phrase is often misinterpreted.

There is a *cause* for everything, and you will need to find the cause of a problem before you can eliminate it. If you take a good look at a problem you are now experiencing, you will see that it originated for one reason: someone forced or pushed another or invaded someone else's reality. But we are not always sure of who made the original hostile move.

Imagine being in a crowd situation in which you are being pushed by the person behind you or next to you. The tendency is to blame this person instead of the one at the back who made the original push and created a domino effect throughout the crowd. Fear of being crushed then develops into hostility between you and the one closest to you.

This is a month to cooperate with people. Do not push. Look for the *real* cause of the discomfort you are feeling. This month invites you to expand your awareness of others so that you can relate one thing to another and find its cause or connection.

There are meant to be differences between people. This lets each of us know who we are. Many of this year's circumstances will be lessons in the appreciation of individuality - humanity's spectacular diversity.

Our experiences are made up from the feelings they give us and the understandings or judgments that follow. Your feelings and your thoughts are not the same thing. It is necessary for you to know the difference between them and allow them to come together in agreement. From this alignment of your consciousness and your Will, your intuition will develop dramatically. From your evolved intuition, you will develop *Free Will*. Otherwise you will forever be in a state of confusion as your controlling mind tells you one thing and your freedom-loving feelings long for something else.

Focus on personal relationships so that a mutual acceptance can be reached; so that peace is in the air and there is a relaxed feeling between all concerned; so that love can flourish or be found. Make this a gentle month. Force nothing. And hold on, inwardly and outwardly, to your personal dreams and desires.

Pay attention to the time consuming details which arise. Look for important connections and clues in all that is happening around you. The circumstances of someone else are likely to provide some insight. Take a back seat. Quietly observe. Get a sense for what is really going on.

From what may seem an unlikely source, you will find the missing link - the connection - between something which appears to have little to do with you, and the course you will be taking for the next nine years. January invites you to find the link between your past and your future which, of course, can only be found in the PRESENT.

~ February ~
1 Year - 3 Month

I don't know the key to success,
but the key to failure is trying
to please everybody.
BILL COSBY

February brings you into the creative 3 cycle which emphasizes HAPPI-NESS. You may have firm material dreams in mind, but they will never be realized unless the specific feeling of personal happiness is your ultimate goal. The first thing to realize is that you are the only one who can create your own happiness.

A dream is often cut short when the reality of what must be done to achieve it sinks in. This month, you will learn the difference between the mere pursuit of happiness and actually living your dream. It is necessary to get specific. What is it going to *take* to make you happy?

Now you must believe in yourself and take yourself and what you have to offer far more seriously. If certain people do not seem to be coming through for you, remember that this is a year of forward movement which requires you to stand alone and face your own reality. You can only rely on *you* for the results you want. The people you are depending on to help you get your plans and ideas off the ground are actually depending on *you* to take the bull by the horns and assert yourself. They need to know if you really are as competent as they suspect you might be! Remember that the evolutionary purpose of the 1 year cycle is to teach you about independence.

3 emphasizes self-expression and creativity. It urges you to create and express happiness by listening to and following your feelings and by doing what feels right for you, *moment by moment.* By recognizing and appreciating the small joys in your life, you will realize that happiness is something you already have if you will only allow it to express itself and expand.

The reason you cannot expand upon your smaller joys is because they are being overshadowed by things that are making you unhappy; things that keep you locked in the past and prevent you from living the life you would like to live. It is time to recognize exactly what is making you unhappy and work on changing these circumstances.

Guilt will tell you that you are wrong to focus on life's joys because more serious matters must take priority. This month, however, your first priority must be to focus on the things that make you happy, no matter how trivial or time-wasting guilt tells you they are.

The more you feel and accept your small feelings of pleasure, the greater your pleasure will grow. Remember the little things that make you feel good, appreciate them, and realize that in this new nine-year cycle of your life there will also be many *new* sources of happiness that you have yet to discover and experience.

Your physical appearance is important now. But perhaps guilt has convinced you that looking good is a vain and impractical concern. Maybe you do not take as much care over your appearance today as you used to. In the other extreme, perhaps your need to keep up appearances is diminishing your freedom to *be yourself*.

Stop allowing guilt to create insecurity in you and to dictate your every move. The purpose of guilt is to stop all movement. The solution is to stop judging yourself and others. Allow your deepest *feelings* to guide you. Feel how good it feels to be yourself. Create a physical image that is pleasing to *you*. To tell yourself that outer appearance is not important and that it is what's inside that counts is a nonacceptance of your own body. Your body will feel this as rejection.

Yes, inner beauty is vital, but do not neglect the physical. Feel your true feelings toward your outer appearance so that a greater confidence can be attained. If you base your appearance on what you believe others think is acceptable, you are not learning the valuable lesson of *individuality* involved. And the significance of appearance not only applies to your personal look. Another aspect, some kind of presentation perhaps, may be involved here.

Your creative and verbal talent is especially important now. The spoken or written word contains the key to your progress this month. Opportunities may also arise through new contacts and activities. It is time to expand your personal or professional network.

3 is the number of communication, and a change is needed in the way you express yourself. What many people fail to realize is that communication requires not only the ability to express oneself, but also the ability to *listen*. Be open to concepts that you have not considered before. The world is changing. New ideas are needed. They will flow freely if you are sociable, friendly, and accepting of those who do not seem to fit in with your usual circle. This year's emphasis on being yourself must be extended to others, too.

This month, a change may take place in the life of a friend, and you are likely to feel its impact quite dramatically. Consider your social connections and the effect they have on you *and* your loved ones. You may be too concerned with what others think of you, or you may not give these people enough attention or time. A change in your beliefs and attitudes toward friends may be needed, one which will enhance your freedom rather than impede it. Now you will know who your friends actually are.

This month you can draw great inspiration from creative and artistic pleasures. Entertain, and enjoy being entertained. Feel how good it is to be *alive*. There is nothing more needed in the world right now than the hope, humor, and optimism of the 3 vibration. This is a special "lighter" month in which life is giving you the chance to discover what makes you happy and what does *not*.

~ March ~
1 Year - 4 Month

Without contraries there is no progression. Attraction and repulsion. Reason and energy, Love and hate, are necessary to human existence.
WILLIAM BLAKE

Your old reality is ending, and your new one has not yet begun. What you do this month will set those wheels in motion. First, you must take care of the outstanding details which are keeping you tied to an old problem. When certain problems seem unchangeable, we tend to repress our feelings on the matter - *"I can't do anything about it, so why try?"*

There is so much deep-seated denial in this attitude that it can turn a relatively small problem into a monster. Break with the belief that you are powerless to *change* things. Feel and sense exactly where you are at this time without denying any of the details. Accept the facts of the situation, as well as how you *feel* about them. You will soon see how to make the positive changes you desire.

It is necessary for you to know your limits so that you can learn how to expand them. The closer you get to your limits, the more you will feel boxed-in and compressed by them. But this is no time to give up. Instead, understand that the restrictive elements of this month are providing an opportunity for you to feel the positive power and the driving force of your own beautiful Will.

Commit yourself to hard work and determination. Concentrate. Otherwise a mistake may be made which, at first, seems accidental or bad luck. A deeper look at the situation, however, will reveal that it was lack of focus that caused the problem.

Much of this month's journey involves mental and emotional effort. Assess the positive aspects as well as the negative ones. Form a practical plan of action to protect your overall goals while honestly assessing whether your current course is any different from the one you set for yourself nine years ago.

It is time to see yourself in a new and more positive light in which you *can* juggle the various aspects of your busy life. Be aware of not only the small details but also where these details fit into the larger picture. The restrictive events of March are occurring so that you can clear your life of the unnecessary material and emotional clutter that you have accumulated over a long period of time. This is preventing you from seeing beyond what you think are your limits.

Your mind is positively buzzing right now. Your consciousness is churning with diverse and conflicting thoughts. Take some time for yourself and actually *listen* to the chaos in your mind. Listen to all the different opinions and judgments that are battling for your attention. Then set *new* priorities.

Be practical. Put everything in its place. Create a workable system in all areas of your life. Organize and clear the decks. Do so with confidence. Sort it all out, detail by detail. Then observe the walls of what *were* your limits move further away from you. Your expanded belief in yourself has pushed these boundaries to a place where they can no longer pressure you.

Recognize the need to change certain beliefs, habits, and attitudes. What you once considered practical or proper may be impractical and improper in today's reality. Only your stubbornness to change, which will manifest as feelings of impatience and frustration, can prevent you from turning this month's obstacles into some kind of breakthrough. Having cleared the strongest barriers of all, your own denials, you will realize that if you judge a situation before you experience it, you have no way of knowing what the experience actually is, or what it has to offer.

Don't blame others for this month's delays, distractions, and detours. In this 1 year cycle of independence, it is you who must take the lead and initiate things you thought could only be done by someone else. Knock on some new doors. Break free from your dependence on others who are clearly preoccupied with their own concerns right now. Your belief in yourself is being challenged. Accept this challenge and you will be given a new understanding - a new skill which will help you do what you already do even better.

Remember that last year was the end of an entire era of your life. This year represents the beginning of a new one. You are on unfamiliar ground. Your feelings are all you can count on to know where you stand. Your feelings are all you can count on to achieve success. Your intuition is the collective voice of all your feelings. It is your natural instinct. It is your Will.

And your Will, when it is allowed its freedom, contains a personal navigational system of such extraordinary accuracy that it makes anything in today's technology look like a toy.

No matter what your plans for the future happen to be, the foundation for those goals must be based in your feelings. Feel them. Listen to them. ACT on them. Let them tell you what you really *want*. By the end of March you will have reached many new understandings which will help you to construct a strong foundation on which to build the rest of your life.

~ April ~
1 Year - 5 Month

Life is what happens to you
while you're busy making other plans.
JOHN LENNON "BEAUTIFUL BOY, (DARLING BOY)"

Both the 1 and 5 energies relate to sudden change, adventure, freedom, and progress. What at first seems like an upheaval or a continuation of last month's restrictions, may well turn out to be just what you needed to set your goals in motion.

You may experience feelings you have never felt before, or a change in your feelings toward a certain person, place, or situation. Things you have always taken for granted can now be seen from a different angle. This will give you a more realistic view of your current conditions and how they fit in with your long term goals.

Life is pointing out the physical, emotional, and intellectual alterations you need to make in order to move ahead. A complete change in your reality is taking place. Therefore, a complete change of attitude is called for.

You may even end up with different goals than you started out with. This is a good sign that you are learning to flow with life's ebbs and tides and that you are noticing and taking advantage of new opportunities for expanding your horizons. You are surrounded by potentials and resources that have suddenly appeared from nowhere. Look for them. They *are* there.

There are new people on the scene, new places to explore, and new optimism in the air. Try to feel as loose and free as possible as you change your perception of your own capabilities. You haven't been using them as well as you could.

If others appear to be blocking you, you may still have much to learn about freedom - your's and other people's. You are currently traveling through a cycle of energy that *is* freedom. In fact, you have so much freedom right now that you may feel overwhelmed by it, and you may be mistaking freedom for the frustration of not knowing what your next step should be.

The circumstances and attitudes of others can only prevent you from moving forward if you allow them to. But, are others *really* opposing you? Or are guilt and fear making you oppose yourself? Are you judging a situation before you have experienced it? Has an unexpected situation thrown you into a panic? Are you afraid that all this change will lessen other people's regard for you?

Remember that love without freedom is a contradiction in terms. Freedom provides the space we need in which to *experience* love. You may not realize it at the time, but an unexpected event is actually setting you free to create a much happier existence for yourself.

Don't blame others for your current problems. These are temporary situations. You *are* where you are meant to be. This is simply the ground you must cover on the way to real happiness.

5 reacts to the magnetism of your expectations. If you don't know what you're feeling, you cannot know what to expect. If you cannot differentiate between a thought and a feeling, your outer reality will produce the same confusion. If you do not expect positive change, then a lack of positive change is precisely what you will get. Thinking positive is not enough. What are you *feeling*?

Has nothing new occurred? Are you stuck in the same situation with no hope of change in sight? Could it be that you did not *expect* a change to occur? Perhaps you need to reconsider what change really means. It means CHANGE - a complete and drastic alteration in the way you observe, comprehend, relate to, approach, deal with, resist, and compound your situation. Align your thoughts with your feelings. Allow your Will to know what it really wants.

5 brings the physical side of life into focus. It urges you to be more active and to nurture your body. Moderate your intake of food, alcohol, and drugs. Don't take foolish chances which can harm your body or general well-being. *Change* is all around you. If you get too caught up in this month's variety of events you could find yourself accident-prone or in the wrong place or wrong time.

The very nature of the 5 cycle is anything that is different to the norm, giving you a chance to see the different options available. Pay attention to and *sense* everything that is going on. Keep your wits about you in this unfamiliar territory.

It is time to recognize a mistake so that you can stop repeating it. It is this mistake that has always caused problems for you in the past. Once you recognize it and refuse to take that route again, it will no longer be a mistake. It will be *experience*.

By now you should realize that the 1 year cycle is made up of first time experiences. Some will feel good, and others will not. Certain areas of your life will change - for ever. For you, this year represents your first step into broader horizons. You are in new and alien territory. You simply have to learn your way around, that's all.

The 1 year asks you to be independent. You already know just how dependent you have been on certain people and things. Now, you must take full responsibility for yourself. Once you do this, you will experience a much deeper understanding of your various relationships. You will instinctively know why others are behaving as they are. Great improvements in important relationships are possible. In some cases, there may be a parting of the ways.

This year, you are learning how to create. To start with, you are learning how all human beings create their own reality. In order to create a reality that you really love, you're going to have to be very honest with yourself about your current situation. Even if you have a passionate goal, if you don't know where you stand, you will be unable to sense the direction in which to take that goal. Accepting where you are is not defeat. On the contrary, it is the courageous act of facing reality. If you cannot accept your own reality, your life will forever be a dissatisfying illusion which you yourself have painted.

Toward the end of April you will realize that for the past 18 months, your emotions have taken you backwards through life. It has not been a comfortable ride. Your frustration is derived from a deep desire to move forward. But in order to do so, you will have to release your grip on the past. The past is your experience. Bring your past into the present. And then *feel* the future you want.

~ May ~
1 Year - 6 Month

The study of change is the study of survival.

EDWARD T. HALL

An important relationship is now in the spotlight and is showing you that love and freedom, when they are balanced, are part of the same thing. Understand the need for balance between your personal ambition and your relationships. Each aspect must coexist in mutual understanding and be connected by your love of both. The decisions you make this month need a friendly base in which to flourish. Stop trying to control a situation which needs to unfold in its own natural way.

The events of May are likely to revolve around family, those you love, the people whose support and involvement will ensure that your life's journey is not a cold or lonely one. You may realize that you have depended on someone or something far too heavily for your own good. Nothing and no one can be taken for granted in the 1 year. There is now an emphasis on home, responsibility, devotion, healing, forgiveness, and peace.

Changes in your personal life are inevitable now. Someone close to you may affect your plans. Because so much emotion is involved here, you may find that an uncomfortable extreme rises to the surface. Extremes result when differences in understanding split an issue down the middle, and we often hurt ourselves and each other in the process.

Accept that everyone is living and evolving at their own pace. You may want to seize control and lay down the law, but this will only create another extreme. Do not take on responsibilities that are not yours. This is not helping. It is interfering. Rather than setting rules for yourself and others, concentrate on establishing what your true responsibilities are and carry them out lovingly.

When you take on responsibilities that are not yours, you will resent the restrictions that always follow. You may think you are responsible for someone else's problem or that they are responsible for yours. You may believe it is your responsibility to keep everyone happy. You may think that you have no responsibilities at all. Now you must assess where you *truly* fit in to this situation.

While others are caught up in their own changes, you will find yourself with a new problem to solve or an emotional situation to deal with. Appreciate the feelings and needs of all concerned. Do what you can to help. Rather than assume that you hold the answers to other people's problems, encourage them to find their own solutions. Avoid the temptation to jump to conclusions. A know-it-all, self-righteous, or judgmental attitude is a sure sign that you are denying some powerful feelings, such as fear, grief, and anger. Until the lessons of love and responsibility are learned, this leg of the journey may jolt you from one extreme to another.

New beginnings in love will develop from new understandings *about* love. Focus on the rich pleasures of romance, beauty, home, and family. Many positive changes can take place in these areas if you are being yourself and giving others the same respect. Matters concerning home and family, neighborhood and even pets are likely to surface. Spruce up your residence. Make repairs. Or, are you wondering where your home - your real home - actually is?

What you considered to be your home, and those within it, are undergoing drastic changes of their own. An old reality is ending. A new one is forming. It is vital that you renew your faith in yourself and in life. The recent upheavals were necessary so that you can start to create the future you actually *want* for yourself. No matter how restless you feel, understand that you *are* in the right place to gain the experience you need. The people around you, be they wonderful or dreadful, can teach you something which will benefit your long-term plans and broaden your view of the world.

This is the time to begin or continue a project that is dear to your heart. Take an independent and self-confident stance. When you stop judging yourself, you will see yourself in a much more positive light. You will always be what you judge yourself to be, and until you change the image you have of yourself and what you are capable of, you may never reach your goals. Then you will have to deal with the frustration of not knowing why.

You have reached the outer edges of a brand new beginning in your life. Will you walk confidently into it? Will you take a greater responsibility for your own well-being and happiness? Will you accept this new path of love, balance, and connection?

The circumstances and attitudes of others may appear to interfere with your agenda. You may find yourself traveling roads you had always sought to avoid. This is a marvelous indication that you really are ready to take a different, exciting, and more responsible road out there in the big world.

~ June ~
1 Year - 7 Month

To learn is to change.
Our destiny is to learn and keep learning as long as we live.
GEORGE LEONARD

Slow down. There are very few guiding lights in your life right now. Your intuition is your only means of vision for most of June. Pessimism is understandable, but unnecessary. You may be starting to question whether this really is a brand new cycle of your life, or whether it is merely a repeat of the same old restrictions disguised in different forms. The truth is that your intuition is screaming at you to let go of certain old beliefs and attitudes, so that your new beginnings can actually begin. Until then, you will be frustratingly stuck in a tiresome game of wait and see.

Someone or something you thought you could count on is no longer available to you. You are unsure of what lies ahead. Don't criticize. Be quiet. Be alone. Be honest. *Feel* what is happening to you.

You will then discover that you are on the very brink of a major turning point in your life, but fear is causing you to resist this change. Guilt does not want you to know that you are feeling fear. In fact, guilt does not want you to know that you are feeling guilt. When guilt is denied like this, it reverses itself and becomes *blame* which you then unwittingly project onto someone else. Move away from guilt by ending those judgments you have made against yourself and others. This will bring you into the *present*, which is the only place from which you can move forward.

If exhaustion or illness arise, don't worry. This is only a temporary phase designed to slow you down to the pace of June's introspective cycle. It is a test of your faith in yourself. No, this is *not* the time to give up on your hopes and dreams. On the contrary, it is time to learn what must be learned in order to make those dreams come true. Study and research are called for now. Do your homework and tie up any loose ends which could come back to haunt you in the months and years to come.

You need rest and solitude. The state of your physical body or your mind, is likely to ensure that you get both. Don't worry about being alone. No matter how many people you surround yourself with, the fact remains that you are a singular entity in this world. *You* are the best friend you will ever have. That is, of course, when you are not being your own worst enemy.

Appreciate just how capable you are of leading your own independent life. You have what it takes to create a very different reality if you will only recognize the *new* potential that exists for you. No matter who else is involved in your plans, you are the only one you can depend on for success. Only when you accept this fact will you be able to share your life with others in a state of *ease*.

Face up to the issues you have been avoiding. If you find yourself depressed, pessimistic, or unable to think straight, you may need to release a deeply buried emotion that you are refusing to admit. To admit something means *letting it in*. Admit to yourself how you feel!

Consider the people with whom you interact on a daily basis; those you have no choice but to be around; those you feel have limited you in some way; those who are not supportive of your goals. Ask yourself: *"why am I still with these people?"* If you are honest with yourself, you will see that others are not holding you back at all. No, it is your dependence on their approval that is creating the problem.

When you get to the roots of what you are truly feeling, there will be some exhilarating moments of inspiration and new awareness. Many questions will be answered as your natural energy levels are restored and you move closer to independence. Let the past go, the recent past included. It doesn't matter if you don't have all the answers right now. Just have faith in the future. Believe in *you*.

7 can sometimes make us feel inadequate. It can make us aware of the great possibilities but afraid that we may not be able to make them happen. If these feelings arise, know that the only thing that life requires of you now is your presence in it and your attention to it. Then, your attitude toward yourself and what you thought was failure will change to one of peaceful and dignified self-acceptance. From this standpoint, you will know that you are capable of greater things and that with patience, determination, and focus, you *can* achieve what you were beginning to think was an unreachable goal.

The purpose of June's introspective energies is for you to *feel* your feelings, *release* yourself from the past, *be* in the present; and *perfect* your plans for the future. If you ignore your feelings and rush forward, there are likely to be obstacles in your way. You may find yourself drifting *away* from your desires. There is no need to struggle. In fact, struggling to push your plans along may cause additional frustrations and delays.

You will be presenting yourself and your ideas to the world *next* month. Use June to make sure that you and your ideas are presentable. It is for this purpose that life has slowed you down. Gather information, study all the facts, analyze them. Get expert advice if necessary. Analyze the nature of what you are trying to achieve. Polish, fine-tune, and perfect your act before you present it to others. Don't cut corners. Aim for flawlessness and precision. Strive to raise, not lower, your standards.

Be sure your plans do not depend too heavily on outside factors or other people. Take full responsibility for yourself. Recognize and use your natural talents and assets. Don't fool yourself about this. Whatever you are good at, whatever you enjoy, whatever you have an avid interest in, whatever you love - therein lies your talent. This is the very thing for which your Will is screaming out. This is your calling. Right now, it is calling you to the next stepping stone in your exciting journey.

~ July ~
1 Year - 8 Month

I do not try to dance better than anyone else.
I only try to dance better than myself.
MIKHAIL BARYSHNIKOV

It is time to focus on financial, business, and material matters. There are likely to be some very important changes here. This is an excellent time to begin or expand a project or to activate new plans. Utilize the extra vitality July gives you because you can now make things *materialize*. If you think you have missed the boat, you are mistaken. NOW is the time to act by taking one small but decisive step toward a goal.

Express yourself with authority, dignity, and self-reliance. Act as if you are already successful by believing in what you are doing. Be efficient, organized, and well informed. Be willing to learn new things as you go.

If you have not advanced in some way this month, perhaps it is your acceptance of reality which needs attention. Which direction is still available to you in light of the natural, political, and economic changes that are sweeping the world? Which direction is still open to you in light of the changes that have swept through your own life just recently?

Long-standing beliefs and attitudes about money, leadership, status, or authority may have to be altered. If you cannot see the opportunities that are all around you, it is because you are looking for them in the wrong places.

It is not only fear of failure that can stop you in your tracks. Perhaps you are afraid of success and cling to failure as a way of avoiding what you perceive to be the negative effects of power. This is guilt paralyzing you. To prejudge how increased power would effect you before you have experienced it shows lack of faith in your ability to love and your failure to understand the impossibility of knowing something before you have experienced it.

How many times have you stopped trying just as it looks like you might be succeeding? The reason you could not persevere was because guilt or fear showed you a negative outcome before the outcome had materialized. You were then left feeling guilty and afraid of what you might become or not become; guilty and afraid of overtaking others or not having the personal power to overtake others; afraid of reprisal or guilty about taking reprisals, afraid of losing someone's love or respect, or guilty about your own lack of loving intent.

All that guilt and fear is the result of a war-like competitiveness that we have judged to be normal. Success comes when you are doing what *love* is driving you to do. Do what you love and allow the events of your life to unfold naturally. Force, revenge, impatience, or outright aggression are sure signs that you do not trust yourself. Without trust in yourself, it is absolutely impossible to trust others or expect them to_trust you. Peace, partnership, trust, and cooperation are the keys to success in the new millennium.

Genuine Free Will does not allow your loving intentions to be twisted in any way. There is no need to lose or harm anyone else in the process of empowering yourself. Remain constantly aware of the mechanics of what you are trying to achieve. Notice everything that pertains to your goal, including the very small details which you may have overlooked. Even if you already consider yourself to be powerful, wealthy, and influential, notice how much harder your power, wealth, and influence are to hold on to these days. Notice how the need to compete and keep up appearances reduces your love for what you are doing.

No matter what your current financial position or personal status, you need more freedom to do what you *want* to do. This will come when you recognize the extent to which you are dependent on others or encourage their dependence on you. It is not other people you need to convince of your capability at this stage. You need to convince yourself. If you are wondering how partnership and cooperation can coexist with Free Will, understand that within a group situation, each person has a specific job to do or role to play. When each member of the team does their part, they are able to create something far superior than any individual effort.

This month you will feel a strong surge of personal power. You are likely to meet someone with whom a common goal can be shared or to whom you can assign some detail work. Delegate fairly. Be patient with yourself and others. Use what you *already* have to get what you want. Be aware of your existing resources and contacts. Take stock of your assets and talents and put them to constructive use. Appreciate and protect all that is yours. A talent you have always had but could never find a use for may hold some surprising benefits now. Recognize the connection between what you want and the people around you. Take control of your life not by controlling others, but by following the call of your heart. You will then know that your plans *are* achievable.

~ August ~
1 Year - 9 Month

*Nothing is so fatiguing as the eternal
hanging-on of an uncompleted task.*
WILLIAM JAMES

The 1 year cycle of NEW BEGINNINGS has now merged with the 9 month cycle of ENDINGS. This means that it is time to wrap up a certain situation or, at least, bring it to the end of a particular phase. An entirely different route must be considered. August asks you to prepare, in great detail, for the new direction you will be taking between now and the end of the year.

The time has come to make a firm decision. It is time to put the past firmly in its place - *behind you*. You can only do this by accepting your past exactly as it happened. Until you are totally comfortable with who you used to be, you will be unable to recognize who you are becoming.

This month's tense situations will show you that you can no longer proceed in the same old non-fulfilling way. The stress you are feeling is inevitable when you consider what is actually happening here. You are feeling the pain that comes with wrenching yourself away from what has been your way of life. You are standing at the end of a familiar road with nothing but uncharted territory ahead of you. You are *afraid*. At the same time, old unresolved issues and unexpressed emotions keep pulling you back.

Within the 9 cycle, it is impossible to move forward while matters of the past have not been finalized. You must go in what seems like the wrong direction - backwards - in order to move ahead. You must tie up the loose ends that are binding you to the past. As each issue is completed, the bonds are released and forward movement is again possible, but it becomes highly accelerated, as if you are being catapulted to a better place.

Something you thought was lost may now return. But anything you let go of will not come back. The good news is that you are unlikely to lose anything that you really need or desire. This is both a confusing and exciting time for you.

You are expanding so fast that it is difficult for your current environment to contain you. As your desire for personal fulfillment expands, you cannot help but outgrow certain people, places, and situations. The behavior of others makes this crystal-clear. You may no longer feel welcome in areas that were once comfortable and friendly. Move ahead with your plans, quietly and confidently. Learn the difference between guilt and compassion. Give your ego a rest, my friend, and develop courage instead. Just remember that courage is not the absence of fear, but the acceptance of fear.

As you leave the old behind, strong emotions will arise. Let them flow. Stop hurting yourself by holding it all in. Nothing is more needed right now than for you to release all that feeling which is bursting to get out. You may have to let go of cherished beliefs in order to implement the new insights this year of change has given you. It is not easy to let go of a belief, especially if it is one you have staunchly held or imposed on others. But it is a most gratifying feeling when you finally find that burst of courage which enables you to let go of your own stubbornness. Here lies the source of a tremendous awakening in your life.

9 is the energy of GIVING. It is interesting to observe that giving and letting go are exactly the same thing. Possessiveness will work against you during August. Do not hold on to things or people that seem to be leaving your life. Their own energies are now at work, taking them along *their* natural paths. If they are meant to stay, they will do so of their own Free Will.

On a material level, eliminate anything that is cluttering your life. Sort out the things you want and need from those which are just taking up space. As your need for freedom increases, you will desire more open space rather than more confining clutter. You will instinctively find ways to better organize yourself.

You may not believe that you can cope with having to face so much reality at one time. You may want to ignore certain aspects and focus only on those that are comfortable. But until you take *everything* into account, you will not find the emotional connection that will make sense of it all. Life is not giving you more than you can handle. It is showing you how simple life can be when the reality of everything is accepted. Accept it all, and you'll be amazed at the new beginnings that occur in the months to come.

~ September ~
1 Year - 1 Month

Real change is accompanied by new insight.
DEEPAK CHOPRA

You are surrounded by a double-dose of 1 energy. It is time to expand your life in dramatic and decisive ways. Change the very texture of your life by embracing the new opportunities that present themselves. They may not be immediately apparent, so look for them, recognize them, and be prepared to act on them immediately. Remember that when we are searching for something, we very often find something better and entirely different.

If old, comfortable, and familiar aspects of your life appear to be collapsing all around you, they are doing so to make way for the positive new beginnings you crave. What are you really afraid of? Change? Or the possibility that things will remain the same?

Don't be afraid to take a chance. Success often requires a giant leap of faith. Now it is time for you to make such a leap. Just remember your past mistakes. Be sure you are not about to repeat them. It would certainly be a mistake to do nothing or to allow your own or other people's negativity to deter you.

You now have the opportunity to become a leader. If you have specific goals in mind, you will know exactly what this means. You will know what to do. This does not necessarily mean that you will reach your goals this month or this year. Remember that this is the very first year of a brand new nine-year cycle of your life. What you decide this month will set the foundation for what you want to be doing throughout the next nine years.

1 is a cycle of action, and *now* is the time to act. An important change will occur - *inside* - which will increase your independence. Highly positive aspects are now entering your life. Issues of the past may reappear. Understand their importance or lack of importance and, finally, release yourself from their emotional weight.

There is no need to abruptly sever your ties. If you are unhappy in a certain situation, now is the time to break free. The same negative conditions will stay with you until you do. Rid yourself of this condition as diplomatically as you can. Find the most constructive way out. Take it now, or plan to take it in the next three months.

Begin something new or start a new phase of an existing experience. In order to feel comfortable on this new path of yours, so much change has been necessary. More is yet to come. The real change has taken place *inside* you, and is being reflected back to you in the changes that have occurred in your day-to-day life.

If you look out into your world and see only the adversity, then you must realize that this is the very same turmoil you have still not cleared up *inside* yourself because you have still not released the emotions involved. No matter how wonderful or how awful the people around you are, it is you who have brought them or kept them in your life. They are a reflection of *your* reality.

It is important that you be yourself and allow others to be who they are. You are an original, unique, creative, powerful, and beautiful individual, unlike any other. Some people fear their individuality. They interpret uniqueness as being alone in the world. They choose to follow the crowd and then become entangled in the snare of mediocrity. We are not alone; we are *free*.

The events of September will show you that freedom is the home of love, and that love, which can only come from inside, is what you need plenty of right now. Don't reject it. Cherish it!

~ October ~
1 Year - 2 Month

Perfection is attained by slow degrees;
it requires the hand of time.
VOLTAIRE

Your life has entered the powerful and peaceful 2 cycle of trust, partnership, patience, and cooperation. Take the focus off you for a while, and concentrate on someone or something else instead. Express yourself openly but tactfully. This is not a matter of denying your true feelings and thoughts but of finding out what your current feelings and thoughts actually are.

Make no major decisions because you are likely to feel quite differently by the end of the month. This is not a time to dictate. It is a time to discuss and negotiate. 2 is a cycle in which persuasion always wins over force. A new understanding of teamwork must be reached and implemented. Cooperation is a two way street. Whoever your team consists of, each must feel free to both request and give cooperation as needed. Each must be able to trust the other. Don't push. Wait for developments to unfold naturally. Work quietly toward creating harmony. Mend a few of those bridges that were burned along the way.

The seeds you planted throughout the year need *time* to take root. To disturb them now could impede their growth or even kill them. If you don't focus on someone or something else, the pressure of pushing against this slow energy can make you physically, mentally, or emotionally ill. Be patient. Relax.

Yes, once again, you are playing the game of wait and see. But this does not mean doing nothing. You are now being given the chance to experience the power that comes from cooperation and from tireless and meticulous attention to detail. By feeling at ease and providing an atmosphere in which others can feel at ease, the wheels will turn smoothly instead of constantly getting snagged on each others' insecurities and fears.

Patiently help where you can, without becoming oversensitive to what seems like an intrusion. Operate efficiently and calmly. Stay in the background. Don't be upset if your plans are halted. Whatever is taking the focus away from your own agenda is doing so for the purpose of improving your overall *timing*.

If you find yourself avoiding people, know that the best results can be achieved by facing them and telling them where you stand. Use diplomacy rather than manipulation. This will enable you to solve the problem, put it behind you, relax, and move on.

This has been an active and ambitious year for you. In your efforts to move ahead, others may be wondering where you've been, where you're going, and what you're doing. Good heavens, they may even miss you or need you. You have been moving so fast and so independently that you may have forgotten how to put the brakes on. Slow down. Make time for those who are important to you, those you love. Give them your support; listen to them; cooperate with them; focus on them; *include* them. They too may be confused as to who and what you are becoming.

At some point you will realize that others are not holding you back at all. It is your dependence on their approval or your fear of losing them which is not only alienating you from them, but is also preventing you from creating the life you want. Be at ease with those you love. October offers the missing link which will perfect a certain plan. If you take the time to listen to yourself, important answers will flow to you through the power of your intuition. Strangely, these answers are most likely to come to you while you are focused on someone or something else.

~ November ~
1 Year - 3 Month

Knowing others is intelligence;
Knowing yourself is true wisdom.
LAO-TZU

Optimism, communication, and networking are the keys to making this a gratifying month. Your enthusiasm will rub off on those around you, creating a more positive environment for all concerned. Do not rely on hearsay. Check things out for yourself.

Minimize your responsibilities. Take a break from the mundane realities of day-to-day life. Rest, relaxation, and fun are needed now. A complete change of scenery will change your point of view and bring out your confidence and optimism as never before.

Friendship and social interaction play important roles in a month when your primary objective is to bring the JOY back in to your life. November's experiences will let you know if you are truly enjoying others or merely seeking approval. Are you talking to have your voice heard or do you have something valid to say?

Your concept of friendship will change as you realize that the only endorsement you need is your own. Break away from those whose lack of Free Will will not allow them to accept themselves, let alone you. This does not mean severing ties or abandoning those who love and need you. But it does mean releasing yourself from the fear, anger, or guilt that certain people trigger in you.

November offers positive new beginnings in your relationships by showing you the negative results of hearsay, gossip, and criticism. You will see that discord is caused by people who demand friendship and tolerance from other people before they are able to befriend or tolerate themselves. View your life's heavier aspects from a lighter perspective. Acknowledge the greater possibilities that lie ahead for you and for those you love. Stop worrying about what others think of you. Do what you want to do.

Life is urging you to develop a *new* approach to the way you communicate. Listen as well as talk. As a result, an unusual friendship or alliance may materialize. Bide your time. Know how you *feel*. Only from your feelings can you assess what is really going on. If you cannot feel loving or friendly intent, there is no need to get involved. However, the chances are that this could develop into a lasting friendship or partnership.

Enjoy the arts in whatever form you love. Do what you love to do, whatever that may be. Look for the little joys in your life and cherish them. Relax from the worry of what your next problem might be and have some fun instead. Lighten up and solutions will appear. Don't waste time fretting over what cannot be immediately achieved. Focus on what you can do *today* to improve your circumstances.

Your emotions have led you most of the way this year. Now you must balance your feelings with the power of your mind; the power of optimism; the power of belief in yourself; the power of creativity; the power of friendliness. Accept your entire reality. Not just the negatives. Acknowledge the positive potential surrounding you. Your creative juices are flowing in full-force. Tap in to them. Put your imagination, intuition, and inspiration to work as new ideas arise.

The fact is that you have until the end of November to create something *special*. Something that has come directly from your heart. Its benefits will come back to you in the form of solid experience and perhaps even a little applause.

Pay attention to your physical appearance. Remember that this is a year of change. Why not make beautiful changes to the way you look. Reinvent yourself. Take time out to pamper your body and luxuriate a little. You deserve it.

~ December ~
1 Year - 4 Month

If I have the belief that I can do it,
I shall surely acquire the capacity to do it,
even if I may not have it at the beginning.
MAHATMA GANDHI

Now you are really starting to feel the magnetic pull of next year's slow and powerful 2 vibration. There are many details to take care of as new responsibilities and emotions arise. The circumstances of someone else may be restricting you and making you feel boxed in.

This year's focus on you has brought you to a turning point where you must continue to focus on creating your own destiny and, *simultaneously*, tend to the needs and circumstances of someone else. You are about to become a master juggler.

Problems will arise if you do not slow down, relax, and take everything in your stride. The merging of the 1 and 2 energies can make you feel like you're being pushed and pulled in all directions. You have been through a lot this year. Allow your emotions to flow freely. Let it all out. And then, get back to the work at hand.

This month's 4 vibration lets you know just what your limits are. We all have limits, and it is impossible to move beyond them. But it is possible to push your limits further away from you. You will be able to do this by realizing the futility of struggling with a situation that is going to take longer to change than you imagined.

Start believing in yourself again. Your understanding of human nature is about to expand, and this is the very talent which will help further your ambitions in the months to come.

Organization is the key. Sort out all the details of the situation. Put everything in its place. Keep to a routine, be practical, develop a workable system. Approach all matters with determination. Prioritize. You can achieve so much this month by simply doing what has to be done, one step at a time, slowly and confidently.

Notice the problems you create by being too rigid in your beliefs and attitudes. Notice the opportunities you are allowing to pass you by because you have judged something to be beyond your reach. See how much extra work you make for yourself by seeking the 'proper' way to do things instead of a way that is more appropriate to the situation.

See how confusing life becomes when you get so lost in the details that you lose sight of the big picture. Notice how much importance you are placing on trivial matters. Make a list or plan. Then plow your way through it, one item at a time. As your list shortens each day, you will see that you are far more capable than you ever gave yourself credit for.

Difficulties may come in the form of *someone else's* problem. The fear of their problems overwhelming you will give guilt and blame the chance to enter the situation, creating resentment between people who otherwise love each other. This month's restrictions are designed to teach you something about guilt and blame which can be of great benefit to you next year.

No problem can occur this month which does not have a positive outcome attached to it. In fact, what you now perceive as the last straw may actually provide the breakthrough you've been waiting for. You now have an opportunity to rid yourself of the guilt that has been plaguing you all year.

Acknowledge how much you have changed and grown this year simply by believing in YOU. Appreciate yourself. And appreciate those who stood by you. Even on those occasions when you pushed them away, they still loved you. Let them know just how much their love and loyalty means to you. You are no longer the person you were when the year began. Even those who did not support you are beginning to appreciate your worth.

But the incoming 2 energy is trying to tell you that you are never going to fulfill your potential if you don't face a certain fact. The fact is that you cannot succeed at what you do unless you *focus* on what you do. You will not be able to focus while you are so worried about succeeding.

You have only touched the surface of your special gifts. You cannot succeed while there is still any doubt about your abilities. Don't fool yourself here.

Recognize your fear of success - your fear of greatness. Know that guilt, and the judgment guilt is made of, tells you that you must not allow your greatness to surface. Recognize your fear of what you still have to learn. And your fear of the changes you may or may not have to make. Feel the weight of all that fear inside you. It is slowing you down and holding you back not from success, but from successfully doing what you want to do.

Be afraid, so that you can let that fear *go*! And then, for the first time in two years . . . r-e-l-a-x.

Everything will unfold successfully, *if you allow it to*. You are moving into a part of the journey where you must let down your guard and take each day as it comes.

For the next twelve months, other people will dominate your life to the extent that you may feel unusually humble at times. You will learn that a high self-esteem is impossible without a little humility.

The lives of others will be a lot more dramatic than your own, and the talent you will acquire from this is that of being *indispensable*. You will achieve this by cooperating with those who need a particular service from you.

For now, relax in your hectic environment. Take the time to feel the love in the air. Accept it. Be grateful for it. And, whatever you have learned this year, never forget it. Hold on to it and bring it with you, as midnight of December 31st arrives and you cross over into the powerful feminine energy of the 2 year Cycle. This is the great voyage of patience, sensitivity, and cooperation. When you get there, remember this: *time is on your side.*

The 2 Year Cycle

a slow journey of patience, cooperation, sensitivity, and gradual success.

> *Time is always short, from birth to death.*
> *Why? Because we do not know how to stop.*
> JULIAN GREEN

The 2 year cycle is an inspiring twelve month journey in which you will find an exciting connection between your past, your present, and your future. You will be able to use this information to set your most ambitious goals in motion. But make no mistake, this will take perseverance and great patience. First of all, you must SLOW DOWN. This means doing whatever you have to do more *slowly*. If you accept your past and live in the present, and if you do not struggle with the slowness of it all, the insight you gain this year will carry you into the future of *your* choice.

Let go of all that stress by letting your emotions flow freely. Once they have been expressed out of your body, you can *relax*. Being relaxed is being at ease. Dis-ease (illness) manifests when you are not relaxed or when you are ill at ease. If you hold on to stress and refuse to slow down, your body will become even more burdened by the pressure of the 2 cycle's slower speed. Illness, sometimes serious illness, can result.

You cannot compete with the 2 energy because it has no acceptance for competition or force. There is no need to push yourself ahead this year. If you do, the results you desire will not materialize. However, you will be amazed at what you *can* accomplish when you live your life at the same pace as the cycle you are in.

You may find yourself retreating from aggressive and stressed-out individuals. If you cannot physically move away from them, and let's face it, they're everywhere, you will only prevent their negativity from becoming your negativity, and their problems from becoming your problems, through your own relaxed and patient frame of mind. Stand still and stare at your life, past and present, because you are about to leave the human "race" for a while so that you can be the human being you have forgotten you are.

Make a special effort to understand what is really going on in the lives of others. Even those who appear aggressive may actually be hiding great unhappiness underneath. You will need to be tactful and sensitive to their feelings. Find a way to create harmony. Even if you are the one who feels vulnerable and unsure of yourself, do not respond with aggression. You do not have to prove a thing. Be patient with yourself, and you will find it easier to be patient with others. A little lightness and humor will go a long way in easing this year's unavoidable tensions.

As far as your ambitions are concerned, *correct timing* is what this year is all about. Your goals are being taken care of behind the scenes. *Patience* is called for. This does not mean merely putting up with negative conditions. You are quietly and conscientiously paving the way for future success, and the kind of patience that will be of most benefit to you entails meticulous and tireless attention to detail as well as *listening* to what others have to say.

Take the emphasis off you. Achievements will develop through teamwork and word-of-mouth. Use your abilities in ways that will benefit others. You will be unable to move forward unless you are patient; unless you wait for developments to happen in their own time, and unless you relax your tensions and long-term concerns.

You will feel a need for more warmth and affection in your life, more acceptance for your feelings, and for the feelings of others. True prosperity and security cannot be realized through war-like competition and aggression. Therefore, peace, cooperation, and tolerance are now your only means of moving forward.

From this quieter and more peaceful perspective, you will find ways to change the parts of your life that you do not like. When you learn to live on a moment by moment basis, you will understand that the present is your only exit from the past and your only gateway to the future. The past and future are connected by the decisions you make in the present.

This year you must decide to quiet your mind, develop your intuition and rely on it to make decisions that are right for you. You will know if something is right for you by the way you *feel* about it, and you will be making significant progress even if you think you are not.

You will become much more sensitive to the metaphysics of life and be able to *sense* the reality that surrounds you. You may experience intense flashes of intuition and inner knowing. Strange dreams are not unusual in the 2 year cycle. Don't be afraid of them. They are trying to tell you something very important. It would be a good idea to keep an ongoing record of your dreams. Write them down upon waking. No matter how abstract or bizarre your individual dreams seem, you will soon see a pattern emerging which will provide valuable insight into the issues of your waking life.

When you recognize and feel the nurturing 2 energy in your life, you will want to relax right into it. You will want to flow with it. In this gentle state of being *carried along*, your understanding of freedom and love will expand. You will know that aggression and denial of reality have almost killed our capacity to think, feel, move, and enjoy. This year's events will show you that Free Will is the next step of human evolution. Free Will is the future.

Be prepared for distraction, delay, diversion, deep emotion, and other circumstances that are designed to test and develop your patience. Each situation contains an important lesson or opportunity for you. Patiently assess everything that is going on around you and inside you. Learn to *feel* your way through situations instead of forcing your way through or going into the blindness of denial.

Very little effort is required when it comes to your personal ambitions. They are actually being helped along by this process of delay and intrusion. If you do succumb to frustration and surge ahead, you may force yourself into the wrong place at the wrong time, and you will need more than diplomacy to get yourself out of the mess.

The circumstances and demands of others will slow you down. Teamwork is highlighted, and you are likely to have a specific role to play within a group, partnership, or relationship. Be diplomatic and considerate while you figure out what these people have to teach or show you. Through their behavior or circumstances, some will be teaching you "how to", while others will be teaching you "how not to".

Cooperate. Learn to be comfortable in your backseat role. It may be difficult to see someone else taking credit for your ideas or efforts, or stealing the limelight or what you consider to be your rights away from you. You may even feel that someone is deliberately keeping you in a subservient position.

If anger arises, allow yourself to *feel* it, preferably when you are alone. Get it out of your system. There is no need to confront people unless your feelings tell you it is necessary. Listen to what your anger or any other feeling is telling you, and you will soon understand why your circumstances are as they are, and that other people's problems are much greater than yours this year.

Listen to yourself. Ask yourself, "What is really going on here"? And then hear all the fear and judgment contained in your replies. A strong intent to *feel* what your feelings are telling you will activate your intuition and provide the answers you seek. *Feeling* your intuition takes time, patience, perseverance, and a genuine desire to cooperate with it. Once you do, you will realize that intuition is a tool for improving any situation in your life.

Intuition comes from your feelings and not your reactive outer thoughts. Learn to differentiate between the two. The outer voice always has some kind of judgment attached to it. Intuitive *feeling* is always calm, loving, and knowing. Intuition is the connection - the bridge - between your conscious and subconscious minds.

There is no need to become a doormat in order to cooperate. You are developing a confidence and grace which will allow you to deal with all situations calmly and efficiently without becoming enmeshed in other people's problems. Others will soon realize that without your input there can be no harmony for them. Your ability to take care of details will make you indispensable, but your high self-esteem will not allow you to become so indispensable that you can't walk away from or change a situation you do not like.

If you do not develop a warm and willing attitude toward others, you will find that your main experience is nervousness, conflicting relationships, blame, guilt, anger, fear, oversensitive and insensitive reactions, and unrelenting criticism. If any of this occurs, you may be trying to control another, or you may still believe that others have the power to control you.

Interacting with other people requires you to *feel* their singular presence; to *listen* not only to the words they are saying, but also to the message they are trying to convey; to see them as they are, in their entirety, instead of focusing on one aspect, and to become aware of how you are *connected* to them.

Even the slightest act of control or manipulation is likely to work against you. This year, you must release your control over others and/or break free of their control over you. You will discover how much more loving and loved you have become in the process.

Last year you learned about the importance of your individuality and independence. This year you will learn that everyone is operating according to their own unique energies; everyone has their own story to tell; everyone is of equal importance; everyone *feels*. The way we treat and relate to others affects feelings and behavior and the quality of life.

You will become aware of patterns of behavior which impede your freedom or someone else's. In these turbulent times, being able to tolerate, understand, and cooperate is an exact and extremely valuable talent. This is your year to show just how talented you are.

~ January ~
2 Year - 3 Month

If a man be gracious and courteous to strangers,
it shows he is a citizen of the world.
FRANCIS BACON

January's 3 vibration places an emphasis on friends, creativity, and joy. In its negative form, however, 3 becomes cynicism and insensitivity. The people in your life this month are here to connect you to specific realities which need your attention. You will learn that you are not responsible for other people's problems and they are not responsible for yours. The answers lie within *you*. Slow down. Relax. Allow yourself to *feel* what is going on. Do not judge by appearances. Go very deeply into the situation instead.

What you feel in the company of others is very important now, especially when you ask yourself *"Am I enjoying my life?"* Be aware of how you allow your insecurities to influence your mood and behavior. What if no friends appear at this time? The same question still applies. *"Am I enjoying my life"*?

If you receive an invitation, accept it. Or perhaps you are in a position to issue an invitation. Social interaction will help you to relax many of your concerns. However, others cannot read your mind. It is impossible for them to know what you need unless you tell them. Through open communication about the feelings of all concerned, solutions can be found which will ease the entire situation. If you hold back, your needs will not be met and the situation will deteriorate. Communication is what the 3 energy is all about.

But do be *diplomatic*. The way you communicate is extremely important. Choose your words carefully. Real communication means that you not only express yourself, but also *listen* to what others have to say. This month even the most diplomatic person may wish that certain words had not been spoken. Treat this as a valuable lesson. We all have a certain amount of ignorance in us which needs to be acknowledged. And what is ignorance? It is when we *ignore* the reality of a person or situation. This understanding will enable you to start the year off in a spirit of true co-operation, which means operating *together*.

Feel how lucky you are to be you. The problems of those around you may make this very obvious and cause you to count your blessings. Of course, you may need to recognize your many blessings before you can appreciate them.

Guilt may tell you that it is wrong to express happiness while others are suffering. This shows that guilt serves no constructive purpose as it dictates misery for everyone. When you constantly try to please other people, you are saying that you cannot accept yourself in a state of happiness.

The 3 energy responds to lightheartedness, optimism, creativity, and the warmth that is shared between close friends and loved ones. Don't neglect duties that must be taken care of, but try to lighten the load if you can. Spend more time with those you love.

Free Will means doing what you want to do and not just dreaming about it. Look at those who are really happy and they will be doing exactly what they want to do, where and when they want to do it, in their own style, and on their own terms. They are responsible for solving their own problems and do not complicate their lives by taking on responsibilities which are not theirs. They do not judge themselves or others. It makes no difference whether they are "helping others" or not. The fact that they have taken responsibility for their own freedom is helping the world in ways that very few are able to understand right now.

When we follow their example, we realize that Free Will is the key to PEACE. When we are doing exactly what we want to do, we instinctively want others to have the same opportunity. We feel great compassion, and a strong desire to contribute, to give something back, to this abundant but cruelly imbalanced world. See yourself as equal to everyone with whom you interact. A fellow traveler on the journey of life.

This attitude will create an atmosphere in which everyone concerned will benefit. It will also help you to realize the extent to which you allow other people's opinions to stop you thinking and acting for yourself. It is time to regain your freedom through peaceful and diplomatic means. There is no need for confrontation.

Life is a mixture of mental, emotional, and physical energies. A balance among them must be reached. If you are intellectually inclined or tend to spend too much time thinking and worrying, now is the time to go out and experience physical and social activity. If you hate to be alone or give little thought to the deeper meaning of life, it is time to embark on an intriguing *inner* journey.

Examine the beauty of nature in its tiniest detail. Take it in with your eyes, ears, nose, fingers, and taste buds. Breathe it in. Feel it. Absorb it. Make this an ongoing exercise throughout the month, the year, your entire life. This the first step to understanding that we are all individual parts of one magnificent connected organism.

~ February ~
2 Year - 4 Month

> *It is well to remember that the entire population of the Universe,*
> *with one trifling exception, is made up of other people.*
> JOHN ANDREW HOLMES

Misunderstandings in a relationship may have caused you to lose your focus on something that is important to you. It is time to sort out the emotional mess. It has produced uncertainty about your *identity*. Who are you? What are you doing with your life? Where are you going? You had a goal but a clash of personalities is distracting you from it.

Aggression will not help matters. Remember that PEACE is the main objective of the 2 year cycle. Speak from your heart but do use tact and a little humility when dealing with someone who is not only dealing with his or her own changes and uncertainty, but also with *your* insecurities.

As far as your own goals are concerned, you have arrived at a vital crossroads and a decision must be made. You can either commit to taking a more ambitious route, or you can give up and allow your efforts to slip by the wayside. There is no right or wrong involved in this decision. Your choice must be based on what you *feel* is right for you. But do ask yourself why you cannot handle *both* situations with equal passion. The emphasis on identity suggests that there is much more to you than *only* your relationships or only your work. The emphasis on order suggests that if you were better organized, there would be room in your life for *all* your desires.

Yes, the wellbeing of others must be considered, but you will be unable to take care of their needs if yours are not being met. Others are expecting a great deal from you. Give them your support. Be sensitive to their needs and feelings. But don't be pressured into taking action before you feel ready. This will give you more time for yourself. It will ease your stress and provide new meaning to what you believe is your purpose in life.

You are actually in a position of influence, but you can easily upset the apple cart by rushing ahead without patiently assessing all the details. It is time to get organized. The debris you have accumulated over a long period of time has now become a barrier to your progress. What is still desirable to you and what is not? What are your priorities? One of them should be to find the next step toward an important goal. But you cannot see where this step is because there is either no order or too much order in your life. Simplify! And then observe how wide your horizons actually are.

Order does not necessarily mean sorting out rooms, drawers and clos-ets, and throwing out the obvious garbage. Nor does it mean impulsively getting rid of perfectly good and enjoyable things. In fact, 'things' may have little to do with it. Organizing your mind is called for. Part of learn-ing the lesson of order is knowing who you are, where and with whom you stand, and in which direction you want to go.

Organizing your life means that you are consciously setting the foun-dation - *actually starting to create* - the life you want for yourself. Put every aspect in its right place, detail by detail. Do not get lost in petty details. *Prioritize*. Be aware of the big picture.

The teamwork that is so essential this year will come from combining your own natural way of doing things with those of someone else. This cre-ates a united effort that is stronger than any individual effort. Each person should know their own job and carry it out. Allow your different forms of love and creativity to coexist in the same time and space. Exist *together*. That is the true meaning of co-operation: to operate *together*.

Taking care of the physical clutter in your life can help. Give everything its own place. Create an efficient system. Keep everything organized. Visualize the end result and set your sights in that direction. What if one of the details was changed in some way? How would that effect the big pic-ture? What if someone else takes responsibility for something so that you can focus on another issue? By becoming fully aware of everything that is going on, and by allowing your feelings to guide you, the solution you need will instinctively appear. As you create efficiency in one area of your life, you will have more time to focus on another.

One of the biggest barriers to personal happiness is that we are unwill-ing to open our minds to *alternatives*.You will never know how much clut-ter is inside your mind until you admit that you are afraid of what you may find there and are, therefore, deliberately keeping your mind closed. Experience this fear. When you do, your mind will open automatically. It was denied fear that kept it shut in the first place. When we deny fear, the magnetic energy of our denials draws to us the very situations we are try-ing to avoid. The acceptance of fear helps us to find ways to bypass or deal with frightening situations.

If others know you're sincere, they will want to help. Don't assume that you already know what they are thinking or feeling. Don't assume any-thing. You will make your influence felt by speaking from the heart. Yes, you do have to cooperate with others this year, but this can only be effec-tive if you are true to yourself, your principles, and your needs.

Your dream is not being destroyed by the presence of others. It is simply expanding so that others can be included in it. Letting them in will take courage. The 4 energy brings you to the very edges of your limits so that you can push these boundaries away from you with your increased determination and belief in yourself. As you expand, so too must your limits of tolerance. You will then realize that you really can do two things at once, and that your dream is still very much *alive*.

~ March ~
2 Year - 5 Month

The future will one day be the present
and will seem as unimportant
as the present does now.
SOMERSET MAUGHM

An unexpected situation will change your reality once again. Total honesty is needed. Express yourself in words that others can easily understand. Cooperation, loving intent, and consideration for all sides of the story will help you to reach a much needed compromise. Express how *you* feel, and you will begin to understand the reality of someone else. An important relationship can be strengthened through open and honest interaction.

Opportunity will arise through the circumstances of someone else. By helping someone, patiently being there, listening, relating, soothing, and encouraging, you can prevent a certain problem from escalating. Help where you comfortably feel you can. Do not get sucked into a problem that is clearly someone else's.

First, you must take a completely fresh look at the situation. Do not overreact, but do be prepared to learn something new. A vital change has taken place. Life extends way beyond your current environment, and it could be that your outlook is too limited.

Your own or someone else's behavior will show you that we have to make mistakes in order to learn anything. But because we deny the feelings that arise from our errors, we tend to repeat the same mistakes over and over without learning anything. Entire lifetimes are often spent repeating a single mistake so that no positive change is ever achieved. Look for a different approach this time. When you have learned what needs to be learned from a mistake, it is no longer a mistake. It is *experience*. Without this understanding, your history cannot help but repeat itself. A positive change is achievable and right for you at this time.

When your conscious mind and your emotional Will *accept* the reality of your past and present, your next step becomes obvious. Patience is imperative but now, more than ever, you must hold on to that dream. In this frame of mind, others cannot help but respond positively to you. Give your knowledge freely. Everyone concerned will benefit.

5 is a PHYSICAL energy. Attention to your body is needed. Recent stress may be taking its toll. Express the emotions you are holding in and let them move out of your being. Rather than saturate your body or alter your mind with a diet of food, alcohol, drugs, or violent "entertainment", nourish yourself instead.

Even in the most loving relationships there is often a subtle element of control. Guilt and fear are frequently used tools in this process of manipulation. Peace can only thrive in an atmosphere of freedom. You may be trying to control someone, or it may be you yourself who feels cut off from free and open communication. Nothing can be achieved until these tensions are addressed.

A change of attitude is needed. Stop taking everything so *personally*. The circumstances of March are testing and developing your ability to relax and be free even in chaotic or hostile situations. Peaceful interaction can turn your life into a loving and fulfilling journey instead of this ongoing jumble of stress.

2 emphasizes harmony and relationship and 5 emphasizes freedom and change. Be diplomatic. Be considerate. Be kind. Be gentle. It is now up to you to reconcile differences and bring peace into the situation. Your own progress cannot be separated from that of other people. If one person in your environment is unhappy, this will affect you too. There is a battle of wills going on at this time. It is a fight you cannot win. The peace of mind you crave so much can only be achieved by accepting your situation exactly as it is and by finding ways to coexist peacefully with others.

Instead of fighting for something you do not have, make the most of what you do have. This will trigger a vital change and will enable you to take an important step toward a personal goal. Only by cooperating with your environment, and the people in it, will you ever be able to regain your focus. Accept the reality of others. You cannot change them. You can only change your *reaction* to them.

You are living in a cycle in which partnership and trust are absolutely essential. Relax those high expectations which none of you could live up to anyway. Teamwork and forgiveness will create a clear road ahead for all concerned.

~ April ~
2 Year - 6 Month

*How shall we expect charity towards others
when we are uncharitable to ourselves?*

THOMAS BROWN

Make a new commitment to patience and compassion because you cannot ignore or walk away from this situation. Insensitivity or selfishness will create barriers which can only separate you from those whose wellbeing is directly linked to your own. Try to make things easier for everyone.

Free Will is indeed a matter of doing what you want to do. The chances are that what you want includes friendly relationships. 6 is a cycle of love and balance which emphasizes responsibilities: those which are yours *and those which are not.*

The people with whom you must now interact are relatives, spouse, lover, parents, children, pets, neighbors, friends - those who are family and those you consider to be family. Someone close, or your living environment itself, needs your full attention. This cycle is rich in lessons about freedom - and not just your own.

Keep your goals firmly in mind as you adapt to a new set of circumstances in which you are *not* the star of the show. Continue to believe in yourself while you allow the feelings and circumstances of someone else to take center stage. Stop struggling against your current situation. Deal with everything calmly and patiently. Be flexible. You are likely to receive some kind of praise for your efforts, and this will boost your spirits considerably.

Try to make your environment friendlier and brighter, regardless of how many details you have to take care of. Resist the urge to control everything. You may believe that your intentions are good, but negative 6 energy can make you too concerned or even paranoid about the way others are conducting their life or effecting yours.

Consider the circumstances and history of those involved. Do not lay down the law, place blame, or set the pace. Tolerance and a desire to accept differences will prevent ugly situations. You may genuinely believe you are helping when, in fact, you are interfering. Your responsibility is not to solve other people's problems, but to team up with them and find ways in which everyone can benefit. You cannot teach others how to live. Their idea of life is unique to them, as yours is to you. Their priorities are not always the same as yours. Their experience of life may be totally different from your own.

You are learning how to be free amid other peoples' energies, including their negative energy. Your first responsibility is to yourself because only when *your* needs have been met can you help others with theirs. When a duty feels more like a burden, you have probably neglected to take care of yourself first.

Don't let guilt coax you into overdoing things in the name of responsibility. There is a lot to think about this month, so slow down, relax, and learn. Make *kindness* your key word. This must start with yourself. It is your inner-self which needs reassurance and acceptance now. Only you can provide it. Be gentle with yourself. There is no need to push. In fact, the harder you push, the more likely you are to hurt yourself in some way. And you may not know the extent of the damage until later in the year.

Yes, this month is all about family. But just who are your family? They are the people to whom you are connected on an everyday basis - whether you like them or not. Your family are the people with whom you are *familiar* and familiarity, without loving intent, does indeed breed contempt. Just as others affect you by their actions and attitudes, your existence deeply affects *them*. You may be biologically connected to some, but you are related in some way to *all* of them.

Allow someone else to enjoy the spotlight. Stop fighting the fact that certain people are a part of your life. How can you be happy when you are refusing to acknowledge your own reality? You cannot change other people, but you can change your *reaction* to them and your *judgment* of them. You can let them be who they are. In the process, you will learn who you are.

The time has come to clear the air once and for all. Speak openly. Let it be known that you want peace. This will bring relief in the short term and notably improve relationships in the long term. Aggression will throw you completely off course.

You desperately need some peace of mind. The chances are that your mind is unable to process all the thoughts that are bombarding it, and your Will is overloaded with feelings that are too strong for you to safely express. No, you are not losing your mind. No, you are not on the brink of an emotional breakdown. You are simply experiencing the discomfort of actually *accepting* your own reality. In order to bring ease and comfort back into your life, I offer the following suggestion. It *does* work.

Every day, preferably first thing in the morning, go off by yourself with a pen and a *private* notebook. Write down EVERY thought and EVERY feeling that arises. Nobody else will ever see these notes. You can be totally honest. Get all of that anger, rage, hatred, fear, terror, guilt, shame, sadness, grief, frustration, and utter confusion out of your system and onto the paper. *Feel* these feelings as they leave your body.

Recent events have triggered this month's mental and emotional turmoil, but you are also likely to find yourself releasing emotions that you have kept buried since childhood. Let them out. They have been hurting you for far too long.

When you have released as much as you can, you will inevitably feel lighter, freer, happier, and more knowledgeable. In fact, this healing process will enable you to make a startling connection between your past, your present circumstances, and your future happiness. It will bring you back to LOVE.

~ May ~
2 Year - 7 Month

*I make the most of all that comes
and the least of all that goes.*

SARA TEASDALE

Having to face your own reality last month has left you eager to make some positive changes. However, you may be uncertain of which approach will best suit your long term plans. Do not rush into things. Certain tasks must be taken care of before you can hope to regain the stability you desire. Slow down. Prepare to stop. Navigating your way through this month's peculiar vibration requires a steady mind, and there are very few lights to guide you.

The illumination you need is inside you. The purpose of 7s dimness is to help you find the wisdom that you are holding in your subconscious mind. The reason we are unconscious in this part of ourselves is that we block out and deny its content rather than *feel* what is in there.

Now those imprisoned feelings are fighting to become part of your consciousness. It is time to take a stand, nurse your pride back to health, and focus on your own needs and desires. Go about your daily affairs slowly and quietly. Be independent. Keep a low profile. Help where you comfortably feel you can.

Use this month's quieter introspective energy to assess your general development. Remember how the year started off for you. Realize where you are now. How have you have handled certain people and situations? Notice how you are connected to everyone and everything around you. Was the part you played in bringing about recent changes a positive one? If your approach has yielded favorable results, you will know that you are on the right course. If not, you may need to reread the 2 year cycle from the beginning so that a deeper understanding can be reached. However, it is more likely that you can now be confident of a successful year.

Allow yourself to *feel* the pain of recent events. Only then can you relax from their stressful effects and move forward into a happier segment of the journey. Relax. Not just physically. You need to relax your mind so that you do not have to spend every waking moment reeling from the stress of recent clashes or worried about what your next problem may be. Once again, unexpressed emotions are causing this strain. *Feel* them - and let them go.

You will then realize that you have overcome a massive barrier which clouded your dreams for far too long. Clarify where you want to go from here. Make workable, achievable plans which will lead to the long term results you want. Let your feelings guide you. Study any unusual flashes of intuition. Don't be afraid of strange dreams. Compare them to situations in your waking life.

An emotional *awakening* is scheduled now which will stir your sleeping ambitions. It will be triggered by positive feedback from other people. At the same time, others may come to you with their problems and cause you concern. Someone may even try to use you for their own gain. Keep your wits about you because any problem you encounter can be turned around to *your* advantage.

7 is the holder of secrets. Try to establish the facts of what you are dealing with. Only by knowing the reality of the situation will you know what your next step should be. Continue to relate to others with diplomacy and cooperation. But do be careful with whom you choose to associate. You cannot afford to waste your time or resources. Do not lower your standards. Raise them.

Stop worrying about your goals. They are on schedule. Instead, pay great attention to detail and *listen* to what others are saying. Try to be more flexible and relaxed in unfamiliar situations. Try harder to cooperate with and relate to others. You must widen your outlook considerably. This will enable you to fix your sights on much broader horizons.

The lesson here is that of self-acceptance. But you may have to lift yourself out of a melancholy or fearful frame of mind to learn it. You may even find yourself facing a moral dilemma of some kind as you struggle to understand the true meaning of freedom. 7 can also create a feeling of being inadequate, vulnerable, or unprepared. You may feel that you should be doing more to help yourself or someone else. Relax, fellow traveler. Just do what you can.

Guilt always tells you that you should be doing better than you are. But the guilt you are feeling now belongs to someone else. Let them deal with it. Then, your attitude toward what you thought were your inadequacies will change to a dignified self-assurance. From this standpoint, your ability to relate to others will expand, and you will once again be able to focus on your own happiness.

~ June ~
2 Year - 8 Month

There are only two ways to live your life.
One is as though nothing is a miracle.
The other is as if everything is.

ALBERT EINSTEIN

Enough is enough. A certain situation has become totally self-defeating and can no longer be tolerated. Let others be who and what they are. It is time for *you* to regain your dignity. Yes, it is time to start realizing your own worth again. In the process, you will be able to appreciate the worth of other people whose good qualities, in most cases, really do outweigh their flaws.

The solution you need is right under your nose. Pay attention to the details as you *take what you already have* and give it a new form. This will require time, patience, and great dedication. You are now in a powerful 8 cycle which enhances your ability to make things happen and get things done. Partnership issues and the art of diplomacy are highlighted. Despite constant interruption, you can expect a real boost to your confidence this month.

Don't try to take on too much. Remember that you are in the slow, low-energy 2 year cycle. Don't exhaust yourself by aiming too high at a time when only your smaller goals can be accomplished. These smaller goals, however, are vital stepping stones to your long-term aspirations. Focus on financial matters, your status, and your reputation. There may be an acknowledgement of your talent and/or some financial gain. By providing a service to others, you will be opening doors for yourself. Yes, you may have to share other people's problems but you will also have the opportunity to share in someone else's gain.

Listen to what others are saying. The experience of someone else may help you to understand an emotional experience of your own. Recognize the suppressed feelings you have been carrying around with you for such a long time. Releasing them will provide you with a powerful optimism. Instead of being beaten once again by the negativity of the past, you must now accept the truth of who you are and *feel* the stunning brightness of your future.

Yet another massive release of emotion is exactly what you need right now. Only then will you understand what is unfolding in your life. Only then will you be able to appreciate that your life really *has* become more comfortable, more pleasant, and more *real*.

One thing is certain: unless you learn to prosper independently, there will always be someone else to whom you must answer. There is no one out there who owes you a living. But it is definitely time to appreciate the support you do have by showing certain people that it has been worth their while supporting you.

Do not waste your energy by trying to do more than the situation will allow. Patience and diplomacy are still the keys to your success this year, and you will lose valuable allies if you take an uncompromising approach. Stay alert. Protect your assets. The path you are on right now is brimming with opportunity and hidden connections. Aim to do the best possible job you can, and use the art of persuasion - not force - to get your point across.

We are living in an era of partnership, not competition. What you consider to be your domain is not yours at all. Everyone is existing in their own right. They have no more power over you than you have over them. Resisting the power that others exert over you is not a matter of severing ties or running away from obligations but of changing the way you *react* to other people.

Don't allow the negativity of the past to bring you down any longer. The people around you are simply fellow travelers on the road of life. What at first seems like a conflict of interests is actually a reminder that others have something valid to offer.

Tread carefully. Other people's feelings, rights, and needs must be considered. You are not the star of the show right now, but you do have a lot to contribute. Compliment others on their successes. Encourage those who are having problems. Think things out before making a drastic move. Do one thing at a time, and do it *well*.

You are only a part of what surrounds you. The more you do your part, the more others will start to appreciate your contribution. They will know that the role you are playing in their lives is an important one. This places you in a powerful position, enabling you to live confidently, *feeling* your way through life instead of blindly forcing your way through it. The 8 energy will now give you a new sense of timing, ambition, and direction.

But is there something you need to change about the way you think and feel about prosperity? If your beliefs and expectations are indifferent; if you cannot see the reality of what is unfolding around you; if you do not understand the difference between prosperity and greed; if you do not realize that every single one of us, including you, has the right and the *responsibility* to create our own prosperity, then prosperity may continue to confuse or elude you. What do you *believe*? What do you *feel*? What do you *want*? What do you *expect*? What are you *doing* about it?

~ July ~
2 Year - 9 Month

Truth, love, gentleness, love of peace,
and goodness are powers which
surpass all others.

ALBERT SCHWEITZER

July brings you to a turning point in the 2 year cycle. It is here that certain situations will reverse themselves, leaving you excited and afraid at the same time. The 9 vibration is deeply emotional. It is also profoundly healing.

An important decision must be made, and anxiety is not the best frame of mind in which to make it. A very positive vibration is igniting all of this month's emotional events. There are magical things happening for you out there, behind the scenes. Just remember that *patience* is what this year is all about.

You have traveled more than half way through this particular 12 month cycle and, yet, you are still dragging with you things and issues you should have let go of a long time ago. The only way you can release yourself from the pressures of the past is to finally accept the past as part of who you are; part of the road you have traveled. Treasure it, because your past is your *experience*.

By respecting your experience of life, you are respecting yourself. Certainly you have made mistakes. Who hasn't? Experience comes from learning from those mistakes and not repeating them. This understanding will guide you with safety and dignity to the next stage of your journey.

This is no time to ignore the 2 year's slow vibration. Do not force any issue. If you do, a situation will arise that will force *you* to slow down. Do not mistake cooperation with subservience. By now you must realize that you can no longer allow yourself to be damaged by the demands of others. There is likely to be some adjusting to do now and, instead of blindly complying with someone else's wishes, you must make a decision of your own. You must be true to yourself or you will not find the satisfaction you dream of. Others must live the lives they choose, and you must make a choice of how you will live yours. Issues from the past may arise, but living in the present is where this month's emotional path is leading to. Don't hurry. Don't worry. Time is on your side.

Openly express your fear of being trapped in a hopeless situation. The truth is that this situation has actually placed you in a stronger position. Can you not *feel* that your desire for happiness is now stronger than the fear which temporarily knocked you off course?

A certain phase of your life is over and this will have a strong connection to someone else. Deep emotions will arise. It may be the very feelings themselves which need to be recognized and let go of, especially when you realize that you have judged yourself to be so much less than you are. Those days of letting others dictate the terms of your life are almost over. But you have to admit that most of your current problems are of your own making.

This year's circumstances have put you in a position where you must cooperate, be diplomatic, keep the peace, tolerate, take a back seat, and hold in your natural reaction of *anger*. The peacefulness of the 2 cycle can cause us to not only deny anger but also to deny that we're denying it. We attempt to keep the peace by tolerating. When we do this, the anger finds a way to release itself anyway, usually through an aggressive outburst. Tolerance is no longer enough. *Acceptance* is what is needed now.

There is so much rage in the world today because denied anger is breaking free everywhere without realizing that it is denied anger. Let your anger surface. Express it fully. Release it from your body in a way that cannot harm you or anyone else. Peace and acceptance will replace it. Guilt and blame can achieve nothing. Forgiveness is necessary now. With real peace in your heart you will be able to relate to others from a very powerful and persuasive point of view. The destructive effects of the recent past will diminish.

Concentrate on teamwork, cooperation, and communication. Exercise kindness, diplomacy, and consideration, mixed with plain old common sense. Others still need your support; you need theirs. Your peaceful demeanor will get the attention of someone who is in a position to help you reach a particular goal.

9 is a creative and loving vibration which urges you to let go of your inhibitions and become *emotionally* involved with your circumstances. What a complex month July is. And all for the purpose of teaching you self respect.

~ August ~
2 Year - 1 Month

Destiny is not a matter of chance; it is a matter of choice.
It is not a thing to be waited for; it is a thing to be achieved.
WILLIAM JENNINGS BRYAN

You need to be more honest with yourself than ever before. A total transformation is taking place. The distracting circumstances of August will help to *develop* your abilities. Drastic change is inevitable. Whether you believe it or not, the current conditions in your life could not be more ideal.

You are perfectly aware of what you have to do. Life has been urging you to take this action for a very long time now. What may surprise you, however, is that other people are only too willing to support you. Slow down, relax, observe, relate, feel, sense, understand. The more you are able to do these things, the more easily you will be able to move ahead.

Recognize how calm, efficient, and self-reliant you can be when you are not struggling to explain yourself. Instead of having to cooperate with others all the time, people are starting to see your side of the story and the value of what you have to offer. You can proceed safely now without stepping on anyone else or without fear of others stepping on you. There is simply no *need* to push.

You are undergoing a complete metamorphosis. You are seeing life from a different angle. Strong beliefs you have always held no longer have the same meaning. A softer, gentler, and yet stronger you is emerging. As exciting as this may sound, it can also trigger a great deal of fear as to where all this will leave you when the dust settles. Work through your fears and insecurities.

This is an excellent time to start something new or to start a new phase of an existing aspect of your life. Allow your creative talent to flow unrestricted. Your original and unique expression will be noticed. Realize how efficient and effective you are when you have the freedom to pursue your own approaches and solutions. Pay great attention to detail, but do be prepared for other people's circumstances to interrupt the creative flow from time to time.

Feel your freedom. Feel your power. Feel your uniqueness. Feel the peace and the connections you have helped create. Feel the marvelous change in the quality of your life now that you have let go of all that stubbornness and faced the reality of the world, and your place in it.

There may be a sense of loneliness at times, or guilt about pursuing your own happiness while others are stuck in less desirable circumstances. There may be a feeling that whatever has to be done, you're going to have to do it yourself. But how else could it be? This is *your* life: *your* desire; your creation; *your* dream; *your* responsibility.

Whatever feelings arise, *feel* them. Listen to them. Really *listen*. Experience them. These strong desires will give you a vital clue as to where your true direction lies. Take responsibility for your own well-being. Know when it is time to rest. You are still in the low-energy 2 year cycle. It is imperative that you take things slowly. Continue to relate to others and listen to what they have to say. Somewhere in these conversations will be the answer to one of your most important questions, which is: "What do I *want*?"

So much is going on behind the scenes. Certain areas still require diplomacy and a quiet approach. Stay aware of any sensitive or volatile situations. No matter what your age, you are now in the process of *growing up*. Don't make waves while the tide is turning in your favor. Simply go with the flow of this month's positive vibrations. Count your blessings. You will see that you have many.

The emphasis is on you, yourself. Make no mistake: the lives of others will continue to affect you for the rest of the year. But you now have the opportunity to take a good look at *your* life - past and present - and interpret what it has all led to, (your current circumstances), and where it is leading, (your future direction).

Keep up with the pace of your feelings because they will be coming to you rapidly now. Deny nothing. Express the way you feel, exactly as you feel it. This does not contradict 2s need for diplomacy. It means that you do not have to pour your emotions out on other people. Make your healing experience a private concern if possible. Accept the changes that are taking place around you and inside you. You have been taking care of others this year. Now it is time to take care of yourself. You have been promoting peace with others this year. Now, make peace with yourself.

Relax your concerns about the future. By now you should be confident in your ability to deal with whatever the future brings. Yes, there may be some lurking doubts in this regard, but do not allow them to shake the confidence you have built. Stay calmly in the present, cooperate with others, take care of all those seemingly unrelated details, and the future will take care of itself.

~ September ~
2 Year - 2 Month

Be patient toward all that is unresolved in your heart.
Learn to love the questions themselves.
RAINER MARIA RILKE

Whatever you learned about self acceptance this year, bring it with you into September. You will surely need this knowledge as the 2 vibration doubles its intensity. Situations will arise to test your understanding of patience, cooperation, partnership, diplomacy, emotion, relationship, and intuition. Don't argue your point too strongly. You simply don't have to *do* that any more.

While others seem to be going crazy, stay calm and centered. They are so caught up in their own situations right now, they may be overlooking the positive influence that you could be contributing. You may even feel as if you have been placed in a subservient role yet again. Maintain your dignity. Do not resent the fact that you are not the star of the show. Your time will come, believe me.

Detach yourself from other people's ongoing dramas. If you have learned anything this year, it should be that your life belongs to *you*. If something does not feel right, there is no reason for you to be involved. Continue to relate to and help others where you comfortably feel you can, but make it crystal clear that you have your own direction to follow.

This year has exposed your insensitivity toward others, and the insensitive way others have treated you. It has also brought to light the *over*sensitive responses in yourself and others. September's double 2 vibration allows you to regain your composure and confidence to levels you have never reached before. You can emerge from this year's circumstances with a new peaceful understanding of life and your increasingly meaningful place in it.

You are learning to be sensitive to *reality* rather than to those superficial aspects you once believed were real. You now have a deeper understanding of all your relationships. We do not own each other. Love cannot survive in captivity. If a particular relationship is important to you, do not make a big deal of petty issues. Realize how jealousy or pride can undermine an otherwise loving association. Use gentleness and affection rather than force. Do not depend on anyone else for your emotional security. This can only come from within.

Throughout September, there could be a mountain of details to tend to. Approach what needs to be done calmly, confidently, and with careful attention.

This year has certainly given you a lot to think about: a new awareness of yourself; where you stand with others; and a deeper understanding of the very basics of life. You may find that a certain nervousness occurs from time to time. This natural fear arises from accepting a truth that you previously resisted. By accepting fear as part of the growing process, this emotion will move through you and out of you, and you will be able to see why this year had to be as it was. You will also reach a better *long-term* understanding of what needs to be feared and what does not.

Your powerful mind is expanding. It is trying to create space for your equally powerful Will. Your intuition is now at double strength, so take some quiet time to listen to yourself. Remember that the wisdom you seek will come from within. Open up to it, feel it, and get ready to act on it in October.

If you think you already know how powerful your intuition is, allow this month's double 2 vibration to bring it to exciting new levels. You will then realize that your Will - your emotional self - is spoon-feeding you the very solution you have been seeking.

~ October ~
2 Year - 3 Month

> *People tolerate those they fear*
> *further than those they love.*
> EDGAR WATSON HOWE

The 3 cycle has a special 'lighter' quality which enables you to see that your enormous problems are not so huge after all. It was your prejudgment about a situation that made you believe there was a problem in the first place. Lighten up. Put your problems, and other people's, in perspective. You may find that you were blowing them out of proportion all along, or were just refusing to accept a changing reality. Sometimes, under a new light, a problem turns out to be a blessing in disguise. 3 is a cycle which stirs the imagination, and this may be just what your situation requires.

Something will now trigger enthusiasm in you. As you start to feel the magnetic pull of next year's 3 Cycle, you will want to surge ahead. Let these feelings be felt. But do remember that you are still in the slow 2 year cycle. Just dream your dreams and plot your course. Imagine what you want to be doing - how you want to be *feeling* - a year from now, five years from now.

Developing genuine closeness with others requires you to feel your *true* feelings toward them. This can be difficult. This year, old friends may not have been so friendly, and those you did not like may have emerged as strong allies. However, you may now meet someone of like mind who can make a positive difference in your life. Someone who is in a position to help has started to take you very seriously.

Bring your creative talent to the foreground. The spoken and written word has great significance now. Your ability to communicate *diplomatically* will have an impact on the roles others will play in your life next year.

If someone comes to you with a problem, try to express the lighter aspects of their situation. Don't become part of the problem. Tactfully make it known that others can no longer dump their problems on you and expect you to feel responsible for them. Let them know that most problems can be solved if people would only accept their reality. This year has taught you that real cooperation amplifies the joys of life and love. Cooperation and teamwork provide the only realistic means of ever achieving peace.

October offers an opportunity to create optimism and joy not only in your life but in the lives of others. Interact as much as you can. Social acceptance is important to you, but you may find that, deep down, you want more than that. You are seeking social *position*. One of the basic lessons of this month is that you will never achieve social acceptance or any satisfying position until you have first achieved these things within yourself.

You cannot expect others to create a position for you. You must know where you want to be and find a way to position yourself there. This cannot happen overnight. You are "in training". Acknowledge how inexperienced you are in your new circumstances. Be willing to learn. Others will be reluctant to teach you if you give the impression that you already know it all. You cannot help but learn if you are humble enough to admit that you know nothing. Don't try to be something you are not. Focus on *enjoying* your new situation. Learn as you go. Get out and have some fun. Enjoy the arts in whatever form you love. Entertain. Be entertained. Pamper yourself. Let yourself feel. Let yourself *heal*.

You do not have to be the star of the show in order to enjoy yourself. You will have a genuinely good time if you let someone else bask in the limelight. There is no need to force a thing.

You will know that you have learned this month's serious lessons when you emerge with enthusiasm and self-assuredness and are focused on the beauty, joy and long-term opportunity which is all around you. You will see that Free Will leads you from one pleasant experience to the next and attracts many followers.

~ November ~
2 Year - 4 Month

For a long time it had seemed to me that life was about to begin - real life!
But there was always some obstacle, something to be gotten through first,
some unfinished business....... Then life would begin. At last, it
dawned on me that these obstacles were my life.
ALFRED D. SOUZA

November's circumstances will make you feel that you have the chance to be in charge of your own life again. There are many details to take care of, and the facts about yourself and others must be faced. Sometimes relationships or projects have to hit bottom before you can see that there is nowhere left to go but up.

Even though you are longing for forward movement, everything depends on your ability to accept the current situation for what it is. It is *restrictive*. An impulsive move now could cause you to lose control. Just keep a low profile and attend to the tasks at hand.

Streamline and simplify. You are being given the opportunity get a workable system going - one which will lead to more freedom and happiness. The hard part is figuring out where to begin. Start by asking yourself where you want all this to lead. Then take one small but vital step in that direction. In the process, you will find yourself letting go of unwanted associations and habits that are distracting you from your true goal.

Now you must believe in yourself more than ever. Patience, again, is the key. Face the limitations now confronting you. Know where your own behaviors and attitudes are contributing to the problem. Your commitment to this situation will enable you to build a clear path in front of you so that you can experience the freedom and change of scenery that next month offers.

Some of the people in your life may seem like obstacles, but it is you who is allowing the situation to continue. The first step to organizing your life is to reclaim it as your own. Don't try to impress others or put on an act. Just make it clear, as tactfully as possible, that your life belongs to you and that you are in the process of creating your future.

Examine your feelings. What is preventing you from feeling free? Are you making unnecessary problems for yourself by hanging on to insecurities and control situations that prevent it? Are you reading too much into a situation and allowing paranoia to destroy a sound relationship which is simply going through a sensitive stage? Break through your anxieties - let go of your ridiculous inferiority complex. Be who you are, as you are *now*, and others will automatically support you.

You may find yourself working harder physically, mentally, or emotionally. Make all the effort you can, but do not struggle. It is time to learn the very important difference between the two. You now have more than enough strength, support, and information to break out of that box which you think is imprisoning you.

Do not view the work itself as just another obstacle. Struggle is the obstacle. It shows that you are fighting your reality and that despite everything you have experienced this year, you have still not learned how to relax and be patient.

~ December ~
2 Year - 5 Month

> *We have a genius for overlooking*
> *openings to extraordinary life.*
> MICHAEL MURPHY

Something will occur this month to bring a sense of excitement into your life and enable you to see the great possibilities that lay ahead. At last, the time has come to make a decision which will allow you to take control of your life again.

You are now in a cycle of freedom and change and although you are longing to press ahead with new ideas and plans, you must remember that although some of these ideas can be put into action now, most of them will take place next year in the 3 cycle. Once you accept that fact, you can use December's 5 energy to take a break, relax, and do something *different.*

Feel the optimism in the air. An unexpected opportunity may arise and, if you recognize it and act on it, you will feel a very expansive potential entering your life. Suddenly, the frustrating events of this year will start to make perfect sense. It is time to broaden your horizons and take a chance or two.

At the same time, your own stubbornness, which is comprised of guilt and fear, is urging you to repeat a familiar old mistake. If you do repeat it, you will feel very disappointed with yourself. However, the fact that you have finally acknowledged this mistake suggests that you will never make it again. Even though events are now working in your favor, it could be a mistake to jump at the first opportunity that seems to promise a way forward. Avoid the urge to act impulsively without first assessing your options. Ask yourself: "What if I tried it this way? What if I do this? What if I do that? *What do I want?*"

Stay within the limits of what is actually possible, otherwise your impatience may undo some of the progress you have made. Focus on your physical body and assess the damage that this year's stress has inflicted. Take full responsibility for your health. In your efforts to cooperate this year, you may have done things which were harmful to your body. You may have become dependent on certain substances or activities without even realizing it. What physical dependencies are holding you back? What emotional dependencies are causing your physical dependencies? These are very important questions to address.

There may be a tendency to overindulge in some of the physical aspects of life, such as food, alcohol, drugs, gambling, sex, exercise, spending, or an obsession for TV, computers, sports, entertainment etc. If your happiness depends on these things or anything else of a material nature, if you need to be diverted from reality, then you are not as free as you think you are.

There is no need to cut yourself off from the things you enjoy. But do try to recognize your compulsion for certain things. Redefine your priorities so that you can enjoy the things you like in a state of *freedom*. Consider your addictions carefully. We all have them.

If responsibilities seem to be restricting you, you can be sure that guilt is causing the restriction, not the responsibility. Guilt tells you that you cannot do what you want to do because it would be unfair to someone else. Remember that guilt stops the natural movement of energy. It destroys life. Love needs *freedom of movement* in order to survive. When love is released from guilt's painful grip, it starts to flourish and prosper.

One of your relationships is about to change in a dramatic and positive way, if you can find the courage to change your perception of that relationship. It has been said that *"We are more inclined to hate one another for points on which we differ than to love one another for points on which we agree."* And these are words you would do well to remember this month.

In a year that has urged you to be patient, quiet, cooperative, and low-key, this month's freedom may be confusing. Remember that everyone has the freedom and the responsibility to decide their own course through life. Take a long-term view of your life. Consider your options very carefully. You have so many!

There may be a mysterious sensation connected with this month's events, including the sudden appearance of people who seem different or strange; the reappearance of someone with whom there has been some kind of rift; traveling to a place that feels out of the ordinary, engaged in something with which you are unaccustomed or even uncomfortable. Perhaps you will simply amaze yourself as you realize how vast your potential for happiness really is.

Life's diversity contains things we love dearly *and* things we absolutely despise. It is not wrong to feel hatred for something if hatred is your true feeling toward it. By working through the fear that is causing the hatred, you will know that it is impossible to give love to someone who refuses to receive it.

To claim that we love everyone and everything is a strong denial of reality. Love cannot survive where there is guilt and the world is filled with guilt, most of which is denied. *Intent* to love unconditionally must suffice at this stage of humanity's evolution. Only from our acceptance of this, and from our *good* intent toward others, can we love, enjoy, create, and prosper. The key here is to stop prejudging people and situations before you have truly experienced them.

Soon, it will be time for you to advance in a new and more exciting direction. It is unlikely that you can stand your current situation for much longer and, therefore, something - or everything - has to change. You have been trying to prove yourself to others this year, whether it was knowingly or subconsciously. You don't have to do that any more. Others are perfectly aware of your abilities. The problem is that you, yourself, are uncertain of what it is you have to offer.

All you have to do is accept yourself exactly as you are. Focus on your positive attributes and stop being so hard on yourself. Visualize yourself six months from now as successful, happy, and fulfilled. What changes will you have to make to your current circumstances in order to achieve those goals? It is time to make a firm commitment to making those changes.

As of January 1st, you will be traveling a different route entirely. You will be traveling on a sea of opportunity which focuses on your happiness. The 3 year cycle will increase your ability to create something wonderful and enable you to communicate on a new and exciting level. Now is the time to prepare yourself, and others, for your upcoming change of direction. But it will serve no purpose to express yourself aggressively. It will serve no purpose to try to make those changes before the time is right. *Patience, patience, patience, my friend.*

Throughout December, do only what is manageable. If you take on too much, your efforts will backfire on you. Use this time to gain new skills, new ideas, and new information.

Whatever you have learned this year, particularly about the value of *relationship*, never forget it. Hold on to it and bring it with you, as midnight of December 31 arrives and you cross over into the 3 year cycle. You are now moving into life's lighter vibration of joy, optimism, imagination, friendship, creativity, and communication. Enter the new year quietly and confidently. Everything may not be as it seems. You are about to set sail on an exciting journey where *appearances* can be quite deceiving. The question is, "What do you want?"

The 3 Year Cycle

a journey to happiness
on a sea of appearances

There is a tide in the affairs of men
which, taken at the flood, leads on to fortune.
WILLIAM SHAKESPEARE, JULIUS CAESAR

This year, the tide of fortune is turning in your favor. And as you travel this simpler and more casual twelve-month cycle, you will need to focus on this question: *"What do I want?"*

This year, your *long-term* happiness is the central issue. The 3 vibration opens up the desire and the driving force of your Will so that you can discover - and then do - what makes you happy. You may not believe this until later in the year, but let me welcome you anyway, to the "lighter" side of life.

Problems of the past can be resolved this year. Relationships and important projects can flourish. New opportunities are all around you. This year's dynamic vibration enables you to determine your true desires and realize that they are attainable regardless of what *appears* to be standing in your way. This is a year of great change. However, before the direction of your happiness can be uncovered, you may first have to detect and eliminate the many sources of your *unhappiness*.

You see, Free Will is not just a matter of doing what you want to do. It also means being free within yourself to *feel* what you are feeling and to express those emotions, whatever they may be, in a way that is natural for you. Only then can you *know* what you want. Only then can you *create* what you want.

Happiness is a feeling - an emotion - which can only come from inside. As long as you hold on to unhappy feelings from the past or present, there will be no place for the happiness that this year offers. Old feelings can only be released from your body by acknowledging that they are there, allowing them to surface and be *felt*, and then expressing them outwardly. As the year progresses and you find yourself in the spotlight, you will certainly need to express your alternating fears of failure and success.

You will then find yourself in the comfortable state of knowing who, what, and where you are *now*. From this realistic perspective, a whole new spectrum of options opens up for you. The past becomes the present you have created. And the present becomes the platform from which to create your future.

Decisions must be made and acted upon. Sometimes, you may have to take a courageous leap in the dark. When you have survived such risks, your courage expands and you realize that you are so much more capable than you thought. With this level of self-acceptance, your leaps will turn to bounds, and this year may just turn out to be the happiest you have ever experienced.

Of course, everything has its opposite extreme, and the 3 energy is no exception. The cycle of 'light' certainly has its dark side. 3s negatives are depression, sorrow, guilt, gossip, oppression, destruction, lies, enemies, ugliness, pessimism, cynicism, coldness, rejection, scandal, and even cruelty. If you experience any of these things, know that you also have the power to reverse their effects. Positive 3 energy is comprised of lightness, happiness, innocence, peace, truth, friendship, creativity, communication, youth, beauty, optimism, laughter, and love. Acknowledge 3s negatives when they arise, but focus on the positives. Draw yourself to them.

3 emphasizes independence within loving relationships. This is not a contradiction, but an opportunity to love deeply without having to worry about what others think of you. You will be learning to replace guilt and blame with self-acceptance. You will learn that you no longer require the approval of others. The more you approve of yourself and do what your Will is driving you to do, the more others will accept and approve of you. They will be witnessing the astonishing beauty that comes with true confidence. When this inner beauty is expressed outwardly, it is so hard to resist. 3 is the energy of *attraction* and *charisma*.

Self-consciousness is actually quite ugly. It indicates a feeling of inadequacy which is reflected back to you through your own and other people's criticism. The problem here is that once we know this, we have a tendency to deny that we feel inadequate and cover it up with a false confidence. This causes us to put on a show and keep up *appearances*.

Pretending we are happy becomes an impossible role to maintain because the negativity we are pretending not to have is still there. This becomes painfully apparent by a conspicuous lack of personal satisfaction. The same old criticisms, gossip, inaccurate hearsay, and nonacceptance always follow. Keeping up appearances is a stressful form of denial which can actually make us physically or mentally ill. Appearances are important - but their role has nothing to do with acceptance from others.

Observe the *triangular* nature of your relationships. Remove yourself from situations which are uncomfortably three-sided and create friction because you are trying to keep or bring together certain people who do not belong in the same set of circumstances. By trying to please one person in your life, you may find that you are distinctly upsetting another. It is essential, therefore, that you please yourself first and allow others to decide for themselves who their friends are.

There are some exquisite surprises in store for you this year if you allow your Will - your deepest desires - to guide you to them. Even as you are reading this, the 3 energy is offering you the gift of optimism, which is a positive beginning.

The more you express optimism, the better your chances for success will be. Optimism is an important tool for clarifying and attaining your life's goals. You attract to you what you expect, whether you do so consciously or subconsciously. Guilt tells us that optimism produces false hope and, indeed, it does if we do not *act* to take advantage of the potential it reveals to us. The purpose of optimism is to show us that greater possibilities *do* exist.

Ideas, plans, or projects you started two years ago are now likely to show signs of progress. This will increase your optimism considerably and provide a new basis for action. Aim high. Give your very best effort.

One of 3s unique abilities is to spread itself to others, positively or negatively. The beauty that comes from your confidence, for instance, transmits inspiration to others. Pessimism, resentment, or criticism transmit ugliness and gloom instead. The "spreading" quality of the 3 energy can have a monumental effect on you and those around you. Whatever you feel, say, do, or create, will actually rub off on others and affect their mood.

You will meet your fair share of cynics and those who love to criticize. For a while, you may even be one of them. Other people will have the effect of mirrors reflecting your innermost feelings back to you. You will discover many feelings and beliefs that you have kept well-hidden, even from yourself. You will learn that your unhappiness is the result of your refusal to truly *feel* your feelings-and let them go.

Friends play an important role in the 3 year cycle. Create more free time for yourself so that you can interact with others. Consider the nature of your social activities and the feelings they trigger in you. What is *your* idea of an enjoyable time? Is there any imagination or creativity involved in your social interactions, or is it the same old boring routine every time? Are you living your own life or just following the crowd? Are you seeking friendship or approval?

Your Will wants to be around others whose Will is also free and active. This year's experiences will show you that human evolution is measured by the level of Free Will within an individual, and that direct contact with others is an essential part of human nature which must be *expanded*.

You may become aware of someone whose approach to life you greatly admire. You may even want to use this person as a role model. However, you cannot be like this person in every respect. Maintain your unique and precious individuality. You have good qualities of your own which need to be expanded.

This is a year to focus on self improvement: your health, your outer appearance, and your creative abilities. You may want to change your appearance or eliminate an addiction of some kind. You may want to reinvent your entire personality. Go ahead. Create a look, a form of expression, or a way of life that pleases *you*. You may discover a talent you didn't know you had. It would be wise to pursue this new interest with passion.

The time has come to put your desires and happiness first. Take whatever steps are necessary to *do* what you want to do. Keep your goals firmly in mind and, as you make new discoveries about what you actually want, be prepared to make some drastic changes. *Focus* on what you want. If your attention becomes too scattered, you will have all the opportunities that the 3 year cycle offers, but you will be unable to utilize them.

We are living in a world that is rife with misery and suffering. You may wonder if seeking joy is appropriate or realistic in this day and age. Guilt will tell you that this direction is wrong or impractical. 3 reminds us that life was never meant to be an unhappy experience. By allowing guilt to suck you in, you will be giving it more power to spread itself further into the world. Take your happiness - your right to exist as you *want* to exist - seriously.

Does this mean that you should ignore what is going on around you? Does this mean that you should refuse to help where help is needed? The 3 year cycle sounds like a selfish one, but it is not. You will be unable to attract success through blatant self interest. Life is urging you to reach out to others in a friendly, optimistic, and well meaning manner. A pleasant and generous nature will attract the success you are now seeking. Think in terms of what you can contribute to a situation, rather than what you can get out of it. Then you will see your generosity and kindness being returned to you in many different and exciting ways.

Know the difference between love and guilt. Where guilt exists, love cannot. This year's events will show you that guilt really is the biggest obstacle in your quest for personal happiness. The only way to remove it from your life is to stop making judgments, based on outdated beliefs, as to what is right and wrong. Develop total acceptance for your own freedom and for your natural capacity for decency and compassion.

Life is a struggle only when you struggle *with* it. Calm down and take the time to observe a problem. Accept everything about it. Take one aspect of it and change or rearrange it in some way. Then your situation cannot help but change its appearance. Remember that appearances can be deceiving. Whatever *appears* to be the case must be seen for what it is deep down and not just what it appears to be on the surface. Then, solutions become obvious, or the whole issue may turn out to be a blessing that you couldn't see before because you were so busy wrestling with it. There is a big difference between struggle and *effort*.

Try to settle misunderstandings quickly and view your life from a lighter perspective. When you are in the process of creating the life you want to live, you will wake each morning automatically refreshed and enthusiastic. Sail through this opportunity-filled year with the attitude that nothing is going to get you down. Of course you will have your fair share of problems, but you will *deal* with them as they arise, instead of worrying about things that have not even happened.

Your personal happiness is the theme for this year. And happiness is an emotion which needs to be *expressed*. Soon you will begin to see yourself in a very positive new light. You will develop new and lasting friendships. You will find success where you thought it did not exist for you. *Enjoy* your trip. It's going to be an interesting one.

~ January ~
3 Year - 4 Month

*The longest absence is less perilous to love
than the terrible trials of incessant proximity.*
OUIDA

In a year which emphasizes the lighter side of life, January's circumstances may seem totally out of place. You may have to work hard, physically, mentally, and emotionally, in order to recognize the opportunity being handed to you. This month's 4 energy is making you aware of restrictions which are preventing you from experiencing the happiness you desire. And so, here you are, face to face with a major source of your *unhappiness*.

Certain aspects can no longer be ignored or tolerated. Your limits have been reached. This is an opportunity to improve an important aspect of your life. In order to take advantage of it, you must approach others in a peaceful and friendly way. Dialogue must take place in an atmosphere which allows everyone involved to express themselves with *ease*. Then, what seemed like a difficult situation will become pleasant, enjoyable, and beneficial to all concerned. Be responsible for the atmosphere you create.

Put all your affairs in order. Clear and organize your path. Then you will be able to see where you're going. Create some kind of structure for your day to day affairs, so that everything has its own place and you will know where to find things when you need them. If you do not get organized this month, you may have to deal with the same old obstacles all year. It is time to *simplify* your life.

Happiness cannot enter a place where there is no space for it. You now need to release *your* grip on the unhappiness of the past and get rid of anything that is cluttering up your life, physically, mentally, or emotionally. Sometimes we hold on to things for what we call sentimental reasons. In the process, we may be holding on to grief, guilt, fear, or anger.

On a physical level, remember that what you see as clutter may be very useful to someone else. In a year when friends play an important role, ask if anyone wants your 'stuff' before you throw it out into the environment. Be practical too. Selling your unwanted items may help bring some order to your finances.

If you feel that a rest would do you good, take some time off. Don't allow guilt to tell you that you cannot take time for yourself. At least do not make extra work for yourself by clinging to responsibilities which are not even yours. Don't take it too personally if a certain responsibility is taken off your hands this month. The 4 energy is making life *easier* for you, not more complicated.

The problems you encounter now are the result of frustration building because your own needs and desires are not being met. So much emphasis was placed on the needs of others last year that your basic need for happiness and fulfillment has been neglected. This situation is about to change, but it is not a matter of changing other people. A change must take place within *you* and others will have to adapt to it.

To start with, you will be changing the way you *react* to other people. Yes, you may have to experience some pent up anger, fear, and grief, but releasing these emotions is all part of removing the clutter that January reveals. The release of your buried feelings can help you to develop an optimistic frame of mind which tells you that you can and must take charge of your own life.

Are you taking certain problems too seriously? Are you trying to heal yourself of previous circumstances, or are you prolonging them by refusing to accept they are over? They will never be over while you are holding on to the emotions involved. Are your problems really *your* problems or is guilt telling you that you must involve yourself in other peoples' problems? Again, ask yourself: "What will make *me* happy? What do I want?"

Wake up. The potential for happiness is all around you. You must get out of the "box" you think is trapping you and reach out for it. This is *your* life, but until you deal with the guilt which is riddling you, and just about everyone else on Earth, you will be unable to live or love in any satisfying way.

Guilt turns love into resentment, and then into hatred. It prevents you from experiencing anything that feels good. Guilt tells you that feeling good is wrong. Then it contradicts itself by telling you that you were foolish for not doing what you wanted to do. There is no such a thing as healthy guilt. If your intention is to be loving, and this includes being loving to yourself, then guilt must not be allowed a place in your life. Guilt's theme song is *"I'm damned if I do, and I'm damned if I don't"*, and it's not a pretty tune.

Go deeper into your feelings and you will realize that every time you think you know what you want to do, guilt steps in and tells you why you cannot do it. *Self-acceptance* is the only antidote to guilt, and this is the ultimate lesson of the 3 year cycle. Stop making judgments against yourself and others. Allow your true feelings to emerge and tell you what you want.

Certain plans and ideas can now be put into action. This will require a large dose of optimism, dedication, and creative thinking. January's emphasis on hard work represents the very foundation of this year's journey away from the chains of guilt and toward the joys of your own *innocence*.

Now is the time to alter your physical, mental, and emotional realities in a way that will make your living and working environments simpler and more comfortable. Organizing your life now means that you are setting the foundation for - actually starting to *create* - the life you want for yourself.

~ February ~
3 Year - 5 Month

People are always blaming their circumstances for what they are.
I don't believe in circumstances. The people who get on in this world
are the people who get up and look for the circumstances they want.
And, if they can't find them, they make them.
GEORGE BERNARD SHAW

Virtually anything can happen in February. When the 3 and 5 cycles combine, diversity, excitement, change, and high expectation are all around you. This month, horizons broaden. Love blossoms. Ideas and babies are conceived. New life is formed. Adventure is in the air. Possibilities abound. You will experience the closure of one matter so that another can expand.

There is likely to be a 'pregnant' feeling now; a feeling of expectancy. And, yet, this month can only promise one thing. The *unexpected*. Whatever occurs will wake up your desire to experience life more fully. You will see that it is possible for you to proceed toward freedom and happiness without guilt's incessant harassment. Yes, it *is* possible for you to be happy.

Your life will change this month. Even if you refuse to accept it, change will take place anyway. In fact, a whole series of changes may occur in order to create a chain reaction which will lead to much greater fulfillment. Be confident. Go with it. Remember that it was *you* who wanted change in the first place.

Concentration is essential. There is so much going on around you that you may be tempted to ignore important aspects, or get so caught up in one aspect that you cannot benefit from any of them. You could even become accident prone. You must FOCUS.

Freedom of movement and expression is taking place in your life, and you are likely to feel lighter and freer than you have felt in a long time. Something constructive is occurring, even though it may be hard to recognize initially. Expand your horizons as far as you can. Stretch your imagination. Expect a miracle.

A change in someone else's life will enable you to initiate an important change of your own. A particular *mistake* you have been making most of your life and which has consistently created trouble for you is likely to be emphasized now. When you have learned from this mistake and when you stop repeating it, it will cease to be a mistake. It will then be *experience*.

What are you really feeling? The truth is that you are experiencing so many *different* feelings at this time. The very foundation of your life has shifted and this can create fear, sadness, anger, and all kinds of stress. This month is likely to be a constant exercise in emotional release, followed by renewed enthusiasm. Your deepest feelings are being released in waves - gigantic *healing* waves.

February invites you to swim *freely* in your own reality instead of weighing yourself down with it. There may be a great sadness involved here. But drowning your sorrows in excesses of alcohol, food, drugs, or other distractions is just a form of denial that shows you have no intention of creating real happiness for yourself. Face the facts. What happens this month, no matter how sudden it may be, is providing you with the freedom you need to move forward.

5s emphasis on physical health, and 3s attraction to beauty and appearance makes this a good time to work on improving the inner and outer condition of your physical body - the vehicle which will transport you through life's journey. The way you care for it will determine whether it ends up on the scrap heap (premature death), or whether it becomes a revered classic (longevity).

A word of warning: both 5 and 3 are creative, physical, and sexual energies. When they combine, pregnancy vibrations are at their highest. A physical child may be the form of creativity you are hoping to achieve. If not, forewarned is forearmed.

A change will take place in a close friendship. Its emotional impact will deepen your understanding of freedom. Remember that friendship is one of love's many forms, and that love cannot survive where there is no acceptance for change or Free Will. 5 thrives on movement and change. You will need to keep up with the rapid pace of this cycle. If you are not paying attention, you could literally crash into things that seem to appear from nowhere. You may find yourself in unknown territory. Stay alert and focused.

Change is occurring whether you want it to or not. You are traveling through life's *corridors of change*. Even though a certain change may shake you to the core, accept the fact that it does present you with an opportunity to be free. Act on your instincts - your true feelings - and travel confidently to wherever it takes you.

~ March ~
3 Year - 6 Month

The basis of all relationships is a mystery.
The bonds which unite us to another can be, simultaneously,
as sturdy as cast iron and as delicate as spun silk.
SALLY BROMPTON

In this year of seeking happiness and fulfillment, what better place to look for these rewards than among those you love. What do you *feel* when you think of the word "home"? Somewhere in your vision for the future is a warm and loving place called home. If there isn't, you may have overlooked some important aspects of happiness.

This month, you may uncover an unexpected truth about yourself or a loved one, and what you actually want from life. You may feel perfectly content. On the other hand, you may feel that your domestic or romantic situation is preventing you from experiencing any kind of happiness at all. Something will occur which features the home, spouse, lover, family, pet, friends, relatives, or neighborhood. This will enable you to communicate on a level you have never reached before, to make an important decision, and to move closer to an important goal. In the process, you will realize that you have only touched the surface of your ability to create the life you want for yourself.

6 is a cycle of responsibility, balance, and love. Sort out just which responsibilities are yours and which are not. Are you placing the responsi-

bility for your happiness on someone else? Are you assuming the responsibility for someone else's happiness? Is guilt telling you that you cannot pursue your own needs while someone else is having difficulty with theirs? Are you judging others or allowing them to judge you without considering each others' individuality? Are you setting unnecessary rules? Or are you living unhappily in someone else's lifestyle?

Everyone is responsible for creating their own happiness, no matter what their relationship. A little acceptance and friendliness may be just what is needed to put these issues into a more pleasant and positive perspective. This means opening yourself up to others. Something positive - even miraculous - is happening here. Give someone else the benefit of the doubt, and *listen*.

Balance is the key to making this month a positive one. Your life is rather like a boat journeying across an ocean. If you place all of its contents on one side, it will tip over and sink. So many people drown in the sea of life because their contents are muddled up together with no separation between what feels good and what does not. Eventually, nothing at all feels good. Sort out the contents of your life, including your muddled emotions and conflicting beliefs. Balance your life *evenly* by knowing what is important to you and by making equal time and space for all of these things.

Disagreements and diversity within a family must be accepted as part of what it takes to be a family. Otherwise you will all be tied together by a fruitless common bond with each one yearning to move in different directions.

Even though you are connected by the love within your close relationships, each of you is a unique individual who must lead his or her own life and find his or her own happiness, no matter how many different directions spring up from within one family. If you believe that others are holding you back, it is time to speak your mind. But do be prepared for unanticipated responses which may prove that you are holding *yourself* back.

Listen carefully to what others have to say. Love needs freedom to express itself. Without genuine acceptance of the reality of another, love cannot be expressed. Learn to *coexist* with people whose experience of life is very different from your own.

When the air is cleared, you will be able to extend love to someone who matters to you more than you thought. Your openness will enable them to understand you on a deeper level. Everyone concerned will emerge inspired, happier, and freer.

Focus on your domestic environment and tend to those issues you've been putting off. Bring beauty and comfort into your home, and take care of the things, people, and pets with whom you share your life. 6 emphasizes *love*, while 3 amplifies *communication*. This is a marvelous time for open dialogue in all areas of your life.

Enjoy the pleasures of children and their activities. Encourage them to develop Free Will and create their own happiness. We do not own our children, nor should we try to control them. Our purpose as parents is simply to love them and guide them toward fulfillment and happiness and be there for them if they fall. We must never place guilt on them. Appreciate their *innocence*, their positive approaches, their emotions, their vulnerability, and their need to express themselves openly. They are the future, right before our eyes. They have been born into an angry and judgmental world. Show them that an alternative does exist.

If there are no children in your life, perhaps there is someone else involved here for whom you have taken on some kind of parental role. Or, perhaps it is the child in you who needs acceptance and loving attention now. Stop being so hard on yourself. Allow yourself - and others - to communicate freely. Feel the positive vibration that comes from the *exchange* of Free Will.

By seeing everything and everyone as *free*, including yourself, you will also be able to heal and inspire and find creative solutions to old grievances. We are all part of nature and, in order to grow, everyone needs light, water, warmth, nourishment, freedom, love, and an accepting environment in which to bloom.

~ April ~
3 Year - 7 Month

Kind words can be short and easy to speak,
but their echoes are truly endless.
MOTHER TERESA

Slow down. You are in the midst of a strange looking fog which leaves no room for hasty decisions or unplanned moves. If you feel inadequate or afraid, it is because you need time to think. Time to plan. You may have duties and obligations, but it is important that you take everything in your stride. Do one thing at a time, and do not worry about how you are being perceived by others.

Accept the fact that you don't know where you are right now. You know that success is near, but doubts and unexpected circumstances seem to be getting in the way. You have a burning need to find a definite direction and the chances are that it is right in front of you.

Your emotions have led you most of the way this year, and there will be yet another emotional situation to deal with this month. Now it is time to let your intellect - your mind - take over. Whenever you can, retreat into a quiet environment where there are no distractions. You need to dream your own dreams and think your own thoughts. You need to remember where you came from. Many of your current problems stem from ingrained childhood influences which you are in the process of outgrowing. You have matured.

Let your thoughts take you back over the entire journey - your whole life - so that you can visualize how one step always led to another; how everything you ever did, everything that ever happened to you *connected* you to the next phase of your journey, and how each step has brought you to this place called NOW.

A decision you make this month will pave the way for the next situation in which you find yourself. Therefore you must *focus* on what you want from a positive frame of mind. You must decide what you want to achieve and *plan* your method of achieving it.

Let those buried feelings *out* as you travel back in time. Know that your feelings and your thoughts are two separate energies. They must come together and *agree* on what took place in the past, the very recent past included. They must come together and agree upon what you desire in the future.

Only when the past is fully accepted into the present can you create, or even imagine, the future you want. How long are you going to hold on to that pain? Let it go, dream new dreams. In May, you will be on your way again - full steam ahead.

April is a time to think, feel, analyze, polish, and *plan*. Remember that you do need the support of certain people if your plans are to materialize. Therefore, be careful not to alienate yourself from others just because you are feeling a trifle fragile this month. In other words, don't take it all so personally.

As your dissatisfaction increases, be careful of the words you say. Both the 3 and 7 energies can make you insensitive and critical of everything and everyone. Remember that thoughtless words do hurt others and can ostracize you from those you need and love.

Make clearly defined plans to move forward, but do not make any major decisions just yet. To enter next month's dynamic waves without a specific plan of action could mean that you are still not serious about what you want. Consider your plans carefully. Analyze them. Find their flaws and fine tune them. Have faith in yourself. Accept that nothing at this stage of human evolution is perfect. Stay flexible. Allow for the unexpected. Not knowing how to do something you would love to do is no excuse for not doing it. *Learn* how. Start now!

You may certainly experience other people's negativity this month. But you cannot allow it to bring you down. In fact, you must see it for exactly what it is - *other people's negativity*. You may have to move a few layers of old and deeply buried emotion in order to find yourself again, but in doing so, you will make a new best friend - you. Now, what is your *plan* for the rest of the year?

~ May ~
3 Year - 8 Month

What we vividly imagine, ardently desire, and
enthusiastically act upon, must inevitably come to pass.
CEZANNE

Snap out of it, wake up, and make some positive waves. 3 is the number of communication, and 8 is the number of power. Yes, the power of communication is what this month is all about.

If you start placing trivial concerns before your own goals and needs, or if you find yourself backing away from an obvious opportunity, it is time to face your fear head on. The problem may be that you are *still* not taking yourself seriously. You seem to be afraid of doing something that, in fact, you are perfectly able to do. The fear you must face is the fear of taking full responsibility for your life. You *can* release this fear. You *will* succeed.

A new and potent energy has entered your life. It is time for action and for implementing those plans you made last month. A decision must be made and carried out. *Feel* the positive energy surrounding you, including an improvement in the way others perceive your talents and efforts. Think success. Dynamic forward movement is the way to proceed, using a creative and knowledgeable approach. If you need something, don't be afraid to ask for it. No matter how difficult a certain task appears to be, keep at it. Don't give up.

Do not focus on the rewards alone, as this will reduce your focus on what you need to *do* in order for the reward to follow. Take yourself and your plans seriously. It is important that you *believe* that your life has taken a turn for the better, no matter how turbulent the waters may appear. The power of belief must not be underestimated. This month's combination of energies represents a big step forward into a future which you have designed by the strength of your desire, *belief*, and action.

Pay attention to your thoughts and your feelings. You have more ability to make things happen this month than you have had in a very long time. Implement the ideas you have been thinking about - not next month, not next year, NOW.

If you have to rely on a friend or relative to assist you, it will work out well for this person, too. See how much more effective you are when you know how to delegate. Don't be afraid to learn new things. In fact, until you do learn what must be learned, it will be difficult to proceed no matter how much effort you exert.

Don't let anyone or anything undermine your confidence. Your determination to achieve what you have set out to do will draw opportunity to you. There may be an immediate improvement in your finances, business affairs, or relationships, or an opportunity will arise which will allow these improvements to occur later.

Personal growth and the creation of a satisfying life often require a courageous leap of faith. Now is the time to jump in and become passionately involved. Do not limit yourself. Do not lower your standards in any way. On the contrary, raise them! If you *believe* that you can have what you are aiming for, the magnetism of your belief will draw it to you - and you to it. Throw yourself into the situation and do what needs to be done. The dress rehearsal of the past four years is over. This, my dear, is the real thing!

Understand that each step you take towards a goal is a goal in itself. If you find yourself struggling with a certain task, remove yourself from it, if only for a few hours. Walk away and focus on something completely unrelated. This much needed diversion will relieve your stress, rejuvenate your senses, and will enable you to tackle the problem with a clearer understanding of how to proceed.

What if things are not going well? What if you have lost instead of gained? What if you feel empty and disappointed? What if your conditions are now below your usual standards? What if there is no hope in sight? If you look closely at everything that has transpired in the last two years, you will realize that this month's events are showing you aspects of your own *power* that you have not used before. From this experience, you can learn *how* to bring prosperity into your life. Yes, effort and determination are called for. You will have to keep going until you get it right! But, what a wonderful gift it is to finally know what you actually *want*.

One way or another, the events of this month have rewarded you richly. You know that the time for trying is over, and the time for doing is here. Your plans may take longer to materialize than you had imagined but, still, what was yesterday's future is today's reality.

~ June ~
3 Year - 9 Month

> *There seems to be a door on the way to*
> *remarkable success that can be passed through*
> *only by those willing to persevere beyond the point*
> *where the majority stop and turn back.*
> EARL NIGHTINGALE

After five months of development, June's 9 vibration insists that certain issues must be brought to an end. An emotional situation must be put in its proper perspective. Decisions must be made. Loose ends must be tied up. You have reached the END of a certain phase of your life.

One issue will be so obviously in need of ending that your decision will not be difficult to make. Other situations may require you to be very honest with yourself. You may have to face a part of your life that you have been refusing to acknowledge, and make a change you hoped would never be necessary.

You are in a cycle of tremendous growth provided that you can let go of things, attitudes, issues, and even people that no longer serve your best interests. It is time to decide upon your next step. You may not actually take this step until next month or later in the year, but an ending which takes place now, in your heart, will set you in a new and more rewarding direction.

Face the facts, no matter how painful they feel. Take control of your life. You are now clearing some space in your world so that new opportunities can come in. You may have to find a courage you thought you did not have in order to recognize the truth about yourself and someone else. A change must take place in the way you see yourself and especially in the way you express yourself. The negativity of the past must not be allowed to contaminate the positive new reality that you have recently created.

This month you are going to see just how much you allow other people to influence you and just how damaging this is to your quest for personal happiness. Be aware of your fear of what others think of you. This fear is often disguised as love and it creates so many problems in your life.

A problem which arises this month may be far more deep rooted than you can currently admit. You see, it is not always a matter of trying to please everyone. A current problem may be based on your feelings for one person in particular. This could be a parent or the beliefs of a parent, even a parent who is deceased. It could involve a spouse, lover, friend, relative, associate, boss, or some other figure who influences your thoughts and feelings.

This person is not holding you back however. It is your *reaction* to this person that is preventing you from doing the things you desire in life. When you are overly concerned about other people's opinions of you, *guilt* is keeping your stagnation in place. And it would seem that guilt is what you need to let go of more than anything else in your life right now.

You have some very real needs which must be taken care of if you are to find the happiness you desire. Just because someone else does not take these needs seriously does not mean that they are not serious needs. If you have difficulty defining your needs, they are those very basic and simple things that make you *happy* and for which you are now longing.

The chances are that someone or something may leave your life in order to trigger your buried emotions. This may test your ability to remain optimistic, but its purpose is a cleansing and healing one with your future well-being in mind. Make no mistake, June is an emotional and transforming month, full of fabulous highs and sobering lows. Issues of the past will return so that you can put an end to certain hostilities or misunderstandings once and for all. Accept what is happening and *feel* how good it makes you feel.

June is a cycle of endings. It is also a cycle of giving. Giving is never about sacrifice. If you feel that you are sacrificing in order to give, then you are not giving because you want to, but because something else is telling you that you should. Accept that guilt is dictating to you here and that giving, purely for the enjoyment it brings, is one of the most satisfying feelings there is. No matter which form your giving takes, it cannot happen until you *let go* of something. Assess for yourself what needs to be released; what no longer has any constructive or loving purpose in your life; what clearly has prevented real happiness for so long - and let it go. Perhaps it is a feeling which needs to be released. Pride perhaps? Anger? The need to control or change someone or something? Let it go and you will feel the exciting vibration of your *new* potential.

From the act of forgiveness, your optimism and belief in yourself will return. You will also realize that others are taking you seriously and are a little in awe of who you are, what you have accomplished, and what you *can* accomplish. This goes to show that not all endings need be dramatic or traumatic. They can feel like the weight of the world being lifted from your shoulders, so that *joy*, peace and a sense of *self-worth* can be experienced again. After all, it is happiness you're trying to achieve, is it not?

~ July ~
3 Year - 1 Month

*Your resistance to change is likely to reach its peak
when significant change is imminent.*
GEORGE LEONARD

It is time to change a situation that has been plaguing you for a long time; an ongoing drama which *always* stops you in your tracks and causes you to lose your focus just when it looks like you're going to succeed. Make no mistake, this situation is NOT going to change until you change your reaction to it. First, you must be clear in your mind as to what your usual reaction actually is.

The time has come to take full control of your own life and concentrate on what is important to you. If not, the negativity of others will become your own and everything you have worked so hard for can unravel before your eyes! Be aware of the manipulative tactics of those who are afraid to see you succeed or those who cannot relate to your personal needs. Be aware of your own faults too, and make some kind of compromise.

If, after the air is cleared, you are trying to make friends with someone, it will help if you relate to that person in a *friendly* manner. Forgive for your own sake as much as for the sake of someone else. This person may not be as much to blame as you would like to think. One of the reasons you were so unfriendly in the first place is because you were afraid of being distracted.

Fear of success produces emotional situations which allow us to blame others for the possibility of failure. Move away from an emotional trap that you or someone else has consciously or unconsciously set. There may be a strong emotional bond between you and whoever is involved. All the more reason to nip this problem in the bud before it destroys this month's enormous potential.

Let your anger work for you. Admit just how angry you are. Your ego is not out of control. In fact, this positive shift in your ego is long overdue. Your ego is the gauge by which you measure your self-worth. It is how you know who you are. In some people it is sadly underdeveloped causing feelings of inferiority and submission. In others it is inflated and exaggerated causing feelings of superiority and the need to control.

When your ego is balanced, you will emerge with confidence, calmness, enthusiasm, independence, and love. You will know who and what you are and how you want to live. You will *be yourself.* Knowing who you are, what you want, living the way you want to live, and being yourself, is what this month is all about.

Accept that life is made up of positives *and* negatives, choose to travel on the bright side of the street, and get back into the game. The end result may take longer to realize than you had imagined, but it is better to do the job well than skip over the details and end up with something inferior. Put the past firmly behind you and prepare to forge ahead with a new level of confidence. Tie up the loose ends of a certain project or situation. Focus intently on what you are trying to achieve long-term, and on what it will take to realize this goal. Take yourself and your dreams *seriously*.

A change in the way you communicate is a priority now. Your use of words has a specific role to play. Express yourself with confidence, not just the appearance of confidence. Feel the power you have to turn your whole life around. It is time to look FORWARD again. Yes, the time has come to communicate your true feelings. Dispense with all that guilt and blame, and just watch how others suddenly start to cooperate with you.

1 is the energy of leadership, independence, progression, and originality. Realize just how far you have progressed this year. Demonstrate your self-reliance and your ability to lead your own life. Do not depend on others for the results you want. Depend only on YOU. Bring your special style, originality, and individuality to the forefront so that your social and creative talents can shine. Your unique way of expressing yourself is likely to inspire someone else who can help you in some way.

Whatever steps you have been contemplating, now is the time to act. Feel your confidence rising and do not allow the narrow vision of others or your own doubt, fear, or guilt to stop you from pressing ahead. Do not trivialize your basic needs and feelings. Realize the value of what you have to offer this world and start to put it out there! ENJOY what you are doing once again.

This positive shift in your consciousness will effect many different areas of your life. You should initiate this yourself or utilize a change which has occurred in the life of someone else. As 1 is a cycle of independence, consider those situations and habits that are keeping you dependent. Take positive steps to eliminate them.

While June was a month of endings, July is a month of new beginnings and fresh starts. There is no better time to change destructive habits and excesses which may give the appearance of freedom but, in reality, are taking your freedom away. Without change we stand still. You are made of energy and energy *must* flow without restriction. Imagine how free you will be without this addiction which may be nothing more than *guilt*.

This month's changes may force you into a more independent stance whether you want it or not. You may find yourself more alone than you expected. This confirms that if you depend on others for the results you want, you will be swept along a road that is meant for someone else. A feeling of abandonment confirms that you are at last in a position to take full control of *your* life.

Allow others to be who they are. Expect the same consideration from them. Don't concern yourself with their reactions. Just DO what you want to do. Feel the excitement you create, that breathtaking combination of electricity and magnetism, when you are being who you really are and doing what you love to do.

~ August ~
3 Year - 2 Month

All things come around to those who will but wait.
LONGFELLOW

An important task needs to be completed as quickly as possible. After that, you will be able to slow right down, stand still for a while, and relax. Yes, I did say relax. Can you remember what that *feels* like?

In a state of relaxation, you will be able to recall, realistically, all that has transpired this year, especially within your various relationships. You will also realize just how far you've come; how much old emotion you have moved out of your body, and out of your life; and how much new understanding has moved in.

You have been learning how to captain your own ship for quite a while now, and you have brought yourself to many new interests, ideas, people, places, and feelings. You have done so well. Now it is time to take a little rest. It is time to gaze at your life and understand your *relationship* to everything and everyone in it. Certain relationships may cause a great deal of concern, but don't allow this, or anything else, to undermine your confidence during this enlightening but slow month which is designed to improve the very timing of your goals.

June brought certain issues to a conclusion. July made it clear that only *you* can make your dreams come true. August is a month when you must rest and revitalize, consider the other people in your life, and contemplate what your next move should be. There are many details to take care of, including important issues which need to be approached in a relaxed, patient, and confident manner.

An important goal must now be given the time and space to develop of its own accord. You, too, need time to replenish your physical, emotional, and mental energies. Any aggressive moves on your part will result in delay, frustration, resentment, and loss.

Whether you realize it or not, you are now part of a team. Cooperate willingly. The circumstances of other people will provide you with distractions which will take your mind off *you* - and this is how it is supposed to be.

Soon you are going to need the cooperation of others yourself. This month will teach you how to cooperate and become closely involved with others without losing yourself in their problems or without allowing other people's negative behavior to suck the joy right out of *your* life. *Hold on to your joy*. Protect it!

Remind yourself that your plans are actually benefiting from this month of delay. As you become emotionally involved with those around you, you will realize just how special *your* life is and why you must protect yourself from people and situations that drain your precious energies.

This month, the circumstances of others will make you realize just how fortunate you are. But do remember that it is your *cheerfulness* - your refusal to be brought down by the negativity or problems of others - that will open the eyes and mind of someone who has possibly been causing you grief.

Try to use good humor and creativity to relate to others. It is not enough to simply hear what they are saying. 2 is a cycle of *relation* and, in order to relate genuinely to another person, you must listen to what they are saying and *feel* the feelings they arouse in you. The feelings that certain people arouse in you may be unpleasant. This is simply life's way of making you AWARE of what you are dealing with and HOW to deal with it. Certainly, you must make your feelings crystal-clear, but all-out aggression is not the answer to this particular problem. You simply don't have to react that way.

To relate to someone means that you recognize and *feel* their situation - their reality. Through a mutual perception of the problem, solutions can be found which bring beneficial results to all concerned. Peacefully share a problem or situation with whoever brought it to you, and see how it solves itself. Find the connection between someone else's problem and something that is on *your* mind, and you will be given some important information. Find that connection, and you will know what your next step must be. By the end of August, you will know that the waiting is over and that YOU are in full control of your own journey.

~ September ~
3 Year - 3 Month

Beware as long as you live of judging by appearances.
JEAN DE LA FONTAINE

If a strong sense of elation or optimism is not what you're feeling this month, then there are likely to be some old emotional issues from your past which need to be cleared up. Allow these feelings to move through you and out of you. Dig up the emotions that you've buried deep inside and let it all out.

This month's double 3 energy gives you the choice of either moving toward happiness by following your own desires or living unfulfilled because guilt has said that your desires are unattainable or inappropriate. The decisions you make and the actions you take will determine the quality of your life for a long time to come.

The opportunity for great happiness is out there waiting for you. If you are to reach out and claim this destiny for yourself, you must now *do* what you want to do; what you love doing; what guilt and fear have been telling you that you cannot do. Your desire to lead your own life must now replace any doubt or confusion as to how others may fit in with your plans.

Your future is in your own hands now. You are the maker and breaker - the sole creator - of your own destiny. It is time to use some of that courage you have been building throughout the year.

Whatever you started in July will now be showing signs of progress. Seize every opportunity to move forward. Bring your experiences of the past into the present. Begin to *create* your future. The mere dreaming of it is not enough now.

You are not responsible for other people's problems or for their unresolved emotional issues. At this stage, it makes no difference what others think of you or your plans. If you wait for their approval, the opportunity will be lost. Accept yourself and your desires fully. Take responsibility for your own life. In doing so, you will find life itself.

Your creative and communicative aptitude is at an all-time high. Take every opportunity to express yourself verbally or artistically. Spend time with those who are creative, emotional, and expressive. These people have an important role to play in your life for the rest of the year. Learn from them. Appreciate their emotional personalities which is what makes them creative in the first place. Remember that creativity is not confined to artistic endeavors. Each situation has the potential for a creative or a destructive outcome. Recognize how your actions and words effect others and choose the road of PEACE.

Take the time to enjoy and appreciate the people you love. They probably want to enjoy the "new you", too. Your social life can provide meaningful insights. Your family life can become part of your social life. Stay focused while you are enjoying yourself.

Appreciate the wonders of nature and the spectacle of the arts. Go to the theater or a concert, or visit a museum or a natural splendor. You may receive an invitation which can lead to a beneficial contact. 3 is the ultimate networking vibration. Entertain. Be entertained. Enjoy everything that comes your way and try to see the lighter side of any situation. Being noticed is part of the magnetic attraction of the 3 energy. Others will certainly be noticing you this month. Pay attention to your outer appearance and take the time to pamper and nurture yourself.

Your enthusiasm and confidence, or your defensiveness and insecurity, will rub off on those around you, creating either friendly or unfriendly environments. Set your imagination free and allow it to roam wherever it wants. Who knows what brilliant ideas will surface when you release the barriers that your fear of rejection has placed around your creative mind?

~ October ~
3 Year - 4 Month

> *Great things are not done by impulse,*
> *but by a series of small things brought together.*
> VINCENT VAN GOGH

October may find you wondering what your next move should be. Remember that you are in the 3 year cycle - the "lighter" side of life. Make sure you don't react too aggressively or passively. In fact, the way you *react* to this month's delays may be more important than what actually takes place. The 4 energy is simply pointing out what is still standing between you and your goal, and the WORK that must be done to realize it.

It is time to get organized. This year's 3 vibration may have created a tendency to base your knowledge on hearsay rather than fact. Determine the *real* facts about everything in your life right now, including the appearance of certain people whose presence does not seem to be helping matters.

Prioritize. Set a new agenda. Put every detail in its place. Don't let this month's delays and distractions cause you to forget that happiness - the *lightness* of life - is what you are working towards.

Deal with each situation as it arises in a relaxed, confident, and dignified manner. Create a system that simplifies, not complicates, your life. Be efficient, practical, methodical, and enthusiastic. Find creative ways to bring *order* to areas of chaos. Determine which problems are of your own making - caused by your own rigid attitudes, beliefs, or your inability to face reality. Misunderstandings in a friendship or relationship may require you to be more sensitive to someone else's feelings in relation to *your* circumstances. Feel your fears. Feel theirs.

Social interaction is still an important part of this year's activities. Use it to ease October's inevitable stress. Or perhaps some order is needed within your social network. In a year when friendship has been such an important factor, there is still so much to learn in this respect. Are friends and family influencing your ability to think for yourself? Do you need to break away for a while so that you can figure things out for yourself, form your own opinions, and make decisions that are right for *you*? Or, are you so detached from others that you never listen to them, even when you know their advice is sound and timely? A balance must be created between your aspirations and your fear of rejection.

Notice how you make extra work for yourself by insisting on doing things your way when there really are simpler and more efficient approaches. Get away from pettiness and mediocrity by focusing on what actually matters instead of whining over trivial things or participating in gossip and destructive criticism.

Realize that the faults you see in others are actually your own faults; the ones you cannot admit to; the ones you deny, being reflected back to you. Let others be who they are or who they pretend to be - *you* must get organized so that you can move forward again. Feel just how powerful your Will is when it is free. Now is the time to take control of your life by making decisions which, last month, you found impossible to make.

A new situation will enter your life this month. Whatever it is, make sure that you react to it in a way which best serves your long term interests. In fact, whatever occurs this month will come back to you next year in one of two forms: it will either create harsh and restrictive circumstances - or - it will lead to breakthrough and great success. Think about this carefully. October is no time for rash or thoughtless moves. It is a time for taking yourself and your dreams very seriously indeed.

~ November ~
3 Year - 5 Month

Why not go out on a limb?
Isn't that where the fruit is?
FRANK SCULLEY

Opportunities abound during this exciting, fast paced, accident prone month. Focus on what you are doing because the erratic speed of the 5 cycle can push you, quite suddenly, onto unfamiliar ground. Be flexible and prepared for any eventuality because *anything* can happen this November.

5 is the number of sudden change and freedom. Keep these two elements in mind as you rush from one situation to the next. At the same time, you may begin to feel the more serious and practical vibrations of next year's 4 Cycle which emphasizes the WORK that must be done to fulfill your goal.

A change in your working or domestic life may occur. This can create excitement and enthusiasm and, simultaneously, make you feel restless, impulsive, and anxious about what your next move should be and where it may lead. Stay optimistic as you look for important clues and connections that can be found through social contact. This is unlikely to take place in your usual social environment. So get out into the big world and 'mingle'.

If you have followed this year's numerological roadmap, you will have gained new insight about your own life, your loved ones, your friends, and life in general. You will have developed a new way of thinking and expressing yourself.

If you cannot feel the optimism that November offers, perhaps there are certain emotions still trapped inside you. Perhaps you are still denying that you are denying. You will be unable to make significant progress until you set those feelings free.

Freedom is the theme for November, but you will never be able to reach your destination if you are too afraid to take the first step. Feel your fear and allow it to guide you - in safety - through this particular segment of the journey. Use this emotion to learn the difference between what needs to be feared and what does not. This is how courage - and common sense - are developed.

But let's assume that your enthusiasm, sense of adventure, and optimism are flowing to the full. What are you going to do with your freedom this month? The 5 cycle urges you to use this time as constructively and creatively as possible.

You may not think that travel or vacation is particularly constructive at this time but, for you, right now, it is. You have been searching hard for happiness, and it's about time you actually experienced some of it. If a vacation is out of the question, then at least enjoy friends, social activities, or a place you have never been before.

Do something *different*. This is no time for limitation or intolerance. Move away from old routines that serve no constructive purpose. Open yourself up to the sheer enjoyment of life in all its splendid diversity. Everyone out there has a story to tell and a desire to fulfill, just like you. Notice how the stories of others are connected to your own. Listen to your intuition constantly.

Not everything out there is likable. But until you let yourself experience new people, places, and things, you will have no way of knowing what is likable and what should be avoided. Your horizons are changing and you are now emerging as a much more confident, mature, and complete human being who is not afraid of people and situations just because they are *different*.

Try to moderate activities which can give the appearance of freedom but are, in fact, nothing more than addictions. It should also be said that when the 3 and 5 energies combine, there is a tendency for something to be conceived. Often this results in pregnancy and, so, if you are not planning to start or expand your family at this time, take whatever precautions are necessary to prevent it. But this tendency for 3 and 5 to produce new life is not always confined to the conception of a physical child. It can also result in the conception of ideas (a brain child), plans, projects, creative solutions, and great vision.

Be aware of all the changes that have taken place this year. Some you have made yourself, some were the result of changes in the lives of others, and some simply happened. Now, a change will occur in your attitude toward work, career, identity, finances, and your general long-term prospects.

Your approach to these matters should be more dynamic now. You are starting to take yourself and your capabilities much more seriously. Your personality is changing accordingly. You know you can succeed. And you know that you will have to make even more changes in order to reach your current goal.

This is an exciting time for you and, by taking a different avenue or a new approach this month, and following your feelings at all stages, you will transport yourself to the right place, at exactly the right time. Swim with the freedom that November offers. *Experience it.*

~ December ~
3 Year - 6 Month

I must create a system, or be enslaved by another man's;
I will not reason or compare; my business is to create.
WILLIAM BLAKE

Love is the greatest joy of all. Forget your preconceived ideas about what love is. Now you will be able to distinguish real love from all the other misconceptions you have believed love to be. This month will show you just how much love exists in your life, how spectacular love can be, the many different forms love can take, and how easily we take love for granted.

Focus on home, family, spouse, lover, children, parents, relatives, pets, and close friends; those who represent the deepest matters of your heart. Peace and balance should not be difficult to achieve, given all you have learned this year. This is a time of forgiveness, acceptance, or at the very least, tolerance.

Create a satisfying balance between your family life and your outside interests. Don't impose your problems or your views on other people. Negative 6 energy brings out the tyrant, know-it-all, and controller in you. These characteristics have no place in your life.

Where there is misunderstanding or ill will, you should be the one to attempt to restore peace and harmony. Let others be who they are. Resist the urge to judge them. Express to those you love that you do, indeed, love them. *Communicate*, and let them communicate their feelings back to you. Devote your time and energy to the people you love without dominating the scene. Let others feel at ease with their own existence. What rules have you set for these people? How are you influencing their ability to solve their own problems? How are these people effecting *your* Free Will?

Love must be FREE. It is now up to you to rescue the love in your life from whatever is repressing it. This task is likely to come in the form of an added responsibility of some kind. You may find yourself being oversensitive to the situation. But this will not help matters. Calm down. The solutions you need are inside you. They will reach your conscious mind when you are relaxed and centered.

Make your home a beautiful and inspiring place by providing a secure, loving, and healing atmosphere. Take care of any maintenance or repairs.

Let your love spread to others. That is what love does when it is free. Your ability to create something wonderful, be it a painting or an atmosphere, is now at a very high level.

The problems of others are real and painful for them. Provide love, not criticism. Someone who is close to your heart really *needs* your understanding now. If you want to know what love is, the answer is all around you. It is also inside you. Love yourself first and you cannot help but find others more lovable.

Next year you will be traveling the 4 road of hard work, painstaking attention to detail, and coming to terms with who and what you are as a human being. Sometimes the 4 cycle can seem like a year-long obstacle course. But, now, because you know about this in advance, you can prepare for it with confidence. Each obstacle you encounter next year will limit you in some way. The purpose of the 4 vibration is to develop your belief in yourself. You will be expanding what you believe are your limits by recognizing and taking advantage of your limitless potential. You will be learning the difference between struggle and effort. And you will be able to create a sense of order for yourself within this chaotic world.

For now, however, simply take in and feel everything that has happened to you and your loved ones this year. Appreciate the positive steps the 3 year cycle has enabled you to take. Whatever you have learned, never forget it. Hold on to your dreams, your poise, your confidence, and your optimism. Take these things with you as midnight of December 31st arrives and you cross over into the powerful 4 year cycle of work, organization, new identity, and BREAKTHROUGH.

The 4 Year Cycle

a journey to breakthrough
on a sea of obstacles

Doubt yourself, and you doubt everything you see.
Judge yourself, and you see judges everywhere.
But, if you listen to the sound of your own voice,
you can rise above doubt and judgment,
and you can see forever.
NANCY KERRIGAN

Welcome to the 4 year cycle of identity, priority, and effort. The events of this hard working year will leave no doubt that the time has come to set new priorities and work tenaciously toward a *specific* long-term goal. Without this vision and commitment, this year could be a confusing and bumpy ride.

The 4 energy reacts to the strength of your Will. Where the Will is strong, great accomplishments can be made. However, it is in the 4 year cycle that we realize that our Will is not as free as we believed it to be because we have repressed it with a limited vision of our potential. The Will is made of *feelings*. Knowing how you *feel is* the only way to know what you want to create in your life. It is from our feelings that all creativity is born.

At first, the 4 energy can make you feel restricted and boxed-in by circumstances you think are beyond your ability to change. The part of you called the Will feels confined by your very thought of having no control in a particular situation.

However, the part of your Will that is free is now trying to rescue the lost parts of itself. Don't worry if you do not understand this immediately. As the year unfolds in its own way, many new understandings will come.

4 is a serious and practical energy which needs a specific goal to work towards. This energy responds best to routine, efficiency, order, and organization. The 4 energy needs to know its destination in advance so that it can maintain its profound sense of purpose. This year, you will be developing a greater sense of your own purpose. You will be setting a definite course or direction for yourself. You cannot just drift along and hope for the best. You need a specific and meaningful goal to focus on and be responsible for.

Seriously consider every aspect of your life. Confront yourself with the vision of where each aspect is leading. Be practical, face the facts, and look for solutions which will change your adverse circumstances. Yes, 4 is a serious and life-changing cycle.

Organize your life according to what is important to you. Certain things you believed were important may be the very same things that are now restricting you. Blaming others is just another form of restriction because it implies that you are a victim of someone or something else. It is actually you who is causing your own restrictions by refusing to prioritize.

Break free of circumstances and beliefs that are keeping you physically, emotionally, creatively, and intellectually confined. These issues are preventing you from being the person you know you can be. This year, you will be facing the reality of YOU, and it may not always be a pretty sight.

It is time to weed out the useless and trivial aspects of your life, especially those beliefs and attitudes that simply don't matter in the grand scheme of things. These trivialities are confusing the larger picture of your life. Focus on what really matters to you and, even then, face the possibility that half of those things don't matter either. What matters is your freedom to create - and exist - in your own right.

It is time to stand alone and gaze honestly at those aspects which you believe are holding you back. You will soon realize that many of them are of your own making. Are you too set in your ways or are you too frivolous and uncaring? Are you too stubborn to accept your past and present mistakes? Are you unrealistic about your talents and potential? Are you unhealthy due to poor diet, substance abuse, or lack of exercise? Are you unrealistic about finance and materiality? Do you avoid facing reality by creating distractions for yourself? Do you base your actions on your own feelings and beliefs, or those of other people?

Be honest with yourself as you consider your options. Weed out those ideas you know are not working for you. Through this process of elimination, you will see the direction you *must* take if you are to build the identity and the new circumstances you want so much. And there we have the essence of the 4 year. It is a cycle in which you must *build* what you want. Hard work is inevitable. Belief in yourself is the key.

Review your financial affairs. Organize this area of your life. The events of April and May will bring these matters to your attention. Save money where you can because next year's change of cycle will provide you with the atmosphere and the opportunity to invest money in yourself or in something that excites your heart. Be practical and efficient with this year's limited resources. Understand how money works and be aware of what is happening in the deceptive world of economics.

The 4 year cycle is a road full of limitations and roadblocks. In fact, this year, you are traveling life's very own obstacle course. The 4 energy brings you to what you believe are your limits. In turn, you will learn to expand your Will to such an extent that this increase in your personal energies will push your limits further away from you. In this way, although you will still have limits - we all do - they will not be boxing you in and pressuring you. The more you believe in yourself and take whatever action is necessary, the less limited you will be. A firm goal must be set, a commitment to it must be made, and effort must be exerted.

Every time you feel yourself struggling this year, stop what you are doing and face the current facts about the situation. Struggle is the painful result of reality being denied.

You will be coming to terms with your own identity this year. You will realize that you have significantly underestimated yourself. Your sense of identity does not come from what you do in life, but from the way you *feel* about life and your place in it. Yes, your professional life may take up much of your time and energy, but there is much more to you than what you do for a living. What do you do for a *life*?

Your progress is unlikely to be rapid. The 4 cycle allows only slow and deliberate movement. You may frequently encounter delays and hurdles, as well as bouts of loneliness and pessimism, only to pull yourself together again as you remember what this year is all about - making an effort to live as you *want* to live.

In the process, you will encounter obstacle after obstacle, snag after snag. Why must it be so frustrating? To show you that no matter what barriers stand before you, you can deal with them and you can even use them to your advantage. This year offers accomplishment, breakthrough, and recognition as its ultimate rewards.

A practical plan is required, as well as diligent and patient attention to detail. The emphasis is now on work, determination, organization, confidence, a little desperation, and a lot of guts. This year you will be getting your act together. And you will be breaking out of the prison that you or others have built around you.

You are about to break away from an old and limited way of life. That's the hard part. You will be entering a new world of love, happiness, creativity, and Free Will. That's the incentive. This may not be the easiest of years but, with determination, this can be one of the most fulfilling cycles you will ever experience.

~ January ~
4 Year - 5 Month

We are never prepared for what we expect.
James A. Michener

You are likely to experience an ominous feeling that much effort is required of you. Restlessness and confusion seem to be ruling you. Your freedom to move back and forth may be compromised. Hastiness or aggression will not make things move any faster.

Effort and attention to detail are needed as delays and unexpected obstacles add to your frustration. The more you accept the reality of your situation, the easier it will be for you to deal with everything efficiently and in your stride.

An unexpected event makes this a month of *change*. It also brings opportunity. Do not allow fear or guilt to cloud your perception. The opportunity presenting itself may be disguised as something else entirely. Look beyond what is immediately apparent to see the *different* potential on offer. Take it slowly, calmly, and methodically. Pay attention to the details and, despite some confusing distractions, focus on the matter at hand.

This month's unpredictable vibrations have sent you a situation through which to expand your horizons. You may find yourself with people and in places that are new to you. You must now take care of issues you have never had to deal with before. Your life has just altered course whether you know it or not, and your adrenalin is running high.

One change leads to another, and you will need to make some changes of your own so that you can turn an important corner in your life's journey. This is a time of steady maneuvering. Therefore, you must get organized. Perhaps an old but comfortable situation has become counterproductive. A certain situation may come to an end or needs to be brought to an end. Face the facts, let go of the old, and welcome the new.

You need FREEDOM: not freedom from your responsibilities but, rather, the freedom to take care of your responsibilities with *ease*. Know what is important to you and what is not. Free yourself of whatever obstacles are blocking your path. Free others of your control over them and release yourself from something or someone who has been controlling you for far too long.

Make moderation a rule this month so that nothing can block (or blur) your vision. You have begun a new segment of your life's wondrous journey. It may not feel like the smoothest or friendliest of roads right now. But here you are anyway. Keep your eyes on the road. Keep your wits about you. Assume nothing. Be courteous to everyone. And, above all, keep your desires and goals safely in your heart.

~ February ~
4 Year - 6 Month

You may not realize it when it happens,
but a kick in the teeth may be the best thing in the world for you.
WALT DISNEY

The 6 vibration emphasizes love and responsibility. Matters of the heart now take center stage and you will need to focus on the details - the facts - surrounding your current situation. One fact is that February is a deeply emotional month which involves your feelings towards a spouse, lover, child, parent, relative, close friend, pet, neighborhood, or the home itself.

Your personal life is in the spotlight, and only your complete acceptance of what is happening here can prevent a conflict of interests. The 4 year cycle lets you know what your limits are, and there is a good chance that your limits have been reached. Relief will come when you let your emotions *out*. You will then be able to regain your self-respect and balance.

It is time to accept your reality just as it is and to change a situation which is causing so much stress. It is time to stand back and gaze at your life and realize that sometimes things have to fall apart before they can fall into place. What at first seems like a loss, is actually an opportunity to move forward.

Calm down my friend. This month is all about finding solutions, restoring your ability to love without fear of loss, balancing the scales, and creating PEACE with yourself and with those who matter to you. Don't prolong the agony by denying that there is a problem. Face your reality, stop struggling, and *work* on it. A decision to be totally realistic must be made. The solution and the healing you need will follow.

Where there is animosity, try to understand what is really going on. Find the cause and you will be able to change the effect. The 6 cycle promotes love and healing which can be experienced in many different forms. Love is all around you this February. Feel it. Accept it. Express it. The more love you express, the more will be returned to you. Be patient. Strive to understand what is happening in the life of someone else.

Know the difference between helping and interfering. You don't have to be right all the time. It is okay to admit that you don't have the answers right now. In fact, there is likely to be one emotional situation for which there is no answer. All you can do is accept it for what it is.

Engage in peaceful and practical discussion. You may realize that something you thought was love is actually guilt in a clever disguise. Be alert to all the people around you this month. Life may be connecting you to someone or something that could be a catalyst for greater order and stability for you, even though it may not be apparent at the time.

Try to provide a warmer and more loving atmosphere for those you love. Guilt and blame serve no constructive purpose. Take a good honest look at your home or working environments. Wherever there is disorder or confusion, sort out the mess one step at a time. Understand the difference between struggle and effort.

On a material level, make necessary repairs and attend to the maintenance or restoration of anything that *belongs* to you. Create extra space by letting go of things that have outgrown their usefulness. Clutter takes up valuable space. It creates a block which prevents new energy from entering your life. Check on the value of unwanted items and sell them. This will help to bring more order into your financial life. A more creative approach to money must be implemented.

We are living in exciting but confusing evolutionary times in which everyone must learn to solve their own problems according to their unique needs and knowledge. Free Will is the *magic* which is currently missing from creation. Free Will is the mastery that comes with taking full responsibility for yourself.

~ March ~
4 Year - 7 Month

Knowledge comes, but wisdom lingers.
ALFRED, LORD TENNYSON

January brought change. February made it personal. March will clarify what has happened in your life since the beginning of the year. Continue to take care of the details and go about your work quietly and conscientiously. Most importantly, spend some time alone, *with no distractions*, so that you can think, contemplate, feel your feelings, and plan your future moves.

Worry and pessimism are often the most disorienting factors in a 7 cycle because 7 points out areas of your life with which you are dissatisfied. If such feelings arise, know that they are on schedule, and remember that there is nothing quite as capable as stopping the flow of life as unexpressed *feeling*. Let it all OUT.

Fear is inevitable, since you have no idea where you are right now. Relax your tensions about having nothing to contribute. The only thing that life requires of you now is your presence in it. This is your contribution during March. The truth is that you have been lost for a lot longer than you care to admit. What you are experiencing now is the acceptance of that fact.

Slow down, to a crawl if necessary, so that you can stop struggling against your current reality. Face the facts of the situation, and the fog that is surrounding you will start to fade away. Yes, you have had quite enough of your present lifestyle and you are realizing that you are capable of much better things. The direction you need will soon be plain to see and you will being sowing the seeds of new life along that road for the rest of the year.

In the meantime, learn to appreciate your own company without feeling lonely. Know where you have made mistakes and strive to stop repeating them. Let your feelings help you to realize just how special and capable you are. Accept the reality of your situation and ponder all the details involved. Weigh them against your own long term hopes and dreams. What do you really want to achieve in this precious lifetime of yours? How do you want to feel - what do you want to be doing - a year from now; five years from now; ten years from now?

Ask yourself: *"what is really happening here?"* Then wait for the answers to reach your conscious mind. Listen to them. FEEL them. When you use your intuition in this way, you are helping yourself to draw up specific plans for the future.

It may take the words, actions, or circumstances of someone else to open your mind, but only you can answer the questions you are asking at this time. The answers are right there inside you. Relax. Listen. Feel. Believe in your ability to create the life you want for yourself.

Reflect, meditate, and analyze. Review the past. Accept the present. Envisage your life not in fragments or segments, but as one continuing journey over which *you* have ultimate control. While it is true that this portion of your journey may feel a little rough, lonely, or humbling, your present circumstances should be viewed as a small and temporary part of the whole adventure; a turning point for your future happiness. Keep in mind that after the events of *next* month, your life will never be quite the same again.

In the meantime, a small change of course is scheduled. You must think for yourself, feel for yourself, and be your own navigator. Draw up precise plans and agendas for your journey, for your aspirations and desires. Map out your best route. If your feelings urge you to take a certain action, take it.

Analyze all the possibilities and *believe* that you will succeed. Be patient. That lonely feeling will lift when you accept your current position, that of coming to terms with just how dissatisfied you are.

For now, the 7 vibration asks you to expand your knowledge. Part of bringing order and ease back into your life is to release yourself from those judgments which tell you that you can't do something because you don't know how. LEARN HOW.

~ April ~
4 Year - 8 Month

> *Keep in mind always the present you are constructing;*
> *it should be the future you want.*
> ALICE WALKER

Snap out of the introspective mood of March and set your feet firmly on the ground. It is time to get down to business. Material and financial security and work related matters should be the focus of April. Effort, confidence, efficiency, and determination will bring astonishing results to a particular project, as well as improvements to your health and relationships.

However, what was once a comfortable and familiar situation may seem to be falling apart now. Don't worry. Without this upheaval, you would not be able to see the *new* potential that exists for you.

Self confidence, optimism, and honest emotional expression will definitely pay off now. 8 is the powerful and karmic vibration of reward for past and present actions. The 8 energy attracts back to you whatever you have put out into the world and prevents you from stagnating in a situation from which you may have believed there was no relief.

Yes, your efforts of the past three years will be rewarded now. In most cases, this reward comes in the form of a business or financially related success or an opportunity to move away from something which no longer serves your best interests. The time has come to build upon your talents so that you can take a large step forward towards ease and independence.

Business and material interests should be advanced by applying efficiency, system, and an enthusiastic attitude. Although attention to detail is still very important, try to delegate where possible so that you can focus more on *the big picture*. You have a specific job to do and you'll do it more efficiently if you are not distracted by other people's responsibilities or your own guilt and insecurity.

The rewards of the 8 cycle are attracted to those who have a realistic sense of their personal power to achieve, and to those who think and act decisively. Visualize the result you desire and take the steps which will bring you closer to it. You now have the power to broaden your horizons considerably.

The turbulent events of the past few months may have depleted your belief in yourself, but now it is time to rediscover your confidence. Maintain your dignity and express yourself assertively, knowledgeably and, if possible, *tactfully*. Whether you realize it or not, you have so much to offer this world. Stay aware of the practical theme of this year. Be cautious of long shot speculations, get-rich-quick schemes, and all other redundant proposals. Stick to what you know is right for you.

Prosperity is not for the few. It belongs to every single being on this Earth - if only everyone knew that prosperity must be felt on the *inside* first. It is possible to be without funds and not feel poor. When you feel poor, you feel this way because you have underestimated your ability to change things.

When you feel the richness of your potential, you cannot possibly feel poor because your potential - your capability - is your first and foremost resource. The events of the past few months have surely taught you that there is nothing you cannot achieve if you focus your mind on it and put your heart into it.

Don't allow greed or guilt to dictate your actions. They could spell disaster for you. While it is true that you may experience *anger* this month, try to understand that it is not others who are causing your problems. It is you, yourself, who must stand up, be counted, and claim equality with someone else.

Appreciate what you *already* have, and use it to get what you want. Never relate "having" to purely material assets. What you already have includes your creativity, knowledge, your belief in yourself, and all the other nonmaterial attributes and talents that are often overlooked. Whatever your responsibilities and needs are right now, they are as valid and important as anyone else's.

So, how do you *feel* right now? What is your *ego* up to these days? What have you actually learned about Free Will, prosperity and materiality? April's vibration offers a very special bonus - a feeling that outweighs any kind of material reward. It is the feeling of accomplishment. It is from the appreciation - the love - of this feeling that much greater *accomplishments* will come.

~ May ~
4 Year - 9 Month

There must be a beginning of any great matter, but the continuing unto the end until it be thoroughly finished, yields the true glory."
SIR FRANCIS DRAKE

There is now likely to be an emphasis on ENDINGS and TOLERANCE, and on your ability to be a "good little trouper". Yes, you need to know that you are loved and needed, but there is no need to overextend yourself in proving to others just how giving and dependable you are. Maintain your self-respect while helping and cooperating in a month that asks you to self-lessly give of yourself.

Emotions may be running high. In fact, the biggest obstacle you are likely to face during May will be made up of your own feelings. You are facing the fact that you really have denied and buried a multitude of emotions over the years. The time has come to accept them and free yourself of their heavy burden. The dramatic events of this month will help you to get a life-time of emotions out of your body, out of your mind, and back into life, where they belong.

Anger may surface when someone makes you aware of one of your shortcomings. There is no need to deny your anger, but there *is* a need to stop denying that you are actually angry with *yourself*. Whatever this problem is, only you can bring an end to it. Once you do, you will be able to proceed comfortably again. If you do not, it will certainly escalate throughout the year.

9 is a cycle of endings, letting go, and giving. These are all separate functions yet they are strongly connected. You see, by releasing old emotions you are *letting go* of them and bringing an *end* to the situation to which they pertained. Through this process you are *giving* you and any others involved the chance to leave the past behind and move into the rich potential of present time.

Finish up anything that needs to be completed. Get it over and done with. By ending certain projects, plans, or situations now, you will be opening up more space in your life. Wherever there is space, there is potential for new opportunities to enter.

Allow yourself to experience any fear that arises. *Listen* to your fear and hear its advice for the most compassionate and constructive way to bring a certain matter to a conclusion. Once this is done, you will realize that much discomfort and 'dis-ease' has left your life. The endings and conclusions that take place in May will be a lot easier to deal with now than at any other time this year. Both you and those you love will benefit from your new level of self confidence.

There may be some delay, frustration, or a sense of loss. Life can certainly have its cold moments and you must accept that fact. If someone or something seems to be leaving you, understand that you do not own this person or this situation. Strive to understand the *cause* of the separation and allow this free spirit to fly. If it is meant to come back to you, it will do so of its own Free Will.

You may have an urge to be very generous now and you should realize that there are many forms of giving. These include the giving of your time and effort, giving of yourself in a particular field or service, giving a sympathetic and understanding shoulder to cry on, giving practical assistance or friendly advice. You can benefit, in ways you could not imagine, when you let go of a certain resentment or insecurity and openly encourage - assist - someone who seems to be doing well.

Learn to give *only* because you want to and not because you think you should. This will enable you to *break through* the barrier of being controlled by guilt, fear, or jealousy. You will eliminate that nauseating feeling of being a 'door mat' for others to stomp on, and you will realize that you can use someone else's example to turn your own life around.

You will also want to be more giving. Learn to say no when no is what you want to say, and yes when yes is what you want to say. Stand up for yourself. Get back in the driver's seat and take control of this journey of yours, without trying to control anyone else.

The combination of the 4 and 9 cycles can feel very restrictive indeed, until you realize that it provides a valuable lesson in seeing *all* sides of the story - not just the side we prefer or the side we are afraid of. Look at the big picture instead of getting lost in one of its many details.

A lot has happened in the last five months. You have experienced a multitude of deep emotions. It is now time to bring an *end* to those feelings by expressing them and releasing them back into life. There is still a long way to go on your 4 journey, but you are over the worst of it now. Use this month to tie up those loose ends, especially the emotional ones. Then walk confidently into June's cycle of independence and new beginnings.

~ June ~
4 Year - 1 Month

There is no reality except the one contained within us.
That is why so many people live such an unreal life.
They take the images outside them for reality
and never allow the world within to assert itself.
HERMAN HESS

Look at how self-reliant you've become. You are standing on your own two feet again, or at least you will be by the end of June. There is always some kind of *change* within a 1 cycle, and one of the most noticeable changes at this time will be in your desire to create a new reality for yourself.

By now you must be sick and tired of being buffeted around like a feather in a hurricane. You are coming in for a landing now. Yes, there may be a few obstacles on the ground to circumnavigate. But if you remain fully aware of your environment and are ready to protect yourself, there is a very good chance that you will land safely on your feet in friendly territory. First, however, a negative influence, which could very well be one of your own attitudes or habits, must be seen for the destructive force it is, and eliminated.

You may feel a little self centered this month. This is how it is supposed to be. Do not let guilt get the better of you here. Independence and self awareness is the theme for June. The obstacles you encounter now are an indication of how dependent you still are on outside factors, including the approval of others. You now have the power to take matters into your own hands and *change* an uncomfortable situation by changing your view of it.

The 1 energy represents The Self. It heightens your perception of who you really are. And, let's face it, your sense of identity has been, and still is, a significant factor in your life this year. You are now being urged to recognize and cherish the characteristics that make you totally unique so that you can *be* that unique individual.

Self realization is a powerful and beautiful feeling. It is one of the most important aspects of human growth as we leave the "I AM" (1) cycle of the 1000s behind, and embark on the "WE ARE" (2) cycle of the 2000s.

See where guilt and blame are preventing forward movement. It may take great emotional effort to break through guilt's barrier and to utilize this month's opportunities instead, but this is exactly what you must do. Break from the old and limiting and embrace what is new and progressive. Believe in yourself, and get on board an opportunity which is yours for the taking.

As a stream of new understandings arise, your outer reality will change along with them. If you used last month to make the necessary endings, this month of change and forward movement will be all the easier to accept because there will be less clutter standing in the way to confuse matters.

Start something new or, at least, start a new phase of an existing project or situation. Do something you want to do but have never had the courage to do. Do something *different.* The number "1" is the "first" energy in the numerological spectrum, and the fact that there is a first time for everything may be made very clear to you this month. In order to move ahead, you may have to do something you have never done before. You may have to see yourself as you have never seen yourself before.

Recognize the roles that others in your life are playing. What can you learn from them? Or they from you? Allow your *feelings* to determine their purpose in your life. Move ahead with any progressive steps you have been contemplating. Do not be afraid to take a chance - a leap of faith - provided that you have assessed all the *details* involved.

Be honest with yourself about any weaknesses you may have and try to strengthen yourself in these areas. Independence will be difficult to achieve while you are still dependent on something or someone else. The 1 energy asks you to be yourself. Being yourself includes being *flexible.* Learn to adapt and bend your uniqueness to achieve what you want. Do not alienate yourself from the very people you need by ill timed or inappropriate actions, or by insisting that you already know everything there is to know. This is a time of learning *new* things.

There is a constructive purpose for the feeling of aloneness you are now experiencing. You wish you had a little encouragement or help with your work, your plans, your dreams, and even your basic needs. The chances are, however, that you will be left to fend for yourself. Although you certainly need others for love and support, it is important not to *depend* on them for your own happiness or for the results you seek. If people let you down this month, it is all part of June's lesson of self reliance.

At the end of the month, slow down a little. You do not want to go crashing into the gentle, emotional, and peace loving 2 cycle of July.

~ July ~
4 Year - 2 Month

The meeting of two personalities is like the contact of
two chemical substances: if there is any reaction, both are transformed.
C.G. JUNG

You are now in very special territory. You have entered the powerful and peaceful 2 cycle in which relationship, teamwork, patience, and cooperation are emphasized. This is a gentle and loving cycle, provided that you abide by its one and only rule: do not force anything.

Now that you know where you are, slow down. Stand still for a while and sense - feel - what is happening to you. Your ability to peacefully navigate your way through this particular section of the journey, after six months of being buffeted in all directions, will determine the quality of your life for a considerable time to come. It will also help to determine who your friends are and who they are not! Most importantly, you will find out if you, yourself, are being a good friend.

You have had to be very practical this year. This has caused you to hold many of your emotions in instead of letting them out. It had to be this way. You had to remain strong on the surface. But now it is time to let those imprisoned feelings out of your system.

An event will occur which is charged with emotion, and you will be forced to feel your feelings deeply. Whatever triggers this situation is also giving you the opportunity to release other seemingly unrelated emotions that you have been holding in for *years*.

This is a time of great healing for you. It is a process that cannot be rushed or ignored. Slow down, feel what you are feeling, and let nature - your nature - take its course.

Learn as much as you can about the 2 energy, because as we travel the new millennium, all of humanity is under its influence and will remain there for the next one thousand years. 2 represents the feminine polarity of nature and does not seek superiority. But it must have equality in order to retain its balance. Be sure to read Part III - LIFE, LOVE, and LIBERTY IN THE NEW MILLENNIUM: *the healing power of emotion* - as this describes the 2 energy in great detail.

The powerful magnetic pull of 2 is now being felt strongly here on Earth. Its vibration is very different from the aggressive masculine 1 energy which influenced life throughout the 1000s. This vibrational transition is causing much confusion. It is creating highly dangerous situations as some people go to extremes to prevent these unstoppable changes from taking place. Those who seek to destroy the peace-loving 2 vibration are in total denial of the cyclical nature of life and are unaware that everything there is, including themselves, is made up of both masculine *and* feminine energy.

Some monumental changes will occur regardless of how much we fight them. 2 is the principle energy of Free Will, and *force* is the one factor it will not tolerate. 2 is sensitive to everything. It denies nothing. Your current circumstances will bring this understanding a lot closer to home. You must either learn to relax in stressful environments, or remove yourself from them entirely. Do not push or manipulate. Cooperate instead.

This can be a confusing month. You know you must work hard all year and yet the 2 vibration is urging you to relax, be patient, and bide your time. Hard work does not always pertain to your job or vocation, although it often does. You may find that living for a month without forcing anything is a barrier in itself that needs thoughtful handling. Loosen up and learn as you go. Consider what has happened to you in the past four years, and see how the past has made the present inevitable.

Proceed quietly with your affairs. Cooperate where you can using a calm, diplomatic, and caring approach. Be the part of the team you are meant to be. Pay attention to everything that is going on around you because the words or actions of others may prove to be important. A situation will occur which requires you to focus on someone or something else. What at first seems like an intrusion will give your own plans the time and breathing space they need to develop of their own accord. Do not push yourself or your plans ahead because there are obscure aspects going on behind the scenes which will soon determine the direction your life is taking. When delays or frustrations occur, understand that their purpose is to improve the overall *timing* of your goal. Help where help is needed and remember that 2 is the energy of peace, cooperation, and understanding.

2 is also the energy of RELATIONSHIP. This is one of the elements that will help establish peace during the 2000s - and in your own life this month. The 2 energy shows us that everyone and everything on Earth is related or connected in some way. Your connection to someone else needs to be seen for what it really is so that a new opportunity for peace and partnership can make itself known to you.

Focus on building better relationships, and you will hear or sense something which will make you realize that there are much greater possibilities for *you* and, possibly, someone close to you. You already have the makings of a great TEAM. However, trust, or some other fundamental aspect of teamwork may be missing.

Use all your senses to feel the significance of what is happening or being said. Get *into* it. Be respectful and patient. Cooperate with those around you, create a harmonious atmosphere, care about the outcome, and be sensitive to all the feelings involved, your own and other people's.

You will soon see that this month's distractions, and even this month's losses, are directly and positively *connected* to your own long-term goals. The solution you have been seeking has been handed to you through your ability to COOPERATE, SENSE, and RELATE.

Both the 4 year and the 2 month produce a surplus of details to take care of. This month there will be more than usual. Deal with them calmly, one at a time, and realize how indispensable you have become to the team.

You may feel deeply emotional or nervous at times but, by the end of July, you will realize just how meaningful and productive this seemingly humble month has been. The fact is that you cannot have a genuine high self-esteem without a little humility.

You will also realize that you have not lost your heart after all. By the end of July your compassion, understanding, and love, will be back where they belong. You will realize that your story, along with its cast of many characters, is not ending. It is simply coming to the end of a chapter. It is in August that you will begin the exciting task of creating the next chapter of your ever-changing story.

~ August ~
4 Year - 3 Month

Stop thinking in terms of limitations,
and start thinking in terms of possibilities.
TERRY JOSEPHSON

At last. A break from the monotony and routine. Remember fun? If you have not scheduled a break for this month, try to take one anyway. Part of having order in your life includes having the freedom to enjoy it. This is an excellent time for a vacation, away from everything that has become the norm, and from those situations which have truly drained your energies throughout the year.

You will need more strength than ever next month and this is the perfect time to recharge your batteries, replenish your energies, and rediscover that most vital part of your being, your imagination. It is time to dream new dreams.

If you cannot take a vacation, take some short breaks which include interacting with close friends and enjoying nature or the arts. Add creative touches to your living and working environments which may liven up the senses of the serious people you have become attached to of late. 3 represents the lighter side of life. You would do well to get yourself into a lighter frame of mind as you travel through its invigorating and optimistic energy.

This is a time to entertain, to indulge yourself in a little luxury, and experience some of life's social and creative joys. However, do not make unnecessary work for yourself when you entertain. It's purpose is to share your enjoyment with others and not to battle with the stress of oneupmanship. A little kindness is what is needed in your life right now. This starts with being kind to yourself.

Spend a little money on you now. One of the main lessons of the 4 cycle is to understand the meaning of limitation. If you want to reduce the limitation in your life - *stop limiting yourself*. If you think money or time are still a problem, take a good look at the reality of your situation, as it is *now*. Take in every detail. Then change one of those details; alter it in some way. Rearrange your circumstances so that you *can* take a break from it all, treat yourself to something nice, and have some fun.

There is no need to lose sight of your long-term goals and plans, or to go overboard with your spending. You may make some valuable contacts for the future while you're out there having a good time. Use a light-hearted and friendly approach to your networking endeavors. Loosen up. Bring enjoyment back into your life. Use your imagination. Say goodbye to an attitude or belief that has taken the fun out of your life for far too long.

This is a month for creative breakthroughs of all kinds and, once again, it is your ability to utilize and stretch your imagination that will facilitate them. Change your focus to the lighter aspects of life, and watch the obstacles, blockages, and delays, which are so typical of the 4 year cycle, lose their power over you.

This year has changed your whole outlook on life by forcing you to look at things from a *different* perspective. If you are a nonsocial or serious soul, you have been thrown into situations where you must mix with people who seem frivolous and annoying, and with whom you have nothing in common. If you consider yourself to be socially inclined or creative, you have been thrown into situations that require a more serious approach.

By now you will know that this had to occur so that you could find out who you really are and what you really want. You will be asking yourself how you can change things so that you can live more freely, and you will know that with patience and effort, you can achieve your new-found goal.

You have traveled far this year. You have faced a lot of reality. Next month, a major breakthrough will be in sight. So, for now, let optimism abound and hold on to that dream with all your might.

~ September ~
4 Year - 4 Month

"Even the woodpecker owes his success to the fact that he uses his head and keeps pecking away until he finishes the job he starts."
COLEMAN COX

The double 4 vibration of September creates a significant turning point in your life even though you may not realize the change of course you have taken until next month. Focus on the work that must be done and tackle everything with efficiency and determination. Get organized. Take care of the chores and details from which you know there is no escape. Make sure your system is running effectively. Maintain a down-to-earth attitude.

Keep your goal firmly in mind, but do be prepared for more detours, delays, and other frustrating circumstances. Take everything in your stride. Counter those feelings of restriction by making time for the things you enjoy, by taking frequent breaks, and getting adequate rest. If a major problem arises, don't panic. You have not traveled this far through the arduous obstacle course of the 4 year without learning that all problems have solutions if they are handled realistically. This means knowing what the problem actually is.

Your work may indeed be cut out for you, but life is not throwing you anything you cannot handle. If necessary, read the entire 4 year cycle again, from the beginning, because the solutions can be found in what you have already experienced.

Remember that even though strong feelings of responsibility may arise, you are *not* responsible for the happiness of others. Help where help is needed, without taking the weight of someone else's problem solely on your back. They, too, must do their part. You may even find that your only responsibility this month is to show others that a little *organization* in their lives could turn their current problems into breakthroughs of their own. Then again, this may not be your responsibility either. It is, after all, impossible to give advice to someone who refuses to accept it.

Face the facts. 4 is such a precise and orderly energy that its influence may have caused you to create many rules and regulations for yourself without realizing how limiting they have become.

Earlier in the year it was necessary for you to place certain restrictions on yourself so that you could get organized. By now you should *be* organized. If you are, perhaps it is safe to relax some of your self imposed stipulations. Be kind to yourself. Be patient with yourself.

Are you aware of how *angry* you have been just lately? You may not want to admit it, but those who know you are well aware of the rage that is brewing in you right now. If you do not let this emotion out, privately and safely, it will find a way of releasing itself anyway and, at that point, it will not care about your privacy or safety. Try to understand *why* you are so angry.

Remember that you needed to learn about limitation so that you could reach, feel the pressure of, and then push your limits away from you. Now as you push those limits even further away, a powerful feeling is emerging which lets you know that the breakthrough you have been working toward is close at hand. By the end of September, you will find yourself yearning for the freedom and expansion that only a complete change of attitude and lifestyle can bring. Your anger is actually being triggered by another emotion - FEAR. You are afraid that something will prevent those changes from happening. What you need to know more than anything right now is that these unexpressed feelings are all that is standing in your way. Feel them, accept them, and express them out of your system.

This year, the very clarity of your thinking has evolved. You have become at ease with who you are. You know the importance of self-acceptance and that all goals are attainable if you believe they are. This is no time for impulsive moves. Don't take risks with your health, resources, or general wellbeing. There will be a time in the near future when you look back on this year of self-discipline, isolation, and hard work, and you will realize with amazement just how much it enabled you to GROW.

~ October~
4 Year - 5 Month

> *There is still a tendency to accept certain*
> *tenets or doctrines on hearsay, without making*
> *the effort to check out the logic or rationale upon*
> *which they are based. And that is as true of*
> *relationships as it is of philosophical dogma.*
> SALLY BROMPTON

The narrow road of the 4 year cycle just got wider. Suddenly you have choices and a decision must be made. October's 5 energy will create a situation in your life in which you will have to choose a particular direction: (a) back to the old ways which allow others to control your existence, or (b) forward, to your own Free Will and happiness. Is there really a choice?

Do not reject the freedom that this month gives you. It's purpose is to put you in touch with your *physical* self. Assess the condition of your body. There have been some stressful episodes this year which may have taken their toll. Remember that your body is the vehicle which transports you through your life's journey. Therefore, its maintenance is vital. You are entering an exciting fast moving phase of your life which requires a healthy reliable body, and now is a good time to repair any damage.

Do something unusual, different, daring and exciting this month. Experience new places, people, and activities. Bring a sense of adventure into your everyday life.

Opportunity is all around you. Listen, watch, and feel, so that you can recognize it when it knocks at your door. The degree to which you focus on your circumstances will determine just how much power you will have to change things and get things done. Be aware that others can help you with your goals. Be resourceful. Do not be afraid to ask for the help you need.

You may start to feel afraid of your own power now. And this fear must be felt and honestly expressed. You may find that what you are really afraid of is the anger you have still not released. Let this imprisoned feeling *out* when you are alone.

There is no need to be aggressive. In fact, keeping a low profile may be your best course of action until the end of the year. Soon you will feel the satisfaction of the enormous strides you have made, and you will develop your courage to even higher levels.

Free Will always contains a genuine intent to express LOVE. Being afraid of yourself, of change, or of freedom, creates a sense of paralysis. Unexpressed feelings stop you from taking even the simplest of steps toward improving your circumstances. Then you must rely on others to tell you what is right and wrong for you. This cannot bring happiness, only more anger.

Let go of all the judgments you have made about yourself and someone you love. Then you will become free of the guilt and blame which has attached itself to this relationship. You will be able to see once more, or perhaps for the first time, the loving connection that exists between you and this person.

Routine matters may seem rather out of place this month. Look beyond the restrictions of this year. Direct your sights toward new ambitions, new goals, and new interests. Expand your current interests beyond past expectation. AIM HIGH. Enjoy the sense of excitement and enthusiasm which are the themes for October. Enjoy social interaction, and the company of new and old friends.

Follow your feelings. Let them to take you to where you are meant to be. If you find yourself overindulging in the physical aspects of life, you are probably doing so to the avoid guilt and blame, which always arise when you know that you must face the facts. Feel your fear in this regard, and let the truth come in.

Overindulgence is a diversion you create for yourself to avoid reality. This can include an overactive appetite for food, alcohol, drugs, gambling, extravagance, sex, 'keeping busy', and addictions of all kinds, including T.V., computer, reading, and the pursuit of trivia. It is amazing what we are able to think up for the purpose of avoiding the truth about our lives. Try not to scatter yourself in this way.

The events of October will shed some light on the theme your life will follow next year. You may already be feeling the magnetic pull of next year's expansive 5 cycle, making this month a kind of testing ground. It is encouraging you to sense and understand the power of 5, which inevitably means change and freedom. Some kind of change that occurs during October will offer an unexpected possibility, a chance to walk away from a negative situation. See the advantage of such a move and be prepared to utilize it.

In this 4 year cycle, when your work and your identity are such major factors, an important change will occur in these areas, or may create a change in your attitude toward your work and your identity. Does your sense of identity come only from the work you do? Is your work satisfying or soul destroying? Are there other areas in your field in which you would be more content, or are you in the wrong field altogether? Where does your work fit in to your overall vision of happiness?

This month, truth is everywhere. Truth is reality. The wars that are ravaging so many lands and killing so many people are true. The innocence of a little child is also true. The serenity of the ocean is true - and so is its horrifying power of destruction. It is true that every single person on this Earth is a Free Spirit. But it is also true that the vast majority has given away its freedom to others simply because they do not want the responsibility of being free. What is *your* truth?

They say there's a fool born every minute. But who are "they"? First they told us that butter was good for us. Then they decided that margarine was better. The world switched from butter to margarine. Then, wouldn't you know it, they discovered the negative aspects of margarine and butter came back into fashion. The only truth that is certain is that which we discover and experience for ourselves. The 5 energy urges you to develop your freedom of mind by realizing that many so-called authorities and experts have ulterior motives and hidden agendas. Think for yourself. Make your own decisions. Anything else is suppression of your freedom.

5 urges you to learn and profit from your mistakes. When you stop judging yourself harshly for mistakes you have made, you will also stop guilt in its tracks. We are *meant* to make mistakes in order to learn something. Our ability to learn from our own mistakes and the mistakes of others is one of life's gifts. It is a gauge by which to measure truth from falsehood. But when we keep making the same mistakes over and over again, refusing to learn anything from them, we cannot progress. Our lives then go around in monotonous circles instead of the spiraling evolving cycles of Free Will.

When we make the mistake of believing what "they" tell us without investigating for ourselves, we just get buffeted around, back and forth, like sheep, from butter to margarine and back to butter.

Find your own truth, make your own mistakes, and learn your own lessons. 5 will love you for your effort. When you have truly learned the lesson involved, and you no longer repeat a mistake, it is no longer a mistake. It is *experience*.

Feel as relaxed and free as possible. Accept your workload with renewed enthusiasm and take some breaks for fun and relaxation. Your progress should give you all the incentive you need to see this 4 year cycle through to a satisfactory conclusion on December 31. In the meantime, there is still much to be accomplished.

~ November ~
4 Year - 6 Month

They who cannot forgive, break the bridge over which they, themselves, must pass.
GEORGE HERBERT

The magnetic pull of next year's 5 cycle will create a change in your close relationships and/or your home environment. November brings you into the 6 cycle of peace, love, and understanding. There is now an emphasis on those people and things for which you feel very deeply. There must be a new understanding here. Love without freedom is love in chains. And those chains are made of judgments that are not necessarily correct.

Pay attention to the circumstances or needs of spouse, lover, children, parents, home, relatives, pets, neighbors, close friends, or community issues. ORDER, here, is either required or needs to be relaxed. The balancing of extremes is an important factor in this month's activities. Forgiveness and understanding should now be your primary objectives. But neither of these things can be achieved until you look at and accept the absolute truth of the situation.

Responsibilities are highlighted. You may need to clarify which are yours and which are not. Don't take on commitments without considering the change and the freedom that *next* year offers. On the other hand, you may find that an additional responsibility now may actually be the catalyst for next year's expansion. Consider your options carefully, and use this month's healing energies to bring peace and balance back into your personal life.

This month's combination of energies brings to light all the restrictions you have placed on yourself, and others, during the course of the year. Some are responsibilities which you think are yours but, in fact, are someone else's. Guilt or blame has a large role to play in this little act. You are in a cycle of love. But guilt and blame are love's great destroyers.

If you feel that someone in your family or circle has made you feel guilty, understand that it is not they who have caused the feeling but you who has accepted the guilt. You cannot deny or bury feelings of guilt and hope the problem will go away. It doesn't happen like that. By throwing it back at the person you think has caused it, you are not removing guilt but merely reversing it into blame.

There is usually no need to confront the other person involved. You can only remove guilt by recognizing it and replacing it with an acceptance of yourself and an understanding that there are always differences within a family or intimate unit. Sometimes, additional feelings must be recognized, accepted and released, such as fear, anger, sadness, and hatred.

Do not let guilt tell you that hatred can't exist among family members or close friends. Most of us have not yet recognized that we actually hate ourselves. Therefore hatred - denied hatred - between family members and loved ones is very common. Face your true feelings about those closest to you. When you have discovered the truth of your feelings you will be able to understand what has *caused* them. You will then be able to forgive yourself and them. Only then can love return.

If peace and love are what you desire, then provide it. If stability and security are lacking, provide it. If trust has disappeared, provide it. If understanding is needed, provide it. Listen, respect, accept, and realize that *everyone* has their own reality and their own personal energies. You cannot assume to know what is best for someone else, nor they for you.

You do not have to be right all the time. The need to always be right prevents you from learning the truth and is the seed of anger, resentment, rage, and war. It is possible to have strong opinions on various matters without being an opinionated person. Perhaps, you need to remove yourself from those who insist that they are always right and you are always wrong. Or, perhaps it is you who needs to change this dangerous habit. If we are to ever experience peace on Earth, it will have very little to do with governments and armies. It will be the result of understanding and respect within intimate personal relationships and communities where people are not afraid to admit that they don't know everything.

Make November a time of healing, beauty, warmth, and harmony. Give care to those you say you care about. If someone close to you seems more like a limitation than a loved one, realize that this may be the very person who can teach you what you need to learn at this point in the journey, even though he or she may not know it. What you need right now is respect. And the kind of respect we are talking about is the kind that comes from within oneself.

Pay attention to your home and make it a loving, peaceful, comfortable, and joyful place to be. Plan to spend as much time there as you can this month. Whether you live alone or with others, beautify your living space with creativity and originality. Bring fresh life into your domestic environment, and remember that you are responsible for the atmosphere you create.

Change is in the air. In fact, you may even find yourself thinking about a change of location or residence. Such thoughts are right on time. Next year's 5 energy is calling!

November is a time to enjoy the pleasures of children and their own extraordinary evolutionary process. Young people are already more emotionally advanced than adults. They have a keener sense of reality than older people, and they are less likely to deny their feelings. It is vitally important that we do not retard their progress by instilling in them the very mistakes we are trying to eliminate in ourselves. Even if there are no children in your immediate family, this is a perfect time to respect young people in general. They have been born into a world of hatred and violence. They try hard, in their own ways, to change those ugly factors, only to be criticized by adults who are afraid for them or who resent them for their youth and their courage to seek alternatives. They are the future of life itself, right before our eyes. We so often see them as the problem when, in fact, they are the solution.

Young people need encouragement, not criticism or restriction. If we are to teach them anything, it should be about their own right to happiness and peace, their own self-worth, their own Free Will, and their own power to heal themselves. Life is changing so rapidly, and today's youth are adapting to these changes with a clearer grasp of reality than most adults. We can learn a lot from them if only we will open our minds and hearts to them. The truth is that we are all learning how to live. We are *all* children and we have so much to learn from one another.

Make time for pets, too. They are living beings. They think. They feel. They love. They grieve. They respond to your feelings. They are *alive*. If there are no pets in your life, or if you are not particularly fond of animals, or if you think that human rights must always be placed before the rights of animals, realize that human rights are gauged by the way we treat animals.

The 6 cycle urges you to expand your artistic and creative abilities. Create something special. Employ the elements of love, beauty, healing, and balance. Express yourself as spontaneously as you can. Make this month a different experience for you and those you love. Experience love - *differently*.

~ December~
4 Year - 7 Month

Integrity without knowledge is weak and useless;
but knowledge without integrity is utterly dangerous.
SAMUEL JOHNSON

Slow down. Relax. This has been a hard working year of practicality, logic, reason, and great tenacity. You have come a long way. You have learned so much.

Next year's theme is FREEDOM, and you will need to keep this in mind as you break through whatever barriers and limitations are left. Timing is an important factor now. Be careful not to push too far too soon. Rather than force opportunities your way, wait for them to come to you instead.

7 is an introspective and psychological cycle. Therefore, most of the organizing needed now is likely to be inside your own head and heart. You may experience a strong feeling of aloneness which makes you sense that something very important is missing. You may want to blame this on others or on your own mistakes and imperfections. However, what you are really missing and longing for is something that you, and all of us, lost a very long time ago - Free Will.

Next year, freedom will be yours if you know how to accept it and respond to it. Use this month to contemplate the possibilities involved. Consider everything you have experienced this year, and you will know why Free Will is the only course available if you are to achieve happiness and fulfillment.

Your feelings of loneliness are temporary ones. Acceptance of this will wake up your Will, your body, and your mind - and you will start to feel *alive* again. The more you learn about yourself this month, the more you will want to learn. You will need to be aware of all your feelings and thoughts. The 7 cycle urges you to take time out for yourself, to be alone, to rest, think, meditate, analyze, and plan. Make this a quiet and serious month in which to chart your course for next year's 5 adventure.

There is no need for rigorous action now. Just plan for the action you will be taking in the months to come. You may feel a little withdrawn from others, and your physical energy may be depleted. What better reason to take a rest.

Relax from the physical, mental, and emotional anxieties of the past twelve months and start to look calmly and confidently towards tomorrow. Feel the excitement in the air. Visualize only the most positive outcomes and *believe* in your ability to make them happen. You see, the ball is in your court now. It is up to you to do what you know is right for you and any others involved.

You may feel that everyone else is on a different wavelength this month, but it is probably you who is out there on some far-off plain. The introspective energies of December may make you difficult to approach or understand. The 7 cycle urges you to venture inside yourself, take the lid off your mind, and see what's in there.

By maintaining an optimistic attitude and a dignified distance from others, you will be doing yourself a great favor. If you feel depressed, look for the real cause of the problem. Ask the right questions - those questions you have been avoiding. Very often we focus on a minor detail in an effort to avoid facing the root of the problem. Be honest with yourself and *feel* what your feelings are telling you. Push your limits away from you once again. Prepare for freedom.

There may be a tendency to criticize others, finding imperfections and flaws wherever you look. You may even be accused of being inflexible, ignorant, or a know-it-all. Instead of criticizing those around you, just let them be who they are. Your future happiness will be influenced by the extent to which you are able to dispense with pettiness and show others that you believe in happiness and freedom - for *everyone*.

A year ago, you found yourself up against your personal limits. But your experiences this year have enabled you to grow and expand to such a degree that your limits have had no choice but to expand along with you. You still have boundaries, but your determination has pushed them further and further away from you so that they are no longer crushing you. You have reorganized your life so that you finally have some new choices.

The feeling of emptiness that December reveals is actually a space within you which has opened up between your old boundaries and your new ones. As empty as it feels right now, it is actually filled with a spectacular framework of potentials which point the way to your future happiness. This space can be filled with whatever *you* desire. It is up to you to climb upon that framework and look for and *feel* the opportunity it offers.

But do not plan too far ahead. That free and seemingly empty space is next year's 5 cycle, and there is nothing predictable about it. 5 is the number of the unexpected and the unpredictable. It is also the number of ADVENTURE, and it is brimming with life, answers, and new experiences. Now, it is directly ahead of you.

As difficult as this year has been, whatever you have learned, never forget it. Hold on to your new found strength, your new sense of identity, and your expanded belief in yourself. Bring all of this experience with you as midnight of December 31st arrives, and you cross over into the 5 year cycle of change, freedom, and *new* experience. Happy landings my friend.

The 5 Year Cycle

a journey of change, freedom, & new experience.

A man should never be ashamed to own he has been in the wrong,
which is but saying that he is wiser today than he was yesterday.
ALEXANDER POPE

Welcome to the exciting and unpredictable 5 year cycle. Its energy is that of change, freedom, variety, choice, the sudden and unexpected, the unusual, and the physical. This year will be quite an experience for you - *new* experience.

You now stand at the halfway point of an entire nine-year cycle of your life. The first four years are behind you. The last four are yet to come. The circumstances of this year will enable you to know the difference between the "old" you, the "present" you and the "potential" you. Expect a substantial change in your life, or a sequence of smaller changes which will lead to a whole new way of life for you.

The 5 year cycle provides opportunities to turn your life around by setting off in a direction that is totally different to any you have taken before. The best way to approach this journey is with a complete change of attitude. Last year's 4 cycle was limiting and restrictive. This year, you must focus on being limitless and free.

Opportunities will surround you all year, but you must be able to recognize them when they appear. This will require an open and adventurous mind. Learn to pick and choose carefully between your various options. Take only those which pertain to your true desires and not just your temporary whims. If you try to take advantage of every opportunity that presents itself this year, the confusion of so much diversity will limit your ability to focus. This could prevent success in *any* area.

If your cyclical energies could be seen as roads or highways, route #5 would be the widest and busiest. This is where all traffic seeks a change in course. Without a basic goal or sense of direction, accidents occur and people find themselves in places they don't want to be. Start out with a firm ambition in mind, a specific sense of destination. But do be flexible. Even the best laid plans can change or be changed without warning signs of any kind. Remember: 5 is the number of the sudden and the unexpected.

You are now on a fast-paced journey which is filled with excitement, opportunity, and action. It is an adventure into life. It is a time to discover what is actually out there for you by experiencing things you have not experienced before. This year is likely to be full of new people, new places, and new possibilities. An opportunity may fall right into your lap, or you may find yourself going back and forth, in all directions, as you consider whether a particular change of course is what you want or not. A decision *must* be made, and courage may be required.

The choices you make should be based on your feelings about the situation, along with a conscious understanding of the probable outcome of your choices. This does not mean that you should judge something before you have experienced it. It means that you must be aware of how one change can create a chain reaction of many changes.

It is essential that you know what you are feeling on a moment-by-moment basis. Denied feelings remain trapped inside you and take *away* from your freedom. This year you will be releasing all that unexpressed emotion which has weighed you down for far too long.

The world is opening up for you now. It is inviting you to experience life to the fullest. Yes, experience itself is what is on offer to you this year. In order to receive it, some mistakes may have to be made. Remember, however, that a mistake *becomes* experience when its lesson is learned and not repeated.

Now you must apply the process of realizing your mistakes and allowing them to evolve into expertise. Alexander Graham Bell, for instance, invented the telephone by accident. He was actually trying to invent a hearing aid. One of the biggest mistakes you could make this year is giving up on something you feel strongly about before you have given yourself the opportunity to experience it *in a state of freedom*. You do not always have to lose what you have in order to get what you want. It is guilt, disguising itself as fear, that makes you feel this way.

Loosen up and feel the freedom that exists within, regardless of your external situation. This powerful feeling will help you to change your outer circumstances. The 5 vibration is acutely attuned to your own expectations and desires. It is also the principle energy involved in sex and reproduction. Conception most often takes place when the 5 energy is active. What will you conceive this year? A child? An idea? A plan? What are you *expecting*?

Don't reject the changes that the 5 year brings. Without change, we stagnate. Some changes will occur suddenly and unexpectedly, while others will be initiated by your own effort. Expect the unexpected. Be prepared for anything. Concentrate on feeling free and fortunate. Understand that you are where you are so that you can prosper from the experience of it.

Be aware of the absolute reality of your life at all times. It is upon your reality that you must base your choices and make the appropriate changes.

Assess the aspects you believe are holding you back. Most of them will turn out to be your own restrictive beliefs and thought patterns which you are keeping in place because you will not accept that there *are* alternatives.

When freedom of mind and emotion is achieved, you will see that other people are not holding you back at all. Situations you think are beyond your control are not stopping you from moving forward. The truth is that you are causing your own stagnation by not changing what needs to be changed *inside* you.

Get away from old routines and do something different. Look for those new directions. Do not scatter your attention and spread yourself too thin, jumping from one thing to another without actually accomplishing anything. Focus on what you *want*. Your curiosity can lead to greater possibilities or to disappointment.

5 is a very sexual and physical energy, and these areas of your life will be very much in focus this year. However, do not fall into the trap of *overindulgence* in the physical aspects of life which include food, alcohol, drugs, sex, gambling, taking foolish chances, and extravagance. Such behavior gives the appearance of freedom, but is actually an addiction of some kind. Excesses can create unexpected reversals which will impede your progress. That would be both sad and unnecessary this year.

Place a special emphasis on your body. Take care of it. Respect it. Strengthen it. Become more aware of your physical senses and abilities. Use your senses creatively. Get adequate rest and relaxation. Love your body and enhance your physical comfort.

See things as they really are. Accept that one person's reality is not the same as another's. Honesty is essential because freedom cannot flow outside of reality. Start by being honest with yourself and you will see that honesty has nothing to do with laws, rules and regulations. It has to do with straightforwardness, truth, and self-acceptance. Head games and manipulation are likely to backfire on you. Try to be genuine at all times.

This is a year for accomplishment, fun, travel, expansion, and contrast. Your horizons are much broader now, so stay clear of dull and mundane routines, beliefs, and attitudes.

5 has all the elements of being in the "fast lane". If you set out confidently, with a specific goal in mind, you will be able to relax and enjoy these action-packed episodes. You will feel love, peace, exhilaration, and self confidence instead of fear, turmoil, loss, and exhaustion. Set your sights high and delight in this year of change, variety, adventure, opportunity and, above all, FREEDOM.

~ January ~
5 Year - 6 Month

Whatever your age, your upbringing, or your education,
what you are made of is mostly unused potential.
GEORGE LEONARD

Freedom? What freedom? You are tied to certain circumstances and commitments. You have responsibilities. There are people and situations you love and need. There are people and situations who love and need you. How can you have freedom and keep what is essential to you? What *is* freedom anyway? If you find yourself thinking such thoughts this month, it is a sure sign that the restrictive realities of *last year* have spilled over into this one.

You are now in very different territory. The 4 year cycle is over and, no matter how it seems, you are free. You *are* free of a mistake which created the restrictions you are now experiencing. It is unlikely that you will ever make that mistake again.

This month's events will show you that love and freedom are the same thing and that one cannot exist without the other. January gives you the freedom to focus on responsibility, relationship, and your domestic situation. The love within these important aspects can now be rescued, set free, and allowed to flow naturally. After last year's misunderstandings and heavy emotions, you have entered a cycle in which healing can finally take place.

January is a time of change in the home or within close relationships. Issues will arise around love, marriage, children, parents, siblings, pets, financial and physical security, and/or location. You are being urged to consider your responsibility and your own needs in these areas. The more restricted you feel about them, the more obviously a change is needed.

There may be a feeling of restlessness about *where* you need or want to be. One's sense of belonging is a vital factor in the quality of any relationship. If you feel that you are in the wrong place, even if you do not know precisely where you want to be, know that this uncertainty is part of humanity's current evolutionary movement. Eventually we will all end up in a place which feels right for us provided we have the firm intent to find it. For you, it could happen this year if you do not allow impulsiveness or fear to steer you in the wrong direction.

Make this a month to consider the circumstances and needs of your loved ones and those with whom you share your life on a day-to-day basis.

If there is ill feeling, try to bring peace and acceptance back into the fold. See all sides of the story and not just your own. Do not think you have the answers to someone else's problem without considering their Free Will, their personal energies, and their unique circumstances. If someone is pulling the strings and controlling *your* life, you must consider your own freedom, your own desires, and the reality of your circumstances.

Freedom has now entered your personal life so that you can balance the extremes that exist within your relationships and which are preventing love from flowing freely. The cynicism and coldness of last year must now be replaced with forgiveness and hope.

6 teaches us that we are each responsible for our own happiness. Where there is blame there is also a denial of this primary responsibility. The need to be right all the time is a sign that you tend to blame others for your own unhappiness. Release the denied guilt and fear that has thrown an otherwise loving relationship into a restrictive one. Once you accept your freedom to create your *own* happiness, you will find that love reemerges. Appreciate what you have and realize that you are now free to enjoy it.

This year will be an exciting journey. Invite the ones you love to join you when they can. Remember that they have their own journeys to make, and by taking an interest in their lives, you will be bringing some much needed balance into your relationships. Make this a time of unity and common goals, to be achieved by each person following their individual desires and needs.

Allow others to gain their own experience in life while you seek to expand yours. Learn the difference between helping and interfering. Let go of any tendency to set rules and regulations which are inappropriate to this year's theme of freedom and expansion. Wherever there are rules, love and freedom suffer. Yet, the chances are that you are still at the mercy of certain rules which were set in place last year. Don't worry. As this year proceeds, you will find ways to lessen their restrictive effect on you.

Freedom is not something to be grabbed at the expense of someone else. This is control, and control is the opposite of freedom. Recognize your need to control situations; to control other people; and replace these tendencies with acceptance, understanding, encouragement, and kindness. Loosen up and feel the freedom that is already inside you - the form of freedom that *nobody* can take away from you. Then you cannot help but extend greater freedom to those around you.

Be honest with yourself when you consider the mistakes you have made in the areas of love and relationship. You may have to change some outdated attitudes and beliefs. If you learn what needs to be learned from these mistakes, you will never want to repeat them.

Don't let guilt or blame stop you from admitting your mistakes in the first place. Guilt does not want you or your relationships to be loving, only guilty and accusatory. When you have learned from these mistakes, you will experience the *freedom* that a loving and balanced relationship provides. Give those you love a sense of inclusion in your life. Do something unusual and exciting with them. Bring fun and laughter into your relationships and loosen that rigid attitude which belongs in a cycle that is over.

This month's emotional nature gives you a much wider latitude and provides a new direction through which your creative talents can flow and expand. As old commercial tactics become more and more unpopular, the world is opening up to creative output that has come *from the heart*. Use this new perspective to further your own ambitions. Your ability to create or entertain can provide a warm, harmonious, and peaceful atmosphere around you.

The emphasis is on mutual love. Forgive or ask for forgiveness. The healing 6 cycle ensures that the more love you give, the more will be returned to you. Love is in the air. Get *into* this frame of mind - or *out* of an association where love does not exist.

Take care of any household issues that you have been putting off, including general maintenance and repairs. Discard anything, material or emotional, that is cluttering up your living space. You will not want these mundane matters to deplete your freedom later in the year.

Pay attention to the needs and emotions of children and be a part of *their* lives this month. If there are no children in your immediate situation, be aware of the innocence and importance of young people in general. They are the future, right before your eyes. They need acceptance, love, support, and encouragement. 6 is a cycle of teaching. It is vital, therefore, that we stop trying to instill in the young the very mistakes we are trying to rectify in ourselves.

The most valuable lessons you can teach children, and any others who come to you for advice, is that the choices they make of their own Free Will are the choices which will create happiness in their lives. Of course, we are all children in the evolutionary process, and we all need to learn this lesson.

~ February ~
5 Year - 7 Month

Married in haste, we may repent at leisure.
WILLIAM COSGREVE

How many opportunities have you lost over the years because you impulsively rushed to grab them without practical consideration or preparation? Slow down, my friend. This is no time to repeat the old mistakes of playing it safe and losing the opportunity, or of rushing headlong into unknown territory without some kind of plan or map. You now need a fresh approach and a change of attitude.

This month's 7 energy provides the ideal opportunity to observe what you *already have*: study it, analyze it, and see its greater potential. Then you must fine-tune every detail and bring it as close to perfection as possible. You will be presenting yourself and your ideas to the world in March, so you had better use February to make yourself and your ideas presentable. Learn to express the joy of what you are doing rather than confining yourself to a set of rules that no longer have a place in your life.

7 is a cycle of wisdom and introspection. In order to use this energy to your advantage, you must spend quiet periods of time by yourself, without distraction. This will enable you to think, sense, study, learn, focus, modify, polish, and *plan*. It will also bring exciting new ideas for the change of direction you seek.

A sudden emotional situation may throw you off course. In reality, it is pushing you closer to the course you actually want for yourself. Analyze the facts of your situation and you will see the *new* options which are opening up for you. Your feelings of doubt, pessimism, and anxiety will melt away. They are just the echoes of last year's stressful 4 cycle which are finally leaving your life. Let them go.

Straighten up. Pay attention. Feel your freedom. Feel your imagination stirring from its lengthy sleep. It's time to put a smile back on your face as you realize the enormous potential before you. There is no need to rush. Make this a slow month of renewed dignity and careful planning. You have so much to offer the world, but it needs to be presented and packaged in a different and more charismatic format. When you understand this, you will see that the world has so much to offer *you*.

Different ideals lead to different attitudes and approaches. These, in turn, lead to the different results you desire. An entirely different wavelength is needed now. Let yourself go. Let yourself get into it. This means being *emotionally* involved. Analyze, visualize, and *feel* your freedom. Use it to create a more desirable situation for yourself and, possibly, others.

The 5 energy enables you to profit from past mistakes. Recognize and admit to your mistakes, especially those of giving up on something before you have truly experienced it, or stubbornly holding on to things that no longer serve a purpose. Know that it is you who sets your own limits and it is you who can expand them. Do what you love to do, but do it differently. When this lesson is learned, you will be able to turn a mistake into expanded talent.

This month, your mind is likely to be far more active than your body. Many new understandings will make themselves known to you if you will just open your mind and your heart to them. Make your plans and have the intent to see them through. Spend plenty of time alone. There are still many emotions stuck inside you that need to be released. Feel them, accept them, and express them back into life. Your feelings need to be free, too!

Feelings of anger should be recognized when you find yourself being intolerant or critical. Feelings of fear should be accepted when you find yourself forcing a positive attitude when, in reality, you are just denying that you are afraid. Feelings of grief must be allowed their natural course, too. It is impossible to feel happiness when unexpressed sadness is weighing you down. Allow such feelings to arise and then move out of you. Then you will be able to enjoy and prosper from your new circumstances. Then you will be able to pick and choose, *with ease*, those things you want from life, instead of being overwhelmed by too much choice.

Wisdom is never handed to us on a plate. It is acquired through the clarity of our feelings and thoughts. Now, your feelings are trying to contact your thoughts and instill in them the wisdom of knowing what freedom actually means. Venture deep inside yourself. Feel and accept what you are *really* feeling. You will not be able to reach your destination if you do not know where you are. Where you are is *on the shore*, preparing yourself for an exciting voyage of discovery. Recognize and accept your current position, and prepare to set sail in March.

~ March ~
5 Year - 8 Month

Never forget that change is a positive force
that is generally for the better and that life
is a performance for which none of us
are given the opportunity to rehearse.
SALLY BROMPTON

Wake up. Snap out of it. You will never reach your destination if you are afraid to take the first step. There are places to go, people to see, work to do, and unusual possibilities to explore. Commit yourself to efficiency, professionalism, and responses which come from your heart. You are now beginning to understand the enormous potential at your disposal through the changes taking place in your relationships and general circumstances.

In a month when your personal power is evolving to a much higher level, be aware that any power struggles you are engaged in may be the result of unaddressed fear. You may believe that others are holding you back through their lack of acceptance for your ideas. You are afraid that there is nothing you can do about it. It is now absolutely essential that you release your dependence on other people's approval so that you can freely follow your own road. The others involved are traveling a different route entirely.

March is a month of action and high expectation as you present yourself to the world with a different kind of confidence. 5 can bring unexpected results, so don't be deterred if your plans are interrupted or propelled into a direction you had not considered. Ride it out - see where it leads. And remember the basic 5 rule: do not judge something before you have fully experienced the *feelings* involved. Be aware of everything that is going on. Keep in mind that change is the theme of the entire year and that the most important changes will take place *within*.

Throughout March, you will feel a heightened sense of your ability to make things happen to your advantage. 8 is a material energy, and you will now be made acutely and suddenly aware of the importance or lack of importance that you place on material things.

At the same time, you may experience a driving force which shows how able you are to manifest the material situations and things you need. Your power to manifest things includes flexibility and attention to detail so that you can see the hidden opportunities as well as the obvious ones. Another part of this power includes being able to "sense" avenues of success. It includes knowing and then doing what must be done for the desired results to materialize. Don't be defeated by your mistakes - learn from them - gain *experience* from them.

8 often influences matters of career, business, money, and status. Changes in these areas will take place now, and you must be aware of those past mistakes which pertain to your professional or financial dealings, or to your rights as a human being. This is no time to be stubborn. The quality of your physical or material life now depends on your ability to gain the experience being offered. Change those old beliefs which have always prevented satisfaction in the past, and feel the freedom that always follows the release of stubbornness. Go in whatever direction your feelings - your Will - takes you.

If you are indifferent here, the only experience you are likely to have is the indifference of others. The odds are in your favor. Know what you want and go for it. Opportunity is everywhere if you are open enough to see it. Stay on track with these dynamic vibrations and allow abundance to enter your life. It is time to grow and prosper or, at least, accept an opportunity that allows for future growth. Act in a businesslike way and, above all, believe in your own capabilities.

8 's a karmic cycle which gives you a return on whatever you have put out into the world. It is the cycle of reward for past and present actions. 8s rewards are often of a financial, material, or business nature because these are the areas in which most human beings *desire* reward. However, be aware of other areas in your life that have suddenly improved. An enormous level of satisfaction can be found away from one's commercial ambitions.

Allow yourself to feel the satisfaction that comes from *all* improvements. Satisfaction means you are no longer hungry; no longer lost; no longer searching. It is this feeling of satisfaction which produces personal power. It also develops the charisma and magnetism which ensures continued success. Know when you are SATISFIED.

~ April ~
5 Year - 9 Month

Out of clutter, find simplicity.
From discord, find harmony.
In the middle of difficulty lies opportunity.
ALBERT EINSTEIN

You have now arrived at the point of your 5 journey where you must say farewell to an old and limiting aspect of your life and feel the emotions that always follow a significant ending. Everything is related to endings and completions this month, so don't expect anything new to happen until these conclusions have occurred. A sense of finality must be experienced, otherwise you will be weighed down by denied emotions and unwanted circumstances for the rest of the year. A phase of your life has ended. You must accept that fact and let it go.

The first four months of this year represent your journey *out* of the past. April signifies the end of that particular road. Endings are a prelude to beginnings. Bring an end to old tensions and fears. What your narrow view once thought was hate has evolved into love because you have allowed yourself to *feel* this hatred. Endings do not always have to be painful. Often they can feel as if the weight of the world has been lifted from your shoulders, signifying that the pain is over and a new and more comfortable reality is forming. Let the pain of the past go. Feel it. Express it. END IT.

Parting with old emotion is always followed by optimism and self acceptance. Sometimes we think it is impossible to find the positive aspects in a particular loss and, if this is how you feel, it is because *so much* emotion is involved. Give yourself time to adjust to a change for which you just weren't prepared, and let those emotions flow as freely as possible.

The 9 cycle confronts us with so much truth at one time that it may seem preferable to deny the reality of it all and look for a way out that does not require such a high level of self-reliance. Fear of success is the fear of taking full responsibility for your life - past, present, and future. This fear must be expressed and released now. Anger toward others may be an indication that you are angry at yourself for being afraid. Get deep into your reality and know that you stand on the dividing line between your old unsatisfactory conditions and a new, brilliant, and free way of life. End the indecision and choose which side of the line you want to be on. April is a time for courage, tolerance, giving, and understanding. Use its power to put an end to misunderstanding. Accept the truth instead.

Make this a warm and loving month in which to discover the power that comes with loving yourself. Without self-love, it is impossible to love another or for another to love you. Renew the love within your relationships by ending your need to control them. Let them be, and they will *be* beautiful.

Once again, your emotions provide an opportunity for creative and professional expansion. This is not a time to start something new but to tie up loose ends and put unusual finishing touches on existing situations or projects. It is from the heart that inspiration flows and this month, your heart is positively gushing. Let your *experience* of life become the vehicle of your success.

April is a time to forgive. Most importantly, it is a time to forgive yourself. See where you are still beating yourself up for things that simply don't matter any more. The past has gone. You are free now. You may not yet be free of the consequences of a past mistake, but you are free of the mistake itself. From this understanding, the rest of your life cannot help but seem brighter.

9 is a cycle of giving - simply for the sake of giving. Do not expect anything in return, not even a 'thank you'. Give because you want to, and not because guilt or fear has told you to. This month, giving may include giving *in* or giving *way*. It may even mean giving *up*. There are many ways to give. One of them will apply to your particular situation now. To give is to let go of something. GIVE - and a new door will open for you.

~ May ~
5 Year - 1 Month

> *The one unchangeable certainty is that*
> *nothing is unchangeable or certain.*
> JOHN F. KENNEDY

This is a month of dynamic forward movement, new ideas, new people, new enthusiasm, independence, and sudden development. Change is all around you now. You may even find yourself being "supported" in an unexpected way, by unusual individuals who have been drawn to your talent, originality, or your strong belief in yourself. There will be some who disapprove of you, of course. This is part of life too. Just accept it. However, if you really do approve of yourself, you may not even notice it.

Yet, despite plenty of encouragement, you may feel vulnerable or abandoned. This is because the 1 cycle requires you to *stand alone* in your new circumstances and experience the power of your individuality and independence. You are in new territory now. You are being urged to focus on you, your life, your feelings, your desires, your ambitions, and your ability to live in freedom, no matter what your circumstances may be, while allowing others to do the same.

The freedom to be yourself and lead your own life is now a matter of priority. Here you are in a new situation. A significant change has taken place. If it has not, then it is up to you to make a meaningful change yourself. If there are still conditions which are making you afraid or unhappy, now is the time to break through these barriers so that they no longer feel restrictive. Are you still holding on to areas of dependence which need to be eliminated? Wherever you are dependent, you must dig up the buried feelings which will lead to the root - the *cause* of the dependency.

Assess these weak points and strengthen your claim to freedom. Although it is necessary for you to focus on you, this month, it is not necessary for others to focus on you. Other people have their own agendas, priorities, and problems. Be sure that the attention you are receiving now is not solely for the purpose of improving someone else's situation while your own best interests are being neglected. Be aware of the games people play.

BEGIN something. This can be a new activity, job, friendship, relationship, business, project, or hobby. It can be anything at all, provided it has relevance to the reality of your life or to a change you wish to make to that reality. Make sure you start something, even if it is just a new phase of an existing experience.

Accept and celebrate your uniqueness. Be who you are. Allow the 'unusual' element of this year's 5 vibration to lead you to places and people who appreciate what you have to offer. You have so *much* to offer right now. The changes taking place in May are likely to remove you from those who do not appreciate you and place you in an area where what you have to offer is actually being sought.

Recognize when you are behaving in a self-destructive way and try to balance these tendencies. Right now, negative behavior may include an overbearing approach, aggression, impatience, subservience, indifference, overindulgence, stubbornness, cowardice, or recklessness. There may be a tendency to overcompensate for what you inaccurately perceive to be a personality deficiency. There may also be a tendency to under or over estimate the importance of what you are trying to achieve. Make no mistake about it. What you are trying to achieve *is* important. It can change your life for the better. Just understand that others have important goals, too, and that the world does not revolve around you alone.

1 is the energy of the EGO - your sense of self. Ego provides a gauge for measuring your own self-worth and the importance of your efforts. At this stage of human evolution, we all have egos which are either over or under developed. Your awareness of this will enable you to balance your ego by feeling your feelings and relating them to your reality.

Feeling at ease with yourself and others simultaneously is, perhaps, the best description of a balanced ego. Balancing your ego will help create balance all around you. The more comfortable you feel around others, the more at ease they will feel around you.

Recognize the mistakes you have made in the past regarding your ego, your expectations of other people, and your sense of self-importance. Be sure you do not repeat them now.

Particular attention should be paid to the individuality that exists within your various relationships. Take the time to assess where this month's changes have actually led you. Your very reality has been altered and it is important to know just where you stand. You can only know where you stand by *feeling* what you feel.

Once you have accepted the reality of your current position, you will be able to proceed with focus, confidence, enthusiasm, and flexibility. Appreciate and enjoy this month's opportunity to substantially transform your life, your relationships, and your view of the world.

~ June ~
5 Year - 2 Month

*No one wins a conflict unless both feel understood
and enlightened about the theme or nature of the other.*
ARNOLD MINDELL, THE LEADER AS MARTIAL ARTIST

Slow down. Stop. Wait. Look. Listen. *Feel.* You have now entered a very special energy which requires you to sense your way through it by *cooperating* with your new environment. At the same time, you will be tying up the loose ends from an old situation. This will enable you to know exactly where you are and what is happening in your life.

Do not assume or force anything. Relax and blend in. You are not the star of the show this month, but you are a valuable part of a team. Your understanding of *relationship* is now being put to the test. Patience and modesty are the keys to making this month a successful one.

Take care of those little details that others prefer to avoid or overlook. Be emotionally involved in the situation. Understand the workings of the 'machinery' involved and do your part to keep everything running smoothly.

There will be detail after detail to take care of so that someone else can take the lead. Experience this with enthusiasm because your own starring role is yet to come. When it does, you will need this kind of willing cooperation yourself. Right now, you may need to test the two-way street of cooperation by speaking up and confidently asking for what *you* need.

There is no need for aggression or fear now - and this is no time to hide or run away. Just relax and enjoy playing second fiddle for a while. Other people's problems are probably much more dramatic than your own right now. Yet, you can rest assured that much is going on behind the scenes which will soon bring improvement to your life. Be patient. This means listening attentively to what others have to say and paying meticulous attention to detail.

2 is a cycle of patience, truth, cooperation, diplomacy, efficiency, intuition, and connection. These are the elements available to you this month. These are the keys to giving new life to an emotional seed you planted in May.

If you find yourself panicked, frustrated, or angered by delays and distractions, know that any aggressive moves on your part are likely to be met with even more delay, distraction, and disappointment. Put your own plans,and ego on the back burner and focus willingly and dynamically on someone or something else instead. Focus on the reality of what is going on all around you. You will soon realize that this month of distraction and intrusion is actually improving your overall *timing* and is providing vital clues to the direction you will be taking in the near future.

You may have to slow down considerably in order to recognize the people or person with whom life intends you to cooperate this month. Your help *is* needed somewhere. Calm down, be patient, and try to understand what is going on in the life of someone else. Relate openly to this person.

Do not force your ideas or opinions on anyone. Do not force anything at all. Nothing can be intimidated, coerced, or attacked within 2's magnetic field without it reacting to you in the same way. It is essential that you understand this.

There is no need to become a doormat for others or to be afraid of making a wrong move. Maintain a high self-esteem. When you are at ease with yourself and with others, your self-esteem will be very high anyway. Changing your focus from yourself to someone else allows an exchange of important information to take place. Slow down. Wait. Look. Listen. Feel. RELATE. This information will come to you when you least expect it. Remember that 5 is the number of the unexpected.

Consider the gentle nature of this month. Accept that mistakes have been made regarding your understanding of patience, relationship, and cooperation. Mistakes have been made in how you have dealt with the mundane and boring realities of everyday life. Know exactly what your mistakes of the past have been and be sure not to repeat them now.

When this experience is gained you will feel the stress and anxiety of recent events leave your life. Your consciousness will expand, and you will sense the true *connection* between you and someone else. Aggression and warlike competition is not the answer. It is freedom *from* these things that must be sought now.

2 is the energy of PEACE. Make peace with yourself. Then peace with others is inevitable. Success will come in the form of team work. It will come from your heart and from the hearts of others. When this experience is gained, you will have reached a new stage in your evolution. Relax - this is only the beginning. Much greater insight is on the way.

~ July ~
5 Year - 3 Month

We are always getting ready to live, but never living.
RALPH WALDO EMERSON

Start out this auspicious month with the attitude that nothing is going to get you down. July brings change to your friendships and social life, and you are likely to feel a great surge of energy which pertains to your own happiness and creativeness. The 3 vibration urges you to feel the joy of simply being alive.

So lighten up a little and take advantage of this month's opportunity to feel good about yourself again. 3's emphasis on friends and acquaintances may draw you to unusual or different people. There may be a parting from those whose ideals are in opposition to your own. Life is giving you the chance to discover where your happiness is *and* where it isn't. An adventurous frame of mind is called for.

Remember that you cannot please everyone. The more you try to do so, the less others can appreciate your efforts. One of the main lessons of this year is to acknowledge the diversity of human life and to allow everyone to be who they really are, including you.

Be careful not to fall into the trap of keeping up appearances. Take a good look at the nature of anyone you are trying to impress and ask yourself *why* you need to do this. The more you try to emulate someone else or conform to others' beliefs or lifestyles, the less regard you have for your own uniqueness and freedom. Learn to respect the individuality of others without losing your own precious identity. And remember that your present circumstances are temporary. Without this understanding, you may be setting yourself up for difficulties in next year's 6 cycle by tying yourself to a responsibility you don't want.

July invites you to let down your guard and feel the beauty of self-acceptance. You are being given a chance to live your life free from the turmoil that occurs when you worry about what others think of you. The 3 cycle is showing you that freedom is the state in which your friendships must now flow. Real friends do not have to impress or placate each other. Even if thousands of miles and a lifetime of years come between friends, they will still be friends, no matter what. Even if all that is left of a friendship is a memory, the friendship still exists within that memory. The bond of real friendship cannot be broken.

So take a real hard look at the people you are calling your friends and ask yourself if this is the way you really feel about them. Where have you made mistakes in the past that pertain to friends and your need for approval? Where have you made mistakes in the past in knowing the difference between a true friend and a passing acquaintance? Learn from these mistakes now and refuse to repeat them yet again.

July is a month of lightness, beauty and creativity. Something will happen this month to trigger strong feelings of self satisfaction, confidence, and purpose. These things *are* lightness, beauty, and creativity. There may be a tendency to ignore this part of the journey but, in doing so, you will miss out on an important experience which can magnify success in many areas of your life. Yes, you are where you are for a specific purpose.

3 is a cycle of creativity and 5 is a cycle of freedom. The implication of this combination of energies speaks for itself. Socializing is not only good for the soul this month but can also lead to important contacts, ideas, and vital areas of inspiration. 3 is the ultimate networking vibration. Keep your wits about you. Do not get caught up in purely superficial matters. Avoid over-indulgence in matters of a physical nature. This could spell trouble that could spill over into August or beyond. This is no time to blur your vision with excesses.

If a vacation is out of the question, try to minimize your duties wherever possible. If you do have responsibilities to take care of, enjoy taking care of them. Whatever you find yourself doing, do it with delight, so that your mood becomes contagious. Use this month's vibrations of optimism to stimulate your imagination.

You should also be aware that July's combination of 5 and 3 energies has created a very high pregnancy vibration in which babies, ideas, and plans are often conceived. Stay focused on the vision of your goals. What will you conceive this month? What will you create?

~ August ~
5 Year - 4 Month

Truth is the cry of all, but the game of few.
TRISTAN BENARD

The focus is now on WORK, DETAILS, REPUTATION, and IDENTITY. As you travel through this month's 4 cycle, you will soon become aware of its serious and orderly nature and of how disorganized certain aspects of your life have become. This is a time of setting priorities, eliminating pettiness and chaos, and getting your life in order.

Whatever the problem is, don't waste too much time agonizing over it. Look for a constructive solution instead which will bring a complete change to the situation. Change is what this year is all about. Not just little changes which really don't amount to anything. The 5 year cycle is about real change - drastic change - a completely different way of living, thinking, doing, and feeling. Remember your life just six months ago, and you will see how much change has already taken place.

Solve a problem by digging up its cause. Then the problem will no longer have a basis on which to stand. Are there still some old beliefs or attitudes in you that cause this problem to resurface over and over? What mistakes are involved here? What mistakes did you make last year or the year before, which are still being paid for now? It is time to change your approach and your attitude.

4 is an energy which responds positively to effort. A problem you are facing now certainly requires great determination and courage on your part. This is because of the enormous difficulty you have in admitting to this particular mistake. But until you do admit it, learn from it, and stop repeating it, this same old mistake will continue to create the same old problems.

It is time to face the cold hard facts here and experience the elation of a major breakthrough. Work at it, chip away at it, stretch yourself, and do not give up. In this year of change, nothing is unchangeable. Even severe limitations can now be changed into opportunity. Sometimes it is not the limitation that needs to be changed, but the fear of change itself.

Yes, August is a difficult month. But it offers you the chance to overcome obstacles of all kinds so that the path ahead is clear and free. You are now realizing the extent to which you are still limiting yourself and the extent to which you can *expand* your level of self- acceptance. This will enable you to take advantage of the double 5 energy of September.

Exert some serious effort to sort out a mess which has been part of an ongoing pattern in your life. Get organized. Create a genuine sense of order. Delays and postponements are common in a 4 cycle, but do not let this weaken your spirit. Do not let your impatience or impulsiveness create more problems for you.

You are traveling through an obstacle course right now. Expect the unexpected. Stay alert. And do not be fooled by 4s stern exterior energy. Do not allow minor setbacks to deplete your enthusiasm. How many times have you made *that* mistake? Retain your optimism.

Know that the physical, mental, and emotional work must be done, and get on with it. This is a time to be practical, logical, and totally honest with yourself. Freedom is the ability to function constructively in whatever happens to be your reality at the time. If you do not like your reality right now, then it is time to do what you must do to change it. 5 is the energy of the unusual and the different and, if you are honest with yourself, you will have to admit that different attitudes and approaches are needed in many areas of your life.

This month invites you to make a place for everything you love and to move away from unloving circumstances. Wake up and pay attention. Feel what is happening to you. It is a tremendous opportunity to grow.

~ September ~
5 Year - 5 Month

You gain strength, courage, and confidence
by every experience in which you must stop and look
fear in the face. You must do the thing
you think you cannot do!
ELEANOR ROOSEVELT

The 5 cycle is working overtime. You are faced with a situation that requires you to make the very changes you have been putting off. Decisions must be made. Action must be taken.

By refusing to deal with these issues, you are preventing new opportunities from entering your life. Stay alert, because opportunities are everywhere. Pick and choose carefully among them. Rash decisions will work against you. A double dose of 5 energy is making September an expansive and fast-paced month. You may prefer to distract yourself with petty issues or overindulgences, but this behavior is just an excuse to avoid the truth.

It is up to you to choose how you will navigate your way through this unpredictable energy which thrives on constructive change and movement. In order for you to succeed, you will need to develop a strong determination to steer your life in a new direction.

What do you *want*? This is the question to focus on. Do pay attention to what you are feeling because your Will expresses itself *through* your feelings. Now is the time to make those changes which will lead you to the fulfillment you desire. It is time to broaden your horizons and live according to the choices you have made. It is time to change your reality if not to the way you want it, then at least to a place that is closer to it.

A mountain is climbed one step at a time. Continue to take steps and you will eventually reach the top. This is a month of choosing your steps carefully but decisively. What was it about the way you handled previous choices that always caused you to lose the opportunities involved?

Remember, too, that some people climb mountains not only for the challenge, but also for the fun, the thrill, the adventure, and the scenery that can only be experienced before the top is reached.

Don't give up just as it seems that you can succeed. Persevere. Remember: until *you* change what needs to be changed, your life will remain as it is. Now, there's a sobering thought!

This month, an unusual agreement may mark the beginning of an unexpected responsibility, although you may not fully understand this until next year. You may also encounter something or someone whose presence, positive or negative, will be felt for a long time to come. Recognize past mistakes pertaining to *indecision* and *impulsiveness*. These mistakes were always the cause of great disappointment for you.

If events take a sudden turn, remember that the 5 year is one in which you must learn how to flow comfortably with life's diversity; the different; the unexpected. Flow with any sudden movement confidently, responsibly, and with high expectation. Your 5 adventure is not over yet.

~ October ~
5 Year - 6 Month

Respect for the rights of others is peace.
BENITO JUAREZ

6 is a cycle of love, healing, responsibility, marriage, balance, peace, love, and belonging. Apply these words to whatever happens this month. They are likely to have different meanings to different people, and because 5 is a cycle of all that is different, remember that love itself has many *different* forms.

It is possible to love different people or things in different ways. It is possible to love one child differently to the way you love another without letting guilt diminish your love for both. It is possible to love your spouse one way and your work another way, forming two very different marriages in your life. It is also possible to hate someone that guilt tells you that you should love.

The circumstances of this month, when properly understood, will enable you to love everything you *truly* love freely and deeply, by coming face to face with guilt and refusing to be ruled by it. Guilt destroys love and freedom. It destroys life.

You cannot destroy or eliminate guilt, but you can move away from it by refusing to judge a person, a situation, or yourself, before you have experienced the reality involved. The less you judge yourself, the more acceptance you will feel, and the more lovable you and others will become.

This year has given you the freedom to find out exactly who and what you love so that your love and your life can continue to expand. This month may bring a strong urge to protect the things and people you love. Herein lies another lesson. Be very careful not to go to *extremes* in protecting what is 'yours'. This can create restrictions and barriers that imprison the innocent, the love, and the life.

Focus on your relationships, especially with those people you call family. An unexpected event may turn your attention there anyway. Your responsibilities may become an issue now. There is room in your life for all responsibilities that are yours, including your responsibility to live in freedom. This can be a time when a responsibility is taken off your hands so that a different one can be assumed.

The events of this month place an emphasis on the choices you have made in the past and the choices you are being asked to make now. You must find a way to live your life without ever having to say the words *"I have no choice"*. You do have a choice in every single move you make, even though it may be difficult to recognize certain options. Most people believe that where love is concerned, there are situations in which there really is no choice. But if love is what you are really feeling, then the choice you make will be based in love and will automatically be the right one. The choice you make will be the one you *want* to make.

This does not mean that you have to stay in a situation that stands to harm you in some way. You simply need to understand that the choices you make create your reality. Remember that a mistake is a way of learning what works and what does not. It is how you gain *experience*.

Your domestic life will dominate this month. You may have to weigh the reality of this situation with your need to be free. You may have to focus on a specific family member, pet, neighbor, authority figure, or close friend. The home may require attention, repair, legal representation, or renovation. Maybe you are away from home and miss the love it provides.

Perhaps you need to find a balance between your outside activities and the people you love. Perhaps you are falling in love. Perhaps love for yourself must now take precedence over guilt which has disguised itself as love for another. One thing is certain. Love is in the air. Feel it. *Love* it.

Creativity thrives in love. Creativity thrives in the 6 energy. October provides you with an opportunity to do what you *love* and to realize that you have a responsibility to let this form of love flow freely. With this understanding, great strides can be made professionally and personally, and can lead to increased financial security for you and your loved ones. This is a time to expand the love you have for yourself and others.

The events of this month will make it impossible for you to focus in only one direction. You need to consider all aspects of your life and discard those which reduce your ability to love. Create a balance between all those aspects which are important to you. They represent the basis of next year's 6 journey. For the next eighteen months, life will make you aware of your responsibility to make space and time for all that you love.

In the past, mistakes may have been made that caused you to concentrate too heavily in one area while another area was neglected. Now is the time to learn the lesson involved and stop repeating it. Relax with your responsibilities, accept where you are now, and learn the art of smooth sailing - toward where you want to be.

~ November ~
5 Year - 7 Month

The only limit to our realization of tomorrow
will be our doubts of today.
FRANKLIN ROOSEVELT

There will be plenty of food for thought this month. You may feel withdrawn and want to spend some time by yourself, or your circumstances may force you into a position where you must be alone. 7 is urging you to take time for yourself, without distraction, so you can reflect, analyze, and think about all that has transpired this year, and all that you *want* to transpire next year.

Matters concerning responsibility, home, love, marriage, children, parents, siblings, partners, community, pets, and security are likely to be very much on your mind. These will be the focus of your attention for some time to come, as you are now beginning to feel the magnetic pull of next year's 6 vibration. The main question is that of responsibility versus freedom, even though you may not immediately see that this question exists. Life is about to teach you that responsibility and freedom are one and the same thing, and that your creative talent can be used to balance and orchestrate *all* the important areas of your life.

Take comfort in being alone. Spend as much time as possible in quiet, peaceful environments so that you can study, meditate, learn, and appreciate yourself. This will enable you to find the answers you seek. Distraction, noise, hostility, and an unwillingness to spend time alone will create an energy block, preventing you from seeing the reality of your situation. Retreat. Listen to what you are really thinking. Feel what you are really feeling.

If you feel lonely, pessimistic, or even depressed this month, simply accept that this is how you *feel*. Realistically assess the truth of your situation. Relax, take a break, and let your intuition take over. The most constructive solutions can be found inside your own thoughts and feelings. Listen to the questions you ask yourself. *Hear* your answers. Find their balancing point, the point where your thoughts and your feelings *agree* with each other. Incorporate this agreement into your plans.

This is not a time for fast forward movement. It is a time to reflect, review the past and the present, and plan for the future. Be content to be alone. Enjoy your own company. Understand that you are the best friend you will ever have. Be good to yourself. Free yourself. Pamper yourself with a little peace and serenity.

This is an excellent time to explore the fundamentals of life and nature. You may find yourself more interested in metaphysics, science, religion, psychology, or philosophy. You may feel drawn to studying, researching or teaching. 7 is a cycle of wisdom, which is exactly what life is offering you this month. Be aware that others may find you difficult to relate to. The *introspective* nature of the 7 energy combined with the *unusual* nature of the 5 year can place you on a very different wavelength.

However, the energy of the approaching 6 year cycle is urging balance. Regain your confidence. Try not to be so moody and critical. Be flexible. Avoid secrets and conspiracy. Stop worrying about things that have not happened. Judging a situation before you have experienced it could be one of your past mistakes which now needs to evolve into experience. On the other hand, forging ahead through an area filled with danger signs is not a prudent thing to do either.

When your life is balanced and you are aware of all of its contents, excessive worry is replaced by self assuredness. You will know that all problems can be solved or avoided by facing and, most importantly, feeling the reality of them.

And you will understand that you cannot possibly cross a bridge before you come to it. Confusing? Annoying? A little scary? Adventures often are. Whether you realize it or not, you are now reaching a point of stability in an adventure you started almost seven years ago. *Remember?*

~ December ~
5 Year - 8 Month

Choice is the essence of what I believe it is to be human.
LIV ULLMAN

SNAP OUT OF IT. Wake up from the introspective vibrations of last month and get back into the passionate flow of life. It is time to act dynamically. New people and new opportunities are all around you. You now have the potential to change your business and financial affairs, and your status, in the most beneficial ways. The 8 energy emphasizes material and financial issues. You are in a cycle of personal power, spiritual understanding, and increased charisma and magnetism. Expect this month's activities to lead to dramatic, progressive, and clearly defined results. And expect to exert a lot of effort in order for these results to materialize. Do not forget that you are in the process of creating your own destiny.

8 is an energy which provides both material and spiritual prosperity. It responds and reacts to actions taken, and rewards the initiator with a return on whatever has been "invested". Metaphysically speaking, the 8 vibration allows you to reap whatever you have sown and, of course, this can have its advantages and its drawbacks.

Before you go rushing off in what you believe is the direction of financial and physical freedom, remember that whatever commitments are made now will manifest *next* year as responsibilities. Next year's 6 cycle also relates to family and love. Before you make a decision, know that you may have to find some pretty creative ways to maintain a BALANCE between new commitments and your existing ones.

Once you have made a decision, act decisively. Acknowledge the improvements that are now taking place in many different areas of your life. You may even find that certain assets turn out to be more valuable than you thought. But do stay alert to the deceptive games that people play. This month, there is likely to be more to certain people than meets the eye. Therefore, it is important to understand who and what you are dealing with. Get advice if necessary. Try to gain knowledge and experience of the issues that surround you. This is a time to seek expertise and incorporate it into your memory banks for immediate and future reference.

Yes, December offers expansion in your business and financial affairs, but also in matters of the heart. An opportunity may arise which can help improve domestic security or comfort. Approach this month in a positive, businesslike fashion. Act in a practical and realistic manner. Try not to step on others as you surge forward. This can result in disappointment or unnecessary aggression.

The 6 year cycle of love, responsibility creativity, and balance now approaches. You should keep this in mind as you pick and choose among December's options. If you find yourself headed toward anything of an extreme or radical nature, try to avoid it. On the other hand, who is to say what is extreme or radical these days? Well, frankly, YOU are.

You must be the one to decide whether something is right or wrong for you. Not by the opinions of other people, but by being totally honest with yourself. How do you really *feel* about this particular issue. As a new responsibility or ambition starts to excite you on a deeply emotional level, try to make choices which bring personal satisfaction and equilibrium to your life and the lives of those you love.

Enjoy December to the fullest and, whatever you have learned this year - whatever feels good - never forget it. Hold on to the wealth of experience you have gained. Hold on to your freedom. Find a place inside you for everything and everyone you love as December 31st arrives and you cross over to the 6 year cycle of LOVE, RESPONSIBILITY, RELATIONSHIP, HEALING, and BELONGING.

The 6 Year Cycle

a journey of love, relationship, responsibility, and healing.

A community is like a ship;
everyone ought to be prepared to take the helm.
HENRIK IBSEN

Our most basic instinct is survival, for ourselves and those we love. But when we, our loved ones, or our beliefs are threatened, we can take some astonishingly extreme measures to protect the status quo. What we often fail to notice is that the extremes we run to are often more dangerous than the original threat.

You have reached a very important and emotional stage of your journey because your closest relationships will be brought to center stage this year. There are now three powerful lanes of energy open to you. On the left and right, there are the unstable "fringes" of opposite extremes. The center lane contains the only energy that can keep the two extremes from clashing, colliding, and destroying love and life. The center lane provides the only connection between them which can restore peace and harmony. The center lane is BALANCE, and this is where you need to focus now. Welcome to the 6 year cycle.

This is a vital time in your life when you will feel a definite sense of duty and priority. The first step to making this year successful is to accept that you do, indeed, have responsibilities.

But, do not assume you already know what your responsibilities are. As the year proceeds, you will realize that at least one responsibility is no longer yours or was never yours to begin with. You may find that other responsibilities have been overlooked and now require your attention. Your primary obligation is to take care of yourself first and do what is right for you. Otherwise you will be in no position to take care of those who will need your help this year. This is rather like those airline safety regulations which urge you, in the case of an emergency, to place the oxygen mask over your own face first and *then* attend to children or dependents.

You will feel a strong desire to become more self-reliant and secure, and to establish your 'place' in the world. At the same time, you may be required to focus on someone else - perhaps a spouse, lover, child, parent, relative, pet, friend, neighbor, or the home or community itself, and BALANCE their needs with your own. You may have to care for someone who is ill, or whose circumstances may cause you concern. Adjustments and sacrifices may have to be made in order to fulfill your list of priorities.

In most cases, the best way to help others is by showing them that they can and must be responsible for themselves. Other cases will require an unusual level of patience, compassion, and understanding. You may also have to reconsider cherished ideas and beliefs which no longer seem appropriate to these times or to your unique circumstances.

Try to maintain a high self esteem as your plans are delayed, altered, and adapted. Responsibility is the urge to respond to a specific area of need. The way you respond is a matter of your own Free Will, which is determined by the way you *feel* about something. Therefore, this is no time to hold your feelings in. There is no need to enslave yourself to the demands of others, not if you are responding with love. But if your responses come from guilt or the fear that guilt produces, you may be in for a bumpy ride.

This year emphasizes love and all matters of the heart including marriage, family, children, parents, close friends, matters of duty, the home, healing, education, security, peace, and creativity. This year, both the pleasures and the problems of your personal life will predominate. When love is your motivation, almost anything can be achieved. First, however, it may be necessary to learn the difference between love and control. Love and guilt. Love and fear. Love and attraction. Love and hate.

Real love cannot be bought, sold, manipulated, or controlled in any way. Failure to understand this has produced the mistaken belief that love hurts. Love can never hurt. It is only the loss of love that hurts. And it is our great fear of losing love which causes us to hold on to it too tightly so that it can no longer breathe.

If there is any ill feeling in the family or with those you consider to be family, try to understand all sides of the situation and promote peace wherever you can. Sometimes blame and anger must be expressed in order to realize that forgiveness is necessary. Even though you may find yourself in the role of problem solver, it is not your responsibility to solve other people's problems for them but to point out options and ideas through which they may solve these matters themselves.

When the 6 energy is correctly understood and applied, you will experience the warmth and pleasure of love and affection with more intensity than ever before. Your need to control situations will be minimized. You will find that by simply letting people be who they really are, any manipulative instincts will start to feel out of place and contrary to your actual desires, and your emotions will flow openly and lovingly. Others will feel at ease in your presence. This will create genuine unity.

Do not make promises you cannot keep, and do not take on responsibilities that are not entirely yours. If you do, resentment, frustration, or loss of love are sure to follow. Accept that certain demands on your emotions, time, and money will be made this year. Accept that you now have it in your power to heal yourself. You are also able to help with the healing of others. Yes, health and healing are major factors of the 6 year cycle. In fact, it is often in the 6 cycle that symptoms arise so that you can get to the root of what has caused them. The cause is always unexpressed emotions that have become imprisoned within you and are struggling to get back into life, which is where they belong.

Even though you will have your own problems to deal with this year, you may also feel like everyone else's counselor. The 6 energy is so magnetic that it can attract certain people to you, even strangers, who can sense that you may be able to help them in some way. But, because the balanced 6 vibration urges that people take responsibility for their own lives, it is important not to encourage others to become dependent on you. Be aware of how your need to volunteer may interfere with your real priorities. Say NO when it is appropriate.

In the 6 year cycle, new responsibilities almost always arise. New possibilities appear. New places are discovered. New homes are often sought, as people seek their right place in the world - a place in which a strong sense of belonging can be felt. Home based businesses are started or expanded. Additional responsibilities arise in the work place. Relationships and circumstances can be seen for what they really are, if you take the time to look and *feel* deeply enough.

This is a time in which marriages and partnerships are formed or reformed. Babies and new creative ventures are born. Long lost relatives and friends pop up from nowhere. Negative relationships or associations are healed - or ended. Justice is sought and judgments are made. Emotions run high and low. Your very concept of justice may change as you realize that justice for one often means deprivation for another and that real justice takes place on a much higher level than most people are yet capable of understanding.

Wherever there is blame toward yourself or someone else there is also hatred. Therefore, past judgments must be reexamined and the feelings involved must be expressed outwardly. The space being taken up in your body by hate - probably hate that you deny having - is space that could otherwise be occupied by *love*. Eventually, hatred will eat away at your body and erupt as either disease or rage. The 6 year cycle is a time to accept, understand, forgive, and heal.

You may have a tendency to seek acceptance for who and what you are from the family or some other group. You will want others to see you as responsible and dependable. Yes, it can be comforting to know that you are approved of and that you belong in a certain circle, but it is also necessary to stop judging yourself and others by what "society" or "authority" deems acceptable. There is no one alive who is sufficiently educated or trustworthy to determine *your* truth for you or to mandate the direction of your life. Seek no one's approval but your own and follow your own feelings to determine the truth. This is Free Will. *This* is responsibility.

6 represents education. But this word is often misinterpreted and confined to assumptions and judgments that belong in the past. Methods of education, teaching, and learning, must change along with humanity's changing realities. Today, real education involves the personal pursuit and discovery of *truth* over assumption. We all have so much to learn about life. Most of it will be learned far away from any classroom, teacher, politician, guru, or preacher. Don't assume that you - or any one else - has all the answers. There is an extreme energy at work when we insist that we are right all the time - and - when we always assume we are wrong and need others to tell us what is right. Truth requires that you feel and understand - not assume.

6 gives you the power of MAGNETISM. You will attract whatever you focus on far more easily this year. Of course, this can have its drawbacks. Focus on danger, and you'll end up in dangerous situations. Focus on nickels and dimes, and that's all you'll have. Focus on other people's shortcomings and you'll be surrounded by negative behavior. Look for problems and, believe me, you'll find them. Try to focus on the good in other people. Replace outdated beliefs with new and more realistic understandings. Seek peaceful solutions to all problems, and allow others to live their lives without your constant input and judgment.

Responsibility is another word that is often misunderstood. If you are struggling with an obligation reluctantly, resentfully, or fearfully, you are probably doing it for the wrong reason. Responsibility too often implies something for which you have no choice; something which takes away from your freedom; something that is little appreciated, or something that has been forced on you. Love cannot force. Guilt can and does. If a responsibility is not of your *will* then the chances are that it is not yours. Careful thought should be given to your motivation for taking it on. This year's circumstances are offering you the *liberty* to take care of your real responsibilities lovingly and naturally. The balanced energy of 6 renovates, restores, and heals.

This year, you are on a journey of power and priority. It is a journey of learning the truth of how you *feel* about your various relationships. It is a journey of healing the gaps between generations, genders, judgments, and individuals. It is the journey of peace. It is the journey of LOVE.

~ January ~
6 Year - 7 Month

Now is not the time to cling to what was,
but to amend what is.
HELEN HAYES

6 is a cycle of responsibility and problem solving. 7 is a cycle of analysis, introspection, planning, and wisdom. This emotional combination of energies often creates an initial fear of not knowing *how* to take care of a particular obligation. Therefore, it is hardly surprising if you start out the year feeling at "sixes and sevens" with the world or with one person in particular.

There may be a tendency to think the worst. Guilt is likely to take advantage of this and make you feel inadequate, frustrated, or just plain guilty because you are unable to contribute what guilt has told you is necessary. Slow down. Stop everything. There is something you need to clarify *inside* you before you make any further judgments.

Life requires very little of you in a material or physical sense right now. It asks only for your presence and your attention. If this is all life requires of you, then others can expect no more from you either. January is a time to clarify what is actually happening so that an effective solution can be found. Open-minded and realistic planning will unveil vital alternatives and options. Before your new directions can be seen, you may have to recognize and remove a lifetime of misinformation and outdated beliefs that you are stubbornly holding on to, particularly with regard to your closest relationships and family connections.

There is nothing wrong with seeking advice from others. Different points of view can be very helpful. But with January's emphasis on education and learning, the truth you seek cannot be found inside someone else's head. You must seriously analyze your situation, as it is now, in order to recognize what needs to be addressed and how best to address it. Knowing what your responsibilities actually are is part of this year's balancing act. There may be a lot of sorting out to do. Be patient. Trust yourself.

Spend plenty of time alone, with no distractions. Minimize your activities wherever possible. You need time for yourself. You need to *think* and *feel*. Listen to the questions you ask yourself, and hear the responses you give. Listen to how you argue with yourself when alternatives appear. Be aware of your resistance to change. Feel yourself resisting - fighting off - your own changing reality. When you become aware of this inner battle, you will also realize that the time for forgiveness has arrived. Everything starts from within. Therefore, forgiving yourself for whatever you are regretting right now will enable this year's healing process to begin.

Right now, the door of opportunity is knocking. Can you hear it? If not, you must bring yourself face to face with your own reality and accept whatever feelings arise. Your feelings *are* your reality and have much to teach you. How can you solve a problem if you reject the possibility that an alternative exists?

Once you have assessed what your circumstances actually are, consider your own needs and desires. How do you *want* things to turn out? What do you actually *desire* in your life? Then consider the reality of the outside world; this changing, evolving, dangerous world in which *dependence* is no longer an option. Then ask yourself if your Will is free - or is it blind? Are you free, or are you trapped in stagnation because what you have is no longer viable or what you want is no longer possible? Are you free, or are you imprisoned by the fear of your responsibility to *change* things?

January is a time of serious assessment which will show you a new and more satisfying direction. Let go of what is no longer available and realize that your old familiar way of doing things is no longer appropriate. Take charge of your life as you travel through these confusing evolutionary times. Broaden your outlook. Accept what cannot be done and focus on what can. Work on restoring the LOVE which your anxiety now threatens to destroy.

Right now, guilt is holding you responsible for everything that does not feel good. It is even telling you that the mistakes others have made or are likely to make are your fault. Never forget that guilt is the great deceiver. It is twisting the word "responsibility" in a way that makes you feel responsible for someone else's problem. On the contrary, the mistakes your loved ones have made, and will make, the situations they have encountered or will encounter, are part of their *own* learning experience. Your responsibility here is to accept that fact and wish them well as they travel the route they have chosen to travel.

If someone in your life is unable to take responsibility for themselves then, of course, your help will be needed. January's combination of cyclical energies are urging you to accept this responsibility lovingly and, at the same time, find a way to balance it with your own needs.

~ February ~
6 Year - 8 Month

Advice is seldom welcome and those who
want it the most always like it the least.
EARL OF CHESTERFIELD

Approach this month in a confident and businesslike manner. The circumstances of February will affect your finances, your home, material belongings, and your long term security. A change may occur in the way your career or outside interests are affecting your domestic and personal life, and vice versa. This is an opportunity filled month when understanding and warmth can be restored to all areas of your life, creating a more balanced and comfortable feeling all around.

Traditionally, 8 is a cycle of reward. In reality, it is a karmic cycle which returns to you whatever you have put out into the world. It emphasizes personal power and prosperity and is often linked to money and business. A heightened sense of responsibility is likely in your financial affairs and career activities.

Remember that the 6 year cycle relates to education, so welcome the opportunity to learn new things which will help boost your career and finances. You may even learn things which can enhance the material well-being of a loved one. He or she may not necessarily agree with you, however. Never mind. Give your advice, and let them make their own decisions.

You can make things happen by acting decisively, realistically, and responsibly. Do not allow greed to be your motivation. This may cause even your best laid plans to backfire on you. If you concentrate only on profit or on the potential rewards, you will be reducing your focus on what needs to be *done* in order to manifest these things.

Now you need a high self-esteem and a strong faith in your abilities. You also need to recognize when a mistake is not a mistake and when bad luck is actually a blessing in disguise. Be alert and aware, and understand the value of what you already have. What you have here is an opportunity and not a problem. It is not necessarily the way things are that constitute a problem, but only the way you *think* they are. Someone may be taking a path which is not right for you. If it feels extreme in any way, remember that you do not have to follow.

Establish new priorities. Consider how your actions may affect those around you. Maintain a loving balance between *them* and your outside life. Express yourself with confidence and affection. Balance does not require you to stretch yourself uncomfortably between your different responsibilities. This indicates extreme behavior. Balance creates time and space for all that is important to you. By the way, what *is* important to you right now?

Try to overcome conflicts between your business life and your personal life by expressing yourself clearly in both areas. Organize and manage your various activities so that they can coexist freely and peacefully. Clearly specify your outside commitments to your loved ones and tell them you need their cooperation Outside associates should be made aware of your personal responsibilities. By placing your cards on the table you will be protecting yourself from future disappointment and resentment. Understand your own needs and feelings too. Redesign your life accordingly. The creative nature of the 6 energy will help you here.

As this month's 8 vibration relates so strongly to money and security, you may want to review your goals and your sense of duty in these matters. Are you caught up in a chain of dependency or irresponsibility? On whom are you dependent for your finances? Who is dependent on you? What do you want in your life, and how do you intend getting it? February is a time to take the necessary steps which will draw you closer to your true desires. This month, you have the POWER.

~ March ~
6 Year - 9 Month

We tend to think of the rational as a higher order,
but it is the emotional that marks our lives.
One often learns more from ten days of agony
than from ten years of contentment.
MERLE SHANE

The energy surrounding you now is urging you to initiate or accept some kind of ENDING, so that you can move away from an extreme situation and bring yourself into a more balanced existence. Take an honest look at your ever changing reality and you will know that now is the right time - the natural time - for this ending to occur. It will clear the path ahead so that a new opportunity can be seen. Be aware of any obsessive or possessive behavior this month. If it exists anywhere in your life, now is a good time to put an end to it. This is not love.

There may be another less apparent aspect of your life which is ready to end. If this is the case, life will bring it to an end for you. Perhaps you are facing an obstacle which could push you toward one extreme or another. Go into your deepest feelings and accept the reality of everything that is happening to you and those you care for. Listen to the answers that arise from your own emotions which, this month, are likely to be running very high indeed.

It is time to let go of a feeling or belief that is keeping you tied to the past. Do not be afraid of endings. They set you free from the pain of yesterday. But do not deny your feelings *about* an ending. If you cannot get past the feeling, you will be unable to proceed, no matter how much you deny that the feeling exists. Don't rush. It takes time, sometimes a great deal of time, to fully experience and heal from a feeling as powerful and as conclusive as the one you are likely to feel this month.

March may bring a dramatic situation into your life concerning a family member, friend, or a cherished idea, project, or possession. Extreme grief or extreme happiness may be experienced. Remember that you are learning the *true* meaning of love this year, and that love is often hidden beneath certain judgments you have made over a long period of time. Of course, not all endings need be traumatic ones. You may experience an ending in March which feels like the weight of the world has been lifted from your shoulders, unless guilt has convinced you that it is wrong to feel this way. Perhaps it is guilt that needs to be ended now, or some other feeling, belief, or attitude that is preventing love from flowing freely.

Notice where unwanted items and circumstances are cluttering up your day to day life and preventing forward movement. It is time to put an end to these areas of stagnation.

9 is also the energy of GIVING, purely for the sake of the pleasure it creates. But giving is not confined to only material or monetary contributions. Giving comes in many forms. Acceptance, love, laughter, understanding, gratitude, and encouragement are the greatest gifts you can bestow on those around you at this time.

There will be a need to give something back this month. You must do so without expecting anything in return. Not even a thank you. No matter how you find yourself giving this March, remember that in order to give you must first *let go* of something.

~ April ~
6 Year - 1 Month

Relationships are like pressures
that push you in 36 directions of the compass.
But, as in a crowded streetcar, if you learn how to
maintain your balance against all the weights,
you might arrive at yourself.
DIANA CHANG

A change in your personal or professional life will occur this month. It may be implemented by you or caused by a change in someone else's life. Expect a change in your attitude toward those people and things you regard as 'yours'. Notice how current events are affecting your plans. Because so much emotion is involved here, you need to be careful that extreme beliefs and attitudes do not take over and damage the enormous potential for *independence* that April offers.

There may be a sense that you now stand alone in the world and that the burden of finding solutions, for yourself and others, is on your shoulders. Remember that no matter how many people surround you, you are an *individual* with a power all your own. When you accept this, you will see that the more you try to control another, the more resistance they will give you. And the more understanding you show, the more you will be understood.

April is filled with important lessons about uniqueness and individuality. You will need to see others as they are rather than how you would prefer them to be. Imagine yourself in the shoes of someone else. Imagine what life *feels* like from this person's perspective. This is a month of fresh ideas and new beginnings. It is designed to improve the balance between your private life and your outside obligations.

Whatever steps you have been contemplating, especially with regard to your own desires, now is the time to take them. Consider the truth - the reality - of the situation and go with your feelings. Take action. Take a chance. You are now ready for a much greater level of responsibility in a new and more fulfilling direction.

There may be a tendency to want to take control because you feel it is your responsibility to do so. Maybe it is. But, rather than setting rules and regulations for others, concentrate on establishing a realistic strategy which respects the Free Will of all concerned.

Certain responsibilities you took on in the past may not have been yours to begin with. Now you may resent the restrictions they are causing. Perhaps someone else is ready to take responsibility here. If this is the case, bring your own needs back into focus.

Try not to impose a dictatorial approach on others and you will find that April flows beautifully as you utilize your power to change things.

Change is likely to occur all around you. One change can trigger a whole sequence of changes which can catch you off guard. Keep your wits about you and look for the advantages involved. While an important change takes place of its own accord, try to initiate some constructive changes of your own or, at least, move closer toward making those changes. Where conditions are making you unhappy, this month provides the opportunity to *change* them.

Begin something new. April provides an element of 'good luck' to a *new* project because the 1 cycle favors anything that is *started*. You may start a new responsibility or bring added independence into your life by ridding yourself of a responsibility that is not yours. If you cannot begin something new, then at least start a new phase of an existing activity. Whether you make this start yourself, or whether life makes it for you, April marks a positive new beginning in your life.

Emphasize your individuality by utilizing your unique skills and resources. Be creative. Be original. Be yourself. You now have the power to create something out of nothing and are likely to feel energetic and eager to proceed with certain plans. Retain your enthusiasm despite the attempts of someone else, or perhaps your own doubt, fear, or guilt, to curtail your efforts. Try to include others in your activities, especially if you are in a long-term relationship, have children or pets, etc. Make time for all that are family. If you have no biological family to speak of, remember that family are those with whom you are *familiar*; those with whom you share your life on a day to day basis.

This is a good time to embark on a domestic project for the purpose of beautifying the home or adding to its value. A fresh start in a relationship stands a good chance of success when a new understanding has been reached. Someone close may be experiencing a new beginning of their own, requiring the whole family to adopt a new agenda or attitude. Encourage, don't criticize. You may discover a new talent, idea, or 'gift', not necessarily your own, which could benefit you or someone else. Until you try new things, ideas, or directions, you may never know what opportunities are out there for you. Do not dwell on your weaknesses. Focus on your strengths instead. Accept what must be done, then do it.

~ May ~
6 Year - 2 Month

Peace can never be achieved by force.
It can only be achieved by understanding.
ALBERT EINSTEIN

Slow down. Relax. Be very patient as the circumstances of someone else seem to get in your way this month. The art of problem solving, as I am sure you know by now, is one of this year's principle themes. This month, life may send you a sensitive situation to practice on.

The 2 cycle is trying to teach you the method by which we must all learn to solve problems in a peaceful society. 2 is an energy of partnership, cooperation, patience, peace, love, sensitivity, compassion, and connection.

Miracles can happen if you are patient enough to wait for them. Slow down. Relax. Take everything in your stride. Try to understand, deeply and compassionately, what is really going on in the life of someone who is causing you concern.

Your own plans are on hold for a very good reason: to improve the overall *timing* which will ensure success and to heal parts of yourself, probably your emotional self, which need attention. Do not force your plans ahead or you may push them into the wrong place and time. Right now, focus on someone or something else, and do so patiently. By diverting your attention to another person or situation, a new experience will arise from which you will gain some valuable information. This new intelligence can also help restore balance to an important relationship.

If you find yourself saying, "I don't have time for this", take some deep breaths and relax. Forget about making time and squeezing people in. Just *take* the time. The world is not going to fall apart if you take a little time to sort out an uncomfortable situation, no matter how much you want to avoid it. The truth is that your world could fall apart if you don't.

Yes, there are many details that need attention. Take care of them all, but relax while you are doing so. It will be to your advantage to actually look for details that others have avoided. This is no time to push blindly ahead or to deny the importance of what life is now asking you to deal with. Let go of all that stress and go slowly and peacefully instead. Use persuasion, not force. Be diplomatic and courteous. The people with whom you must interact this month are all potential partners in one way or another. Allow them to relax *with* you.

Someone close needs your attention, patience, and understanding. Don't judge or condemn. Making others feel guilty or afraid is a common and deceptive means of controlling them, especially among those who claim to love each other. This behavior no longer has a place in your world. You now have an opportunity to solve a problem which affects not just one, but many people.

You may have to examine your own tactics and motivations very carefully to realize just how subtly you have been controlling others or have allowed your feelings toward others to control your behavior. You may be held fully accountable for past actions. Don't fight it. Life is merely pointing out a mistake you have made so that you do not have to repeat it again.

Insecurity, anger, and fear must be recognized and given outer expression. Own up and take full responsibility for the role you, yourself, have played in this month's conflicts. Blame and guilt can achieve nothing. Find the deep-rooted emotional *cause* of all that is going on in your life. This is the only solution available to you.

Both the 6 and 2 energies influence your *relationships*, and you will want to eliminate the power struggle that exists within them. Love must be free in order to be love. Relax. You *know* each other. It's not as if you are total strangers. The chances are you have known each other for a long time. So why not just relax with that fact and seek healing instead of deeper conflict? 2 is the energy of diplomacy. This means that in order to resolve a conflict, everyone involved must feel as if they have won something. The needs and feelings of all concerned must be taken into consideration. You see, *consideration* is what this month is about.

Insecurity breeds obsession and this, of course, can jeopardize *all* your relationships. Your intentions may be good, but the 6 energy can cause you to become overly concerned, even paranoid, about the way others are conducting their lives or disrupting yours. This can cause you to act rashly. Balance requires that you do not judge a person from only your point of view.

Consider the unique circumstances, the personal history, the freedom, and the *feelings* of that person. Do not try to force someone into a position which is merely convenient for you. This is extreme behavior, and the only thing it creates is war. This is a month in which you are being taught about peace which, of course, starts within.

~ June ~
6 Year - 3 Month

One must have the courage to dare.
DOSTOEVSKY, CRIME AND PUNISHMENT

The 3 energy is so light and carefree that you may have a problem noticing it, let alone receiving what it has to offer. This month's circumstances may not feel light and carefree at all. Certain extremes may rise to the surface and create a tense atmosphere. This only goes to show that the world is sadly lacking in what the 3 energy offers. 3 is the energy of happiness, open communication, friendliness, beauty, networking, and creativity.

This month, 3 reminds you to take the time to recognize and appreciate the happiness you *already* have. It is urging you to turn your closest relationships into loving friendships. Optimism is called for. Get into the frame of mind that nothing is going to get you down. But before you can do this, you may first have to release a great deal of old sadness, pain, anger, or grief under which your natural optimism is buried. Release those old emotions, especially those feelings of resentment, and feel the warmth and new understanding that replaces them.

Whether it feels this way or not, you are now in a cycle of joy, laughter, social interaction, and natural beauty. Yes, these elements are at your disposal throughout June. These are the gifts which will make this month a loving and successful one. These are the gifts which will improve the very texture of your life.

There is no need to force a smile or keep up the phony appearance of happiness. Just allow yourself to *feel* it, and it will be genuine. When guilt jumps on you and tells you it is wrong to feel happiness when others cannot, remember that guilt is an unremitting deceiver.

Other people cannot recover from their problems while guilt is telling them that they are responsible for *your* unhappy mood. This way guilt wins by bringing everyone down. Let others draw from your optimism and cheerfulness.

3 is a cycle of physical attraction. 6 is a cycle of emotional magnetism. This powerful combination of energies can be used for healing yourself, and for helping others to see how they, too, can heal. Seeing the lighter side of a situation will help to activate this loving power.

June is a time for social interaction and friendliness. If you have to work, have fun working. If it is impossible to enjoy your work, it may be time to consider a different way of making a living. We are living at a time in which it is essential for all of us to discover the lives we would love to live, and then start living those dreams.

Try to bring fun into the home. Liven up your relationships. Minimize mundane chores and get creative instead. Let your guard down and be yourself. Express your affection, be helpful, and notice that what you once considered to be a problem is really not so important after all. Focus on what *matters* to you. Socialize and communicate with friends and family. Do not assume that everyone will get along, and do not become trapped in the problems of others. Each of us has a responsibility to solve our own problems and to stop creating problems that need never arise.

In family or social settings, there is often an urge to gossip and criticize, especially when the 3 energy is active. This is 3s way of pointing out that whatever you judge and criticize in others are the very same flaws you hate in yourself but cannot admit to. When you see yourself in people you do not like, what you are actually seeing is the extent to which you dislike yourself.

3's vibrations respond to your own denials because 3 is the energy of creativity, not destructiveness. You may, however, have to contend with a destructive element this month - someone who is far from creative, far from cordial, and far from any semblance of happiness. Do not be drawn into this vacuum of negative energy. This month you may have to deal with one of 6s *extreme* situations, and it may be a lot closer to home than you think.

This cycle emphasizes communication. The more you express yourself truthfully *and* diplomatically, the better the results will be. Know what is appropriate for a particular situation. Balance your sense of humor so that others are not overwhelmed, offended, shocked, or bored by it.

Having fun does not mean that you have to be funny all the time, or that other emotions should be ignored so that you can give the appearance of having fun. It means enjoying what you are doing, that's all. There is no need, whatsoever, for insensitivity. There is no need to control or dominate. The happiness that this month is all about can only come from within and can only have a positive effect on others when it is *genuine*.

A friend may come to you with a problem or a friend may *be* a problem now. Offer ideas that enable this person to solve his or her own problem. A true friend will cooperate wherever possible. A true friend will not take away another's Free Will by assuming responsibility and, thus, controlling this person's life. Neither can you allow a friend's problem to jeopardize your own well-being. Remember your priorities. Do what you feel is right.

Spend some time enjoying the natural environment. Many of the answers you seek can be found in nature. People are only one small part of nature, and you will be amazed at the solutions that come to you by relating the circumstances of your life to nature's eternal current of ongoing cycles, ebb and flow, day and night, beauty and beast, life and death. Human nature is only a small part of the big picture. Only when a broader understanding of this is reached will you see that your current circumstances have a deeply healing and loving purpose.

~ July ~
6 Year - 4 Month

Be certain that the direction you are taking
is the direction you want to take.
How much do you really want
what you say you really want?
SALLY BROMPTON

July's combination of energies emphasize organization, work, effort, responsibility, love, family, and healing. These vibrations respond positively to natural order and simplicity of system. The events of this month will signify just how great or exaggerated your responsibilities actually are. Unrealistic responses from you or someone close to you, are likely to bring delays, frustrations, and disappointment. If this is the case, your obligations may start to feel oppressive. Remind yourself that the purpose of the 6 year cycle is to make you aware of which responsibilities are yours, and which are *not*. Stop making unnecessary work for yourself.

The chances are that you feel responsible for something that is beyond your control. Others may be adding to your stress by holding you responsible for something you may not have done or, perhaps, would rather not admit to. Guilt may be rearing its ugly head in an effort to bring your life to a standstill.

Whatever transpires this July is happening so that you can bring order and ease back into your life. Yes, you may now be asked to pay for past mistakes. But the more you resist this, and the more stress and tension you hold on to, the closer you will be drawn to certain extremes which will only make matters worse. Pretending you are calm is denying reality. *Be* calm.

Balance the events of your life by accepting and organizing them. Be practical and rational. Where there is chaos or confusion, face the facts and sort it out. By now, others will have recognized your role of problem-solver and will be looking to you for solutions. The answers you need lie somewhere under the great deluge of physical and emotional clutter that seems to be everywhere. Take care of all the details that arise as well as those that have been neglected, no matter how boring or time consuming they may be.

Your tolerance level is close to its limits now. It is, therefore, time to expand your ability to tolerate so that you can push what you thought were your limits further away from you. At first you may feel boxed in, restricted, lonely, or powerless to help yourself or someone else. Wishing the problem would go away or denying it exists will make matters worse.

This month's circumstances offer you the chance to transform a problem into a major breakthrough which will improve the entire structure and atmosphere of your life.

Realism, determination, effort, practicality, and love will get the necessary action rolling. One positive action will lead to another. Stop struggling against the reality of it all. Accept that this problem exists and then set about finding the solution. This is no time to be stubborn, judgmental, pessimistic, unconcerned, controlling, or afraid. Respond in a way that can *solve* the situation, rather than exacerbate or prolong it. If you cannot gain the support of others, then you will have to go it alone. Do not waste your time on guilt or blame. The events of this month require you to keep an open mind, a mind that is willing to consider alternatives.

There may be a tendency to want to do things in what you believe is the proper way, or the way guilt has told you is right. This tendency may even be the *cause* of the original problem. There are always alternatives and choices. Be as flexible as you can. If a task seems too big to handle, just chip away at it with determination. Stop struggling, stop panicking, and exert *effort* instead. Have you imprisoned yourself in a responsibility that is not entirely yours? Is a certain situation depleting your ability to think and act for yourself? It is time to break out of that jail. Either remove yourself, physically, from the problem, or expand your levels of acceptance and tolerance.

And what if an obstacle is fixed and unmovable - a long term or life sentence? It may take some time to accept this, but such an obstacle is exactly where it should be. It is a diversion that will prevent you from going any further in a direction that is not right for you. It is an opportunity to discover a more appropriate and effective way of doing things. It may even be an opportunity to discover your true direction in life. Assess all the details of your current situation and you will see the benefits it is offering.

A particular problem may, at first, seem like a huge mountain that dominates your entire existence. Well, you are about to climb that mountain, one step at a time, and carefully. Take the first step and you'll be on your way. If the first step doesn't hold, it simply means that you have not taken all the details into account. Reassess everything and try again. With realistic planning and determination, you will eventually reach the top, and you will do so with a feeling of accomplishment, freedom, and confidence. You will. And you will then see the exciting new array of options that are suddenly available to you.

~ August ~
6 Year - 5 Month

> *The bonds which unite another person to ourselves*
> *exist only in our minds.*
> MARCEL PRIEST

An unexpected development will occur out of the blue. You are now surrounded by the energy of FREEDOM. Some people are at ease in this vibration, while others realize just how afraid of change and freedom they actually are. At this point of the journey, it becomes apparent that others need their freedom, too.

Of course, it can be painful when we see a loved one making a mistake or being used, manipulated, or even endangered by others. If this is the case, a firm stand must be taken. But you must be careful that your reactions are not playing right into the hands of whoever else is involved. If you accuse someone of something that you yourself may be guilty of, then you may be handing them ammunition to use against you. The secret lies in the art of compromise. Yes, you do have an enormous responsibility here, but in order for this matter to be solved amicably, everyone must feel as if they have won something, however small it may be.

The nature of the 5 cycle is an exciting one because it is magnetically attracted to your own *expectations*. Whatever you expect to materialize will materialize. However, your expectations run very deep and are not always what you think they are. They are not mere wishful thinking, optimism or pessimism. Your expectations stem from your *core* beliefs and deepest feelings. The events of this month will show you whether you really are aware of your feelings and motivations or whether you are denying them.

First, observe the small changes taking place around you which are offering you more freedom. There may be an ongoing obstacle related to home, family, or a particular relationship. There may be an aspect you have lived with for so long that you had forgotten it was something you disliked intensely. You got used to it. Quite unexpectedly, that whole situation may disappear or reverse itself. Once you start to recognize these small changes, your level of expectation will rise and more beneficial changes will start to occur.

You are now being urged to recognize a mistake, learn from it, and then profit from the experience. What is the biggest or most frequent mistake you have made in your life pertaining to family and responsibility? Are you now about to repeat it in some way?

In the 6 year cycle, one of the most common mistakes is that of judging someone else's situation and then interfering in their business, because you think you know what is best for them, or that you can "save" them in some way. When this is not your real responsibility (and it seldom is), the obligation you have assumed to becomes a burden for everyone concerned. This can lead to great resentment and even hatred on all sides. By judging this way, you can create serious trouble for yourself and those you think it is your duty to help. Cooperate if possible but, in most cases, let others live their unique lives and solve their own unique problems.

In a month when consequences are a major factor, do not jump too quickly into a new responsibility. How will this new obligation affect your *long-term* freedom and security? What sacrifices will the others in your life have to make? What is your motivation for wanting this new responsibility? Where will it lead? What are your options and alternatives? What does guilt have to say about all this? What do you really *feel*?

Sometimes, what you think is a mistake is not a mistake at all. It could be a sign that a positive change of direction is available. Try to recognize these signs as they appear. This way, you can benefit from what you thought was a stroke of bad luck or a mistake. Often when we are looking for one particular thing, we discover something else entirely which makes us realize the irrelevance of what we were originally seeking.

August's 5 energy stresses the importance of *Free Will*, yours and other people's. It illuminates the various ways in which you are abusing your own freedom, or allowing others to abuse it. In this unpredictable month, when anything can happen, try to avoid impulsive reactions. Be aware of any addictions you may have. Any form of dependency reveals *missing* freedom. 5 exposes one's addictions to relationships, duty, food, alcohol, drugs (including prescriptions), sex, TV, extravagance, gambling, status, or anything else which has the power to control you or those around you. Changes are needed so that you are free to *enjoy* life.

Physically and mentally, you will be at your most resourceful, provided you approach situations with optimism and realistic expectations. Ideas will flow in abundance. Put them into action. Opportunity is now knocking loudly, but you may have to get out of the house or your usual routine in order to hear it.

You may feel that your home is where you want to be, but you may not want to be stuck in the rut of ongoing responsibilities. Try to take a break or vacation. 5 urges travel, changes of scenery and culture - the exciting, different, and unusual. All of these factors are available to you, although you may have to do some juggling to make them a reality.

Sudden events may arise which may actually force you away from the home front. Try to include the people you love in your new adventures, otherwise there may be some burned bridges to mend next month.

~ September ~
6 Year - 6 Month

We do not remember days. We remember moments.

CESARE PAVESE

September's double 6 cycle highlights your responsibilities and duties, making them seem both satisfying *and* restrictive. Focus on the people and things you really care about. This is a time for love, acceptance, forgiveness, and a brand new understanding that comes from the acknowledgement of your own insecurities.

If there are still areas of disagreement or ill feeling, now is the time to set things straight once and for all. Approach others with a real desire to be understood and an equal desire to understand. Accept their right to be who they are and to live their own lives.

There may be some real problems to solve this month - *or* - you may realize that this year-long cycle of solving problems, counseling, and healing is coming to an end. Be sure you are not simply creating problems now for the sake of having something to solve.

What about your own life? Your own needs? Have you stayed true to your principal responsibility to yourself and your own Free Will? With all this in mind, determine what your obligations are now. Your priorities should have changed considerably since the beginning of the year.

The events of this month will strongly affect your feeling of belonging and are likely to involve your closest relationships. Try to understand the individual personalities and circumstances of all concerned. Do whatever you can to provide a harmonious and beautiful atmosphere within this circle.

You may be called upon for advice or practical assistance, and you will probably be only too happy to provide it - *or* - your input may not be sought at all. If this is the case, understand that you are now being released from certain obligations. Perhaps others have finally learned the lessons you were trying to teach them all along. Perhaps they are standing on their own two feet at last. Do not feel offended if others no longer have to depend on you. The crisis is over. This may be difficult to understand at first, but you must now release your dependence on *them*.

Express yourself openly and honestly without imposing your beliefs and rules on anyone else. Enjoy the beauty and warmth of the love that surrounds you. Congratulate yourself on providing a stability you often had your doubts about. 6 is a cycle of *parenting*, and whether there are children in your life or not, you have been a parent to someone or something this year. Perhaps you yourself were the child involved. One way or another, this year has been just as it should be, an *emotional* experience.

Consider any feelings of loneliness. You have spread your love in many directions, yet you feel alone or even abandoned. Could it be that you have still not learned that until you love yourself first, the love you need most of all cannot be yours?

You have learned so much about responsibility in the past ten months, and soon you will embark on a new journey of discovery. *Self* discovery. This will begin in October and will last for fifteen months. There is more for you to learn and discover about yourself than you can possibly fathom at this time.

~ October ~
6 Year - 7 Month

I look over the various parts of my character with perplexity.
I recognize that I am made up of several persons,
and that the person who at the moment has the upper hand,
will eventually give place to another.
But who is the real one? All of them? Or none?
SOMERSET MAUGHM

This is an excellent time for study, research, writing, teaching, and becoming aware of your own special inner strength. Spend as much time alone as you can. Learn to *enjoy* your own company. Think about the people you love. Understand your purpose and position within this group. Exercise your mind and *feel* whatever you are feeling. If there are still problems to sort out, now is the time to analyze the situation and look for constructive answers. But don't force things. Don't overexert yourself. This is a time to think, feel, reflect, and plan your route into the future.

The magnetic pull of next year's 7 cycle is beginning to alter the texture of your life. Your view of the world is changing, and you may start to feel uncertain about life itself, particularly where family and romantic matters are concerned. You may also realize that you want more than this - *much* more - from your life.

You will need to be alone so that you can think things out. If you deny these feelings or distract yourself from them, not only will you still need to be alone, but you will also feel *lonely*. Being alone is part of October's positive agenda.

Pessimism or even depression may surface from time to time because you are unsure of what lies ahead. There can be a tendency to think the worst. This indicates that your fears are coming to the surface and need to be recognized, experienced, and expressed. *Do not be afraid to be afraid.* Only when you genuinely feel your fear will you realize that its purpose is a protective one. Only then will you hear what it is telling you to do or not do.

Consider how the past is now being vividly reflected into the present. This is happening so that you can develop your emotional and spiritual awareness and *plan* your future out of your present circumstances. You are in a cycle of wisdom and understanding, and this is a time of self-appreciation.

Your intuition is made up from your collective feelings. It is trying to make itself heard at this time. Shhhh. Listen. Listen. Your thoughts and feelings are separate energies. They need to communicate freely with each other so that an agreement can be reached inside you. Where there is confusion, relax all mental judgments so that your feelings have a chance to make themselves known. Quiet time alone, with no distractions, will accommodate this healing process. There is no need to become a hermit or to allow your different wavelength to alienate you from others. Just take some time and space for yourself when you need to.

October is a time for *planning*, not doing, not yet. You may feel an urge to criticize everyone and everything around you, as you notice flaws and imperfections in yourself and others. Try to remain flexible and open minded, poised and contemplative. Find the balance between overstatement and understatement.

7 is the cycle of secrets and mystery. Somehow, these two words will fit accurately into your life this month, as you reflect on the energy of someone who is dear to you. Only by coming to terms with a secret you have kept from yourself - a secret *feeling* - possibly about a loved one - will you ever be able to relax with yourself. Be honest. Admit how you really feel about this individual, because acceptance of this feeling will allow sadness or anger to evolve into love.

~ November ~
6 Year - 8 Month

> *To know what you prefer instead of*
> *humbly saying Amen to what the world*
> *tells you you should prefer, is to have*
> *kept your soul alive.*
> ROBERT LOUIS STEVENSON

Snap out of it, my friend. This is no time to feel pessimistic or indifferent. November's powerful vibrations provide an opportunity to take control of your own life. The plans you made last month should now be activated. This will bring a more satisfactory balance between personal matters and your business or financial interests. Devise realistic *long-range* plans which will reduce any conflicts between domestic and outside activities. The events of this month are likely to affect both.

The 8 energy works by knowing what it already *has* and then expanding the value of it. It learns how to use its existing resources to acquire what it *wants*. This year's 6 energy is very creative. It will help you to find ways to create opportunity from existing resources. The incoming 7 vibration of next year will teach you things you did not know before. 7 also offers the wisdom to know that your resources do not always pertain to funds or material assets but rather, to your expertise and talents. Even if you do not have a penny to your name, the combination of this month's energies will enable you to make things happen, get things done, create something from nothing, or take something you already have and increase its worth.

You are almost at the end of the 6 year cycle in which you have learned about responsibility and love. November emphasizes your inborn power to survive and prosper. But in order to survive and prosper in a world that is changing so rapidly, it is also your *responsibility* to know what is happening out there in the big world, and be aware of how others use their powers to diminish yours.

Prosperity is a fundamental part of life. Yet, so many people have difficulty in creating and maintaining it. This is because what we have always believed to be prosperity is, in fact, destroying human life, animal life, plant life, ocean life, aerial life, and Earth herself. Our concept of prosperity must change. Of course, wherever there is a need for change there are always people who would rather die or kill in the name of *tradition* and often in the name of *God*, than allow something new and loving to happen.

The predominantly masculine millennium of the 1000s has now evolved into the feminine 2000s. *Everything* is changing. Why have the last thousand years been a miserable repeat of war and manipulation? Because we did not learn that peace cannot exist without freedom. Women may not be ruling the world in the days to come, but the feminine energy that is in both women *and* men must be allowed to express itself in its own natural way - *emotionally*. It is only from a deeper understanding of this process that peace can be achieved. And it will start with our own personal relationships.

Why do we call ourselves the human *race*? Because, so far, life has been just that. A race for supremacy. One big competition. One big war. As this violent cycle comes to an end, there are still those who are so engrossed in the human "race" that they will do *anything* to hold on to it. Just listen to the extreme views of certain leaders as they quote history and pledge to repeat it rather than change it. Listen to certain religious leaders placing blame, preaching hate, and applauding war as if to say it is God's Will that we destroy ourselves. Life's cyclical nature is scientifically indisputable. So why do we continue to deny the reality that Free Will *is* God's Will?

And why is it so important for *you* to understand all of this during November in your 6 year cycle? Because it is imperative to *your* future that you look at and accept the reality of what is happening in the world. It is vital that you respond to it in a way that feels right for you. 6 is the energy of THE HOME. This planet is your home, and everyone on it is your family. Ensuring a peaceful and prosperous future for yourself and your family is what this entire year has been about. The circumstances of this month are providing the greatest clue to the direction your life will take in the months and years to come.

~ December ~
6 Year - 9 Month

Never forget that the merits of any relationship
are of far greater significance than
any minor flaws or defects.
SALLY BROMPTON

<u>This is a time of giving, ending, and letting go.</u> The phasing out of an activity or situation will add harmony to a relationship or to the household itself. There may be some strong emotions involved. There is no point in holding on to a responsibility that is no longer yours. Remember that it is far easier to end something in a 9 cycle than at any other time.

Domestically, it is a time to discard old unusable things and clean up the debris within the home. End any areas of misunderstanding or discord by allowing your feelings to surface truthfully. End imbalances and power struggles and allow peace and understanding to replace them. Wherever guilt or control are present, love is not. Harmony, forgiveness, equality, and tolerance are the positive factors of this emotional month. Whatever comes to an end now, whether it happens of its own accord or you have implemented it yourself, will set the tone for next 12 months.

For you, next year is a cycle of quiet introspection, study, learning, analyzing, thinking, planning, and feeling. If this is not quite what you had in mind for yourself in the months to come, understand that learning and evolving is our purpose for being here and that each of us has a unique creative role to play within that purpose.

It is in the 7 year that all the imperfections in one's life are relentlessly exposed. It is also in the 7 year that we gain the wisdom and the expertise with which to *perfect* our creative purpose. And the year after that, the 8 energy ensures that we reap the rewards and benefits of the effort involved.

But for now, end this year by showing those you care for just how much you have learned about love and responsibility. Feel the love that surrounds you and let those who matter to you know how much you appreciate them. Love them for who they are instead of wishing they were, somehow, different.

Allow December to be a very special time for love, family, romance, harmony, and beauty. Traditionally, this is the time of year when sentimentality arises, hearts are softened, wrongs are forgiven, and presents are exchanged. Realize that the most valuable present of all is NOW: *The moment; the present.* Fill it with love and give it to everyone around you. Exchange your present with the present of someone else by accepting *their* reality. Forgive. Let go of the past.

Whatever you have loved and learned this year - *whatever feels good* - never forget it. Hold on to the love and the understanding. Bring it with you as midnight of December 31st arrives, and you cross over into the powerful 7 year cycle of wisdom and understanding - *the great inner voyage.*

The 7 Year Cycle

the inner voyage -
a year of learning

> *Life is a process of growing and outgrowing,*
> *and what fits snugly today, be it an idea,*
> *attitude, or belief, may be entirely*
> *the wrong size tomorrow.*
> SALLY BROMPTON

Welcome to the 7 year cycle. The 7 energy flows in an atmosphere of privacy, solitude, and quietness. It is constantly seeking answers to its steady stream of questions about itself and life. It is seeking truth, wisdom, dignity, fulfillment, and perfection. This year, so are you.

Without knowing its purpose, the 7 journey can be confusing or even depressing. Therefore, from the very beginning, you must understand that no matter how much you want to surge ahead, this is a year of learning *how* to create the conditions you truly want for yourself. In the process, 7 will constantly expose you to those aspects of your life with which you have become dissatisfied, so that you can realize just how perfect and satisfying your life *can* become. Only then will you know where your unique talent fits in to this rapidly evolving world.

This is a self centered year in which you will know that you have far more potential than you ever realized. You will be seeking - and finding - the course or lifestyle which feels *right* for you. A more serious side of your nature will emerge, along with a stark awareness that the status quo is simply not good enough any more.

Instead of rushing out to find new opportunity, realize that opportunity is actually looking for *you*. Trying to force or push yourself ahead will only result in the same old feelings of dissatisfaction you thought your forcing and pushing would eliminate. This is not a time to do - it is a time to *be*. Slow down, stand still, and admit that you feel lost on life's great churning ocean.

Last year's responsibilities are no longer the driving force in your life. Suddenly, you are not at all sure of what you want. Even if you are sure of what you want, you will realize that you're never going to get it unless you make a serious commitment to it. Do not panic. Being lost may be the only way to find out where you are. The truth is that you are exactly where you are meant to be, and you are right on schedule.

This is a year of searching and learning. The 7 cycle is one of introspection, emotion, research, analysis, intuition, reflection, self-realization, seclusion, and, above all, FAITH. All of these energies are available to you, but it is up to you to utilize them in a way that will benefit you. This is meant to be a quieter, "inner" year in which you can learn the answers to your most burning and often avoided questions, particularly those which relate to you, to life itself, and your purpose in it.

Understand that the changes you desire will take time and effort. In order for new opportunities to come in, you will have to let go of some of your old beliefs and attitudes. This year, you must seek and find what is perfect and ideal for *you*, and then study and analyze what needs to be learned in order to make it your reality. It will take this entire year to figure things out, so don't assume that you already have the answers. Instant gratification is not on this year's agenda.

An unexpectedly slow pace may sometimes cause frustration and worry. At these times, remind yourself that this is not lack of movement, but a chance to move more realistically towards greater *long-term* goals.

Be patient. Very little activity is required during the 7 year cycle. Instead, this twelve-month journey should be used to devise specific goals and plans for *next year's* dynamic 8 cycle of action and material achievement. It should be used to gain the mental and emotional experience which will make next year's material achievements possible.

Although your life will be moving slowly, it is possible for wonderful and significant things to happen during the 7 year cycle. However, these advances and successes should be seen as stepping stones to the greater potential that will present itself next year. No matter what, you will be made very aware of the imperfections in your life so that you can study and analyze your options.

Everything you experience this year will be influenced by 7s power of *reflection*. Once this power is recognized, your life will become easier to understand and organize. Reflection means not only looking back and pondering the past, it also means looking at everything and everyone around you in the present and seeing your reality being mirrored back to you *through* these people and things.

Whatever or whoever affects you is your reality. If you are honest with yourself, you will notice that many aspects of your current reality feel out of place and are no longer desirable. No matter how spiritually or materially advanced you think you are, the reflective power of 7 will expose a painfully empty space in your life which can make you feel quite lonely. Only by accepting that this emptiness exists will you be able to discover the fullness of your true capabilities. You see, that emptiness is your own sad and unfulfilled *potential*.

Deep emotions may arise. Feel them. Experience them. Do not deny them. If ill health occurs in the 7 year cycle, it is usually an indication that there is so much buried emotion inside you which your body can no longer contain. All of this feeling is bursting to get out, and may do so in the form of what we call *depression*. In reality, it is *suppression* - the 'holding in' of your emotions. Once these emotions have been recognized, and the feelings involved have been released from your body, a tremendous improvement in the state of your mental, physical, and emotional health will occur.

If you find that you just cannot shake these heavy feelings, you would be well advised to go off somewhere quiet and read Part III, *LIFE, LOVE, AND LIBERTY IN THE NEW MILLENNIUM: The Healing Power Of Emotion*, which has been specifically written to help with emotional release.

There is never a need to hurt yourself or anyone else in the process of releasing your emotions. You do, however, need to spend some time alone, *with no distractions*, so that the feelings involved can be given your undivided attention. Sometimes your own feelings may take you completely by surprise, as if they were dark secrets you were keeping from yourself.

In the process, you will experience many sudden insights and revelations which will boost your confidence considerably. You will need more privacy than usual. Make sure you *take* the time and space you need. Know the difference between privacy and secrecy, and between planning and scheming.

There may be a tendency to overanalyze situations. This is a form of denial. To overanalyze means that you have already found the correct answer but are refusing to accept it. Then you go on searching for the answer you would prefer rather than accept the truth. Remember that the truth for one is not necessarily the truth for another, and that the truth has a tendency to drive you crazy just before it sets you free. However, you will soon realize that what you once thought was craziness is simply what it takes to free yourself from humanity's outdated beliefs.

Of course, you cannot expect others to automatically know what you are thinking or feeling, or what is happening to you, or to understand your mood swings and bouts of secrecy. They may think you are on a different wave-length entirely, and they are not wrong. You may be difficult to approach or comprehend this year. Even your closest companions cannot read your mind or feel your feelings. Communicate openly and honestly. Instead of taking your relationships for granted, seek to understand and enrich them.

Everyone in your life is now reflecting your reality back to you. Their behaviors and attitudes can teach you a lot about yourself and provide vital information as to what is really happening in your life and on this planet. It can feel a little lonely when you realize that some of the people you love do not understand what you are experiencing. Be patient. Eventually, they'll get it.

This is a year to study, research, analyze, and learn. The more something grabs your attention, the more you should pursue it. In order to bring this year's plans to fruition next year, study and focus are required. Your intuition, *your feelings*, will be of great help to you, because no matter what subject you find yourself studying, you will be able to sense or feel unexpected ways of using this information. A desire or dream you thought could never happen will soon become within your reach because you will know that it's all a matter of learning *how* to make it happen. Commit to this year's learning process, and it *will* happen next year.

Travel your 7 journey with optimism and enthusiasm. Plan your life so that you can spend plenty of time alone. Listen to your thoughts and feel your feelings. Take stock of your abilities and talents and work to expand them. Be aware of those approaches which are not working well for you. Remember that *everything*, including nature itself, is changing.

Determine where your most avid interest lies. Plan to *specialize* in that field. Use this year to gain knowledge, confidence, and expertise. Learn to appreciate YOU. Acknowledge just how gifted and unique you are. Accept the fact that you are a free spirit. Embrace the diversity of life and your place in it. Rediscover yourself.

Realize that life is not confined to one field or locality. Get reacquainted with the "big" world, along with its beauty *and* its horrors; its excitement *and* its mediocrity. Recognizing these extremes will help to secure a balanced position for yourself.

This is your year to learn the fundamentals of magic. Yes, magic. The secrets of manifestation. The laws of abundance. The Will must determine what it *wants* by the way it feels. Consciousness, which is the spirit or the mind, must then plan for this accomplishment by considering and orchestrating all the facts. You must face your fears and allow them to move through you and out of you. Through this process, you will know what needs to be feared and what does not.

Genuine intent to succeed will release you from the bondage of guilt. Without guilt, your reality can be seen for what it really is, and balance can be maintained. Without this balance, your magic may well materialize, but not as you had hoped. Acceptance of reality is the key and, for this, your total presence is required. Only by being completely *present* in a situation will you find the answers you need to weave the kind of magic you actually desire. This is why the 7 year cycle asks you to *be* rather than do.

Life stretches way beyond our own private environments. Beyond this living planet, we are connected to an entire universe which is brimming with life and energy that we cannot even imagine. Explore every aspect of your *own* reality and, by the end of this year, there will be no doubt in your mind as to who and what you are and where you fit in to the ever-changing kaleidoscope we call life.

If you think you already know your true identity, you may be in for some interesting, and possibly shocking, revelations. The 7 year cycle gives you the chance to discover how perfect you and your life can become when your emotional WILL teams up with KNOWLEDGE.

~ January ~
7 Year - 8 Month

It's never too late to be what you might have been.
GEORGE ELIOT

This month's energies emphasize finances, status, and career. You are likely to experience a loss of enthusiasm for a particular ambition or situation. The 7 and 8 vibrations are pointing out to you that certain circumstances have served their purpose but are now revealing their imperfections and limited long term potential. This is not a time for rash decisions or impulsive moves.

Being aware of the dullness that surrounds you is sufficient for now because the solutions are not immediately apparent. Sail through January's confusing energies by understanding that this entire year will be an exercise in self awareness and fine tuning which is meant to raise your belief in yourself. In fact, you are likely to spend this year working through the guilt, fear, or limiting beliefs which are preventing you from being who you really are. In order to succeed, you must resolve to be patient and constantly aware of your own thoughts and feelings.

Meanwhile, life will go on, and you will soon understand the necessity of this twelve month cycle of deep thought and meticulous *planning*. Any changes that take place this month, or this year, are for the purpose of positioning you closer to your true direction. You may not like where you are, but if you cannot see any other possibilities, stay where you are. On the other hand, if you believe that where you are is perfect, you may not yet have felt the greater potential stirring inside you. Give yourself time. You *will* feel it. This year of self-realization has only just begun.

Approach this month in an efficient and businesslike manner and be willing to learn new things, especially where career and finance are concerned. Be aware of everything that is going on around you, not only in your immediate vicinity but in the big world of economics and politics. Be aware of the instability of money itself, regardless of how vehemently others deny there is a problem. Stay clear of ideas and schemes that have out-lived their effectiveness to produce wealth. Be *aware*.

As more jobs and entire industries become obsolete, it is necessary to face new truths about making a living. There is very little financial security to be found in the traditional workplace. But there are exciting alternatives for those open minded enough to pursue them. An entirely new career dimension is emerging with the new millennium which involves cleaning up the physical, emotional, and social mess of an age that is OVER.

Success can no longer be defined in 20th century terms. Today's success is measured by the levels of *fulfillment* and *enjoyment* that our day-to-day lives provide. We are not on this Earth to labor under the control of indus-try. We are here, in this evolving creation, to *create*.

New fields of creative opportunity involve the environment, philan-thropy, healing, fitness, education, agriculture, the arts, law, natural sci-ence, services of all kinds, entertainment, and many other wide open areas that are creative rather than destructive.

This month, and throughout the year, you will be exposed to today's reality in many unexpected ways. It is up to you to follow your Will and find your own truth, so that real satisfaction and prosperity can enter your life. The answers are unlikely to leap out at you this month, but your awareness of the new possibilities can evolve into solid ambition later in the year. For now, keep your everyday life going, and spend as much time as you can contemplating these exciting possibilities.

~ February ~
7 Year - 9 Month

*If you find that someone is holding you back from
achieving those things you believe you want,
think again. Could it be that they are
merely the outer edge of your aspirations
and that, on another level entirely,
you seek fulfillment of a different kind?*

SALLY BROMPTON

9 is a cycle of endings, realization, emotions, giving, and interpretation. This powerful vibration has entered your life to wake up your subconscious mind, the part of your mind that is asleep. As you start to question your own beliefs, you must focus on your true feelings about your current situation. Life is asking you to end something that no longer serves a purpose. But don't jump to conclusions about this. Think about it carefully. What needs to be ended is your *reaction* to something or someone else.

Long forgotten memories of the past may emerge suddenly and mysteriously. They are being triggered by events taking place in the present. These memories, along with the feelings that were buried with them, must be allowed to flow without further denial because they represent the very things that are holding you back.

See how your current situation is connected to all the things you ever did, all the places you ever went, and everything you ever experienced. Each of your experiences automatically led to another, and then another until you finally reached this place called NOW.

But it is impossible to be fully in the present when half of you is stuck somewhere in the past. You will never be able to look forward if your emotions are always dragging you backwards. Release those buried emotions by feeling them and expressing them out of your body. This will bring you to where you are supposed to be; in the here and now. Yes, February is an emotional month.

Try to see your life as one continuing journey and not an erratic fragmented sequence of unrelated events. Whatever happened in the past must be accepted as part of your unique journey. Regrets are unnecessary because whatever happened to you in the past is only one small segment of your continuing voyage into freedom. Next month you may find yourself plotting an entirely new course.

Do not expect anything new to happen this month. Things are ending, not beginning. In fact, nothing new *can* begin until the necessary emotional endings take place. Getting your feelings out is the most needed ending of all right now. If you cannot be honest with yourself, who *can* you be honest with? How can you believe in someone else if you do not even believe in you?

These endings may affect other people in your life. A compassionate and sympathetic approach will benefit all concerned. The 9 cycle asks you to GIVE, simply for the sake of giving, without any expectation of return or thanks. But do be aware of the many different forms of giving that exist. These include love, generosity, acceptance, time, assistance, and creative output. Sometimes giving includes giving way, giving in, or even giving up. Only you can determine what you need to give and to whom. But remember that giving always entails *letting go* of something.

~ March ~
7 Year - 1 Month

> *To live a creative life, we must lose our fears of being wrong.*
> JOSEPH CHILTON PEARCE

Now here is an interesting combination of energies. Both the 1 and 7 vibrations relate to THE SELF, but in very different ways. 7 urges spiritual awareness and quiet introspection while 1 wants outer action and fast forward movement. 7 has little interest in materiality, while 1 wants all the material pleasures life can give.

Through this pushing and pulling of your desires, you will become aware of your own conflicting nature. This month's circumstances will show you just how independent or dependent you are. You will become aware of how free or enslaved your Will is as you realize how much you rely on the opinion or approval of others. Don't be afraid to say, "I don't know".

A new and powerful energy is starting to emerge in you. Eventually, if you allow it to flow freely, it will enable you to live your life exactly as you want to live it. Perhaps not immediately; perhaps not this year. Part of this month's experience is to realize that what you want from life - your ideal situation - is going to take years to put together. But if you don't start somewhere, your dreams can never materialize.

An important change will take place now, leaving you to figure things out for yourself. Initiate an additional change of your own, or move closer to making that change in the future. Make sure you do not use distractions as an excuse for not starting or changing something. Perhaps what you believe is a distraction is actually a reflection of something that is crying out for your attention.

This is a month of fresh ideas and new beginnings. Start something to help stretch your mind. With so much emphasis on The Self, it is time to get to know the real you, rather than the categorized you. This month's strong combination of energies will react adversely to any area of your life which is restricted by prejudgment or labeling. Free Will and individuality are what you must seek now.

A sudden change may seem to alter the entire direction of your life. No matter how you feel at the time, this upheaval is happening to increase the amount of time and space you have in which to think, analyze, learn, and grow. Do not let an opportunity pass you by just because you don't know anything about it. Learn about it!

By now, this year's 7 energy may have made you feel a little withdrawn, reserved, or even secretive. Others may see a strangeness about you and may wonder what is happening to you. Try not to alienate yourself from those you care for, as this will only add to your pressures, and theirs. Work through the feelings of FEAR that are certain to arise this month, especial-ly the fear of venturing inside your own mind. You may be amazed to know just how afraid you are of your own potential. To activate your genius, you must have the sincere intent to be honest with yourself. You will then be able to *feel* your mind opening up as the truth about yourself is revealed to you. This awareness will help you to reclaim *your* life as your own.

If you ignore this month's important introspective agenda, you are likely to have bouts of aggressive or submissive behavior. You may become cynical and pessimistic. You may engage in episodes of egotism, impatience, and intoler-ance. Or you may become timid, afraid, and unable to act decisively.

Study and analyze the entire concept of Will. If you believe you already have Free Will, you are very much mistaken. At this time, no one on Earth is free, although many are working on it. We live in a world of economic and political slavery. We are enslaved to institutions such as politics, indus-try, religion, and other belief systems. Oh, and let's not forget the institu-tion of marriage.

Think about this honestly and reach your own conclusions as to how free you are. Remember that no one else can give you freedom. It is not theirs to give. Freedom is a state of being which can only come from with-in *you* and for which *you* must take full responsibility.

~ April ~
7 Year - 2 Month

Come then, let us go forward with our united strength.
SIR WINSTON CHURCHILL

Slow down, take some deep breaths, and wait. You have now entered the peaceful feminine 2 cycle. It asks for your patience, gentleness, and sensitivity. 2 is a cycle of diplomacy, understanding, connection, intuition, diversion, teamwork, and interaction. No matter what transpires in your life this month, adhere to this simple guideline: do not *force* anything.

Relax. Relax. Relax. Assess your general development. Think about how the year started off for you and where you are right now. You need to get a more accurate sense of where you stand. Reconsider your *long term* goals and desires, and observe everything that is going on around you: personally, locally, nationally, and globally. Use your intuition - your feelings - to direct you to the next level of understanding. Accept your reality and *relax* with it. Do not lie to yourself about what your reality actually is. It is the denial of your feelings and circumstances that imprisons you.

2s vibration shows us the relativity in all things. It shows us how everything and everyone in life is connected and that there is a reason or cause for everything. April is likely to present you with a major distraction, or a series of distractions, that will test your patience and tenacity. Make a strong commitment to peace, diplomacy, and cooperation. Put your own plans on hold for a while and relate to someone or something else instead. By relating someone else's circumstances to your own, by finding the relativity - the connection - involved, you will also find a vital missing link that you have been looking for.

Remain calm, diplomatic, and helpful. Stay in the background and allow someone else to take center-stage. Interact with others more deeply and genuinely than you ever have before. Be *involved*. Don't be afraid of what you might hear or learn. This year, you will be encountering many aspects with which you may not feel particularly comfortable, but these are aspects you must face if you are to benefit from the information they contain.

Both the 2 and 7 energies emphasize intuition. Yours will be working overtime throughout April. Both energies activate the inner senses, making this a time of heightened intellect and strong emotional movement. Listen. Observe. Feel. Relate.

You will be unable to progress on any level *unless* you are patient; *unless* you wait for developments to happen in their own manner and time, and *unless* you RELAX your tensions and long term concerns. What really matters is what is going on NOW. Learn to live completely in the present, moment by moment, and you will understand that the present is your only exit from the past and your only gateway to the future.

The present - this moment - is the *only* reality even though it contains the energies of your past and future. This understanding will enable you to sense your way through all situations, instead of forcing your way through, freezing in fear, or running away. You will be progressing even if you think you are not.

Be prepared for distractions, delays, detours, deep feelings, and other frustrating circumstances. Understand that your own needs, desires, and aspirations are actually being helped along by this process of delay and interruption. If you do succumb to frustration and force yourself ahead, you may find yourself in the wrong place at the wrong time. Relax and take everything in your stride.

Partnership and teamwork are highlighted. Relate to everyone with understanding and tact while you figure out what these people have to teach or show you. Know whether they are showing you "how to" or "how not to". Help where help is needed. Learn to be comfortable in your back-seat role. Be aware of how you have helped others in the past. See these favors being returned to you this month, and not necessarily by the same people. Yes, it may be difficult to see someone else taking credit for your ideas or efforts or stealing the limelight away from you. Relax. Let it be.

If anger arises, allow yourself to *feel* your anger fully. There is no need to confront others unless it is obviously the appropriate thing to do. Listen to what your feelings are telling you, and you will understand why your circumstances are as they are. Listen to the questions you ask yourself and the judgments you reply with. Then ask your inner self to clarify the situation. Ask yourself, *"What is really going on here"*? Then listen, very carefully, again.

~ May ~
7 Year - 3 Month

Happiness depends, as nature shows,
less on exterior things than most suppose.
WILLIAM COWPER

The purpose of this month's combination of energies is to show you just where your future happiness lies, and where it does not. Recognize how your present circumstances are now reflecting this vital information back to you. What makes you happy? Who makes you happy? Who and what are making you *unhappy*? How are your own repeated actions and stubborn beliefs contributing to your unhappiness? What do you *want*?

3 represents the joys of life. The importance of the 3 energy, however, is sadly underestimated. Its vibration is so light and carefree that we sometimes fail to notice it. Even when we do, we do not always take it seriously. Now, however, in this serious 7 cycle, it is time to understand 3s vital role in your life.

3 is a cycle of optimism, happiness, humor, nature, art, creativity, communication, networking, social interaction, and beauty. Imagine how life would be without these wonderful, joyful elements. Frankly, it would not be worth living. Throughout May, it is essential that you feel, accept, and embrace this exuberant vibration. It will help you to define personal happiness, and it will show you how willing others can be to assist you in creating it.

You may now be only too aware of the flaws and imperfections in some of the people and things you once thought would make you happy. This can result in an uncomfortable tension. The 7 cycle tends to dull the gloss and glamor of life so that you can see the reality instead. There could be concern in matters pertaining to friendship, creative endeavors, social standing, or your (or someone else's) physical appearance. Plan on some significant changes in these areas which will help improve outer appearances or otherwise boost your confidence.

The change you desire to your status, or a change in social conditions, now requires high self-esteem while you learn new social skills, behavior, and procedure. You may feel like a fish out of water. But being comfortable and self-assured in alien surroundings is part of what needs to be learned in order to groom yourself for the substantial opportunity that next year's 8 cycle offers.

You may not feel like socializing at all or, when you are with other people, you may find your mind wandering to more somber thoughts.

However, friends are an important aspect of this month's theme, so it is important that you do not become too withdrawn or reclusive.

You may also find the elements of *social interaction* and *secrets* coming together in some strange way this month. You see, 3 emphasizes friends. But all energy has its opposite reflection and, this month, the question of enemies may arise. 7 puts an emphasis on spiritual openness, but its opposite reflection is plotting and scheming. Whether it is true or not, you may believe that someone does not want you to succeed. Be aware of the motivations of others without becoming paranoid. Or, is it you yourself who is plotting, unknowingly to bring yourself down?

Try to make May a month of personal enjoyment. Allow your positive energy to spread to others through cheerful and enthusiastic expression. If you find yourself involved in a serious situation, acknowledge the reality of what is happening, but focus on finding a positive solution. Do not get caught up in the problem itself. Instead, create an atmosphere of optimism through which the solution will be easier to accept.

Your creative ability will be high throughout May. Take advantage of this by engaging in an artistic pursuit, or something which emphasizes the beauty of life instead of its darker side. Socialize, entertain, and *be* entertained.

Give friends and family the opportunity to get to know you all over again, and vice versa. Appreciate all that feels good in your life, including the accessibility of music, different cultures, and the arts. What happened to your sense of humor this year? This is a good time to rediscover it.

Take care of responsibilities that cannot wait, but try to delay non-urgent matters until another time. Take a good break, a vacation, or a trip to the countryside or coast; somewhere where the splendor of nature can bring added relaxation and refinement into your life. And do remember that there is so much positive energy among the vast pockets of creativity and compassion that exist in the hustle-bustle of big cities.

You may find yourself talking, writing, or expressing yourself more than usual. 3 emphasizes all modes of communication. But do not slip into the negative attributes of both the 3 and 7 energies which urge you to trivialize, criticize, and spread gossip and rumor. Thoughtlessly expressed words can create havoc in your life this month. Their effects can spill over into the rest of the year. There is no need to hurt others just because you are dissatisfied with your life. Communicate creatively, not destructively.

Set aside time and space for yourself. It is during your "alone" time that you will receive a new awareness of what it will take, or what needs to be let go of, in order to find the happiness you want so much. The truth is, you want more - *much more* - than you have ever wanted before. It may take you the rest of the year to figure out how to make a start. Now you know why the 7 year is about *planning*, rather than doing.

~ June ~
7 Year - 4 Month

Faith may be defined as an illogical belief
of the occurrence of the improbable.

H. L. MANKEN

If you get the feeling that you are boxed in from all sides; that life has become a blur; and that one problem seems only to compound the next; do not deny that this is how you are feeling. There is nothing wrong with wanting to maintain your privacy, but there is a huge difference between privacy and denial.

Those who care for you may be worrying about you, so do not make it harder for them by pretending that your problems do not exist or that you have it all under control. You are not fooling anyone. Others may not hold the solutions you seek, but sharing your dilemma will, at least, give you a new perspective on things.

Feelings of restriction, loneliness, and vulnerability may arise. There are likely to be delays, detours, cancellations, and a mountain of details to take care of. Others may be infringing on your time or privacy. Despite it all, approach this month with the determination to do what needs to be done. Stop beating yourself up over what has happened. It was simply a road you had to travel in order to get to where you want to be.

Whatever is happening, try to make effort your key word. 4 often brings you to what you believe are your emotional, mental, or physical limits. The answer is to accept your situation exactly as it is. Only then can you expand your belief in yourself. This increased awareness pushes your limits further away from you. Although they are still there, *we all have limits*, they are no longer pressuring you. Then you will see what your next step must be.

Yes, your life is a bit of a mess right now. You need to get organized. By analyzing and prioritizing, you will be clearing the path for a much easier approach to the rest of this year's activities. Get rid of all that clutter around you. Hard work now will definitely pay off later. However, be aware that the hard work and the clutter involved are likely to be more mental and emotional than physical or material. Wherever there is chaos, find a way to replace it with the desire to change things positively for all concerned.

Life is trying to help you build a solid base for your future. Even the best laid plans may need to be changed to suit changing needs. This month's events are also pointing out to you that your plans must be put into action systematically, one step at a time. Face the facts that you have been avoiding. Sort it all out, detail by detail. Be aware of how your own behavior may have contributed to the problem. When you have squarely faced all the facts about yourself and the other people concerned, you will experience a strong and comforting sense of accomplishment.

The restrictive nature of 4, combined with the introspective nature of the 7, can create a tendency to overanalyze a situation. You may be focusing on its negative aspects instead of seeking a positive *solution*. Try to concentrate on a perfect but realistic outcome. Visualize and *feel* the results you want.

Be aware of how your thoughts, beliefs, or actions may be compounding the problem. Are you blaming others for your problems? For your own shortcomings? Is your point of view too limited? Are you unwilling to let go of something which is preventing you from having what you really want? Are you holding on to situations or people who do not have your best interests at heart? Are you refusing to accept a change that has already taken place? Are you denying your true feelings? Are you *using* or losing your Free Will?

Why must June in the 7 year cycle be so difficult? First of all, the 7 energy can often make you think the worst of any situation. The purpose of this is to build *faith* in both yourself and life. Without it, we cannot see beyond our so called problems. Without faith, there is no *hope*. Then, along comes the 4 energy which places obstacles in your path. The purpose of this is to bring you to what you believe are your limits so that you can see that you are not as limited as you thought.

4 is the number of breakthrough. But when you think about the word breakthrough, it sounds rather painful, doesn't it? 4 also suggests that you *build* the reality you want, which means effort, hard work, getting organized, and knowing what you want to achieve.

And so, between thinking the worst, being confronted with obstacles and barriers, stretching yourself beyond your current limits so that you can break through them, exerting effort to build a new reality, and being unsure of what it is you want to build in the first place, you can see why June in the 7 year is not the most pleasant place to be..... until you understand its purpose.... THEN you can regain your confidence. THEN you can see your different options. THEN you can decide to take things easier; to stop struggling against a situation over which you have absolutely no control. This means calmly *accepting* your current reality.

For now, you can look forward to a positive change in July, even though it is you who may have to set the ball rolling. It will also help you to know that your 8 year is going to be SO different from this one, and you are likely to start feeling this powerful new energy as early as October.

Remember that you alone must decide your future. And there is no reason why it should not be a happy, healthy, loving, successful, safe, and satisfying one. Remember, too, that all change takes place on the inside first. This understanding will lead to the mental and emotional *breakthrough* that June is all about. Yes, this has been a difficult year for you so far, but now you must have faith in the *future*!

~ July ~
7 Year - 5 Month

The highest result of education is tolerance.
HELEN KELLER

The 5 cycle brings your physical body into focus. At this time, your health is a gauge by which to measure your current levels of stress and anxiety. If symptoms arise, it is likely that you are holding emotions in which desperately need to be expressed *out*. Therefore, what you are experiencing is not depression but *suppression* of your feelings. This month there is nothing more healing for you than to let those emotions OUT.

Slow down and inspect the damage. It may not be as bad as you thought. You may believe that the condition of your body determines the way you feel. This is not true. The way you feel determines the condition of your body.

You cannot change everything overnight. If your life is to progress in any significant way, you must devise a realistic plan of action - a sensible agenda - for the next six months.

You know there is so much available to you out there and that there is no reason why you cannot have your own "piece of the pie". *But the TIMING isn't right yet.* You may have experienced some success this year, but it was only a preliminary step. A much greater success lies ahead of you. But while your focus is on those things and people that appear to be limiting you, you will never be able to give your true potential the focus it needs.

You will feel the possibilities this month, but you may have to wait until October or November to act on them. Be patient. Make your plans. Pay great attention to detail. Remember that this year, you must wait for opportunity to come to you, rather than aggressively seek it. The positive changes taking place now can create a positive and permanent alteration in your general direction.

This is no time for impulsive decisions. Perhaps it was your past impulsiveness that produced the unsatisfying conditions you are now experiencing. Remember that the very nature of this year is to study and analyze your options and choose what is best for you. Spend some quiet time alone. Discover your new awareness of *timing*, and reassess what you want to achieve next year. A sense of adventure is likely to elevate the way you think about yourself; your loved ones; your abilities and resources; and your general ambitions.

Not only should July be used to *plan* for your future happiness, but also to change existing plans which are no longer practical. Let go of old, unproductive, but often comfortable conditions or attitudes which are no longer appropriate to the life you are trying to create for yourself. See the imperfections in your previous plans and beliefs and understand why *free will* must be restored to your life, and to the Earth itself. Make choices that are loving, constructive, and positive, instead of destructive, negative, and unfulfilling.

July may bring something unexpected into your life which will heighten your understanding of freedom. You may experience new and different people, places, activities, and ideals. Excitement is in the air. Something will occur to make your heart beat a little faster. Stay relaxed as you flow with your changing horizons. But do *focus* on what you are doing at all times. If you are not aware of the rapidly changing nature of the 5 energy, you can be prone to accidents, mishaps, loss of direction, and other disrupting events.

Remember, too, that your freedom cannot be grabbed at the expense of someone else. This is abuse of freedom. It is also an abuse of freedom to overindulge in addictive pleasures that actually keep you dependent, such as food, alcohol, extravagance, gambling, and any other form of excess that distracts you from reality. Make moderation your code this month. You need a clear head right now.

~ August ~
7 Year - 6 Month

To err is human, to forgive divine.
ALEXANDER POPE

6 is a cycle of love, healing, and responsibility. It is time to focus on matters of the heart. Some issues may run very deep indeed. These are likely to include certain relationships, domestic matters, and the question of *duty*. August reveals the flaws and imperfections, as well as the joys, in your private life, all the way back to your childhood. Study and analyze all that has ever happened to you in the name of LOVE.

Realize that a large part of you is trapped in the past. You must go back and release yourself from the guilt, blame, anger, fear, and grief which are holding you there. It is there, in the past, that you will find the true cause of your present situation. Once the cause is located, the solution becomes obvious. Right now you need to forgive, and you need to be forgiven.

Try to spend as much time at home as possible. Concentrate on what your responsibilities really are, and try to bring peace and harmony into your closest circle. This is not the best time to travel, unless it is to visit family or close friends, or to fulfill a specific duty. Take care of those people and things that mean the most to you. Make your home a friendly place to be.

Someone close to you needs either loving attention or cautious handling. If you are serious about improving your long-term future, now is the time to attend to this matter. If not, your freedom and happiness in the months and years ahead may be jeopardized. The circumstances of August are likely to bring to a head the matter of *whose* responsibility is in question or who should be *held* responsible for a particular mess.

If you are blaming someone else, or depending on them too heavily, it is time to take responsibility for your own life. If they are blaming you, or if their dependence on you is becoming more than you can handle, it is time to remove yourself from this imbalance and insist that they be responsible for themselves.

The problem here is that so much emotion is involved within close relationships and you may want to avoid an outburst with someone you care for. However, in a year when you are looking deeply into the prospects of your *long term* happiness, ask yourself how you will feel if this situation is not resolved one year from now? See yourself five years from now if this situation has not changed. How will you feel *then*?

One way or another, it is time to analyze - not overanalyze - certain relationships so that an atmosphere of love, agreement, peace, and freedom can prevail.

Special understanding and attention should now be given to children. Parents often feel overwhelmed by their responsibility to raise their offspring in safety and can often lay down the law without realizing that children must also have freedom. It is damaging to expect too much or too little from them. It is destructive to focus only on their negative traits while ignoring their real talents and their loving attributes. In today's evolving and dangerous world, young people need inclusion, love, understanding and, above all, encouragement. They need to know that life is not a series of punishments but, rather, it is a series of *consequences*.

For every action there is a reaction. For every cause there is an effect. Peer pressure must be shown for what it is: just part of the big "race", the massive competition between human beings that is now very out of place on this planet. Children must be free to express their feelings, and their feelings must be accepted as part of their individuality. If they are encouraged to follow their hearts' desires - their Free Will - while allowing others the same freedom, they will seldom go wrong. Of course, that applies to all of us.

If there are no children in your life, try to reach an awareness of children in general. Young people have a difficult task ahead of them in making this world a more peaceful and habitable place to live. They represent the very future of this planet. You may find yourself remembering your own childhood this month. This is 6's way of emphasizing the need to respect *all* children - those you grew up with - as well as the innocent child that still lives within you.

Pets may require special attention and appreciation also. They are alive. They feel. They think. They love. They, too, need affection, security, and understanding. We have much to learn from the instinctive nature of animals, and from their ability to love without condition.

You may find yourself angry or worrying about something which has not happened and, perhaps, need not happen. Don't deny your feelings, but don't overreact either. The more you honor another's freedom, the easier it is for love and respect to flow. Accept the *individual* nature of someone who may be casting their disapproving eye on you right now, and you will realize that you cannot change anyone but yourself. You can start by changing your *reaction* to this person.

August is the perfect time to learn the difference between helping and interfering; loving and controlling; accepting and denying. Wherever there is judgment, guilt, or control, love cannot survive. Use this month's soothing vibrations to balance, heal, and revitalize.

~ September ~
7 Year - 7 Month

The will to win doesn't mean anything
because everybody wants to win.
It is the will to prepare to win
that makes the difference.
ROY BLACK

The new awareness that September brings will shed some much needed light on the shadowy road you've been traveling this year. There is likely to be more activity than usual and, yet, you may also have some very introspective needs.

The 7 vibration of WISDOM is surrounding you from all sides now. Rather than cutting yourself off from the rest of the world, it is time to face the world in all its stark naked reality. You have traveled a long way since the beginning of the year. You have learned so much about life and about you. Now it is time to hold your head up high and emerge with your new self image and your expanded confidence.

Things may not be exactly as you want them yet, but you *know* you'll get there. You're planning on it. It would be a good idea to make additional plans which will prepare you emotionally and physically for next year's dynamic activities. Yes, within the next twelve months you will arrive at a much more stable and pleasant destination.

Use this month to fine-tune and perfect yourself and your plans on an inner level. Patience is required. This does not mean putting up with negative people and situations. At this point in your journey, it is more likely to mean paying meticulous and painstaking attention to detail.

Focus on your beliefs, feelings, ambitions, relationships, your expertise, and your dignity. Life is urging you to point yourself in the direction you *know* is right for you. That is what this year has been all about.

What if things go wrong? What if you feel worry, depression, or pessimism instead of enthusiasm and confidence? What if you feel that nothing exciting or beneficial lies ahead for you? Then you must do your homework. Analyze, research, and study. Do not forget that the 7 energy is your mirror of truth. What is it reflecting back to you in your day-to-day affairs and ongoing feelings? Are you unwilling to accept that your old ideas and ways of doing things simply don't work any more? Are you refusing to see the *new* potential that is right under your nose? Analyze. Research. Study. Learn from the reflections of everything and everyone around you.

Relax and meditate whenever you can. Visualize your hopes and dreams in great detail. Review the past and express the emotions that emerge from your memories. You will then be able to see the potential that lies ahead, rather than only what you believe is stopping you from attaining it. *Feel* the present. Relish every moment, because it is only through the present that you can glimpse the future. Be content in your solitude. You are your own best friend and it is vital that you treat yourself as such.

You are unique. You are special. Rather than fall to the evils of peer pressure which insist we should kill Free Will and follow the crowd, start to appreciate just how different you are. It is your very differentness that enables you to stand out from the crowd and reach your *own* expectations of happiness. Mediocrity is a tragic loss of Free Will. The 8 energy of next year will give you the opportunity to *become* who you really are. There is so much to look forward to. There is so much to plan.

~ October ~
7 Year - 8 Month

I never thought people would take
my thoughts seriously; I know I never did.
ALBERT EINSTEIN

Much of this year's new knowledge and understanding can now be used in practical, realistic ways. By now you should be certain of one thing: a significant change must occur in the level of *power* you have in the world. You have not experienced all that you have experienced in life only to remain unfulfilled. Realize the extent to which you can improve your life by improving the quality of what you contribute to it. This month you will be very aware of improvements you want to make either in the work you do, the conditions in which you live, your relationships, or all of these areas.

Now you will start to feel the vibration of next year's 8 cycle overlapping with this year's 7 cycle. This combination brings issues of finance, career, business, status, prosperity, and personal belongings into view.

October provides a preview of the greater possibilities that lie ahead for you. A new sense of ambition will arise. Although certain actions can be implemented now, remember that you are still in the 7 year cycle which encourages planning rather than doing. On an inner level, your horizons can certainly be broadened, enabling you to see that you can, indeed, expand what you once thought were your limits.

There is still much knowledge, insight, and illumination to soak up between now and the end of the year. Your intuition is very strong now. It can bring you to a new level of understanding about the importance of balanced coexistence between the emotional, spiritual, and physical aspects of life. This recognition will not only open your eyes to your own greater potential, it will also open your heart to the needs and potentials of others.

This year's journey has been a profoundly spiritual and emotional one for you. Now it is necessary for you to reacquaint yourself with the more earthly and material aspects of your life.

Opportunities may begin to appear. These should be acted upon decisively and confidently, with dignity and composure. The tide is now beginning to turn in your favor. Take yourself seriously. Have patience. Have faith in yourself. Believe in life.

You may have to take a brand new approach to financial and business matters. You may have to change some of your beliefs as to how money and business are affected by various world events. Remember that the whole world is evolving and great change is taking place everywhere. Not only are we living in a changing world but, also, in a world that *has* changed. And it will change constantly as the process of human evolution unfolds. Many old ideas about prosperity and financial security are no longer valid.

Continue to observe, study, research, analyze, and learn. Try to approach matters in a businesslike and realistic way. Express yourself with confidence.

Be aware. Know what your reality actually is. Do your homework before making strong statements or taking irreversible action. If you are fully alert, there will be no need for nervousness or doubt. *Feel* the dynamics of your own personal power emerge. Be patient. It will not be too long before you will be using these feelings to your full advantage.

~ November ~
7 Year - 9 Month

Nothing we ever imagine is beyond our powers,
only beyond our present self knowledge.
THEODORE ROSZAK

The 9 vibration of November will bring an end to some aspects of your life, including this year's emphasis on the inner self. By the end of the month, life will require you to 'snap out of it' and come back to Earth with both feet planted firmly on the ground. This does not mean the end of your ability to tap in to your intuitive genius. Rather, it represents a new phase of your journey in which you will be able to live successfully in the spiritual, emotional, and material realms *simultaneously*.

This month's circumstances are designed to give you plenty of practice in the art of balance. At times, life may feel like an emotional roller coaster. This has been a long year for you, and you have endured some rough emotional experiences. It is essential that you allow all the feelings involved to emerge and then release them from your body. This gratifying and healing process *needs* to take place. Your body needs it; your mind needs it; your Will needs it; *you* need it. Let those emotions *out*. There is no need to confront others, or to hurt yourself or someone else in the process of outwardly expressing your emotions. Make sure you create *private* time and space for this.

This is not the time to start anything new. Instead, focus on ending things that are no longer beneficial or appropriate. You may find yourself concluding or phasing out certain aspects of your business, career, or financial activities. Such closures are usually made on a material level but will also effect your mental and emotional energies.

The endings made this month are likely to be in preparation for next year's dynamic movement even though this may not be immediately apparent. Timing is still an important factor: any major decisions or actions should be given careful consideration or delayed until next year.

Of course, some endings may be out of your control. If this is the case, you can be sure that there is a very good reason for both the ending and the time in which it is taking place.

Use your imagination. Visualize the possibilities that a certain ending offers. Flow confidently with this month's circumstances by knowing how you really *feel* about things. Soon you will be feeling your way to something new and exciting.

9 is also a cycle of generosity and compassion. With your mind very much focused on next year's financial and material gains, the vibrations of November are urging you to give in some way. There are many ways to give and not all of them require sacrifice. Approach this month with a commitment to fairness, kindness, and tolerance. A charitable, helpful, and optimistic attitude will actually attract opportunity to you this month.

Clear the path for next year's action by completing anything you have been putting off. If something is expected of you but you have not followed through, now is the time to finally get it done or admit that you cannot do it. Get this matter out of the way once and for all and remove its guilty weight from your shoulders.

Take a good look at the material blessings you *already have* and appreciate them. Those things which are of no use to you and are cluttering up your life should be given to someone who does have a use for them. Sell them - or barter with them. Use what you have to get what you want.

This month's endings are part of the natural course of your life. It is a waste of your time and energy to try to hold on to people, situations, or things who appear to be leaving you. Let go. If they are meant to stay, they will. Stop worrying so incessantly about things that have not even happened. Now is the time to END your ridiculous inferiority complex which causes you to believe that you have to lose something in order to gain something.

~ December ~
7 Year - 1 Month

The future ain't what it used to be.
"YOGI" BERRA

1 is a cycle of new beginnings, origins, independence, change, achievement, and ambition. Both the 7 and 1 vibrations relate to expanded awareness, and this combination is likely to make you feel very self-centered. Focusing on you is perfectly natural at this time, but your eagerness to start something new may be a little premature. If you find yourself engaging in episodes of anxiety, impatience, aggressiveness, and egotism during December, this could be a sign that you are traveling way too fast. Be careful how you treat others this month, especially those whose cooperation and support you will need in the months to come.

Whatever you have been planning, December will provide an opportunity to put the *first stages* of your plans into action. Snap out of the 'inner" world in which you have been living for the past twelve months, and focus on your physical and material reality. Make some kind of constructive change, or move closer to making such a change in the near future.

Don't obsess over any weak points you may have, but work on strengthening them. Particular attention should be given to areas of dependency that you may still be denying. 1 urges independence. But how can you be independent if your very happiness *depends* on factors outside of yourself?

Recognize your addictions and obsessions; those things or people you think you cannot survive without, or you believe are holding you back. *Accept* that you have these problems and commit to finding ways to become much more self-reliant.

December is a time for enthusiasm and optimism. Look forward and see the potential awaiting you. Express your individuality, originality, your creativity, and your confidence. The 1 cycle urges you to be progressive and to take the lead. It urges you to look ahead rather than dwell in the past or adhere to traditions which inhibit and control. Being yourself and moving at your own natural pace are the keys to making the rest of your life a successful and happy experience.

Being yourself does not mean going to unrealistic lengths to be different. It means recognizing and appreciating who and what you naturally are without putting on an act, airs and graces, or downplaying your talents or appearance. Being yourself means being yourself. Nothing else. See the beauty in your uniqueness and realize that your very differentness is a gift from life.

If you find yourself frustrated, disappointed, or just plain stressed out, you are probably pushing too hard, too soon. Just as you cannot cross a bridge before you come to it, you cannot enter a new cycle of your life until it actually begins. Your 8 year cycle has not started yet. Be *patient.* If you are not receiving the support you had hoped for, you may need to take another look at just how dependent or oversensitive you still are. Both the 1 and 7 energies can create feelings of aloneness or even loneliness; a feeling that if something is going to be done, you will have to do it yourself.

Relax with your plans. Maintain your confidence. Whatever you have learned in this strange and introspective year - *whatever feels good and real* - never forget it. Hold on to it and bring it with you, as midnight of December 31st arrives, and you cross over into the transformational 8 adventure of SUCCESS, SATISFACTION, and PERSONAL POWER.

The 8 Year Cycle

developing your personal power -
a journey of achievement

> *Whatever the soul knows how to seek,*
> *it cannot fail to obtain.*
> MARGARET FULLER

You get what you want in the 8 year cycle. You really do. However, if you do not know what you want, you will have no way of knowing what you will get! This year, it is time to get specific. It is time to *feel* what is in your heart and allow yourself to be drawn into the fulfillment of your desires. You are traveling a year long cycle in which you will prosper according to the strength of your will, your *desire*, to succeed.

Throughout the year, you will feel a marked increase in your ability to make things happen and get things done. Consequently, your expectations will rise, along with your self-confidence and your feelings of satisfaction.

It is likely that *last* year was deeply emotional and confusing for you. It had to be that way so that you could know what your desires actually are. Now, enough is enough. It's time to get down to business!

You will soon realize that you must now become stronger than you have ever been before. Traditionally, 8 is known as the energy of power, material and financial gain, achievement, reward, status, and self-satisfaction. This year, you will experience all of these things as you seek their *true* meaning. The 8 vibration will provide the means - the personal power - with which to change the status quo and accomplish a significant goal which will alter the entire direction of your journey.

A certain driving force, the strength of which you may not have experienced before, will bring you closer to freedom than you have ever been. It is up to you to decide precisely what you want to accomplish and to eliminate habits and attitudes that have held you back in the past. It is time to make a firm commitment to creating a new and satisfying reality for yourself.

You may start out in one direction at the beginning of the year, only to find yourself in an entirely new situation later on. Progress will come from information or intelligence that you have accumulated during the course of the year. This is not merely a matter of believing something new, but of *knowing* it.

This year's accomplishments are only the beginning of your long-term advancement into freedom and happiness. Remember that desire is a form of love which drives you and often carries you from the inside, toward external success. There is no telling how far it can take you.

This is a very special year in which events and circumstances will lead you from one important experience to the next. Each will bring you closer to your 'right place' in the world. You may find yourself on the receiving end of material, emotional, or spiritual gifts. Others will be more inclined to assist and support you once they see how seriously you are taking yourself and your goals. This year you will be learning about the *business* of living.

A sense of belonging is one of the most precious rewards on offer this year. Your quest, however, must begin with where you *are*. If you are not happy where you are, then it is up to you to take the bull by the horns and do what is necessary to *change* your circumstances.

Your right place in the world is not necessarily a matter of geographical location. Being where you want to be can also refer to matters of love, relationship, health, status, finances, or any area where improvement is desired. Whatever your desire may be, it is important that you treat it as a goal - a real and reachable ambition. Even though your goals may be of an external nature, the ultimate goal must be the inner *feeling* of self-satisfaction. After all, what is success? It is a state of happiness.

This year, you will meet others who are not where they want to be, who are also searching for the warmth of personal satisfaction and belonging. You need to be around those who are seeking truth, satisfaction, and freedom. You can no longer endure the limitations imposed on you by those who do not share or understand your need for independence and fulfillment.

You will know that if something *feels* right to you, it *is* right. You will also realize that what feels right to one may feel totally wrong to another. Free Will runs in all directions. Each one of us has the right, and the responsibility, to choose our own course.

At first, others may oppose you, those who think you may be aiming too high; or those who feel insecure with your ambitions. Or, you yourself may have doubts as to how you can make your desires happen when you do not appear to have the means or knowledge to do so. Or, you may be able to feel the strong potential of the 8 energy, but are unable to pinpoint what it is you really want to accomplish.

Relax. The more you place such obstacles in your way, the less able you will be to *feel* what you are feeling inside; the less able you will be to *imagine* the details of the life you want to live; the less able you will be to dream your dream. Believe that you CAN have what you want! You are exactly where you need to be in order to find the resources and inspiration which will fuel this exciting twelve-month journey.

The power of your feelings is now driving you in a particular direction. This energy can make your endeavors appear effortless. But make no mistake about it, this is not an easygoing year. Consistent hard work and determination are necessary. Difficult decisions will have to be made. Physical, mental, and emotional stress can result. It is essential, therefore, that you take adequate time to rest and replenish your energies, even though you may not think you need to do so. Throughout this tantalizing year of goals and accomplishment, you will need to take frequent and complete breaks from the work load. If not, you could easily burn yourself out by October or November.

This year's circumstances will expose you to many different forms of power. Some will excite you while others will enable you to see the dire consequences of power when it is abused. From these experiences, you will want to develop a greater power of your own because it is only from this position that you will be able to turn your dreams into reality. This is a time of dynamic action, efficiency, and faith.

The 8 cycle enables you to reap the rewards of whatever you have "invested" into your life. These rewards depend largely on how much *love* for what you are doing is involved. Ultimately, you will learn that love has many different forms and is, without doubt, the greatest power of all.

This is certainly a time to focus on career, material progress, finances, business, and status. Twentieth century ideals may have to be changed before you find your correct course. You must reconsider the very concept of money, power, and success as the reality of these things changes before your eyes.

True success, in this day and age, is no longer measured by what you take out of life but, rather, what you contribute to it. You are not here in creation to toil for others, but to create your own unique destiny.

Recognize the power others have over you. Find ways to release yourself from their control. If money or power appear to be all that is driving you, then you are likely to achieve certain goals, but their long-term potential will be far less satisfying.

The 8 year cycle is a quest for inner satisfaction, contentment, happiness. This means that you must do what has to be done to *create* the life you want for yourself. One of the first rewards of the year may come as an opportunity to finally do what you *want* to do. This is a return on your investment of having the courage to search for what you truly desire in the first place. Or, you may have the chance to bring what you already do to a much higher level. Seize this opportunity and bet big on your abilities and potentials.

As strange global events continue to unfold, you will realize that you are the only one you can count on for prosperity, security, and stability. Become informed and aware of what is taking place in the world. This will increase your power levels and will enable you to take precautionary measures to protect your resources and reputation. You *are* ready to turn your life around and make it truly satisfying. This time, you are taking yourself much more seriously. This time, you're going to get it *right*!

Certain obstacles may have to be faced and dealt with but, deep down, you know that you cannot let anything stand in your way. Some of these obstacles have materialized because of misconceptions about today's political and economic reality and an inability to separate guilt from love. Staunchly conservative approaches are no longer working. Institutions are being questioned, exposed, and opposed by those who desire the freedom to decide *everything* for themselves.

Remember, you are now traveling the "power" section of your journey in a world that is rapidly changing. It is hard to keep up with everything that is going on. But, why struggle to keep up when, with focus and dedication, you can be streaks ahead of those who cannot see humanity's *positive* potential for freedom?

You are on a very serious mission this year, and you will know that you are on course when you realize just how much you are enjoying the work involved. An increased sense of self-importance may be felt, and this is a good sign that you are feeling the urgency and the pleasure involved in taking charge of your own life. This is no time for false modesty or for outright arrogance; just practical application to what must be done.

Try to accept all that you are feeling, including the fear and the arrogance, and strive to *balance* these feelings. When you do, you will emerge confident and calm, rather than bullying, manipulative, greedy, or cynical.

Many contradictory emotions will arise for the purpose of understanding and balancing your ego, not suppressing it. When your ego reaches that tranquil place between over-inflation and self-depreciation, it goes peacefully to sleep. Then, many different forms of love emerge.

Your abilities are at their strongest this year. You will be able to make things happen by focusing on the desired results, trusting yourself, and acting decisively.

8s emphasis on abundance and materiality often relates to one's career, finances, and status. Rewards can also be attained in other areas of your life into which *love* has been invested. The sheer variety of reward you receive this year will help build a greater sense of satisfaction in you. In turn, you will learn that the rewards themselves are never as gratifying as the feelings they create.

Maintain a businesslike approach to everything you do. Use all your effort and knowledge to achieve your desires. This is no time for idle dreams or wishful thinking. It is a time for *living* the dream instead of merely fantasizing about it. It is a time to wake up from the emptiness that comes from believing that others control your life. Reclaim your Will and start *doing* what you really want to do.

The 8 energy enables you to expand your talents significantly and to discover talents you did not know you had. 8 brings dignity into your life by teaching you that life has given *everyone* an ability which is uniquely their own. Now is the time to display a talent that, until now, you have had to keep under wraps.

Accept your *responsibility* to live in freedom. Create your own financial and material security. Learn how this process works. You will soon learn that your personal security is directly linked to seemingly unrelated events taking place elsewhere around the globe.

What was once considered sound business sense may not necessarily apply today. Competition is not the answer to maintaining quality. Quality cannot help but suffer when competition turns into war; and it always turns into war at some point. The finest quality can only be maintained by *love* of quality. Remember this as you present yourself and your ideas to the world this year. Concentrate on the larger issues and move away from pettiness and dependency. Delegate as much and as fairly as possible. Aim higher than ever before. Go after what you really want and *believe* you'll get it.

Remember that this year you are experiencing and learning about POWER. You will learn that love is the greatest power of all. It is also the most needed commodity in the world right now. First, you must love yourself, your God-given talent and the passionate feelings it creates in you. You will then find that you and others become so much more lovable and you will want to share your good fortune. Remember that the love you are seeking must start on the inside first. On that basis, your future looks very bright indeed.

~ January ~
8 Year - 9 Month

> *If love is the answer,*
> *could you please rephrase the question?*
> LILY TOMLIN

A situation which has prevented you from living the life you want to live, is coming to an end. Life is urging you to feel and *be* who you really are. If you are still stuck in last year's introspective frame of mind, it is time to snap out of it and face the truth of your present circumstances.

This ending is about to clear your path for a fresh start in February. Your emotions or the emotions of those around you may be running high. Observe and sense what is really going on. Your feelings are telling you what you really *want* by pointing out what is no longer desirable. Yes, something, or everything, has to change. Once you accept this fact, alternatives will start to appear.

You will soon understand that although adjustments must be made, you can fulfill certain large scale ambitions, and you can do it this year. Go back into the past and complete your unfinished business there. Recognize all the attitudes, beliefs, and situations that have kept you from fulfilling a particular dream. This month takes you in what seems like the wrong direction - backwards - so that you can define the things which are preventing you from moving forward. It is a highly emotional but cleansing time.

Consider the unproductive aspects which always slowed you down; that consistent set of circumstances which always ended in disappointment. Realize how guilt, and the fear that guilt hides behind, has so often stopped you in your tracks. The 9 cycle is showing you that it is possible to have exactly what you want without damaging yourself, or any one else, in the process. In fact, if you do not resolve to do what is right for you, you will never be able to do what is right for others.

Your WILL is waking up now. It is reacquainting you to those rich feelings of self-appreciation you had forgotten you were able to feel. Once you have made a decision which is not derived from guilt or blame, your self-esteem will be raised to the level needed to pursue your goal. Others will give you their full support.

Endings must now be made in a way that will allow you to walk away, without regret, if not immediately, then later in the year. Avoid intolerance and impatience. Try to be open minded, forgiving, compassionate, and optimistic. Above all, accept and enjoy the feeling that is urging you to believe in yourself. This is your Will trying to free itself.

Situations may arise to test your patience and tolerance. Their purpose is to show you that you *do* have a choice: you can remain dependent on others for your happiness, or you can take full responsibility for your life by developing a strong intent to fulfill a personal dream.

9 is a cycle of giving, and in the 8 year cycle which emphasizes getting, this may seem like a conflicting combination of energies. But it is not. Giving and receiving are equal parts of the same process, as one cannot be achieved without the other. There are so many ways to give: your time; support; money; service; understanding; sympathy; creativity; etc. But giving *out* is not the only means of giving. Sometimes giving involves giving in, giving way, or even giving up. Only you can decide how to give this month. Just remember that in order to give you must *let go* of something.

~ February ~
8 Year - 1 Month

What is qualified?
I haven't been qualified to be a mayor.
I'm not qualified to be a songwriter.
I'm not qualified to be a TV producer.
I'm not qualified to be a successful businessman.
And so, I don't know what qualified means.
SONNY BONO

February signifies a time of independence and fresh starts. Even though the month may start off slowly, an important change is developing which will provide an opportunity to move closer to your goal. There is a positive reason for this month's change of atmosphere. There is no need for aggression or impatience. Stay confident and focused, no matter what is going on around you. You are exactly where you are meant to be in order to receive or, perhaps, conceive the opportunity you need.

Your feelings, thoughts, and actions represent the planting of seeds which will start to bud in April. Conditions or situations that have worked against you in the past can now be changed. Have the courage to discard old beliefs which have been held in place by nothing more than inexperience.

You will soon have the chance to gain first hand experience simply by allowing yourself to be *emotionally* involved with your own dream. The more emotional this month's events become, the more easily new ideas will flow. You know that the time has come to create a different and more satisfying reality for yourself. You know that this is not going to happen overnight. Therefore, patience, great dedication, and a lot of consideration for others will be needed as you become comfortable in your changing environment.

There is likely to be one idea which creates great excitement in you. You may not know exactly how to get the ball rolling, but don't worry. The "how to" will follow the "desire to". The magnetic pull of your desire - your Will - your feelings - is now drawing you to the *means* of turning your desire into reality.

Certain changes may occur of their own accord. Other changes must be implemented by you. One small change can lead to a whole series of changes and open up an entirely new direction for you. We are all afraid of change. When fear arises this month, allow yourself to *feel* this natural emotion instead of pretending that you are not afraid. True acceptance of your feelings will provide the answers you need. You will then be able to proceed positively and confidently upon the shifting sands beneath your feet.

1 is the energy of independence. It urges you to recognize any weaknesses, excesses, and addictions that keep you dependent on someone or something else. Dependence on anyone or thing other than yourself is an abuse of your Will. So, too, is encouraging others to be dependent on you. This is a month to *stand alone* and assess your own capabilities, potentials, resources, and needs.

Start something new. This may be a new activity, job, attitude, friendship, residence, or project. At the very least, start a new phase of an ongoing situation. If you have a history of starting things but never finishing them, you may need to be extra cautious here. Whatever you start now, even if it is only in your mind at this stage, is likely to set the course for the rest of the year.

The 1 cycle places an emphasis on the Self. It points out your individuality, your originality, and your creative talent. This can make you feel a little self-centered at times, and guilt will try to undermine you for being so self-absorbed. But you *must* focus on yourself during February. Only then will you be able to feel and measure your desires and abilities. Only then will you be able to determine your true identity, instead of forever being told by *others*, who and what you are and what you should be doing.

This month is an exercise in finding your *purpose* in life. This is determined by how strongly you feel the desire to create a particular reality for yourself. As both the 8 and 1 energies influence the ego, you may need to understand that ego is only a problem when it is either over or under inflated. Everyone has an ego. Without it, we have no way of knowing ourselves. Your true feelings will help you find a comfortable balance between egotism and self-sacrifice.

Learn to have patience with yourself, other people, and your goals. Today, nothing of value happens as quickly as we desire. Do not rely on others to get the work done. Much will have to be started, continued, and completed by you. You may feel a sense of loneliness at this time. But this is a good sign. After all, how else could it be? Yes, of course you will want the love and support of others, but it is you, alone, who must do what is necessary to make YOUR dream come true.

~ March ~
8 Year - 2 Month

The world is full of magical things
patiently waiting for our wits to grow sharper.
BERTRAND RUSSELL

SLOW DOWN. Take some deep breaths. As much as you may feel compelled to *do* something, this month's 2 cycle urges you to be patient and wait. In fact, something may occur which forces you to take a slower approach to all matters.

March is all about timing, and this is not the time for forward movement. Instead, it is a time to give your wholehearted attention or support to someone or something else. The way you respond to or treat others now will have a major impact on your overall plans.

2 is the magnificent feminine creative energy towards which all of life is evolving. It is the principle energy of the new millennium. This month provides a preview of what we must all learn in the years ahead. 2 is the energy of Free Will, peace, sensitivity, team-work, patience, connection, partnership, cooperation, intuition, diplomacy, and efficiency.

Now, as you find yourself focusing on the needs of someone else instead of your own, you will know that this is the right thing to do. You will be needing the support of others later in the year, and now is a good time to remember that "what goes around, comes around". Your attention to detail and your high sense of priority will not go unnoticed.

Try to stay as composed as possible as your own doubts, or the doubts of others, distract and frustrate you. The most significant contribution you can make right now is to give someone else your patience, kindness, and understanding. Their circumstances are far more complex and painful than you may imagine. Your own needs are being taken care of behind the scenes where your impatience cannot damage their potential. Don't force anything. Just be as genuinely friendly and helpful as you can.

Try to deal with everything efficiently and decisively. Make yourself indispensable without forcing your presence or your ideas on others. Stay in the background. You are here to help, not to control. Let someone else bask in the limelight. Your own recognition will come later.

The 2 energy teaches us that all individuals are connected to the one large body we call humanity; and that humanity is only a part of an even larger entity called life. This month will provide you with a spectacular opportunity to experience this linkage for yourself. Adopt an open, relaxed, and attentive frame of mind so that you can recognize and absorb this new intelligence.

At some point while you're cooperating, taking a back seat, tending to details, and putting your own life on hold, you will realize that *until* these details are taken care of, your plans cannot proceed anyway. You will hear or see something which you would normally regard as mundane, uninteresting, or even offensive. Observe and listen to everyone with whom you come into contact. Someone different has come into your life to tell you, or show you, what you most need to know at this time.

In order to find that connection, you will need to listen very carefully to others and hear what is really being said. Try to feel what they are feeling, without assuming that you already know. Compare their situation to your own. How is this making *you* feel?

A new sense of direction will suddenly emerge, and you will feel the POWER that comes with this peaceful use of intuition. You will know that although the purpose of this month's events is to take your mind off your goals, it is also to help you *clarify* them.

What is motivating you? If your goals are based on competition, greed, oneupmanship, revenge, or anything that does not have a peaceful and loving intent, you are unlikely to succeed. Find the love in your heart and allow it to direct you. Remember that life is moving away from war-like competitiveness, toward peaceful and loving connectedness.

Aim to do what you love - and to love what you do. As it happens, this is the very advice which can help the people who seem to be creating so much distraction for you this month. Doing what we love and loving what we do is the key to freedom, happiness, and peace on Earth. But this cannot happen until we develop the *courage* to be free and peaceful within ourselves.

~ April ~
8 Year - 3 Month

It takes a lot of courage to show your dreams to someone else.
ERMA BOMBECK

As you phase out the cooperative, backstage activities of March, you may find that you have made a powerful friend indeed. If this is not immediately apparent, it will become so later in the year. You have now entered the inspiring 3 cycle of *creativity* which should certainly revive your sense of enthusiasm. The ideas of the past three months can now be implemented. At the very least, you will know that they are achievable.

It is time to create the arena or environment which will transform your ideas into reality. April provides the opportunity to "test the waters" and see how well you perform to an audience without actually striving to gain the acceptance of others. You see, it is your own self approval that is needed now. This is what others will be noticing and applauding.

This month's combination of energy emphasizes happiness, communication, optimism, appearances, friendliness and the lighter side of life. Your own plans have center stage. The only thing that can stop you from getting them underway is a lack of enjoyment or love for what you are doing. Be sure that what you say you want is what you truly *feel* you want.

Happiness is the same for everyone, even though everyone has their own unique way of expressing it. Happiness comes from doing what you want to do, what you *love*, what you are being driven to do. This is creative freedom. This understanding will help to heal the feelings of fear that arise - the fear that you may not have what it takes to accomplish what you so fervently desire. But you DO have what it takes! And now you are beginning to realize this.

Friends, relatives, and associates are likely to affect your life in a significant way this month. Be aware of what is really going on, and do not allow the negativity of others - or your own - to damage your belief in yourself.

Keep your goals firmly in mind. Allow your feelings to guide you through all situations.

Notice how you still worry and become distracted over petty things. Learn to focus on what really *matters* to you. Recognize when guilt is holding you back by disguising itself as love or friendship.

Reaffirm just how seriously you are taking yourself and your plans. Renew your commitment to what you are trying to achieve, and know that this is the year to make it happen.

Try to take some time off and enjoy some light social activities. Soften a little from the hard-line world of pure ambition. Display some friendliness, warmth, humor, and satisfaction with life. Appreciate just how good it feels to be *alive*. People who do not respect your ideas may actually have something important to point out to you, *or* they may not be friends at all. The events of this month will show you that friendship can only flourish if there is first friendship with oneself.

3 is also the number of communication. The way you express yourself is important now. The spoken or written word has a vital and specific role to play. Let your pleasant disposition spread to other people. You will see that it actually rubs off on others, even on those who have taken little interest in your ideas before, creating a warm environment for yourself in which to live or work.

Aggression by you or toward you represents an energy which could damage this month's potential. Take some time to contemplate such feelings, and experience the truth behind them. Open communication is paramount. It starts with the communications you send to and receive from *yourself*. Admit the truth of how you really feel right now. Perhaps a lot of that anger has already gone.

April may also bring a material object into your life which can become not only a friend to you, but also a kind of tool for developing your ideas and plans. 3s emphasis on friends can also apply to nonhumans.

Some kind of success, or a strong sense that success is possible, will heighten your good feelings. It is in this optimistic frame of mind that you are most likely to meet others who can be of benefit to you. We are living in new and very different times. We are learning what "today" is all about by trial and error. New people and new understandings are entering your life to help you change some of your old beliefs, ideas, and rules. This is particularly true in regard to the negative power of disinformation. Opinions are just opinions. Be sure to check things out for yourself instead of relying on hearsay or gossip.

Strive for excellence in all your endeavors, and you will be rewarded by the knowledge that you are, indeed, a very creative person. Just imagine how creative you *could* be if you were not so concerned with how others see you. Hold on to your optimism as your very concept of creativity, friend-ship, and self-acceptance changes with the times and you become more interested in how *you* see yourself. The atmosphere of April will make you realize that you are far more capable than you ever realized.

~ May ~
8 Year - 4 Month

If you run into a wall, don't turn around and give up.
Figure out how to climb it, go through it, or work around it.
MICHAEL JORDAN

May brings you into the down-to-earth 4 cycle which emphasizes the WORK that must be done to fulfill your goal. There is no time for idleness, procrastination, or wishful thinking. Assess what needs to be done and do it. Start out this month with great determination. Dispense with pettiness and rivalry, and concentrate your efforts where they are most needed.

4 emphasizes your identity - the way you see yourself and the way you believe others see you. In the process of sorting out your beliefs about your-self, you are likely to experience limitations, delays, postponements, can-cellations, mental blocks, and other obstacles. The 4 energy is urging you to take all the *details* into consideration. Only then can you get organized. Analyze your entire situation. Make a firm decision to get through this month's obstacle course, and then feel yourself GROW!

You may start to feel overwhelmed by what it will take to reach your goal. This initial fear is inevitable and is simply reminding you that Rome was not built in a day. Allow yourself to experience it. You may not like the way it feels, but this is nothing compared to the feeling of dissatisfaction - self hatred - you will experience if you do not take advantage of this year's opportunities.

You now have an opportunity to reach for a dream and begin to make it real. You will be amazed at what you can achieve with patience, effort, efficiency and, above all, belief in yourself.

Stand and stare at the obstacles you are facing. Assess which of them can be avoided and which ones will prevent your progress until you have removed them completely. In the 8 year cycle, you will prosper if you take what you *already* have and appreciate it. What you already have are your ideas, resources, talent, passion, and imagination. Appreciating them means *loving* them and using them in constructive ways. It also means expanding them and increasing their value.

Get down to the work involved as quickly as possible. Focus less on the problems and more on creative *solutions*. Don't get so lost in the details that you lose sight of the big picture. Your objective is to get organized so that you can start on the actual work involved. Enlist the cooperation of someone else to take care of the more mundane details. Others will be only too happy to cooperate if they can see that you believe in yourself.

The events of May will teach you to persevere, chip away at, and *break through* restrictive situations. You are now laying the all important groundwork for your plans. It is a serious undertaking but, if you really do love what you are doing, it can also be an exciting one. This month, you will encounter what you thought were your limits, only to realize that your belief in yourself has expanded, and this has pushed your limits to a place where they can no longer pressure you. You are READY to take that vital next step.

Cheerfulness, enthusiasm, and consideration for others, will help you sail through this hardworking cycle. Effort and determination now will pay off handsomely later. Make sure you get plenty of rest because the heavy workload can deplete your physical energy, making you feel tired and drawn. Save some time for fun. An orderly and balanced life includes work, play, and rest.

Consider the things and people that you believe are still limiting you. Are some restrictions of your own making? We often limit ourselves through outdated thinking, or because we feel we must do things in a certain way.

Certain obstacles may appear to be permanent or immovable, such as your responsibilities, your age, limitations of your physical body, or the circumstances of your personal or working environments. By accepting the reality of your life, in all its detail, you will find that those obstacles are being placed in front of you so that you can *change* situations that are making you unhappy and preventing your progress.

If you are certain that a particular problem is beyond your ability to change, then you must consider that life is trying to steer you in a new direction entirely where this immovable burden of yours can actually be included in your plans and become an asset instead of an impediment.

An opportunity may arise for you to heal your physical body or to make changes to other areas of your life with which you thought you would always be stuck. These represent some of the wonderful but less obvious rewards of the 8 year cycle.

Perhaps this month's emphasis on work and healing pertains to your own feelings and thoughts. Acknowledge that you have a fear of drastic change, and feel what your fear is telling you. Remember that you have Free Will. Using it will be a breakthrough in itself because you will finally know what it is you *want*.

This month, your emotional wellbeing depends not so much on what happens to you, but on how you *respond* to what happens. Choose to respond naturally to your circumstances and become emotionally involved with the pressures of getting a goal off the ground.

By the end of May, you will realize just how great a breakthrough you have made. You will be able to look back over the past five months and startle yourself as you realize just how far you have come. You will realize that the journey has only just begun and that it's starting to feel *good*.

~ June ~
8 Year - 5 Month

*The future belongs to those who believe
in the beauty of their dreams.*
CARL SANDBURG

You have entered the electrical 5 cycle which responds directly to your innermost feelings. What you are thinking is not the issue here. What you are feeling, deep down, is what will influence this months circumstances. If something happens unexpectedly, as it probably will, it is likely to be something you expected or suspected all along but did not allow yourself to consciously accept.

If nothing significant happens, it is because, deep down, you felt that nothing would occur. It is important to learn the difference between emotion and thought. Try to experience your feelings without commentary of any kind. Feelings contain no words. Feelings are only *felt*. You will soon know that positive thinking without positive *feeling* is mere self-deception. The adventurous 5 energy will help you to reach an alignment here - if you allow it.

Do not confine your activities to one area. If you do, you will start to feel restricted and may lose the potential for advancement that this month offers. Do something you have never done before. Where routine has become a bore, do what has to be done but do it *differently*. The combination of the 5 and 8 vibrations urges constant movement and changing environments, otherwise a multitude of anxieties may arise to throw you off course.

June is a time for excitement and enjoyment. Your adrenalin is likely to be flowing to the full. Travel is indicated. This is an excellent time for a break or vacation. It is certainly time for a CHANGE of some kind. At times, you may feel out of your depth and a little awkward. Just be aware of everything that is happening around you. 5 is a very fast paced and unpredictable energy. It brings you face to face with people, places, and things that are different, strange, exotic, unusual, and sometimes challenging.

Because things happens quickly and erratically in the 5 cycle, you can become reckless and accident-prone if you are not focused. You can get lost or caught up in someone else's reality. So do pay attention as you travel this cycle of *sudden* occurrences.

You are likely to have more physical energy at this time because both the 8 and 5 vibrations are concerned with the physical and material aspects of life. You may become aware of a deeper appreciation for your physical body. It is time to change the way you see yourself. Appreciate the beauty of your dream. Appreciate the power you have to make it come true. You will then see yourself, physically, in a positive new light because you will see your real beauty - your *inner* beauty - shining through the surface of your outer skin.

At the same time, you will learn that you cannot please everyone. Not everyone is able to share your point of view, and the chances are they never will. Your need to bring these people into your camp may never be fulfilled. Focus instead on those who are friendly to your cause.

Throughout June be careful not to overindulge in physical pleasures that, although enjoyable for a while, can actually impede your freedom. These include excesses of food, alcohol, drugs, (including prescription drugs), gambling, extravagance, communication, and other areas where moderation is called for. Excesses of any kind can create *unexpected* problems for you this month. Do not lose your focus now.

A chance encounter, a simple conversation, or your acceptance of reality can give you the enlightenment or encouragement you need to keep yourself moving in the right direction. Perhaps the only thing that needs to be changed is your own self doubt which guilt has cleverly dangled in front of you. Remember that the 8 vibration is urging you to appreciate what you *already* have. If you are certain that what you already have is not enough, then you must use what you already have to attain what you need.

Something in your life *must* change now. You may want to hold on to - or run back to - an old situation simply because you are accustomed to it. But, this month, life is urging you to accept your *changing* reality. Let go of what is no longer available to you. This will give you the faith you need to walk confidently into new territory. Wherever you see change this month, there is a potential opportunity for you. It is up to you to recognize the opportunities, to discern carefully between them, and decide which ones are most beneficial to your goals. You see, it is *long-term* happiness that you are trying to build now. Accept the fact that this will take longer to establish than you anticipated.

One of the main lessons of the 5 cycle is that of profiting from mistakes. This month, life will make you very aware of mistakes you have made. We have to make mistakes in order to learn. And, *until* we learn from a mistake we have no choice but to repeat it. Now, you must recognize a particular mistake, admit to it, understand the consequences of it, and stop repeating it. At this point it will no longer be a mistake. It will be EXPERIENCE. Are you about to make that same old mistake again? Why not do it *differently* this time.

~ July ~
8 Year - 6 Month

See yourself as you really are,
as well as what you could become.
SALLY BROMPTON

Work will keep you busy this month. But you may be interrupted several times so that you can *balance* your outside interests and your emotional commitments.

The question of responsibility arises. Deep feelings may be experienced as you seesaw between two aspects of your life that are precious to you. Only in a state of balance can you fulfill your responsibility to both.

If you find yourself ill-tempered or irritable, it is probably because you are feeling the enormous stress that guilt has placed on you for listening to your own feelings instead of *it*. Resentment and blame are the result of guilt's nagging insistence that you are wrong to focus so exclusively on yourself while neglecting someone or something else. Then, when you attempt to change your focus, guilt comes flying back at you and tells you that you are just too weak to follow your own Free Will. It was guilt that invented the saying "*I'm damned if I do and I'm damned if I don't*".

Now is the time to replace this belief with an understanding of balance. If you were to place all the contents of a boat on one side, it would tip over and sink. Think of yourself as that boat. You will see that you must spread the contents of your life evenly across the deck. Secure a place for everything that matters to you, including your personal goals. Balance your life so that all your different *forms* of love can coexist in harmony. Your primary responsibility, therefore, is to keep yourself afloat. This is no time to abandon ship. Accept the stress you are under. Feel this experience fully. It will allow you to know exactly where you and others stand, as well as who or what your priority should be.

The only way to maintain peace in your diverse world is to weigh up its various components and accept the absolute reality of it all. Then minimize activities which do not pertain to your current situation. Instead, focus on those people and endeavors that are important to you. Acknowledge what cannot be done and focus on what can. Recognize the extremes that the 6 cycle brings to your attention. Proportion them. This is a very emotional time for you. Communicate openly. Inform others of what is going on, and what, if anything, is required of them.

The 8 year is one of reward, so do be aware of the potential you are being offered this month - *love without guilt.* When you are able to see guilt for the destructive force it is, you will realize that it is not others who are restricting you now. It is more likely to be you, yourself, who is causing your current restrictions by believing that you have to lose something in order to gain something.

6 brings forward all matters of the heart: love; family; spouse; children; parents; siblings; home; community; relatives; health, education, neighbors; pets; and all those things for which you have a sense of familiarity or "belonging". The issues of this month will make you appreciate what you *already have* and will help you to understand that when love is free it heals, warms, excites, and grows. Keep your eyes on your goal. Expand your horizons, and make room for everything - and everyone - you *love.*

~ August ~
8 Year - 7 Month

There is always something new
by looking at the same thing over and over.
JOHN UPDIKE

Slow down. Some fear has arisen which seems to have taken the spring out of your step. This is the 7 energy telling you that you may have missed an important point regarding your future plans. Impatience or self doubt may be clouding your vision now. Work through these fears by analyzing your entire situation.

Knowledge is power. The knowledge you gain this month will enable you to add some unique features to an important project or relationship and will let you know the difference between what needs to be feared and what does not.

Get to know how every aspect of whatever you are involved in *works*. Understand its protocol and procedures. Visualize the mechanics of what it will take to create a successful outcome. Know exactly how you, what you are offering, and the people you are dealing with, all fit in to this machinery.

A deep analysis of your situation can prevent you from jumping to the wrong conclusion and then losing faith in yourself. This year is the start of a wonderful new cycle for you, but you may be holding on to an old situation which is draining the joy right out of your life. Flush out the physical and emotional clutter. Allow yourself to *feel* what is really going on inside you. Stop thinking the worst and let your intuition - your feelings - take over.

The 7 energy can make you feel that you are moving too slowly. You may even think that others are conspiring against you. Perhaps someone is jealous of you. Or, perhaps you are afraid that you don't have what it takes to fulfill a particular goal. The truth is that you are standing on the edge of what could become a wonderful new way of life for you. But you have no experience of that world, and you are afraid.

Your fear is perfectly natural and it is right on schedule. However, there is no need to be intimidated. You do belong in that world. But you do have to *believe* that. Then you have to find your way around. It will take courage, and it will take time.

No matter how much you want to surge ahead, you must realize that outer action is not required at this time. Belief in yourself is what will bring *perfection* to your efforts.

This month's combination of cycles enables you to move yourself mentally and emotionally *inside* whatever you are trying to create. It enables you to see and feel your goal as a living entity. You will see any flaws that exist within it. You can then work on cleaning it up and giving it sparkle. Remember that you, yourself, may be the project that you're working on this year.

Do not look only for negative content. Appreciate all that is positive in your life, too. Whatever your goal is, think of it as your baby - your creation. Give it your love and attention. Nurture it and prepare it for its own entrance into the world *next* month. Yes, you will be presenting your "child" - or yourself - to others in September. Your priority is to take what you already have and breathe *form, definition, and life* into it. Spend plenty of time alone this month, so that you can imagine - "image-in" - the possibilities.

At the same time, a situation may occur which feels like a battle of Wills. Do not overreact. Just make it perfectly clear as to what you can and cannot tolerate. If you feel that you cannot allow your time and space to be invaded any longer, express whatever feelings arise. Speak with dignity, diplomacy, and authority. Do what you *feel* you must do.

Maintain faith in yourself. Self discipline is essential because your ability to fine tune now may determine just how successful you will be in the months to come. Forget about the potential rewards. Focus on what has to be done on the *inside*. It is time to take yourself very seriously indeed.

~ September ~
8 Year - 8 Month

Dreams are real while they are happening.
Can we say any more about life?
HAVELOCK ELLIS

You are now in a very important place in the journey. You are probably feeling this deeply. You are brimming with power; you believe you can achieve your goals; the odds are in your favor; and you know there is no turning back now. It is time to put your cards on the table and show the world just how capable you are. The prospects are exciting, and you have the feeling there is much more to come. For now, however, take one step at a time. Each step you take will prepare you for the next.

Dignity and self-assuredness are the result of knowing the process - the workings - of what you are involved in. Be willing to learn. You are surrounded by opportunity. A power that you were not aware of is emerging in you. But because you are unfamiliar with how this power *feels*, nervous tension can arise. You may find yourself short-tempered with others who perhaps, if you care to notice, have some very real problems of their own. Perhaps they do not understand your intentions. Perhaps they do not wish to understand. Or, perhaps the stress you are now displaying is beyond *their* ability to tolerate.

Allow yourself to feel your fear of failure as it battles with your fear of success. Everything will work out fine if you will just regain your focus and stop trying to get the end result before its right time.

September's double dose of 8 energy is pointing out that you are also holding in a great deal of anger. Pressure in a certain part of your body, often the back of the neck or head, could very well be denied anger which is bursting to get out. Take the time to find the cause of these feelings. Once they are expressed and the pressure is released, you will be able to proceed calmly and confidently.

You do not have to confront whoever has made you so enraged. But you do have to confront yourself with the reality of what has happened to you in recent months. If not, the magnetism of your denied anger will draw petty annoyances to you.

Fear is the cause: fear of this enormous power that you know you have but are not sure how to use; fear that if you allow others to distract you now, you will lose the momentum it has taken you so long to amass.

Life may send you a problem now. Another clash of Wills, perhaps? This is happening to help you *accept* the increased power that this year has given you.

Someone or something may be pushing you and making you feel uncomfortable. You are afraid of losing your focus. So *don't* lose your focus. Even if you feel you are being pushed to your limits - *expand* your limits.

Allow your belief in yourself to push those limits up and out and away from you. You are in the process of creating your own destiny, and this month's double 8 energy places you in a much stronger position than you may think.

Give others a fair hearing without losing sight of your goals. Whatever is pressuring you will then seem less powerful, less significant. This is not a matter of denying the feelings involved or ignoring the problems of other people. It is a matter of knowing that you are capable of dealing with more than one issue at the same time. It is a matter of realizing the personal power you have developed. It is a matter of using this power to increase your levels of tolerance. When you deny what you are really feeling, you only create more intolerance and stress for yourself. Only by dealing calmly and efficiently with this month's distractions can you make the breakthrough that is now scheduled.

Put everything in proportion and you will realize that September's annoyances are helping you to express buried emotion out of your body and back in to life where they belong. Creative excellence can then move in. Work through these feelings and get your focus back on the work at hand - *as soon as possible.*

This month you will be proclaiming that you are a professional - so *be* a professional. You are entering a situation in which you must develop a much higher self-esteem. Loving what you are involved in will enable you to make a difficult job look easy, even though you are very conscious of how hard you have had to work. Remember why you chose this path in the first place - because of the enjoyment and the love you derive from it.

The hardest work is behind you now, so *enjoy* what you are doing once again. Be the person you have dreamed of being. Show efficiency, confidence, and dependability. Let others take care of the petty details. Now is the time for a dynamic display of confidence. Yes, now is the time to *be* who you say you are.

~ October ~
8 Year - 9 Month

Tolerance, patience, and understanding are all in short supply.
It is up to you to recognize how and where everyone concerned,
including yourself, can benefit by your display of these attributes,
even though the need to achieve is paramount to your existence.
SALLY BROMPTON

9 is a cycle of ENDINGS. Its influence will bring certain matters to a close. October's cleansing energies urge you to take care of the details, tie up the loose ends, and get things *finished*.

8 is the energy of material satisfaction. You will need to know when you are satisfied with something so that you can let it go without being overcome by fear.

Being satisfied will prevent you from taking things too far and will enable you to conclude something at exactly the right time. Yes, fear is inevitable as you wonder what the future will bring. Feel it. Express it. Let it go.

Eventually, satisfaction must be reached, otherwise a state of standstill will prevent further movement. Success is achieved *after* your satisfaction has allowed your goal to move forward. Success, therefore, is always behind you or in front of you. It is the feeling of satisfaction which remains in the present.

There are no guarantees when it comes to creating your own destiny, but the endings made now will reveal new potential for you. As you bring matters to a close, do so with the satisfaction of knowing that you have given all you can give. Now it is time for your effort to attract its own success. Whatever emotions this parting creates in you, *feel* them and give them your full acceptance. You will feel even more satisfaction when you do. Expressing your emotions, this month, really does conclude the entire process in which you have been involved all year.

And there may be others involved now - people you love but have had to neglect in order to develop your evolving power. This month's emotional reunions or partings should leave no doubt as to your ability to feel.

If illness, depression, or physical discomfort arise now, it is a clear sign that you are still holding onto things that need to be let go. A complete break from the situation may be needed so that you can lick whatever wounds you incurred in the process of empowering yourself. Loosen up, relax some of the rigidity you thought was necessary this year, and *unwind*. Your passion to succeed is commendable, but it may have caused you to overlook some of your most basic needs.

Of course, your passion to succeed will stay with you for a long time to come. But the first phase of a particular goal is coming to an end this month. Remember to thank those who have helped.

You may also want to thank those who hindered your efforts because, in their own way, even if they opposed you, they were also instrumental in building your newfound strength and confidence. This is a time to understand and forgive and put the past behind you.

The efforts you have made this year have brought you to a brand new level of potential. You have reached the end of your old path. And you did very well Now, although you have come up in the world, you are at the bottom of the next level. To some, this can be frightening. To some, this can feel like failure. It is not. You recently became a big fish in a small pond. Now you are about to set sail on the ocean of greater opportunity. There is much to learn and, this month, as ideas you once cherished are turned inside out, you are likely to learn something new and quite unexpected.

Try to be with those you love and care for. Give yourself to these people in some way, not when guilt tells you it is the right thing to do, but when your own loving feelings tell you it is what you want to do. Oh, what satisfaction comes from love when it is free.

~ November ~
8 Year - 1 Month

Every exit is an entry to somewhere else.
TOM STOPPARD

Now that you have achieved one goal, beware of becoming complacent. Last month's endings have created a brand new set of circumstances for you. Many choices exist now, and there is so much to get done. New ideas are flowing and unexpected avenues are opening up. You have accomplished a lot, but this accomplishment is only a stepping stone, albeit a vital one, to much greater possibilities. New areas of understanding are touching your life.

1 is the energy of new beginnings, independence, originality, change, and self-acceptance. You are likely to experience all of these things in some way during November. You are at the beginning of a brand new phase of your life. This is likely to start with the feeling of standing alone, feeling your own pulse, your own energy, your own satisfaction, and your own remarkable power. You will then realize that this marvelous feeling of being alive can only be achieved when you are *being yourself.*

A great change is taking place in your perception of life. Doors are opening that were not open to you before. "As one door closes, another opens", the saying goes. The problem is that, all too often, we cannot see the doors that are opening because we are still focused on the ones that have closed.

Only by allowing the doors of the past to close completely can we see the enormous potential that lies ahead. This can only be done by recognizing the feelings you are holding in and expressing them outwardly. Once again, let your feelings tell you what you want. Then go ahead in that direction. Remember that you are in very different territory now. Stay constantly aware of your new position. There is no need to prove how clever you are. Actually, it would be a good idea to assume that you know nothing at all. This way, you cannot help but learn what needs to be learned.

There is now an emphasis on you: your individuality; your special abilities; your feelings, and your desires. Accept yourself, faults and all, exactly as you are. Only by accepting your faults can you ever hope to change them. But do not judge yourself harshly for having them. It is from the satisfying feeling of self-acceptance that you will be able to accept the individuality and the faults of the people with whom you are now dealing. You will realize that we are *all* in the learning stages of how to live, no matter what qualifications or titles one may possess.

When this awareness is achieved, you will experience a jolt of positive energy which comes from learning something which is entirely new to you. Your consciousness has reached a new level of understanding, and you know that, yes, one person *can* make a difference. The experience of actually *feeling* yourself evolve into higher consciousness is the new beginning November has in mind for you, regardless of what is taking place on a physical or commercial level. It is a feeling you will want to repeat as often as possible because, quite simply, it feels so extraordinarily good.

This year's 8 cycle has provided you with many rewarding experiences in the material aspects of life. Now, however, your life is being pulled by the magnetic energy of next year's 9 energy. Next year will bring a complete cycle of nine years to an end, emphasizing the emotional issues of your entire lifetime.

November's powerful combination of energies gives you the opportunity to visualize your life as one continuing journey, with each event of the past leading to where you stand today. And, from where you stand today, you can hear the call, and you can feel the exciting lure, of where you want to go from here. This is the call of your Will. Where is it taking you?

~ December ~
8 Year - 2 Month

It is tact that is golden - not silence.
SAMUEL BUTLER

Slow down. Don't push. Take some deep breaths. Relax. You are not the star of the show this month. Everyone else is. Maintain your belief in yourself but be aware of your current position. You are on someone else's turf. This is a time of quiet *being* rather than doing, and of making others the focus of your attention. The 2 cycle does not respond well to force or aggression.

Your circumstances leave you no alternative but to give yourself, your goals, and other people, some much needed breathing space. 2 brings out your emotions more than any other cycle. You can no longer deny all those feelings that you've kept hidden for so long.

Adopt a quieter, calmer demeanor. Let others bask in what is *their* limelight. Yes, you had to concentrate on your own needs this year, but the time has come to bring *balance* back into your life. Realize that others may also have something to offer and that their reality is as valid as yours. In fact, you are likely to be surrounded by people who consider themselves to be more experienced than you. Maybe they are and maybe they're not. Patience and genuine cooperation will help you find the necessary balance.

It may take some effort to adapt to this month's slower, humbler pace and, at the same time, retain your new sense of self worth. When you genuinely feel good about yourself, you have no need to push yourself or your accomplishments on others.

Self-acceptance enables you to feel so relaxed that you can live, moment by moment, without concern of what others think of you, or of what your next problem might be. The love you have built up for yourself can now be *shared* with others.

A partnership of some kind may be established. You are part of a team and, the more you do your part, the more efficiently the team can operate. Others are aware of your increased power. But they can only relax with you when you, yourself, are relaxed. Then the wheels of progress can turn successfully and smoothly without constantly becoming snagged on each others fears and insecurities.

Your ability to intuit is very strong now, and through this emotional energy you will feel a powerful urge to create something of much greater value in your life. Be patient. The groundwork for such a goal will take time and effort. This year, personal satisfaction was the goal. Be satisfied with how well you did.

Even if others are grating on your nerves right now, your connection to them may turn out to be one of the greatest rewards of the year. There is no need to push yourself in any way. Certain details must be taken care of. Don't worry about your own plans too much. The break you are giving them will ensure that they are receiving recognition on their own merits, without your constant presence or interference. Patience and faith are the keys to a successful end to the year.

It is important that you know the theme of the year to come. The 9 year cycle is the end of an era of your life. It frees you from all those emotions you have been holding inside. It enables you to let go of the past by bringing the reality of your past *comfortably* into the present. This will enable you to start a brand new chapter of your life in the 1 year cycle.

For now, as the new year approaches and you prepare to cross over into a new twelve-month cycle of your life, remember this year's many powerful experiences. Remember the many lessons you have learned and feel the strength you have gained from them. Be proud of who you *were*. It was that person who enabled you to be the person you have become. Hold on to this amazing wealth. Hold on to your expanded power. Hold on to your belief in yourself - as midnight of December 31st arrives and the emotional 9 year cycle of *conclusions* begins.

The 9 Year Cycle

the end of an era -
going back to claim your future

> *The old is dying and the new cannot be born.*
> *In the interim, a great variety of*
> *morbid symptoms appear.*
> ANTONIO GRAMSCI

The 9 year cycle brings you to the end of a complete nine year cycle of your life. This is a time of completing unfinished business, reaching conclusions, tying up loose ends, and cleaning up behind you. These actions will enable you to step into the next nine years of your life without the pressure of unresolved matters of the past pulling you back.

It has often been said that as one door closes another opens, but if you refuse to accept that certain doors really have closed, you will be unable to see the new doors and the new possibilities opening up before you. It is time to face the absolute reality of your past and your present, and then decide how you want to create your future.

Your reality is not just a matter of where you stand today or where you want to be tomorrow. It is made up of everything that has ever happened to you, everyone you have ever met, anything you have ever done, and any feeling you have ever felt - or denied. Where you stand today is the result of where you have been. But, before you can move ahead, you must release yourself emotionally, mentally, and sometimes physically, from those aspects which no longer serve a purpose and are chaining you to a point in time that no longer exists.

It is time to integrate your past with the present, so that the potential of your future can be seen and felt. This is achieved by accepting the past exactly as it was, and by feeling everything about it that you've been unable to feel.

This year provides the opportunity for significant evolutionary transformation. There will be alterations and improvements to all areas of your life, even though you may not immediately see the positive merits of certain situations. When the old buried emotion that is weighing you down is released, life suddenly becomes a much lighter experience and is more easily understood and enjoyed.

You may feel a sense of numbness or stagnation at times. This is because you are so close to accepting your full reality, but are holding the emotions involved *in* instead of expressing them *out*. The magnetic pressure that this creates prevents forward movement and draws to you a repeat of the very situations you would prefer to avoid.

We have all been conditioned to believe that emotional expression denotes weakness and is somehow negative. In fact, emotional expression is our strength, our own self-healing mechanism, our only means of freedom, and the ultimate tool of creativity.

People who refuse to accept the past are those who spend their entire lives rehashing the same old situations, making the same old mistakes, unable to accept new realities, dissatisfied with everything, and all the time aging rapidly. They find ways to justify their unsatisfactory existence by blaming others, blaming time, blaming life itself, and sometimes blaming themselves.

Stubborn unchanging beliefs cause people to embrace sayings such as *"Life's a bitch and then you die."*, or *"There's nothing you can do about it, so why even try?"* It often seems easier to accept excuses like these than to accept our responsibility to live *freely*. Some people claim to be apart from or above the journey humanity is taking, all the time resenting that they are too afraid to be a part of it. And, because none of us has truly evolved into Free Will yet, we are all effected by these misunderstandings.

This year, it is not enough to simply have an intellectual understanding of Free Will. You will learn that your *feelings* are your only means of activating personal freedom. This year of endings and conclusions offers you the chance to free yourself of the erroneous beliefs that have *always* caused unhappiness, dissatisfaction, and stagnation. The 9 year cycle teaches you how to break free from the past by releasing *your* grip on it. Without this understanding, you will forever be a victim of something that once happened to you. It is time to heal.

Nothing new happens in the 9 year cycle until the necessary endings are made. The more you strive to begin something new without first releasing the old, the more resistance life will give you. If you do not make an effort to accept the emotional realities of your past this year, you will find that your history will simply repeat itself in your next nine-year cycle.

This is a year to go back over your life's continuous journey and consider everything that has happened to you. There will be things you don't want to remember; memories you may be blocking from your consciousness. These are the very events and situations which need to be addressed now. These are the heavy loads that are weighing on you like an anchor, preventing you from moving forward into the kind of life you desire. The more genuine *intent* you have to allow forgotten memories to resurface, the easier it will become to accept 9's healing process.

It is the sheer weight of old emotion that causes depression, even though we try to fool ourselves into believing that depression can be avoided by avoiding these emotions. This pretense creates deeper denial and, eventually, deeper depression. If you find yourself dwelling on certain emotions such as anger, fear, or grief to the extent that you cannot live a constructive life, then there is a good chance you are using these emotions as an excuse for continuing to deny another emotion which is even more deeply buried.

Being afraid to feel your feelings is a natural response. The only way to deal with this fear is to understand that fear, like all other feelings, must be allowed to follow its own evolutionary process. It must be allowed to MOVE. When you cling on to fear you are refusing to accept its ability to help you. And, by stopping its movement you, in turn, become paralyzed by it. Feel your fear, accept its presence, and allow it to move through you - and out of you. This process develops courage; the ability to recognize those things which really do need to be feared, *and* those which need not be feared at all. New understandings will follow, and other buried emotions will pursue the same outward course.

You must resolve to be totally honest with yourself. Understand that mere positive thinking can do more harm than good if you are not simultaneously *feeling* positive. Your thoughts and your feelings are two very different energies. They must be experienced separately so that you can tell them apart. However, when your inner feelings and your thoughts agree and align with each other, miracles begin to happen and Free Will is born. One of these miracles is that each time you release a buried emotion, something positive *always* occurs afterward.

In order to express your feelings, you must accept that they are there, search for them, recognize them, and understand their *cause*. The 9 vibration takes you in what seems like the wrong direction - *backwards* - but this is the direction you must take in order to find the unfinished issues which are preventing you from going forward.

It is natural for the 9 year cycle to be an emotional one. Not only will you be dealing with emotions from the past, but also with new emotional situations in the present which, in effect, help trigger the old feelings which need to be released. This year's circumstances may actually be reenactments of past circumstances in different forms. They may represent the consequences of past actions, beliefs, and attitudes. It is impossible to live fully in the present if part of you is stuck in the past. Therefore, you will want to go back and retrieve those parts of yourself that are stuck there.

This is a 12 month cycle in which generosity and humanitarianism play important roles. By achieving a greater depth of feeling in yourself, you will sense just how powerful feelings are. Not just your's - everyone's. You are likely to reach a more compassionate understanding of other people's needs. You will become aware of how you and others are compounding certain problems by denying your true feelings and refusing to face the reality of your situations. You will also become very aware of the difference between compassion and guilt.

If you find yourself helping others reluctantly, or allowing the actions of others to hurt you in some way, you are probably doing so because guilt has convinced you that it's the 'right' thing to do. Maybe it is and maybe it isn't. But the only way you will ever be sure is by letting your own feelings guide you. It is in the 9 year cycle that we realize the extent to which guilt has kept us from achieving happiness and how much we have denied guilt by reversing it into blame.

Unhappy memories will arise so they can be healed. This will create a space within you for happiness to resurface. Old inaccurate beliefs will be replaced by new truths and potentials. As you accept what *has* happened to you in the past, you will develop a clearer picture of what you *want* to happen in the future. The old you becomes the present you, and your Will - your desire - then determines the future you.

Not all endings will have unhappy emotions attached to them. Certain situations will be concluded, bringing you much relief. Don't always assume the worst. Accept that your past is simply the ground you had to cover in order to get to where you want to be. Your understanding of this will make your 9 year cycle one of the most exhilarating and dynamic journeys you will ever travel.

~ January ~
9 Year - 1 Month

We only truly evolve as people
when we dare to get to know ourselves
and remove the layers we hide behind.
GERI HALLIWELL

As the 9 and 1 vibrations merge this month, you will realize that your life is not providing the fulfillment you hoped it would. You may feel that there just has to be more than this. You seem to be trapped in a room which has no door; stopped in your tracks at a time when you feel you should be moving forward. This month, the 1 energy urges you to LEAD your own life. But what kind of a leader would say, "Hey, follow me even though I have no idea where I'm taking you"?

The 9 cycle is telling you to stop blindly pushing yourself forward, go back into the past instead, and realize where your past actions and beliefs have *led* you. The 1 cycle urges independence, while 9 points out just how *dependent* you are on so many different factors. The 1 energy tells you to be yourself, while 9 asks "How can you be yourself when such a large part of you is lost somewhere in the past"? 1 is the energy of material attainment while 9's influence makes it clear that material attainment alone cannot bring happiness. 1 says "Hold on" and 9 says "Let go".

Your emotions are being pushed forward and backward at the same time, creating a feeling of being torn between two issues. You know that something has to end but you cannot make that ending because you're afraid to know what the outcome will be. "Someone tell me what to do", your subconscious pleads, and then replies, "Only *you* have the answer".

This brings you to the conscious conclusion that you now stand alone in the world to face your own reality, make your own decisions, and create your own reality. An important change must take place in your under-standing of *independence*.

1 is a cycle of *new beginnings* and, in this 9 year of *endings*, January repre-sents the beginning of an entire year of conclusions. The new evolves out of the old but, by refusing to accept the emotional reality of your past, the old has no choice but to repeat itself.

Your feelings must be allowed to move in all directions; forward, back-ward, to and fro, so that you can recognize the emotions from the past that are still trapped inside you. Ask yourself how you would *like* to feel so that a sense of what "can be" is also felt. Visualize your life with a past, a present, *and* a future. See exactly how your past has created your present and how the future you want can be created out of your present circumstances.

You know you are entering a new phase of your life and, yet, you may experience great frustration and fear of failure while this transitory period plays itself out. It is as if you are waiting in the wings and are afraid you have missed your cue. You know your time will come, but why won't it come quicker? It is because your present position is this:

You are living in both the "letting go" cycle of your past, and the "learning the ropes" cycle of your future. You have no idea what to expect from the people involved in either cycle and they, too, have no idea what to expect from you. Try to be as gracious and patient as possible, and don't blame yourself or others for the inevitable delays.

You may feel ready to break new ground, but do realize that you still have so much to learn about the new reality you wish to create for yourself. This is a time of letting go of those parts of you that no longer serve a purpose; and of revealing those courageous parts you always believed should be kept hidden.

Last year, your efforts catapulted you to a new position in life in which you and others became aware of your talent. Your *past* reached its peak. This year, others are viewing you from a different angle, as if the future is trying to figure out where you fit into it. You are now dealing with the reality of your whole lifetime and there is a lot of ground to cover. You are going to find that no matter how many different circumstances arise this year, they all represent one experience only - the experience of releasing yourself from the past. So be patient with yourself - and others - as you GO BACK to claim your future.

~ February ~
9 Year - 2 Month

I was angry with my friend;
I told my wrath, my wrath did end
WILLIAM BLAKE

SLOW RIGHT DOWN. Take some deep breaths. There is no need to struggle or push. Try to relax with whatever is going on. There are people or things in your life that you truly love and do not want to lose. But there are other aspects that you have only been pretending to love because you consider them inseparable from the things you do love. Fear of losing what you love has imprisoned you to situations or people that you just *can't stand* any longer. The sooner you admit this to yourself the sooner a solution will be found. Something has to *give*, but you are not sure how to proceed. Slow down, relax, and take some more deep breaths as you allow this reality to sink in.

A decision must be made. By the end of February, you will have made it. Use this month to relax completely. Your decision must be based on the reality of what you want as well as what you do not want. Impulsive moves are likely to work against you.

Great patience and attention to detail are required. Take some more deep breaths, and forget about pushing yourself ahead. Keep a low profile. Your own plans, goals, and circumstances are being taken care of, on some other plane, while you tend to important matters which pertain to your *relationships*.

Do not force anything. 2 is the gentle energy of sensitivity and caring. 2 promotes peace, patience, diplomacy, partnership, and cooperation. 2 is the energy of intuition, balance, and ease. Most of all, 2 is the number of emotion. The emotional act of feeling your fear has also stirred the anger inside you, enabling you to finally lose patience with your situation. Some very deep feelings have now risen to the surface.

You have allowed certain circumstances to go on for too long because guilt told you that you must not hurt someone else's feelings, that you must give up on a dream because that is what love or decency requires of you. Now, however, you know that this situation cannot continue.

Great understanding, honesty, and patience are required as you assess the facts of the matter. Has guilt tricked you into sacrificing yourself in the name of responsibility, peace, or love? What are your options? You must find a solution which allows you to *keep* what you love and move away from what is hurting you.

Teamwork and cooperation have important roles to play. Slow down. Relax. Keep taking those deep breaths. Understand the meaning of the phrase "there is a reason for everything". It means that there is a *cause* for everything. And it is that cause, from the past, that you must now find through your natural ability to sense things.

The combination of the 9 and 2 energies is powerful and cleansing. If you are honest with yourself, you will experience feelings of anger, hatred, shame, sorrow, grief, or pain this month. These feelings need to come out, but do remember that your healing process is a personal concern. There is no need to confront others when releasing your feelings, even though it may take the words or actions of someone else to push these feelings to the surface. Make sure you give yourself the privacy and the time you need for this process. The situation cannot continue as it is. In fact, your life cannot move forward until this matter is resolved.

Proceed calmly and confidently with your day-to-day affairs. There are many details to take care of. If you find yourself pendulating between the extremes of having too much patience and having none at all, realize that you are now being stretched between the extremes of your situation. Being aware of these extremes will help you to find a point of *balance* where you can express yourself spontaneously without hurting yourself or anyone else.

Allow others to express themselves freely, from *their* point of view. Their realities can be respected, even if they are not fully understood. What is of interest to you may not interest others, and vice versa. Rather than forcing your point on other people, find a persuasive form of expression which enables them to *understand* what you are trying to convey. If you cannot get your point across at all, do not push too hard. You cannot expect others to fathom something which you, yourself, are struggling to understand. And you cannot be expected to involve yourself in something which clearly goes against your grain.

2 is a very gentle vibration. It is *you* that you need to be gentle with this month. Face the reality of your situation, find the cause, release the feelings involved, and then *relax* with your new understandings. Slow down and cooperate with your environment and with those around you. Some friendly interaction with others will help take the pressure off yourself for a while. Don't force anything. By the end of February you will have made an important decision and it will probably come as quite a relief to you.

~ March ~
9 Year - 3 Month

It is hard not to exaggerate
the happiness you haven't got.
STENDHAL

It is time to conclude an issue, project, or situation which is no longer working for you. This ending can be an enormous relief, providing you do not deny the inevitable feelings of sadness that arise when you say farewell to an old friend or an old belief. March will keep you busy tying up the loose ends of this month's emotional hellos and goodbyes. Don't allow guilt to deplete your energy or optimism.

Let this month's intense emotional movement transport you back to times when you were laughing, feeling good about yourself, feeling the satisfaction of achievement, feeling loved, and being in love. Again, don't let guilt tell you that it is wrong to wallow in the past or that you must keep up the *appearance* of being strong and in control of your emotions. Guilt's function is to stop the emotional movement which allows life to flow freely. This month, you will be going back into the past so that you can retrieve the many episodes of *happiness* that are buried there.

Do not forget that this year represents the end of a complete era of your life. Life is now asking you to make a firm decision which will end that phase of your life where other people's negativity sucked you in so easily. Your unique journey has its own direction to take.

Do make sure, as you travel backwards, that what you are remembering and reliving is not just an *appearance* of happiness. We often deceive ourselves into believing that we were happy just because we were able to give the *impression* of happiness. It is not difficult to mimic the outer appearance of happiness for short periods of time, even when we are deeply unhappy inside. It is the *inner* feelings of happiness, and not just the pretense, that you must search for now. You may have to dig pretty deep. If you cannot find old happiness at all, you will first have to remove the layers of *sadness* that are burying it. Yes, the 9 year cycle is destined to be an emotional one, but a very healing one.

Expand your creative ability by stretching your imagination. See the *new* potential that exists for you in this evolving world. March invites you to tap in to the hidden potential you have had to keep under wraps until now. You are beginning to shed those parts of you that no longer contribute to your well-being. Meanwhile, those marvelous aspects of yourself which you always thought you had to keep hidden are beginning to emerge. Hold on to your optimism throughout this month's confusing, exhilarating ride. Be real with other people and watch the real way they respond to you as you find your *natural* way to communicate.

Friends are a major aspect of the 3 cycle. It is within the arena of friendship that much memory can be reclaimed. Try contacting an old pal. Perhaps there are some loose ends to tie up there. You may find that a current friendship has lost its flare or, perhaps, the nature of a friendship is causing a problem. A friendship may end, or a misunderstanding can now be cleared up.

3 shows us how we seek the approval of others before we make a move, and how discouraged we become if we do not receive approval after making a move. Remember, the only approval you need is your own. Anything else prevents you from moving at all.

Keeping up appearances is fear of rejection. You must now deal with your fear of how you are perceived by others. Allow your fear to evolve into *self-acceptance*. When you truly accept yourself for who and what you are, as well as who you *were*, the magnetism that this creates draws to you everything and everyone you *love*, instead of those people and things with which you have nothing in common. Without full acceptance for yourself, you cannot fully accept anyone else. Nor can anyone else fully accept you.

Look back over your life's experiences and realize just how hard you have been on yourself. What is the worst that can happen if you do not get your life exactly as you think it should be? This is a very serious question. And when you are able to answer it, you will release yourself from the painful grip of guilt. Guilt always tells you that you should be doing better than you are. Sometimes we deny the guilt in ourselves and turn it into blame. We transfer our own guilt onto others by implying that they should be doing better than they are.

The things you want to happen may forever elude you until you let go of the magnetic feeling of *need*. Neediness attracts neediness. Guilt attracts guilt. Satisfaction attracts satisfaction, just as money attracts money and love attracts love.

In a month when you are searching for the secret of personal happiness, you will realize that the only times you were genuinely happy were those times when you were not concerned about what others thought of you.

~ April ~
9 Year - 4 Month

Don't be dismayed at goodbyes.
A farewell is necessary before you can meet again.
And meeting again, after moments or lifetimes,
is certain for those who are friends.
Richard Bach, Illusions:
THE ADVENTURES OF A RELUCTANT MESSIAH

The purpose of the 4 cycle is to bring you to your limits so that you can know what your limits are. Once you accept that these boundaries exist, you can use your intent and determination to push them away from you. Instead of allowing your usual limits to crush you under their weight, your own expanded belief in yourself will push them up and out and away from you. It is time to use the power of your Will to create more space for yourself, physically, mentally, and emotionally, regardless of who seemingly pushed you to your limits in the first place. If you look carefully, you may notice that someone else has reached their limits too.

On a physical level, make this a month of efficiency and hard work. Use common sense. Organize yourself and get everything in order. Keep to a sensible routine, create a workable system, and recognize the serious nature of what you are trying to accomplish. Whatever this work entails, remember that its purpose is to make life *easier* for you, not harder or more complicated.

Know when it's time to rest so that your physical energy can be replenished, not drained. There are many details to take care of now. Your determination to deal with them all will provide the power you need to reach your limits and push them away from you. And, "hey presto!". Suddenly, your potential expands and you can accomplish things that, last month, you thought were quite unattainable. Expansion has taken place in your conscious mind. Now, great fulfillment can be experienced by organizing your life, dispensing with pettiness, and analyzing what you are left with.

Expanding your emotional limits means *feeling* the pressure of all those buried feelings of the present and past, and being aware of how free you will be once they have been released from your body.

Expanding your spiritual or mental limits means understanding this process and having the firm intent to participate in it. Until this understanding takes place, you are likely to feel overworked, boxed-in, and unable to move in any direction. Let it all out and experience the good feeling that comes from a sense of closure.

It is impossible to prejudge the effect of this process before you have experienced it. You may be afraid that it will leave you feeling heartless and empty. Are you assuming that if you had total freedom you would not know what to do with it? That others would try to take it away from you? That you would lose love? Or that this level of freedom would be too difficult to maintain? Only by allowing yourself this experience will you ever know, without a doubt, that total freedom to do what you want _is_ love, and that the emptiness and heartlessness you fear is actually the fear of living a life without ever truly knowing love's many forms.

Certainly, some feelings of heartlessness may arise now. And you can be sure that guilt will have plenty to say about it. But until you acknowledge these bitter feelings and allow them to leave your body, you will never be able to discover the enormous power they are burying - the power of your own love. Even if you expand your experience of this in the smallest way, it will bring expansion to all areas of your life.

This month's emphasis on work can provide even more personal growth by expanding the limits of what you think is your _identity_. Restriction is often caused by measuring your worth by the work that you do, instead of by the satisfaction derived from _all_ that you do in life. If what you "do" is just part of the cold reality of having to make a living, you may find that making a living has become a difficult or unpleasant process in itself.

Much of this month, (and this year), is likely to focus on what you _want_ to do. Humanity is evolving to a state where Free Will is our only alternative to self-destruction. Free Will means doing what you _love_ to do. This is how prosperity is being attained now, and how prosperity will be attained in the future. The answer lies in whatever makes you happy, and this can only be determined by the feelings your activities invoke in you. It is time to go back and rescue an activity or idea that once made you _feel_ passionate, but was abandoned because your circumstances changed, or because you or others decided you could not make a living from it.

Old beliefs about what is practical may no longer apply in our changing world. We know that where there is happiness there is love, and where there is love there is creativity and life itself. It is on this foundation that your true identity can be built and your true talent expanded to a level where you can not only make a living, but also live the life you want to live.

~ May ~
9 Year - 5 Month

One's knowledge cannot go beyond one's experience.
JOHN LOCKE

May brings you to an important crossroads which can leave you wondering which way to go? Fear and anger, which may be very well hidden
even from yourself, are demanding to know why all this change is necessary, and why you can't just get "back to normal".

First, you must recognize and feel your fear and anger. Then you must
find their cause. Realize how the past has made the present inevitable. You
will soon know that your craving to get back to normal is actually an unrealistic wish to get back to the past - which is full of the same old mistakes
which led you to your present circumstances. By facing this reality you will
know that the only option left is that of real and constructive *change*.

Guilt does not want you to have the freedom of learning from your mistakes. Guilt is very clever at disguising itself as blame. By lifting the blame
off other people, yourself, or situations beyond your control, you will clearly see where you have made mistakes and how you are still repeating them
to this day.

One reason humanity has learned so little in so long is that we have
made judgments against ourselves for making mistakes instead of using
our mistakes for their intended purpose, which is to learn something.
Once you admit that a mistake has been made; once you learn what needs
to be learned from it and do not make that mistake again, the mistake
itself evolves and becomes - EXPERIENCE.

End those beliefs and judgments that are preventing you from being the
person you want to be. Be aware of everything that is going on around you,
otherwise you could become accident-prone, reckless, or unable to keep up
with a situation that is changing before your very eyes. There is now an
emphasis on your physical body. Take care of it and realize just how vital a
part of you your body is. There may be a tendency to block out - deny - your
present reality by overindulging in alcohol, food, drugs, sex, gambling, or
some other means of avoiding the emotions involved. This month, your
physical condition is a good indicator of just how much buried emotion
you are carrying around with you.

Choices and changes must be made. You may feel lonely standing there at the crossroads of your life with no idea where any of these roads will lead. But you are not alone. Millions of people, all over the world, are standing at their crossroads, too. But it is you *alone* who must make the choice of either moving forward into a happiness of your own design or returning to 'normal' and stagnating miserably for another nine years. Is there really a choice?

With freedom and change in mind, free yourself from normal routines and activities or, at least, approach them in a different way. Free yourself from the word "normal". It is just another word for average. It is normal conventional thinking that has almost killed Free Will on this planet.

Freedom of thought, movement, emotion, and expression - for everyone - is the only alternative to war. Make peace with yourself. Everything starts with the self because if there is no peace within, there can be no peace in your outer reality either. Tradition is breaking down all around us, and the world is embarking on a peaceful revolution of love and creativity.

The magnetic 5 energy is attracted to and responds to your *expectations*; not necessarily what you *think* you expect, but on a deeper level, what you *feel* is going to happen. When unexpected things occur, as they may this month, they are usually things that you did expect deep down but were unable to bring into your conscious mind. On the other hand, you may be thinking very positively about change this month but nothing changes. This shows that deep down you did not expect anything to change and that positive thinking is always outweighed by denied 'negative' *feelings*.

~ June ~
9 Year - 6 Month

The one thing we can never get enough of is love,
and the one thing we never give enough of is love.
HENRY MILLER

A selfless and realistic attitude is required as you face certain facts about love. There is likely to be an emphasis on the home, responsibility, spouse, lover, children, parents, pets, relatives, health, close friends, and other matters of the HEART. Issues of the past will return so they can be felt, released, and understood.

These personal areas of your life are heavily influenced by deep bonds and feelings. Lack of emotional movement indicates deeply denied feelings about those closest to you. A positive ending will take place when you *let go* of that anger, fear, or grief. You will then realize just how much love is buried underneath the anger, fear, or grief that you've been holding inside for so long. It is probably your anger, fear, or grief which has caused a physical problem that needs your attention now. Many people believe that the condition of our physical bodies affects the way we feel. On the contrary, it is the way we feel which affects the state of our bodies.

Love must be free in order to be love. Judgments, control, rules, and conditions are the result of fear that has been denied. Love that is "held on to" is not free. Love can only be felt, given, and received in a continuous free flowing exchange. Guilt does not want you to realize that you really do hate some of the people you claim to love, because guilt does not allow you to feel your true feelings. When you do feel your true feelings, anger and hatred may certainly be felt, but these emotions can evolve, like any other feeling, into love. Guilt wants to keep anger and hatred firmly in place by making you deny that anger and hatred are what you are feeling. Working through your true feelings about those closest to you is going to make this month a very warm and loving one, despite the apparent contradictions involved.

Remember, too, that a mental acceptance for unconditional love is as far as humanity has come in realizing this concept. No one on Earth is presently capable of loving everyone and everything. This is because not everyone or everything can or wants to receive the love you have to give. It is impossible to love those who horrify and disgust you without denying your feelings of horror and disgust. All you can do is accept that everyone is evolving at their own speed, and that their speed may not be the same as yours.

So many people believe that love is lost when they no longer share the same interests. This is not true. We are all searching for a reality that feels right for us. For some, this may involve a geographical move. For others, it means pursuing something they feel passionate about. Your ideal reality can only be determined by the direction in which your feelings take you. Consequently, even those who love each other deeply may not share the same ideals.

An acceptance of the *individuality* of those you love will help reduce the confusion and conflict within these precious relationships. It is important that this is not a one-sided acceptance. You, too, must be accepted for the individual you are, and June's healing energies will provide an opportunity to make this clear to someone who may not be giving you the acceptance you need and deserve. You will also realize, however, that until total acceptance for yourself and what you are trying to achieve takes place within YOU, it is impossible for anyone else to fully accept you.

Your Will knows the path it wants to follow. Listen to it, feel it, and let it take you there. It also wants you to be around others whose Wills are free and active. Old judgment has been that family and close friends should always stick together, *no matter what*. But this belief causes so much denial of reality, emotion, and happiness. Genuine love and closeness can only remain within a group if each individual is free to be who they really are, learn what they need to learn, and go where they need to be. Without this understanding, familiarity does, indeed, breed contempt.

With so much emphasis on the home, you may find yourself wondering where home for you really is. Childhood memories may emerge. Thoughts of the old neighborhood, siblings, parents, children, or others close to your heart may arise. There is a lot of unexpressed emotion involved here.

In a month when responsibility is also a key issue, you may realize that by trying to control another or allowing someone else to control you; by assuming that you are responsible for everything or not responsible for anything; by focusing too much on one area of your life and neglecting other aspects, neither peace nor love can exist within your relationships. A balance must be found which makes room for *everything* you love.

Your primary responsibility is to free your Will and encourage others to free theirs. In most cases, this results in being able to *share* happiness with those who matter to you. In other cases, the time will have come to move away from those who cannot allow love to live in freedom. A responsibility which may now be placed upon you need not feel like a burden if you approach it with love instead of guilt. If you are uncomfortable about a certain responsibility, or with your role within a relationship, make your feelings known. You can ease much of your stress, and other people's, by being honest with yourself, and with those around you.

Allow everyone to be who and what they are. Teach children and other dependents about their own Will and that life does not punish but responds to actions taken. Allow them to be active participants in the creation of a close and loving family instead of the burden that many children today believe they are. The truth is, we are *all* children. We are all just learning the meaning of life, love, and liberty.

~ July ~
9 Year - 7 Month

> *The definition of courage is grace under fire.*
> ERNEST HEMINGWAY

No matter what transpires this month, there is likely to be an element of *strangeness* about it, as if a fog has descended on your life. You are unsure of what your next move should be. You want to *do* something, but the feeling persists that "you're damned if you do and you're damned if you don't".

This is the voice of guilt. It is creating a feeling of inadequacy; a feeling that you have little or nothing to offer. Guilt is telling you that you must constantly be doing something, because doing nothing and getting nowhere in this human 'race' is not acceptable. Stop judging yourself by someone else's standards. Accept the presence of guilt and then move away from it. Only then will you be able to benefit from the 7 cycle through which your life is now traveling.

July is a month in which life is asking you to slow down, preferably to a crawl. Stop doing, stop racing, and simply be. *This* is your contribution to life right now. Just accept the stillness of it all and know that you do not have to prove a thing. This is a month in which you can do or contribute little else, so why frustrate yourself with the need to be *seen* as busy, productive, and in control? It is time to discover the perfection in the human *being* rather than the flaws in the human race.

This feeling of perfection will come when you are quiet, alone, and at ease in your solitude. Take private time and space for yourself. You have some private thinking and feeling to do. The question is, *"What do I really want?"*, which can only be answered by another question: *"What do I really feel?"*

The reason you have been unable to make headway this month, or perhaps this year, is because you do not know which direction to take. The only way you will be able to see your options, let alone make a decision, is to go inside, back in time, and determine what it was in the past that led you here; to this state of being lost.

If you find yourself criticizing or blaming others, it is probably an attempt to cover up or deny criticisms you have of yourself. If you search your feelings now, you will discover an important connection between mistakes you see others making and mistakes you have made yourself, perhaps in a different form.

Much can be changed and accomplished by recognizing the link that is being mirrored to you by the actions of other people. Others may criticize you. Don't let this deflate your belief in yourself or in what you are trying to achieve. In fact, see the negativity of others for what it is. It is the negativity of *others*. Use its emotional impact to make yourself even stronger.

Issues of the past may reappear. Deal with them once and for all. In the 9 year, anything you haven't dealt with is going to deal with you. Be careful when it comes to secrets of any kind because they are likely to surface during July. Try to bring a secret out in the open, or accept that this matter is unresolved. Work through the fear or guilt you are holding in as a result. You may even find that an issue no longer has a need for secrecy. But if you stand to hurt yourself or someone else by "coming clean", ask yourself what would really be gained by making a painful revelation.

In most cases, the only person you need to be honest with and reveal your secret to is *you*. Perhaps this emphasis on secrets means that someone else's secret will be revealed to you and may effect you in some way. Maybe someone will shock you as they reveal how *they* really feel.

7 is a cycle of KNOWLEDGE. It is a perfect time to study, analyze, research, and fine tune. Instead of saying, "I can't do what I want because I don't know anything about it", LEARN about it.

Realize where you have allowed fear to hold you back in the past. See the futility of clinging on to it. You are now on a cyclical curve of self-empowerment through LEARNING, and there is so much to learn if you will just give yourself the freedom to do so.

~ August ~
9 Year - 8 Month

Mediocrity knows nothing higher than itself,
but talent instantly recognizes genius.
SIR ARTHUR CONAN DOYLE
THE ADVENTURES OF SHERLOCK HOLMES

August is a time to efficiently wrap up the loose ends of your financial and business activities. Accept your losses *and* count your blessings. The events of this month may appear to be all talk and not enough action and, yet, there is probably more reward involved here than your ego is willing to admit.

There is now much to learn about what you really want and what no longer appeals to you. Life has pulled you to a crossroads and careful consideration should be given to your finances, your ambitions, and your personal power to make things happen.

8 is a cycle of *prosperity* and *satisfaction*. The events of this month may start to challenge your belief in yourself. Someone else's negativity may surface, yet again, in an effort to deplete the confidence you have worked so hard to gain. You may feel hurt, angry, even defeated. Try to understand why this is happening.

8 is the energy of self-empowerment. Your circumstances are showing you just how you have allowed other people's negativity to affect you in the past. Remember that the 9 year cycle represents endings and completions. This month marks the END of that era in your life in which you allowed others to wipe the smile from your lips, the glow from your face, and the enthusiasm from your heart, through their words, actions, or limited views. You can no longer allow other people's negativity, or what you perceive to be other people's negativity, to become yours. You cannot change other people, but you can change your understanding of them and your reaction to them.

Pick yourself up, feel how empowered you are, and continue in the direction of your choice. Life is inviting you to grow, flourish, and excel. But are you aware of it? Will you accept it? What are your alternatives? See yourself a year from now - or five years from now - if you have not resolved this conflict between your own needs and the power others have over you. See yourself a year from now - or five years from now - if you *do* accept this freedom and start to live the life you want to live and be the person you want to be.

Money may come in or important agreements may be finalized, but the results may be less than you had hoped for. You will receive what your efforts are worth, but it will be difficult to hide your disappointment. Until, of course, you realize that this months events have not defeated you at all. On the contrary, your ambitions have suddenly grown by leaps and bounds. You want more out of life - much more! And you know that you are the only person on Earth who can make it happen.

The events of August are enabling you to shed the guilt and fear which have always placed limitations on your true ambitions. As you conclude business and financial matters, you will know that your old way of life has reached the end of its usefulness. Those aspects you once regarded as important simply bore and aggravate you now. Face this reality. One particular party is over, and it is time to go back to the drawing board of your own imagination. That is where the next invitation to happiness is waiting.

The 9 year cycle is a time of *total completion* in which no loose ends should be left untied. Consider any debts you may have and, if possible, pay them. You may have a debt you have forgotten about - to a friend or relative perhaps - and this must be addressed now or by the end of the year, so that its guilty shadow cannot follow you into next year's brand new energy.

Be patient with yourself and others as you rethink the very nature that your life has taken on. This year has been an erratic journey, to say the least. Consider how you feel about totally changing the lifestyle to which you have become so accustomed. Contemplate how much of the "old you" was created out of a fear of loss; a need for status; to give the appearance of happiness and success while, all the time, your real desires and potentials were being denied simply because you needed the reassurance and approval of others. No matter how free or how powerful we believe ourselves to be, it is in August of the 9 year cycle that we realize the truth.

Now, a new direction toward real happiness and success, through doing what you want to do, is squarely in your hands - no one else's. The choices you make in the next four months will determine just how satisfied and prosperous you will be in the years to come.

The only person you have to satisfy is *you*, so make August a time to appreciate what you already have in terms of love, support, talent, desire, resources, a willingness to learn new things, and a determination to be free. It is from an acceptance for where you are today that you will create the tomorrow of your own design.

~ September ~
9 Year - 9 Month

So we beat on, boats against the current,
borne back ceaselessly into the past...
F. SCOTT FITZGERALD

Let it go. Let it out. Let it be. Get it done. Get it over with. Get everything you have been putting off out of the way. Let September's double 9 energy take you on its roller coaster ride of ups and downs and turnarounds so that, once and for all, the real truth about your past can be buffeted to the surface where you can finally *accept* it for what it is.

Like never before, go back over your life's journey and remember everything you have done, everyone you have met, everywhere you have been, everything you have lost and gained, given and taken, your thoughts, your feelings, your love, your happiness, your anger, your fears, your passions, your ideas, your laughter, your tears, your satisfaction and your guilt - *everything*.

Even if you staunchly believe you are living 'in the moment', September's deeply emotional events will show you just how cleverly you have mastered the art of denial. And you will know that continued denial is no longer an option.

If you find yourself depressed but do not know why, you can be sure that you are resisting memories that are now pushing themselves to the surface. Accept them, finally, as parts of your life that have *gone*. The past is always present. However, only your full acceptance of what has happened to you in the past, the recent past included, will make this reality a comfortable one.

September's emotional vibration is all about your *intent* to move on to better things. Painful emotions remain with you when you do not accept and *feel* them. They need to move through you and out of you so that your life can proceed in a more positive direction. Yes, this has been a very emotional year for you. So why are you holding all that pain in instead of letting it out?

Release your grip on the past by feeling what needs to be felt. Then feel yourself moving into present time. And from present time, you can point yourself in the precise direction you want your future to take. Accept that the past has gone and that you can no longer dwell in it by denying its emotional effects on you. Accept your past as the route your unique journey took. Your past is your truth, your *experience*. Your past is what it took to bring you to where you are today. It is what it took to make you the person you are now *and* the person you want to become.

Your ability to be proud of your past will lift the fog that has enshrouded you throughout this year. You will finally know why the 9 year cycle must be this way. You may not have all the answers yet, but out of the thinning fog a new optimism rises; a new sense that the best days of your life are ahead of you.

As acceptance after acceptance is made, you will realize that each release is replaced with a new opportunity for a brighter future. Understand the natural process that is taking place in your life. Once the past is fully accepted, it will be time to turn yourself around and look *forward* instead. The future you are creating is inviting you to take a glimpse at it.

A brand new nine year cycle of your life begins on January 1st. Right now, this new phase is empty and open to anything you wish to do with it. Plan to fill it with life, love, happiness, prosperity, laughter, and freedom. Bring an end to those situations, beliefs, and attitudes that you don't want to drag with you.

Be aware of just how much negativity has already left your life this year. There is so much to be optimistic about now.

If optimism is not what you're feeling right now, remember that each emotion that is stuck somewhere in your body is weighing you down or eating away at you. This does not make emotion the enemy. All that your feelings require is the freedom to express themselves. The truth is that the fear you have about having to feel these denied emotions is *nothing* compared to the fear you have, and may be denying, of not being able to feel at all.

This month's intensely healing vibrations urge you to stop denying that you are afraid of what the future holds for you. It is this denied fear which is preventing the future from opening up for you. No one can know for sure what our futures hold, but we can make the best of the present by aiming ourselves in the direction we want our future to take. This can only be in a forward direction.

The fears that all men have are denied because society has brainwashed little boys into believing it is cowardly and wrong to be afraid. Women's fears have become deeply denied because of the antiquated belief that little girls are less important than little boys.

Whatever your gender, remember the child inside you. Realize that fear is a natural movement within life. To cut off from it is to cut off from life itself. Fear is a natural and vital part of life which allows us to sense possible danger and deal with it appropriately. Without this understanding, fear becomes terror, and then we are then unable to move in any direction.

By allowing fear to take its natural course through and out of the body, we become confident; we become focused; we become strong; and we become able to differentiate between that which should be feared and that which need not be feared at all.

Most of us have photographs of ourselves as babies or children and if we don't have them we can usually get them. One of the most healing things you can do for yourself is to look at your infant or childhood image and remember - *feel* - your own young life, your smile, your little hands and feet, your little face and body. Then feel the vulnerability, trust, and innocence inside that child before judgment and guilt got hold of you.

Look at that picture and ask yourself, *"How could anyone ever hurt this little child?"* Recollect all that has happened to this child along the way and feel the grief and the stress of a lifetime that you - and that child - are holding on to. This will enable you to release your dis-ease and heal. It will enable you to accept, protect, and love yourself once again. Look at that little person in the photograph and then look at yourself in the mirror. Whichever way you look, you are still that child.

You may feel an emptiness inside after this month's emotional releases because of the sheer weight of the pressure that has left your body. Guilt may try to fill the space you have just created by telling you that it is wrong to be so emotional. Guilt does not want this healing to take place. Recognize guilt's wretched voice and move away from it, without denying its existence.

Feel your newly acquired self-acceptance which wants to take that child in the photograph and give it love, happiness, health, prosperity, security, and freedom. You and that child have come a long way together. Now, the quality of your journey depends on how willing you are to accept, forgive, believe in, and love each other. Have you forgotten that *happiness* is also an emotion which needs to be expressed as it arises?

What are you looking *forward* to? Tie up all those loose ends and details that are standing between you and your goals - between you and your deepest desires - and then rejoice in the knowledge that a wonderful new life awaits you.

~ October ~
9 Year - 1 Month

I am where I am because
I believe in all possibilities.
WHOOPI GOLDBERG

Some kind of change is scheduled for October. You are starting to feel the magnetic pull of next year's powerful 1 cycle of NEW BEGINNINGS overlap with this year's equally powerful 9 cycle of ENDINGS. Something will occur which will restore your optimism and revitalize your imagination.

The less unfinished business you have to deal with, the clearer you will be able to see ahead of you. October promises to show the first signs of next year's exciting and life-giving potential. Suddenly there is light on your path once again.

This emotional year of endings and completions is almost over, and you will find that you can move forward now. But you should do so cautiously. You need to be sure that a new venture is not just a different form of a past mistake.

Until December 31st, the 9 year cycle is your reality, but from now until then you can start to position yourself closer to the life you want. When you enter the 1 year cycle next year, you will need a plan of action. Make sure your plan is flexible because 1 is also the number of change. And *everything* will change next year.

1 is the number of independence. If the feeling arises that you are now alone in the world, or that the cooperation you need is not available, it is doing so to point out areas of *dependence* that you are holding on to. Yes, you will need the cooperation and support of others, but you cannot depend on others for *your* happiness, success, or well-being.

Do what you have to do, by yourself if necessary, and you will soon see that the cooperation you need is all around you and will be given freely if you do not demand or expect it.

The combination of the 1 and 9 cycles makes this a month of give and take, ups and downs. It can provide a huge increase in your self-confidence if you are willing to stop taking everything so personally and consider that others are no longer the cause of your emotional problems. Rather, it is your unwillingness to let go of old pain, old resentment, old grief, old guilt, and

old blame which is causing an uncomfortable rift between you and someone else who really does need to be understood, accepted, and forgiven.

The *change* that this month brings is pointing to next year's potential.
Focus on you. Focus on who and what is precious to you. Work through
any nervousness, fear, or pessimism that arises. These feelings need to
evolve into October's positive atmosphere.

Work on finding a comfortable balance between dependence and
defeatism and impatience and aggression. Make sure that feelings of egotism or inadequacy do not get the better of you this month.

Begin something new - nothing major because major beginnings cannot succeed within your current energy cycles. Start something which will
prepare you for next year's monumental changes. The 9 cycle has taught
you that nothing new can begin until the ground has been carefully weeded and prepared for the new seeds of the future. This is the cyclical reality
of nature. Although some positive action should be taken now, your own
nature is telling you to "hurry up and wait."

This year's encounter with the past has placed you in a position of
tremendous freedom to move in the direction of your choice. As each
moment passes, the past must be allowed to move into its natural position,
behind you, where it cannot impede your freedom to move forward.
Feeling your feelings, as they arise, moment-by-moment, until they are
completed, is the natural sequence which ensures continued freedom.

While some feelings are blissful and others are painful, feeling all your feelings will restore precious energy to your life. Cutting them off before they
have had a chance to complete themselves will inhibit and damage you. Apply
this understanding as a way of life, rather than just a mental concept.

Notice just how original and creative you are when you are not waiting
for the approval of someone else. See how deeply loving and loved you are
when your love is not seeking acceptance but is simply accepting itself. Feel
what it is you desire and deserve in this life of yours and expect to get it,
because from this acceptance of your own desires you will also see *how* they
can be fulfilled.

~ November ~
9 Year - 2 Month

You must stoop a little in order to jump.
F. SCOTT FITZGERALD

SLOW DOWN. Relax a while. Resist the urge to race ahead into new territory which is not yet ready to receive you. 2 allows nothing to be forced without disappointing consequences. The seeds you planted last month must now be given the chance to take root and grow. Be patient.

The circumstances of November will create many details which will keep you so busy that you will have little time to focus on yourself or your plans. Relax with this situation and, despite the delays, intrusions, and detours, do what has to be done.

Some stress may have to be experienced in order to understand why it is so necessary for you to accept and relax with - cooperate with - your current environment. This diversion is actually aiding your plans and goals by providing just the right timing and conditions they need. It is also providing important information which will make implementing your plans so much easier next year.

You are in a cycle of intuition and sensitivity. It is from your ability to sense things that this vital new information will be derived. Be aware of everything going on around you as something will be said, done, suggested, or perceived that relates directly to your own needs and plans. Strange as it may seem, this missing link will be found when you are focusing on someone or something else.

Nothing can be forced this month, including your search for the "missing link". It will happen naturally after the release of a deeply denied emotion which you have been too afraid to face until now. It will happen when you least expect it. When this revelation does occur, it will feel like a light bulb being switched on inside you as your feelings finally make *full contact* with your mind. Your natural ability to sense or intuit will expand through genuine acceptance of your circumstances, along with the feelings that arise *because* of your circumstances.

November provides an opportunity to experience the actual feeling of evolving into higher awareness. From this astonishing feeling, you will know that the goals you have set for yourself are only a pale glimpse of what you can *really* do. From this realization a beautiful calmness emerges that has all the tenderness and warmth of love, because love is exactly what it is.

By extending yourself to others now, you will experience love of yourself, love of your Will, love of others, and love of life. In a month that tells you to take a back seat and focus on someone or something else, you will be amazed at the richness of the rewards this offers. The experience of evolving human consciousness provides the real meaning to the term "information age".

~ December ~
9 Year - 3 Month

> *I am enough of an artist to*
> *draw freely upon my imagination.*
> *Imagination is more important than knowledge.*
> *Knowledge is limited. Imagination encircles the world.*
> ALBERT EINSTEIN

What a year this has been. So much emotion. So much reality. So much truth. And here you are at the end of it; at the end of an entire nine year phase of your life. Or is it eighteen years, twenty seven years, or more that you have been rehashing the same old mistakes? Of course, now your mistakes have evolved into practical *experience* and need never be repeated. Congratulations are certainly in order as you realize just how good it is to be alive.

You see, it is not your claim to freedom that has caused this year's difficulties, upheavals, and traumatic events. Rather, it was the process of *breaking away* from those situations, attitudes, and beliefs which always stood between you and your higher potential.

You may believe that you have achieved a lot in your lifetime, or you may think you have achieved relatively little. But if you have accepted the truth of your past by releasing the feelings involved, you will know that the enormity of your potential is yet to be realized.

At the same time, you may feel totally exhausted by this year of facing and feeling reality. If you cannot see the benefits of this year's emotional journey, then perhaps you are trying to do too much, too soon. Concentrate on doing less so that you can enjoy doing more of what you love to do. Be good to yourself, my friend.

You are on this Earth for a distinct purpose, which is of your own design and your own desire. But if you bury yourself under a blanket of trivial matters, you may never be able to fathom what your purpose is. Nor will you be able to appreciate those people who have loyally and lovingly traveled with you this year. There were probably times when you were not easy to be with.

Remember what was said at the beginning of the year: *The 9 vibration takes you in what seems like the wrong direction - backwards - but this is the direction you must take in order to find the unfinished issues that are preventing you from going forward.*

Your year of forward movement and new beginnings has not yet begun, and it is necessary for you to accept this fact. You cannot cross a bridge before you come to it, nor can you enter a new cycle until you are there. Be patient. Focus on the present. Appreciate what you have in the here and now, rather than lament what was lost in a different time.

December's 3 energy emphasizes friendship, lightheartedness, optimism, creativity, beauty, and humor. These are the harmonious notes on which to end this year of endings. Take these gifts and share them with the people you love. Make December a month of fun, relaxation, socializing, and appreciating the smaller joys of life. There is no need to keep up appearances through extravagance or indifference. Be yourself, and allow others the same freedom.

You now have an opportunity to tie up some last minute loose ends pertaining to your various relationships. This has been a year in which your whole concept of friendship and love has been radically altered. Some endings were inevitable. Emotions ran deep. Your ability to forgive will provide the perfect ending here. Your understanding of Free Will ensures that never again will you allow the senseless forces of guilt or blame to stop you from being your own best friend.

The seeds you planted in October may now begin showing signs of growth, which will create distinct feelings of optimism. This is a good time to get creative. Give your long neglected imagination a free range to go wherever it wants to go. Your imagination has no limits at all other than those you impose on it the moment it seems to go beyond what is 'normal'. Remember that normal is just another word for average or commonplace.

When you set your imagination free, you may not like everything it shows you. But you are also free to pick and choose what is right for you. The contents of your imagination are fighting for release now, just as your emotions have been all year. Set your imagination free by letting go of those judgments and preconceived ideas which have always kept your deepest desires and your greatest ideas from ever surfacing.

Relax and enjoy the last segment of this particular journey, so that you can enter the upcoming "1" year cycle with dignity, confidence, and *with* the people you want to be with.

Dare to look beyond the known horizons. Bring your unrestricted imagination and your pioneering spirit with you as midnight of December 31st arrives, and you cross over that line into the 1 year cycle of change, independence, fresh starts and new beginnings - into a new reality - a new era - of YOUR design. *Just imagine* ....

CYCLES

Cycles of engergy
life of the Universe
rotating, gyrating
climaxing, giving birth
blessed creation
forever a miracle
throbbing, pulsating
and reaching the pinnacle
Love at the center
joy all around
color's the vision
music's the sound
dance is the movement
notions abound
and the healing of laughter
goes round and around
Cycles of energy
dancing in liberty
moving and grooving
in sweet synchronicity

blessed creation
visions that cannot wait
imagination
opens the gate
Love at the center
joy all around
color's the vision
music's the sound
dance is the movement
notions abound
and the healing of laughter
goes round and around
Cycles of energy
make us sensational
glowing and knowing
and warmly vibrational
blessed creation
the world is your protege
no limitations
Maestro - come out - and *play!*

ÇYÇIEŞ OF ENErǫY
PARt THREE

Life, Love, and Liberty

in the new millennium

the healing power of emotion

Why should we use all our creative power?
Because there is nothing that makes people so generous,
joyful, lively, bold, and compassionate, so indifferent
to fighting and the accumulation of objects and money.
BRENDA UELAND

Life, Love, and Liberty

in the new millennium

the healing power of emotion

> *We tend to think of the rational as a higher order,*
> *but it is the emotional that marks our lives.*
> MERLE SHANE

How else can you measure the quality of your life if not by the way you *feel* about it? To feel is to sense or intuit. Sensitivity, intuition, emotion, feelings, are all different words which describe our sixth sense which, in turn, defines the WILL.

We *all* possess this sense. It is as natural as taste, sight, touch, hearing, and smell. As our consciousness expands and evolves, we are realizing that emotion is an essential source of our personal power if only our consciousness - the mind - would allow our feelings to emerge fully and be *felt*.

Our minds are reasonably tolerant of what we believe are 'positive' feelings but, because not all of our feelings feel pleasant, we tend to cut ourselves off from those so called negative emotions and pretend they are not happening. Although feelings are being constantly triggered inside us, we are not fully aware of them and, eventually, we become weighed down by all that unaddressed and unexpressed emotion without actually knowing the cause of our unhappiness.

Rather than risk the heaviness of depression, we suppress our emotions and rely largely on our minds to steer us through life. Of course, this has enabled us to expand our minds to the great evolutionary proportions of today and, as our minds evolve to higher levels of understanding so, too, does everything else on Earth.

But we are also experiencing a sense of loss as we notice that our relationships, in their many different forms, are not providing the warmth or the love we imagine they should. The mind, alone, is not a very warm place to be. Yet, it is from the coldness of pure intellect that we try to fathom why it is so difficult to maintain existing relationships, to form relationships we believe would be good for us, or why we find ourselves in situations, or with people with which we have little or nothing in common.

We have reached a level of consciousness where further expansion is impossible until we accept that we are so much more than consciousness and physical mass. *Going within* has been a marvelous and enlightening experience, but we have now entered a new cycle of time which forces us to look at reality and to feel things about it that we thought our minds had long ago learned to control. Now we know that positive thinking without positive *feeling* is nothing more than self-deception.

Surprisingly, emotion is a largely unexplored dimension of our existence. Emotional freedom, or Free Will, is the unstoppable next step in our evolutionary journeys - the next great frontier of human understanding. It is the key to peace, love, and creativity. It is the theme of the new millennium.

Free Will is also the theme of this book. It has been written for those who are seeking the freedom to live their lives according to how they feel; spontaneously doing whatever they feel driven to do; creating realities in which love, truth, peace, and happiness are abundant. We are discovering more and more about our unlimited nature, the unlimited nature of creation itself, and the power of love and satisfaction over purely commercial ambition. Our twentieth century concept of success has changed. Regardless of how much money or prestige we may accumulate, if we are not *enjoying* life, then we are not successful.

Today, our creativity is exceeding all commercial and conventional boundaries. When we *feel* something deeply enough, we can bring it to life, give it form and substance, and prosper from it in ways that far outweigh commercial success alone. It has long been known that emotionally expressive people are *creative* people.

Although money and material satisfaction are important, they are not the ultimate rewards involved here. Releasing yourself from the *heaviness* of life is the ultimate goal, so that the *lightness* of freedom and genuine happiness can be experienced. At that point, we find abundance in all areas of our lives.

Love and joy are the highest forms of energy in the Universe - the highest highs. But, at this stage of our evolution, none of us is able to remain in a state of love or joy for very long before we start to feel ourselves being dragged down again by the sheer weight of our own unexpressed feelings; dragged down not only to a lower level of emotional energy, but also into less desirable situations in our day-to-day affairs.

We believe that our happiness is depleted by outside realities. We try to comprehend our lives looking outward, facing one problem after another, dealing with the occasional and inevitable crisis, and forever concerned about what our next crisis may be.

There are also those dreaded times when our sense of loss is so acute that we have no choice but to feel the awesome power of our emotions. Then, through burning tears and constricted throats, we face the world and vent our rage. Or we retreat from the world in fear of being seen as the emotional creatures we really are. And we beg to know, from whatever higher power we believe in, "why is this happening to me?" Only by accepting and expressing our feelings as the natural release mechanisms that they are, can we ever evolve and fulfill our God-given potential for love and joy. Our emotions are the fuel of our evolving journeys.

> *Although the world is full of suffering,*
> *it is also full of the overcoming of it.*
> HELEN KELLER

When we look at this world and the dangerous absurdity in which we live, it can be difficult to believe that humanity really is evolving to higher dimensions. We sense the potential for peace, only to have our hopes dashed by the fear that others cannot accept this possibility and will destroy life before we even get a chance to understand it.

Although we desire a safer and more loving existence, we are often unaware of our own contribution to the world's chaotic situation. We judge and blame others for the ills in society, and for the problems in our own personal lives. Then we look to different 'others': politicians, scientists, doctors, religious leaders etc - to solve our problems for us and make the pain and the fear go away.

But when we analyze the solutions and dogma being handed down by those who are often less aware of reality than ourselves, we realize that our dependence on others to make decisions for us and to tell us how to live, has given them a power they are not qualified to have. Others cannot give us freedom because, quite simply, it is not theirs to give.

There are those who believe they are not personally involved with humanity's present confusion; they focus only on what they believe is the *positive*. In doing so, they are failing to notice their own role in the *negative* and are unable to change what needs to be changed. There are also those who focus only on the gloom and doom of this world. From this perspective of hopelessness, it is also impossible to contribute to positive change.

Yes, it can be frightening to look at this world as it *really* is. It often appears that evil is on the rise, outweighing our good intent. However, a closer look at what is really happening on Earth shows that what seems to be the expansion of evil is actually evil being *exposed* far more frequently and courageously than ever before. Such exposure shows us that evil is not so much on the rise, but on the run. Such exposure also brings us face to face with outdated judgments as to what is "right" and "wrong". But in the midst of such colossal change, it is all too easy to prejudge the unfamiliar before we *feel* the reality of it, and then miss the opportunity to learn something new and constructive.

In order to find the truth, we must learn to look at life from the balanced position between purely positive or negative points of view. It is from a state of balance that we realize that our problems, no matter what form they take, are the result of our resistance to accept our personal responsibility to live in freedom.

Our transformation begins when we accept that denial of reality is what we are evolving *from*, and that FREE WILL is what we are evolving to.

> *The important thing is not to stop questioning.*
> ALBERT EINSTEIN

It is scientifically accepted that everything in creation, including people, is comprised of a consistent vibrating substance which we call energy. Within this energy there are distinct differences in vibrational speeds and characteristics. In order to sustain itself, all energy must flow freely to pursue its evolving journey through creation; a journey which operates in measurable cycles of time and space.

The purpose of these cycles is not to keep us confined to one unchanging system in which we are conditioned to compete with, and destroy each other. On the contrary, their purpose is to provide doors of opportunity through which to discover exciting new creative dimensions of human potential. We are not here in creation to be slaves to industry. We are here to *create*, not destroy.

But until we learn what needs to be learned within each cycle, all we do is repeat them, along with the same old mistakes we have always made, without actually getting anywhere. Perhaps this is why the human species has failed to learn much about its own nature in all the time we have existed, and why history has always repeated itself at regular and predictable intervals.

It is no coincidence that humanity's first important discovery was the wheel. The circle, or cycle, has far more significance than many people imagine. The wheel was the first invention because its shape is the first element of life. It represents humanity's desire not to merely go round in circles, but to move *forward* with greater ease. Our circular planet also moves in regular and measurable cycles. Earth's constant motion accounts for the four seasons, day and night, time and tide. Earth is a small dot on the universal map and, yet, an integral part of an incalculable planetary system in which *cyclical predictability* is its common denominator.

But it is the emotional cycles of human life - how people *feel* - that account for trends, wars, laws, creativity, economic and ecological shifts, and evolution itself. Just look at how emotional our lives have become.

The way we feel determines the course of all creation and destruction. Human life is unnecessarily complicated, and so difficult to change, because we are reluctant to recognize the power that our feelings give us. It is only through the spontaneous expression of our feelings that we will ever know what it *feels* like to be a whole human being.

The cycles of life may be invisible to the physical eye, but the way they affect us can be clearly seen in our day-to-day affairs. The more components something has, the more intricate it is, and the more cycles within cycles occur. Time has many traps, including old cycles of belief and judgment that offer no possibility for positive change. The more we revolve mechanically around clocks and calendars, the less spontaneous we become as we try to stay on or ahead of time. Yet, we fully expect time to catch up with us and, when it does, our time is 'up', and we die.

Now, with Free Will as our objective, we can use life's natural cycles to actually transcend time and exist as human *beings* - instead of the human 'race' against time and each other that we are all presently engaged in.

For years, I struggled to understand how we can have Free Will when we are so heavily influenced by the numerology of life. I realized, however, that these cycles provide the mental, physical, and emotional *framework of potentials* with which to break free from the traps of time by learning what needs to be learned within each cycle.

Numerology provides the way *out* of our present system of destruction and into the freedom of joyful and creative living. Knowledge of our individual cycles allows us to flow freely *with* nature instead of against it. It shows us that the scientific argument of creation vs. evolution is quite absurd because we cannot deny the creative nature of life or that the nature of creation is to evolve!

When you are being yourself and doing what you love to do, you lose track of time and you are happy. And is it not happiness you are looking for? Time doesn't fly when you're having fun, it stops. This state of loving who we are and what we are doing is the nucleus of Free Will, peace, love, and creativity. Through our own natural cycles and the feelings they trigger, we can recognize who we really are and what we really want. When we balance the power of our feelings with the power of our minds, we discover *how* to make our dreams come true.

> *There is no such thing as a perfect relationship,*
> *and the most successful ones are between people*
> *who regard themselves as individual, independent entities,*
> *rather than someone else's appendage.*
> SALLY BROMPTON

Who we are and what we want determines the personality of our Will, which is often very different from the personality we present to the world. We are usually so busy trying to create personalities which we hope will live up to the expectations of others, and doing things we don't even enjoy, that we have no time for attaining our *real* desires. We imagine that love comes only from our relationships, and we often fail to realize that love must be given in order to be experienced, and that love has many different *forms*.

If you are unhappy with yourself and with what you are doing in life, you will reflect your dissatisfaction to those you love. Then you will suspect that the relationship itself is the reason you are unhappy. So much true love is lost because people believe they are no longer free to *change* things when they are in a relationship.

In fact, the first thing we seem to do when love enters our lives is to place rules upon it and chains around it. But when two people love and trust each other and remain free and independent individuals, they reflect their personal satisfaction back to each other - and the love thrives. This is just as true of relationships with children, relatives, and friends as it is with our romantic partners.

Some people are afraid of love. They believe that love hurts. This is not true. Love is incapable of inflicting pain. It is the *loss* of love that hurts so much. It is our fear of this loss which causes us to hold on to love too tightly so that it cannot move freely between the people involved. That is where GUILT enters the situation and begins its slow and deceptive process of tearing love apart.

Feelings are natural energies which must flow and evolve freely. It is hard to accept that there is a substance among us which is not natural - not made of the energy of which all life is made. Guilt is merely the opposing echoes of judgments that humanity has made throughout time. Sometimes its judgments are correct and often they are totally wrong. The more we base our beliefs and decisions on these judgments without *feeling* the reality of the situation for ourselves, the more guilt we create. Its presence prevents the movement of all natural emotion. Ultimately, it will cause us to destroy life itself unless we learn to recognize it and remove ourselves from its influence. We must do this *without denying its existence*.

The most frightening thing about guilt is that many people have either become complacent about it, or they revere it. Some of the most judgmental doctrines on Earth hail guilt as the voice of righteousness and use it as a means of enslaving others to the same judgments. We see the violence, hatred, war, and all kinds of despicable acts taking place, and we are disgusted by the absence of guilt in the people involved. But what we are seeing in them *is* guilt which they are denying. Denied guilt is pure evil.

During the course of this journey you will learn to recognize guilt as it contradicts everything you feel and think. The moment you decide to do what you want to do, guilt will rush in and tell you why you can't do it. And then, after it has stopped you from doing what you want to do, it will rush back at you and tell you that you were wrong to back down, and that you are inadequate and should be doing better than you are. It convinces you that you do not have what it takes to pursue your true desires and that your desires are inappropriate anyway.

Whatever is making you unhappy in life, you will find that guilt is stopping you from making the changes you need to make. If you think it's fear, be aware that guilt thrives on fear, and this is where it often hides. Guilt cannot be felt and released like natural emotions because it is not an emotion of any kind. *Guilt is what stops emotion from expressing itself.*

Learn to distinguish it from your thoughts and feelings. When you start to recognize its contradictory, deceiving commentary you may, at first, feel overwhelmed by it. It is in every move you make and every thought you think. The theme song of guilt is: *I'm damned if I do and I'm damned if I don't.* It's not a pretty tune.

Learn to recognize this great echoing nothingness which never shuts up, so that you can withdraw from its influence, and from the people who would use it to control you. The only way you can do this is by developing your freedom to feel, think, and decide *everything* for yourself, without prejudging a situation.

Feelings are neither positive or negative. They are a natural part of your being which are triggered by the various realities of your journey. It is our conditioning, both the correct and incorrect judgments we have been imprinted with since birth, which determines how we *react* to our feelings. Guilt has no true power except that which we give it.

All the violence and upheaval we are seeing in the world today is the result of the Will of humanity breaking loose in a state of denied guilt which, of course, calls itself "blame". But blame is made of the same unloving, unfeeling stuff that guilt is made from. Judgment! We are judgmental beings because guilt tells us that we must always be right.

Today, however, we are learning just how wrong we have been about so many aspects of life. Now we are learning *how* to learn. Instead of bombarding each other with our opinions on matters that we have not even taken the time to study, intelligent people are no longer ashamed to say, "I don't know". Admitting our ignorance is a huge step forward for humanity.

> *Better to light a candle than to curse the darkness.*
> CHINESE PROVERB

Guilt itself cannot be destroyed, and its presence cannot be denied. But when we *accept* reality, it has the effect of pushing guilt away without our having to deny it is there. Each time you recognize guilt and refuse to be ruled by it, you will gain more Free Will to live as you *want* to live.

You will experience love, compassion, and innocence instead of the fear and anger which guilt creates by making you do things you don't want to do, or by stopping you from doing things that you do want to do. The Will is natural, guilt is not. The Will is creative, guilt destroys.

There is no such thing as 'healthy' guilt. You will face guilt frequently on your journey to freedom, but don't let it govern your course because it will keep you at a standstill. Free Will will guide you from one loving experience to the next.

Mistakes will be made and, oh, how we judge against those who make them: especially ourselves. Do we really want more laws to prevent us from making mistakes and, thus, never learning anything new? The more laws we create, the more we sacrifice our freedom to learn. Isn't it better to *learn* to live in freedom than to be so afraid of freedom that we just give it away to those who seek to dominate us with *their* denied guilt? There is only one way to live in freedom, and that is to recognize mistakes, learn what needs to be learned, and change our approach accordingly. Like everything else in creation, a mistake needs to evolve. When it does, it is no longer a mistake. It is EXPERIENCE.

I dream for a living.
STEVEN SPIELBERG

The inventors of the aeroplane made thousands of 'mistakes' before it was actually airborne. Those early aviation attempts often appeared humorous and embarrassing. Sometimes they were fatal. But from each mistake made, those pioneers learned something new. We are now able to fly around our world, and beyond it, because a group of people, who were once thought to be crackpots, were brave enough to endure the frustration of their mistakes so that something could be *learned*. Their achievements were the result of their ardent passion to do what they wanted to do. In their case, it was to fly. That was their desire; their love; their *will*.

If you look at your life's mistakes in the same way, you will be exhilarated by your innocence and your potential, and you will prevent the guilt of your past, present, and future mistakes to weigh you down.

Let fear be a counselor and not a jailer.
TONY ROBBINS

Through the pages of *Life Cycles*, you are embarking on a journey which leaves denial behind and exposes you to reality. If this sounds a little frightening, accept that it *feels* frightening. You see, when you deny your fear, it manifests in your life as terror. The magnetic energy of your denied fear draws you to the very situations it hopes will trigger you into releasing it. You cannot do what is necessary to protect yourself if terror or panic is paralyzing you. This is why spontaneity of feeling is so essential. If you express your feelings of fear, as you feel them, you will have no denied fear to draw horrific situations to you.

The feeling of fear evolves when: *(1) you face the reality of what is causing it; (2) you understand the options available to you based on the nature of the problem; (3) you make a choice which will determine an outcome; (4) you accept the outcome.* With practice, this process can proceed and repeat itself in a split second. It can protect you from dangerous situations. It can even save your life.

Without an acceptance of fear, you will have no way to distinguish those things you *do* need to be afraid of from those things which need not be feared at all. Courage is not the abscence of fear. Courage is the acceptance of fear. It is peace of mind. Panic, however, is the result of fear being denied its natural course and is what I can only describe as a form of hell. When an emotion has been expressed, it evolves into understanding, and then into love. True understanding always evolves into love. We evolve by allowing our feelings to evolve.

Like all energy, our various emotions must be allowed to flow without obstruction to a state of completion. A feeling cannot complete its cycle until it is recognized, *felt*, and expressed out of the body. When we deny or cut off from a feeling, it remains trapped within the physical or mental body and becomes greatly distressed. It then manifests in our personal lives as disease, misfortune, or some other form of adversity.

> *Do not the most moving moments of*
> *our lives find us all without words?*
> MARCEL MARCEAU

There is a tremendous difference between a thought and a feeling. Thoughts are made up of words, ideas, and images, and are a form of electricity. Feelings are felt. Their magnetism can be *felt* moving inside the body. Although they can be described after the fact, feelings themselves contain no words, but they do speak a language all their own.

In order for a feeling to complete itself and evolve, it must be accepted fully into the body and mind, and then expressed outwardly through whichever sound is natural for it; whichever sound is natural for *you*.

The vibration of your unique sound provides the vehicle on which your feelings leave the body. But we are so afraid that our natural guttural emotional 'noise' will be heard by others that we prevent true expression and healing by trying to rationalize our feelings with words. And, because the fear of seeming abnormal is so prevalent in society, it is wise for us all to heal ourselves in an environment of privacy until a wider understanding is reached.

There will be times when you feel it is in your best interests to hold your emotions in, particularly where anger and hatred are concerned. In these instances, it would be wise to allow these feelings to *move* through the simple act of writing them down. Their actual release can be achieved at a time you feel is right and safe for you. Emotional healing must take place within each individual first. Global healing will not suddenly happen. It will *spread*, one person at a time, one day at a time, and during a cycle which is right for that person.

> *It is difficult to get people to understand something*
> *when their salaries depend upon their not understanding it.*
> UPTON SINCLAIR

Creativity and healing are impossible without emotional involvement because our feelings draw out our thoughts with their magnetism. Our various feelings have a powerful and tenacious survival instinct. Unexpressed feelings dutifully eat away at the body that is imprisoning them. Their violent struggle to be free then creates dis-ease within the body. Suppressed emotion causes *all* disease.

Of course, we run to a doctor when symptoms arise. Doctors are trained in the surgical or chemical removal of symptoms, but not in removing, or even acknowledging, the emotional *cause*. The pharmaceutical and medical industries will never be able to eradicate disease because they refuse to consider that illness is the result of emotional denial. After all, if self-healing is recognized as a natural and automatic process, these empires would soon crumble. If there is no money to be made, industry will do anything it feels necessary to prevent a widespread recognition of our own potential to heal ourselves. Even when the healing power of emotional release become undeniable, the pharmaceutical industry will doubtlessly produce a pill which they will claim does the job for you.

Yet, conventional medicine *is* evolving, albeit reluctantly. Even this mighty field cannot help but be swept into nature's process of self-improvement. Many hospitals are now employing holistic practitioners along side their state-of-the-art technology and highly specialized doctors. This merging is inevitable because the more specialized doctors become, the less they can focus on the whole being, including the *feelings* of their patients. People are demanding humane, holistic, and natural approaches to health matters, and the fact that we are now spending billions of dollars per year on alternative medicine is helping to improve the health care system.

Because we heal ourselves by expressing emotion out of our bodies, some outer symptoms may arise in the form of a cold or aching sensation in certain parts of the body. You are probably aware that you are more susceptible to colds when you are emotionally 'low'.

There is no medical cure for the common cold because the symptoms represent the materialization of unexpressed feelings which are trying to push their way out of the body. This makes the common cold not an illness, but an opportunity to be *well*.

However, instead of allowing emotions to leave the body freely, our use of chemicals pushes them back down again. So, if cold-like symptoms arise during the course of your healing journey, try to ride it out without medication for a while. Eliminate distractions which deter you from feeling what needs to be felt. If you feel miserable, get to the root of what is *really* making you unhappy: not the outer symptoms, but a deeply buried feeling from the past which is pushing its way to the surface.

The more spontaneous you are with your feelings, the less likely you are to get a cold and the more freely and happily your life will flow. Remember that the emphasis is not on 'catching' a cold, but on releasing it.

> *A little learning is a dangerous thing* .....
> ALEXANDER POPE

Do use common sense here. If you think that what you are experiencing is more than just a 'common cold', see a doctor. You see, self healing certainly is a matter of Will, but if you do not know precisely what your Will is, or how to use it correctly, healing cannot take place.

The concept of self-healing is often misunderstood. Your intention may be to heal yourself naturally, but lack of knowledge could actually make your health worse. It is impossible to heal yourself if you do not know *how*. Good nutrition and exercise are essential, but until healing takes place at the roots - your trapped emotions - it may be necessary to seek the aid of a doctor or other qualified healer until you fully understand the process of genuine emotional release.

We have all been conditioned to believe that it is wrong or weak to show certain feelings, such as anger, hatred, fear, grief, or pain. These natural emotions may now be so heavily denied that you do not even know they are there. All you need is the genuine INTENT to allow these feelings to surface and to start expressing them as they emerge.

Emotional freedom does not mean that we should be crying or yelling twenty-four hours a day. It means that when we consistently allow ourselves to *feel* our feelings, we realize that many of the things we feel so negatively about are actually superficial matters: a measure of our intolerance for ourselves and each other.

When someone argues or complains all the time, it is usually because they are angry. They are angry about something far more significant than the petty issue they appear to be obsessed with. They are using anger to camouflage a different emotion, pain or grief perhaps, which was triggered by a past event, and are unaware of how happy they would be if they would allow themselves to heal from the experience.

Emotional freedom develops real tolerance and not the stress we currently think is tolerance. It allows us to become at ease with life's realities so that our feelings, in general, are pleasant and creative ones. Each of us has a lifetime of denied emotion to release, and this cannot be done overnight. Spontaneous emotional expression is a natural, permanent, and ongoing function of life. Therefore, we must learn to *love* our feelings, no matter what form they take, just as we are learning to love our minds and our bodies.

There is no need to dump outbursts of emotion on others, even though it may take the provocation of someone else for you to recognize the feelings which need to be expressed. Healing is a personal affair, and you must make private time and space for yourself where your self-consciousness will not deter the process. If you believe it is impossible to create your own space and time for this, then you may be in serious need of reclaiming some personal freedom.

> *Peace cannot be kept by force.*
> *It can only be achieved by understanding.*
> ALBERT EINSTEIN

Make no mistake, there are many people who are unable to relate to this material. It is a violation of their Will, and a waste of your effort, to impose your understandings or your feelings on them.

There are also people out there who fully understand where this is leading and will do anything they can to oppose Free Will, either because they are afraid to accept the responsibility that comes with freedom, or because of their addiction to power and control. And there are millions of others, all over the world, who understand that freedom of Mind, Body, and Will, is now the only acceptable direction for human life.

During the course of your journey, you will learn that you do not have a soul but, rather, you *are* a soul: a complex being, who happens to reside in your particular physical body. We are comprised of Mind, Will, and Form. When these three elements achieve genuine acceptance for each other, absolute balance is achieved, and the soul emerges as a perfect four-dimensional entity.

You may wonder where *spirit* fits in to this equation and I have to ask, "what is spirit if it is not consciousness - masculine energy - the mind?" It has been our marvelous, masculine, spiritual minds that we have been expanding so dramatically in recent years. "Going within" has meant venturing into the far corners of one's mind. And, because mind and spirit are the same thing, I believe that in the near future, we will drop the phrase Mind-Body-Spirit, and replace it with Mind-Will-Body. Then, we will finally be acknowledging and accepting feminine energy as an equal and vital part of life. This is exactly what is taking place on Earth today. The masculine mind is discovering and learning to accept its feminine counterpart - the love of its life - its own feelings - its WILL.

No one can tell you *how* to feel your feelings or what a particular feeling feels like. It is up to each of us to regain our sensitivity here through our own effort, intent, and action. Working with others on this can be helpful but it is not necessary. Working with others can sometimes retard the process. Only the individual can interpret his or her unique emotions along with their *causes*, and then make the appropriate outward releases. As well as accepting your own emotional reality, it is necessary to accept that others must have the freedom to express their feelings, too. This is how peace is achieved.

The future ain't what it used to be...
YOGI BERRA

Numerology provides us with a chronological map of Earth's cycles. We are now experiencing the magnetic effects of the emotional and feminine 2 cycle of the 2000s before we have fully comprehended the intellectual, competitive, and masculine 1 cycle of the 1000s. And as exciting as this era may be, it is also a confusing and dangerous time in which we are coming to terms with our fear of change.

We are living in a world that is not only constantly changing, but in a world which has already changed. It is only from this spark of acceptance - the shock of it all - that our minds can open wide enough to see beyond the gloom and doom, and recognize humanity's fabulous potential for peaceful coexistence *and* individual fulfillment.

We have entered a new cycle of time and space in which we are learning how to be the spiritual and emotional beings we *are* in this material and physical world we're *in*. We are learning to be free and independent, even within relationships and group situations. We are also learning how to protect ourselves from those who feel threatened by freedom.

The millennium of the 1000s took us through a massive cycle of time and space which was masculine in nature. This is why our world was always considered a "man's" world. It is why we have always called ourselves "man"kind, and why God has always been depicted as male. The 1000s emphasized the physical, competitive, progressive, independent, pioneering, territorial, self centered, and aggressive aspects of life. This cycle expanded the masculine intellect which exists in both men *and* women. Now, our minds have evolved to such an extent that they can evolve no further until the feminine Will - emotion - is recognized and accepted *by* the mind.

As we travel the 2 cycle of the 2000s, we are starting to understand the feminine aspects of life, which are sensitive, intuitive, caring, diplomatic, creative, and peaceful. 2 is connected to everything through partnership, relationship, and cooperation. It represents the emotions of both men *and* women.

Feminine energy does not seek superiority. It was the very notion of superiority in the sexes which created the world's imbalance in the first place. Feminine energy demands equality, not by emulating masculine energy but by accepting itself as the powerful and *different* force of nature that it is. 2 = balance = equality.

What some see as a "war of the sexes" is actually the feeling of fear between two energies who know they must live and interact in balance, but are confused as to what is expected of themselves or from each other. In the process, we are realizing just how confused humanity is about sexuality itself and that we have judged sex from only a traditional masculine point of view. This view is riddled with shame which, of course, is just another word for guilt.

Even the word "history" (*his* story) reveals the imbalance through which we have tried, throughout time, to preserve the truth. Now we are starting to listen to *her* story. We are listening to and acting upon a barrage of issues concerning women, their rights, and their connection to life itself. The Will's energy has been with us all along, just as women have. But, because we did not realize its unique power, we denied it and put it down, just as women have been denied and put down throughout history. And, yet, it was the emotional feminine Will, and not the mind, which constantly changed the world and continues to do so.

It is the emotional feminine Will of all men and women which votes governments in and out, shapes economies, and produces trends. The Will exposes atrocities throughout the world which, in turn, stir the emotions in us all. It was the emotional feminine Will which, in 1989, in the name of freedom, tore down the Berlin Wall and rose up in Tiananmen Square. And in 1997, it was the emotional Will of men and women all over the world that was devastated by the sudden death Princess Diana. She was perhaps the most visible reflection of emotional feminine energy. Isn't it unfortunate that Diana's emotions were so often considered to be her flaws when, in fact, they were her strength and her beauty?

It was also the emotional feminine Will of African-American *men* which, in 1995, marched a million strong on Washington to claim equality as human beings. The Million Man March was criticized for various reasons, including the fact that women were excluded.

But those who criticized were not seeing the true evolutionary dimensions of this event - the reality of black males choosing to take full responsibility for their own lives, for the lives of the children they created, and to heal the terrible rift that was occurring between them and black women.

Its timing, towards the end of the masculine 1000s, was perfect. It secured a pathway into the new millennium for black women to claim their equality not only with black men but with all human beings. The Million Man March was an emotional and magnificent display of racial harmony and was a celebration of black *women*.

But, alas, for as long as we label ourselves the human "race", how can we help but be rac-*ists*? Racism will continue to retard our progress until we realize that the human "race" must end in order for a free and peaceful *humanity* to begin.

Ignorance of our cyclical nature has led us to believe that competition is the way to proceed through life. This is how the word "race" came about when describing the diversity of human existence. Everything we do is a race or contest of some kind. And because we are still denying the effects of guilt, the race has become diabolical. It is no longer competition, but war, being declared at all levels. This is the 'racism' our judgments and beliefs have created.

We deny our racist behavior, insisting that there are different meanings to the word race. There are not. Race means CONTEST. And what is a contest if not a declaration of superiority?

A bend in the road is not the end of the road .....
unless you fail to turn.
ANONYMOUS

What a vicious cycle we keep in place with our judgments of how life 'is'. Our inclination to compete has placed our very existence in jeopardy. However, our desire to learn about peace has taught us that the problem is not only a matter of color or culture and that the evil of racism penetrates all aspects of life, all nationalities, 'classes', and belief systems. Racism effects everyone on the planet, even those who claim they have risen above such ignorance.

There are many dangerous 'races' being run today in total disregard for the well being of our planet and the life upon it. This includes the well-hidden race for world domination which is being disguised as freedom by certain factions of industry, military, politics, religion, and science. As our ability to feel becomes stronger, we know that the freedom we have always taken for granted is a mere illusion.

But the survival instinct of the human Will is now stirring. By recognizing our past mistakes, we know that we cannot continue as we are. We know that violence and control are not the answer. We know there must be more to the human experience than only materialism, technology, war, dependence, destruction, disease, work, worry, taxes, unconsciousness and death. We have started to search, en-masse, for the "meaning of life". In our desperation to find true understanding, we are finally becoming *emotional* about it. We know that we are on a path of destruction and that a change of course is imperative.

> *Peace is not the absence of war.*
> *It is a virtue, a state of mind,*
> *a disposition for benevolence,*
> *confidence, justice...*
> BENEDICT SPINOZA

The 1 energy of the 1000s teaches us that all is attainable through Free Will if we do what we really love. And, yet, we continue to do things we do not love or desire simply to give the *appearance* of being ahead in the "race".

FREE WILL is the only alternative to the stagnation of guilt or the evil of denied guilt. It teaches us that great strength, and greatness itself, comes through love of ourselves and compassion for others. The emphasis on individuality, on doing what you want to do, and on Free Will, is not a matter of selfishly bulldozing your way through life without regard for others. It is a matter of using your individual and unique desire, talent, and intent, in harmony with the desire, talent, and intent of others, to create a more hospitable way to live.

The 2 energy of the 2000s is making us more willing to utilize our talents in the context of teams and groups. Each individual must recognize and accept his or her purpose within the group, so that the maximum effect can be attained. But it is only through the Will - the way we *feel* - that we will ever know who our group is, and what we can contribute to it. It is only through the way we feel that we can know when our experience with a particular group has been completed and it is time to move on. Otherwise we become stuck in places and with people with whom we have nothing in common, unaware of why we are so unhappy.

In order for us to know our purpose within the group, we must contribute our *love*. And I do not mean this in an abstract way. Love has many forms. Our individual contributions, therefore, are specific. What is it that triggers love in you? What do you love to do? What do you love to experience? What brings you satisfaction? What are you good at? What do you have a passion for?

What makes you happy? Whatever your answers are, these are your contributions. And your answers may change as the future unfolds.

We all desire positive change yet we still cling to the familiar, knowing very well that this often contributes to our ongoing and escalating problems. We are afraid of the new 2 energy because its "feel" is unfamiliar to us. It is time to slow down! It is time to feel our fears and let them go!

It is scientifically accepted that the Earth itself has reduced its speed. Yet, the human 'race' has accelerated its pace. We are finding that the more we rush, the slower we proceed. Never before has humanity had so much information and technology at its fingertips. And never before have we been so confused by all this 'progress'. Yes, *everything* is slower in the new millennium because peace is the essence of the 2 energy, and peace cannot exist at the frenetic pace at which we have been traveling.

Of course, all is not 'peace and love' when the 2 energy is misunderstood. It is hard for us to dispense with age-old beliefs and ideas, even though we know these judgments have always prevented lasting peace. When the process of peace is approached only from an intellectual masculine point of view, without understanding the age-old *emotions* involved, hostility is prolonged. To achieve peace, we must learn *how* to achieve it. First we must find peace in ourselves.

Another characteristic of the 2 energy is that it uses the power of *nature* to destroy anything that pushes against it. 2 does not seek superiority, but equality. It does not tolerate force. It knows that any push for control creates an imbalance in which life tips over on itself and cannot survive.

Fear about the Earth slipping from its axis and destroying us all, and many other environmental concerns, have emanated from an awareness of the sexual imbalance that we have created throughout time. Although these concerns are legitimate, such catastrophic events can be prevented by a mass awakening, *now*, which restores complete freedom of movement, thought, and emotion to Earth's energy flows. This global awakening has truly begun.

Meanwhile, we will continue to experience extreme weather conditions and other natural disasters, the harshness of which will accelerate the movement of our *emotions*. If you do not understand how human beings influence Earth's weather patterns, you need to know that everything on Earth, in Earth, and surrounding Earth, is operating through the same planetary network of electromagnetic energies. An imbalance or blockage in one part of Earth's energy system, in people for instance, cannot help but affect all of its parts. Direct assaults on the planet, such as pollution and nuclear testing, produce violent repercussions as the planet expresses the feelings of pain and rage that such attacks trigger in her.

The Earth expresses outwardly what she feels inwardly. We experience this as "natural" but extreme ecological conditions. It is not only our assaults on the planet which cause her to react in this way. Emotion is an energy in itself, the quality of which affects the planet profoundly. All over the world there are vast pockets of emotion such as misery, terror, and rage, which weigh heavily on the planet's ability to move freely. It is essential for us all to free our Will energy and to encourage others to do the same.

Violent storms, flooding, volcanic eruption, earthquakes, animal extinction, extreme temperatures, etc., are the effects of our planet trying to heal herself. At the same time, human survival instincts are also being activated. The mass Will of humanity is beginning to speak up. Just like the Earth itself, we must learn to express our feelings so that we, too, can heal.

*I am learning that if I just go on accepting
the framework for life that others have given me,
if I fail to make my own choices,
the reason for my life will be missing.*
LIV ULLMAN

The fact that the feminine 2 cycle has replaced the masculine 1 cycle does not mean that women will be ruling the world. Women certainly do have an opportunity to change what has always been a man's world into a *balanced* world. But there is an unaddressed anger which exists between men and women. We deny these feelings to a large extent because the love between men and women is natural and desirable and is vital for the survival of our species.

But until our sexual anger is truthfully expressed and released from within, it will remain an unpleasant barrier between the sexes. If we are to continue to exist, let alone coexist, we must accept that each of us is made up of both masculine and feminine energies which need to be balanced. Only when this level of harmony is reached will any of us know just how magnificent love can be.

Women's rights are a huge issue today because we are living in a cycle which is right for this balancing process to occur. We are seeing not only an improvement in the way women are perceived and treated by men but, first and foremost, a huge surge of self- awareness and acceptance by women themselves.

Sexual balance is taking place even though some women have developed more masculine energy than feminine energy in the name of competition. Sexual balance is taking place even though some men are so afraid of the increasing power of women that they will go to any lengths to curtail it.

Sexual balance is taking place even though some women are so afraid of losing the men they are dependent upon and so afraid of the responsibility that comes with freedom that they openly denounce their own equality. Sexual balance is taking place despite all that.

Men are discovering that an acceptance of their feminine energy actually enhances their masculinity because along with balance comes increased intelligence and creativity. And many women are discovering the immense creative and intellectual power that comes from accepting themselves exactly as they are.

Far from making us an androgynous society in which sexuality itself is denied, our current journey toward feminine recognition serves to bring equilibrium to this world. But first we must realize the enormous role that guilt (shame) plays in suppressing the natural flow of sexual energy. Something is very wrong with the judgments that war is righteous while sex - the very basis of all life - is reprehensible.

It is the balancing of mind and emotion - spirit and will - masculine and feminine - that is breaking down the structure of such judgment and is forcing us to embrace reality instead. And this is producing the spectacular creative and humanitarian renaissance of our times.

We live in a world far more slavish in its
obedience to ancient custom than we like to admit.
RUSSELL BAKER

Meanwhile, female babies in India and China and other places around the world are still being slaughtered by their own parents because females are considered to be of no *value*.

In Egypt and other sub-Saharan countries, little girls still undergo a savage procedure in which their clitoris is removed with a razor blade, often at the local barber shop, *without anesthesia*. This ancient belief, which goes back to the time of the pharaohs, considers it *wrong* for a female to experience the natural and loving sensation of orgasm, and that females are merely the property of males.

In Japan, elderly women are now severely crippled because, as young women, they were enslaved to a tradition in which their feet were bound tight, causing them to walk in the tiniest, most subservient of footsteps until, finally, their arches collapsed under their weight. The slavery of women and children is still practiced in many African and Arabian countries.

It should be said, however, that great strides are being made in these and other countries, by brave women and men, who are bringing these matters to the attention of the world and are demanding basic human rights and equality for women.

Still, it makes us feel glad that we live far away from such places, doesn't it? But, think again. These barbaric acts against the feminine are echoed strongly and consistently in our so called "civilized" society and are often a lot closer to home than we care to admit.

For instance, why does a woman, in civilized society, throw away her very identity by changing her name (which, in most cases, is her father's name) in marriage? Why are the bride's parents expected to pay for the wedding? Why is the groom given his parents' blessing while the bride is given AWAY?

Tradition? Perhaps. But surely the parents of those slaughtered or maimed little girls throughout the world will claim that their practices are also a matter of tradition. Tradition which is upheld to this extent is totally illogical in a world where everything evolves, especially when it is held in place by the erroneous judgment that male is superior to female.

Why do we use words like bitch, son of a bitch, and mother, when speaking adversely of someone or something? Even the word "bastard" is a derision of female energy. It implies wrong doing on the part of the female because she was not legitimized by marriage to a man when her child was conceived or born. We use these words with such nonchalance. But is the ease with which we use this kind of language a measure of our ignorance, our blindness, our denial, of the deep-seated hatred we *all* have for the feminine?

> *Ultimately, human intent is the most powerful*
> *evolutionary force on this planet.*
> GEORGE LEONARD

During the 2000s, humanity will discover its vast powers of intuition and will realize that we are all connected and related in a vast variety of ways. This will enable real peace to manifest rather than the mere tolerance which now passes as peace. Yes, tolerance is a vital beginning provided it is exercised with the genuine *intent* to achieve peace. Otherwise, tolerance is nothing more than denied anger which becomes hatred and, eventually, erupts as rage and war.

Guilt has told us to deny anger; to cut off from this feeling entirely. In doing so, we have become a society with so little Free Will left that we are all victims of one kind or another. While we see ourselves as victims, we cannot possibly have consideration for others because we are so preoccupied with protecting ourselves from whatever we believe is going to attack us.

It may seem heartless to tell someone who has experienced trauma to *get over it*, but that is precisely what they must have the intent to do. The only way any of us can move past our old wounds is to express our feelings about them fully, without feeling guilty for doing so. Guilt does not want you to heal. It only wants you to feel guilty. Remember that the past was the course you had to take in order to gain the understanding and the experience you have in the present. And your present understanding and experience will enable you to create the future *you* want.

> *Other people seem wrong when*
> *their perspective doesn't match yours.*
> DEEPAK CHOPRA

We want to be seen as normal even though normal is just another word for commonplace or average. We frequently judge, criticize, and resent those whose Will is strong enough to enable them to live freely. We label them eccentric, selfish, or even crazy. The social structure we call political correctness has, in many ways, expanded our victim status because it is based in guilt. It labels everyone who is not clumped into the mainstream as a minority. At the same time, political correctness insists that we tolerate each others' labels and categorizations, regardless of how we actually feel about them. This is a massive denial of guilt, fear, and hatred.

In reality, it is impossible to have acceptance for everyone. It is impossible to accept those who horrify and disgust us without denying the feelings of horror and disgust. Those who cannot accept themselves cannot accept acceptance from anyone else. Our negative feelings toward other people will only be able to move out of us when we stop denying that we have them.

It is our loving *intent* which will prevent us from expressing hateful feelings in a way which could harm ourselves or someone else. Self-acceptance is the key because the more we learn to love and accept ourselves, exactly as we are, the easier it will be to love and accept others, and be accepted by others in return. Every desire and intent, starts on the inside first and is reflected back to us in our outer reality. The way others treat us is always an accurate indicator of how we are treating ourselves on an emotional level.

If we do not want to be judged, we must stop judging others. This does not imply that we should condone behavior which is harmful or offensive.

It does suggest that we encourage others to be free individuals instead of criticizing their precious individuality.

> *I must create a system, or be enslaved by another man's;*
> *I will not reason or compare; my business is to create.*
> WILLIAM BLAKE

When we first discover our greater potential, we often fear the new level of thought and feeling we have suddenly reached. It is logical that when one's mind suddenly expands and exposes new realities, certain fears and denials will arise as we face what we always thought would be *the unknown*.

Often we refuse to believe that we've experienced something evolutionary because old mental programming - old judgment - tells us that such a thing is not possible. We need to be more aware, therefore, of just how drastically our reality has changed, and continues to change and that denied fear keeps the old programming in place.

Humanity is waking up now. We are slowly facing our expanded reality. It is not always a pleasant awakening, but it is reality nonetheless. In many cases, those who are assuming control and declaring 'change' at every turn are referring only to economic and 'power' issues and are actually attempting to change things back to the way they *were* - the very same road of denial and homophobia we are in the process of evolving from. People want to be free. People do not want to be led, especially by those who can no longer FEEL anything.

Freedom itself is evolving to a new and exciting stage, making it impossible for today's intelligent leaders to set firm agendas, stand on specific political platforms, or to enforce laws which are decidedly out of place. It is comforting to know that politicians are not immune to the evolutionary process. There really are some evolved and visionary leaders out there who, unfortunately, must now learn to deal with a plague of 'old-school' opposition.

We, ourselves, are generating the information needed in order to make our lives more livable. If you think that satellites and computers are the basis of the information age, realize that these technologies are only reproductions of human capacity, and are only as effective and accurate as what has been programmed into them *by* human beings. The most valuable information at our disposal is coming from within.

Each one of us, no matter what our age, sex, creed, ethnic origin, or circumstance, has information to share at this time. Everyone has valuable information to offer because everyone is involved in this emotional journey to freedom. Everyone has their own story to tell and their own way of telling it. *This* is the information age which, through FREE WILL, can only evolve into an era of far greater significance: THE AGE OF PEACE.

Good luck my fellow traveler. God bless. And may your journey be magnificent.

Bibliography and Other Resources

INSTANT NUMEROLOGY *by Sandra Kovacs Stein - Newcastle*

NUMEROLOGY: THE COMPLETE GUIDE *by Matthew Oliver Goodwin - Newcastle*

NUMEROLOGY HAS YOUR NUMBER *by Ellin Dodge - Simon & Schuster*

WHAT NUMBER ARE YOU? *by Lilla Bek and Robert Holden - Aquarian Press - UK*

YOUR CHILD'S NUMEROLOGY *by Robert Stein - Ballantine*

LIVING IN THE LIGHT *by Shakti Gawain - Whatever*

CREATIVE VISUALIZATION *by Shakti Gawain - Bantam*

THE ARTIST'S WAY *by Julia Cameron Putnam*

ILLUSIONS *by Richard Bach - Dell*

JONATHAN LIVINGSTON SEAGULL *by Richard Bach - Dell*

VOICES OF TRUTH: *Conversations with Scientists, Healers, and Thinkers by Nina L. Diamond - Lotus*

EMOTIONAL INTELLIGENCE *- Daniel Goleman - Bantam*